Great Walls and Linear Barriers

Great Walls and Linear Barriers

Peter Spring

Pen & Sword
MILITARY

First published in Great Britain in 2015 by
Pen & Sword Military
an imprint of
Pen & Sword Books Ltd
47 Church Street
Barnsley
South Yorkshire
S70 2AS

ISBN 978 1 84884 377 6

Typeset in Ehrhardt by
Mac Style Ltd, Bridlington, East Yorkshire
Printed and bound in the UK by CPI Group (UK) Ltd, Croydon, CRO 4YY

Pen & Sword Books Ltd incorporates the imprints of Pen & Sword Archaeology, Atlas, Aviation, Battleground, Discovery, Family History, History, Maritime, Military, Naval, Politics, Railways, Select, Transport, True Crime, and Fiction, Frontline Books, Leo Cooper, Praetorian Press, Seaforth Publishing and Wharncliffe.

For a complete list of Pen & Sword titles please contact
PEN & SWORD BOOKS LIMITED
47 Church Street, Barnsley, South Yorkshire, S70 2AS, England
E-mail: enquiries@pen-and-sword.co.uk
Website: www.pen-and-sword.co.uk

Contents

Maps and Linear Barrier Lists

Acknowledgements

This book has been a long time in gestation although its completion owes much to an intense period of activity made possible by semi-retirement. Essentially it would not have happened, however, without the impulse from my wife, Anna, who challenged me to stop going on about new walls being built – at a time when, after the fall of the Berlin Wall, received wisdom was we were entering an age without walls – and actually try to write about them. Also, the encouragement and advice of David Harrison was essential to completing a proposal and then commenting on the text, as well as keeping up the momentum of the work. Thank you also to Philip Sidnell of Pen & Swords for accepting the proposal, Barnaby Blacker for editing, Matt Jones for production and Alex Swanton for the maps. I am very grateful to Lawrence Joffe for his expert reading the text.

It would have been impossible to have written this book earlier than the 21st century. Most of the walls and linear barriers were found on the basis of certain hunches as to where to look which were then investigated using tailored internet search terms or following certain geographical or man-made features – for example, Roman roads — on online maps. The anonymous contributions on Wikipedia were invaluable to background research and one can only recompense by making a contribution to its costs. Email made it possible to contact experts and I am grateful for the replies from, Alexandru Madgearu, Alison Gascoigne, Sören Stark, Eberhard Sauer and Jim Crow. Thank you for the time and materials given to me by the National History and Archaeology Museum Constanța (the site of ancient Tomis and Ovid's exile) which is near the Valurile lui Traian of the Dobrogea. (A visit is recommended to get a flavour of the extraordinary and largely unrecognised archaeological wealth of Romania.)

The internet provided images of linear barriers almost entirely unavailable in published texts. I am particularly grateful to the fascinating online Great Wall Forum which expands the subject matter of walls visually far beyond any conventionally published sources. Thank you to the following for providing images: Sergey Bieloshapko, Seamus Cullen, Brian Feldman, Elena Filatova, Geopan, Andrey Kolchugin, Andreas C. Lehmann, Kin Jim, Nagy, Brian Thomas Mcelherron, Pascal and Nathalie Mercier, M. M. Miles, Adrian Mihălțianu, David Pettegrew, Leonid Rosca, Eberhard Sauer, Kim F. Siefert and Mirko Slak. I am grateful to the following for images available through the Creative Commons license: Maxim Bielushkin, Btxo, OlofE, Wolfgang Kuhoff, Pakeha, Heinrich Stuerzl, László Szalai, Frank Vincentz, Vity OKM, www.derbent.ru, 1.2 Tadam. Thank you to my sister Emma for a drawing of the ancient Egyptian wall frieze.

The maps are an amalgam drawn from multiple sources with a fair bit of deduction from various texts. There is a lot of otherwise unavailable material on foreign language websites. I have tried to give the sources in the bibliography and apologise for any oversights. The maps are very much work in progress and errors are entirely my own responsibility. Their value lies hopefully in revealing broader patterns rather than the precise location of individual linear barriers.

Finally, on a personal basis, I must say thank you to my wife and children for putting up with long absences and distracted presences while writing this book and to David Harrison for his patience accompanying me on various foreign trips which demonstrated that linear barriers, despite having been very substantial objects, can prove extremely elusive on the ground.

Technical Matters

Names

Many linear barriers have more than one name. It would be comforting if one could impose some over-arching consistency as to which to use but this is not really possible with a subject that covers lengths of time and space where the units measure in thousands. The best that usually can be done is to take the most familiar or common name and be consistent in its use. This, however, can result in some inconsistencies. For example, the linear barriers on the Great Hungarian Plain to the north and east of the Danube are collectively known by the Hungarian name, the Csörszárok. Yet this includes a linear barrier described in French as the Petit Fossé. Near to the Csörszárok in Serbia lie a number of earthworks that are most commonly known by the German collective name Römerschanzen. As said, the only consistency reasonably possible is to be consistent in the use of one name in this text.

Some linear barriers are only known in different scripts. For example, there are linear barriers in the Ukraine which are only described in Cyrillic, for example, Траянові вали Подністров'я, or in direct translation from Ukrainian, Trayanov Vali Podnestrovya. Since this linear barrier has only been found in Ukrainian texts the direct transcription will be used.

An apology will have to be made in advance as sometimes the use of names may inevitably look somewhat confusing. For example, the Roman Emperor who conquered Dacia is generally known as Trajan. Walls attributed to him in Romania and the Ukraine are known respectively as Valul lui Traian and, in transcription, as Trayanov Vali. Therefore, in the same section of this book there may be three spellings.

Distances

Distances will be given for simplicity in kilometres and metres unless there is an explicit mention of a measure like a Roman mile. Most numbers come with a strong health warning as those linear barriers which have survived at all have often lost significant sections or were never originally continuous. Also, it is uncertain precisely how long were some distances used in ancient texts such as the *danna*, *beru* and *parasang*, as they were not absolute lengths but measures of how far it was possible to travel in an amount of time (in itself likely to be an estimate in the absence of portable time pieces) which varied hugely according to terrain.

Names and distances in quotations

Quotations from primary or secondary sources may use spellings and measurements that are different to those standardised in the rest of this book. Generally, the form used in the quotation will be respected. This may, however, result in different spellings of the same person or entity within close proximity.

In the case of Chinese walls some texts use Wade-Giles system while others employ the more recent pinyin. In this book the pinyin system will generally be given. Where quotations have used Wade-Giles a transcription will be provided in pinyin in brackets where the English spelling is different.

Distribution terminology – zones and clusters

Linear barriers are not randomly distributed. This is hardly surprising given that the great effort required to build them meant they were constructed in response to the onerous demands of a specific locality or a broader strategic need. Most linear barriers tend therefore to be found in zones and even within those zones they are not randomly distributed but found in clusters. In an attempt to provide some order to the multiple barriers discovered, extensive use is made of the concept of zones and clusters, particularly with respect to maps. (The zones used to categorise the linear barriers in the text are shown in the associated maps.)

Organising material with boxes

There is a challenge to writing a fairly flowing narrative in that it can be disrupted by descriptions of individual linear barriers. Therefore, such descriptions are distinguished by the use of boxes – hopefully enabling the reader to follow the narrative more easily. The amount of text allocated to different linear barriers might seem rather arbitrary as some better-known or very long linear barriers might appear to get less coverage than obscurer and shorter barriers. In part this is because there is little point in adding to the weight of words on the likes of Hadrian's Wall or the Ming Great Wall of China, therefore leaving more space, in what is a comparatively brief survey of a huge subject, for less well known walls. Also, it is a matter subject to the vagaries of available information and, indeed, curiosity. This is the internet age and it is possible immediately to fill the gaps on almost any barrier covered in this book by placing its name in a browser. Information is being updated continuously and frequently images are now becoming available too.

Sources and notes

Many of the linear barriers found in this book have been discovered using Google to search within geographical or politically promising areas where certain patterns predicted that such barriers might possibly be found. Often the material turned up in local guides, blogs, and personal websites. Functionally, it is almost impossible to impose a highly academical methodology to such content. The notes and bibliography try to give sufficient information to rediscover such source material. That said, what can be found is constantly changing and expanding and the interested reader is invited to see what new information can be discovered by placing key words into Google: suggestions include Змиевы Валы (Zmievi Vali), Valurile lui Traian and Folkevolde. The increasingly efficient translate function produces fascinating results. Also, the image search can conjure photographs and maps. There is a wealth of new material coming out of eastern Europe, particularly the Ukraine.

Maps

There is considerable uncertainty as to the precise location and length of many linear barriers – some of which may only be known from literary sources. On balance it is considered that it is more useful to try to show the location of linear barriers on maps – particularly as patterns may emerge even if the site of individual linear barriers is uncertain. The maps, however, should be regarded very much as work in progress.

Photos

Apart from a few well known linear barriers there are no stock photographs. Linear barriers have, however, attracted great interest from local people and many marvellous images can be found on the internet. Unfortunately tracking down the photographers and gaining approvals is often a very difficult task. The result has been that many excellent images have not been included. Readers are, however, invited to put the names of linear barriers into google images and many photographs will appear. The results can be particularly prolific if local languages are used, for example: Ukrainian Змієві вали (Zmievi Vali); Russian Засечная (Zasechnaya); and Bulgarian Еркесията (Erkesia).

Part I

Introductory

Prologue

In the early seventh century BC the steppe nomads of Central Asia burst through the Caucasus into the Middle East and onto the stage of history. The Scythians chased the Cimmerians out of the Pontic Steppe on a helter-skelter ride through Asia Minor, Palestine and Assyria.[1] The Cimmerians probably went through the central Caucasus and defeated the kingdoms of Urartu and Phrygia, causing the suicide of Midas. The Scythians careered down the east side of the Caucasus along the Caspian Sea shore. Then for twenty-eight years they were, wrote Herodotus, the 'masters of Asia'[2] evincing élan, farce, arrogance, and, when actually fighting, invincibility that would have done credit to the wildest companies of Napoleonic era hussars and cossacks (the latter coming from much the same area).

All sorts of strategies were used to contain the nomads from the steppe. At first the Assyrians tried offering brides and bribes, and their king Esarhaddon gave to the Scythian leader Partatua rich presents and his daughter. Then, when the Scythians were in Palestine, the Pharaoh Psammeticus, 'met them with gifts and prayers, and prevailed on them to advance no further'.[3] Jeremiah launched jeremiads, warning the Israelites, 'Their quiver is as an open sepulcher, they are all mighty men. And they shall eat up thine harvest, and thy bread, which thy sons and thy daughters should eat: they shall eat up thy flocks and thine herds: they shall eat up thy vines and thy fig trees.'[4] The crafty Medes then built alliances with the Scythians and together they took Nineveh and destroyed Assyrian power in 612 BC. But everyone became fed up with the arrogant nomads who exacted regular tribute and additional imposts from many nations and plundered at will. The Medes finally devised a successful strategy, namely treachery: they invited the Scythians to a banquet, got them blind drunk, and massacred them. The remnants of the Scythians limped back to the Crimea.

The nomads – as a result of the tough survival lessons learnt eking out the harsh existence of nomadic pastoralists on the steppe – had developed and mastered a remarkable military technology and organisation. The composite bow and the hardy mobile horse were used by groups where every man was a warrior, and which could coalesce into much larger bodies. For over two millennia, the nomad appeared able to defeat, almost at will, the armies of sedentary states when a major horde gathered and the fight was on ground open enough to allow for manoeuvre. When nomads mastered siege technology – or co-opted those who had – there was almost no defence against them and eventually, under the Mongols in the thirteenth century, the steppe nomads conquered the largest empire the world has ever known.

Until a new technology was developed based around firearms and fixed and mobile linear barriers, the sedentary world had to survive not just against nomad *chevauchées* –

great raids – and armies of conquest, but also endless more minor raiding. Moreover the taking of booty and people would debilitate and ultimately exhaust any settled state if the nomads were not somehow managed and contained. Thus, for more than 2,000 years, settled states had to use holding strategies until the means to defeat the nomads on the steppe itself could be fashioned. These were the strategies tested against the Scythians, like paying bribes, offering princesses in marriage, invoking divine intervention and, ultimately effective in this case, treacherous massacres. Also developed were tricking nomads into attacking each other, employing nomads to do the fighting, and adopting nomad fighting practices.

There is consistent evidence of another strategy. If Scythian history is picked over, walls and other linear barriers feature surprisingly frequently. Herodotus said that, in his time, there were still traces of the Cimmerians in Scythia including Cimmerian walls. When the Scythians returned to the Crimea after a great raid lasting many years, they found that their women had set up home with their slaves, who they had previously blinded. The children of these unions built a trench across the Crimea to obstruct the return of their parents' masters. Later this trench served as a border of the royal Scythians domain from which they launched attacks on the Cimmerian Bosphorus. This will be mentioned again in chapter 5.

The Chinese *Book of Songs* described how in the ninth century BC: 'The king has ordered Nan-chung (Nan-Zhong) to go and build a fort on the frontier.'*[5] This was built against the Xianyun who were, another poem described, 'very swift'[6]. 'Many scholars believe that they (the Xianyun) were probably the first true horse-nomads to confront the Chinese, and were most likely related to the Scythians of the west.'[7]

In Central Asia, in the pass at Derbent, a wall was built in the third century BC when as: 'The Greeks abandoned Samarkand and the territories north of the Hissar Range for the first time, the pressure of the Scythians was so insistent that the Graeco-Bactrian kings were obliged to build the frontier-wall of Derbent.'[8]

In the Ukraine it is believed that the Perekipsky Val, restored in the seventeenth century, had been built originally in the Scythian times.[9]

In the Crimea, Strabo described how during the reign of Mithridates VI (120–63 BC) the Scythians made their attack, near *Ctenus*/Inkerman, on the fortified wall that extends across the isthmus.'[10] Also, in the Crimea there were linear barriers running north to south across the Kerch peninsula of which: 'There can be no real doubt that both long dykes were strategic structures designed to control lateral movement across the eastern Crimea, not least by pastoralist Scythians.'[11]

The Hellenistic king Asander of the Bosphoran Kingdom (44–47 BC) built the Uzunlar Wall across the Kerch peninsula against nomads whose description and location well matches the Scythians.[12]

---

* Nan-Zhong in pinyin. This translation uses the word 'fort' but other translations say 'wall'. Early Chinese historians, when discussing previous walls, refer to that of Nan-Zhong indicating they believed Nan-Zhong did build a wall.

Josephus mentioned the opening of the Iron Gates in the Caucasus – supposedly built by Alexander the Great – to let the Scythians through into Hither Asia* during the fourth year of Vespasian (AD 73). 'The Alans, which we have formerly mentioned somewhere as being Scythians ... about this time laid a design of falling upon Media ... with which intention they treated with the king of Hyrcania which lay around the southern Caspian; for he was master of that passage which King Alexander shut up with iron gates.'[13] The gates must have been built as a gap in something – presumably a wall extending across a pass.†

There are also references to a wall built in the reign of Valerian (253–60) for in the face of 'The excursions of the Scythians, and of the Marcomanni, ... The Athenians repaired their walls... The Peloponnesians likewise fortified the Isthmus, and all Greece put itself upon its guard for the general security.'[14]

Thus, from China, across Central Asia, the Ukraine, the Crimea, the Caucasus to Greece, there were contemporary reports of Scythians and linear barriers to keep them out but also built by them. And the Scythians were only a part of the story for, after this early seventh century BC encounter between horse-borne steppe nomads and settled states in Hither Asia, there were increasing reports of walls and other linear barriers.

The irruption of the nomad Scythians and the Cimmerians from out of one steppe range into another region was a process that would be repeated several times over the next two millennia. Ironically, in the later fourth century BC, the first trans-steppe nomad explosion, starting with the Xiongnu nomads in the east and petering out with the Huns in the west, was ignited by a burst of expansionist and aggressive wall building by Chinese states to the north of their usual territories. The second great east to west Eurasian Steppe irruption was that of the Turks starting in the sixth century. And the third was the Mongols and Tatars in the thirteenth century. All three trans-steppe nomad irruptions provoked great flurries of linear barrier building along the borders of the steppe and the sown (that is regions amenable to agriculture); and for two millennia, from Europe to China, linear barriers appear to have been a very significant element of the strategic mix that literally held the line against the nomad threat.

This book tries to cast a new perspective on walls and linear barriers as an essential part of the strategy vital first for holding the line against, and then eventually defeating the nomad threat, a process largely completed in the seventeenth and eighteenth centuries. It also looks at linear barriers more generally in terms of the relationship between settled states and barbarians, both nomadic and non-nomadic, and peoples on the move, or migrants.

---

* Hither Asia is the area extending from Persia to the Mediterranean.
† Josephus said in the *Antiquities of the Jews* (1, 6, 1), 'Magog founded those that from him were named Magogites, but who are by the Greeks called Scythians.' In many legends Alexander built a great wall between two mountains to block off Gog and Magog. The story also appears in the Koran.

Introduction – Why Walls?

Reason for interest in walls

What provoked interest in the mobile nomadic Scythians and their perhaps surprising relationship with static walls? And why consider the broader question of the role of linear barriers in history?

It started with the bothersome question which arose from the collapse of the Berlin Wall in 1989 which was rather over-optimistically hailed as the start of a new era without barriers. While it was true that the Iron Curtain's physical manifestations did come down, more generally the opposite appeared to be the case – for all around the world new barriers have been and still are being erected to stop the flows of peoples, protect natural resources, defend hostile borders and assert control of regions where political claims were dubious. Familiar examples are the walls and fences with which Israel has isolated itself from the surrounding region. The US is separating itself from Mexico. Barriers are also being built between the nations of the Indian sub-continent and the Arabian Peninsula. Greece has been considering constructing a fence along the Turkish border to stop migrants.

While searching for modern barriers particularly using broad searches on the internet, earlier examples kept appearing. In 1930s Palestine, for example, there was Teggart's Wall, and earlier still, in biblical times, the Wall of Alexander Jannaeus. In Russia there was a whole series of wooden barriers, many made out of living forest, built between the fifteenth and eighteenth centuries. While most people have heard of the Great Wall of China or Hadrian's Wall, it became clear that that were dozens, indeed hundreds, of pre-modern linear barriers.

The sheer volume of these discoveries was rather puzzling as received wisdom appeared to be that wall building was both militarily and morally misguided – as reflected in the failure of the Maginot Line and the Berlin Wall. But if it was misguided then why did peoples regarded as particularly clever – like the Romans and the Chinese – indulge in wall building when the practice might be more dangerous to the constructors than the threat it was intended to keep out? Perhaps ancient peoples were wiser than some modern people have been prepared to admit, and linear barrier building might actually have been an activity of proven utility, allowing for inevitable failures due to human error and eventual change of circumstance? These seemed questions and challenges worth exploring. Walls appeared a massive subject, largely unstudied on a broad basis across time and geography.

Patterns and hunches for searching for walls and linear barriers

While researching the question of pre-modern linear barriers, rather than randomly happening upon new barriers, it gradually became possible – on the basis of certain hunches developed from observed patterns – to predict where walls might be found. Four patterns proved particularly useful to this inquiry.

Political patterns

- **States, nomads and barbarians** – Walls appeared to be built by states and empires, large and small, some to keep out settled 'barbarians', others (mostly outside Europe) to keep out nomads – but all reflecting the need for more civilised polities to protect themselves against people they perceived as 'less developed' and with whom it was impossible to forge reliable agreements. (Generally, it seemed that civilised empires and states did not build linear barriers between each other because relations could be regulated through written agreements. Also, if war did break out, linear barriers were unlikely to be effective against the great armies such polities could put into the field and thus pointless.)
- **Warring states** – Not all walls were built by empires to stave off nomads or barbarians. For example, the first long walls built by the Chinese were constructed in the Spring and Autumn and the Warring States periods between the seventh and third centuries BC as defences against other Chinese states. Many walls appeared to be built by multiple states at war with each other that were at similar stages of development, in areas of increasingly constrained resources, largely the result of growing overpopulation.

Geographical patterns

- **Land corridors** – Certain geographical locations appeared particularly productive of linear barriers. Mountains, seas, rivers and marshes provide natural barriers that both channelled the flows of armies and peoples on the move and rendered man-made barriers impossible or superfluous. But land corridors between such mountains and seas, rivers and marshes were, however, very often found to have linear barriers across them. Also, linear barriers were often discovered in these land corridors at the point where the natural obstacles defining the corridor came closest, for example isthmuses on peninsulas and passes.
- **Valued land** – Some linear barriers protected and defined land which, for some reason, was more valuable than the surrounding area but was not covered by buildings. An obvious example is irrigated areas around rivers and oases in otherwise arid or semi-arid regions where uncontrolled entry by hostile forces could not be countenanced. The land might, however, be valued for other reasons, for example it provided a defensible foraging area when the broader polity was under attack. Or it might have had a political or even sacral significance that rendered it more important than surrounding areas.

These patterns helped predict where searches might be focused in order to find more linear barriers; but the barriers, once found, raised further questions. Some were discovered in advance of recent frontier lines, so perhaps their role here was aggressive, to secure the hold on conquered land and to assert power. In other situations, however, linear barriers were not found where they might have been predicted, according to the patterns outlined above, raising questions as to why linear barriers might not have been built. Generally, it might also be asked whether linear barrier building was a successful strategy and what other strategies might be deployed in the face of various threats?

Challenges to analysis

The challenge of producing a balanced analysis of the abundant linear barriers found became clear. For a start the subject did not seem to have been tackled before on a systematic basis. Then where it was tackled it was fragmentary rather than comprehensive, and discussion seemed frequently to be unbalanced by what might appear to be an anti-wall prejudice. For example, looking at early linear barriers it is said of Sumer's *Muriq Tidnim*: 'As for this great wall, it proved even more ineffectual than such barriers have always been in the end. No more is heard of this vast and vain work.'[1] And in ancient Egypt: 'The Wall of the Prince which Amenembat had thrown across the Eastern Delta had proved as inadequate in the face of determined assault as such passive defense lines always are.'[2] A recent book is dismissive of Chinese long wall building: 'And so, in the ninth century BC ... the Chinese first turned to a policy that would remain a comforting, albeit counter-productive, last resort for the next 2,000 years: wall-building.'[3] Also consider, in the context of China, South America's so-called Great Wall of the Inca, built in the fifteenth century: 'Like the Chinese wall, it was intended to keep out barbarian invaders. And it proved equally ineffective.'[4]

It often appeared difficult to mention linear barriers without bringing up the case of the Maginot Line built by France in the 1930s to defend itself against Germany. Yet this seemed somewhat irrelevant as it was not a continuous linear barrier and, anyway, was not itself breached. For example: 'It seems that the "wall psychology" of the later Sasanians engendered feeling similar to that widespread in France before 1940, when the Maginot line was thought to be impregnable.[5]

Walls were often criticised in terms of efficiency and rectitude: they did not work and they were even considered to be inherently immoral by philosophers, moralists and poets. Ultimately, it appeared only a militarily deficient and morally corrupted ruler or people would resort to wall building. Also, there often seemed to be a near desperation to interpret the function of linear barriers as anything other than military: they were expressions of power sufficient in themselves to deter, exercises in state-building and in personal aggrandizement. Sometimes, the supposed functions could seem almost bizarrely non-military, for example, grand-scale landscaping, even water filters, giant vegetable plots, and obstacles to evil spirits.

Often it seemed that, for some modern historians, all walls were iniquitous, as being constructions designed to perform so distasteful a function as impeding freedom of movement. This was the case even if the clear intention of the group whose freedom was being impeded might have been to kill, enslave and plunder. Historical perspective seemed to be suspended – with the result that barriers which appeared to have worked during the lifetime of their builders and indeed for several subsequent generations, were deemed valueless in more modern times. This might be because – when they faced a threat different to or greater than the one they were designed to counter – they ultimately failed.

As the questions about the significance and status of walls and other linear barriers took shape, an effort was made to find books that might clarify the subject. Apart from Hadrian's Wall and the Ming Great Wall of China it was hard to find many dealing with individual walls – let alone walls collectively – and such few books as there were appeared to underline, by the particularity of their analysis, the lack of more general surveys. These books tended to deal with linear barriers in places and times where historical archaeological analysis has been very intense: that is classical Greece and Rome, and Britain. Thus, there are books on the six kilometre long Dema Wall of Athens[6], the linear defences of the small Salganeos Plain[7], and the Hexamilion (literally six mile) Wall traversing the Isthmus of Corinth[8]. In Britain, apart from books on the two Roman walls of Hadrian and Antoninus Pius, there are books on Bokerley Dyke[9], Aves Ditch[10], and Offa's Dyke[11].

Quite recently, however, some books have been published which examine a number of specific linear barriers or related issues: *Mauern als Grenzen*[12]; *Walls, Ramparts, and Lines of Demarcation*[13]; *Borders, Barriers, and Ethnogenesis: Frontiers in Late Antiquity and the Middle Ages*[14]; and *Do Good Fences Make Good Neighbors?: What History Teaches Us about Strategic Barriers and International Security*[15]. Therefore, the subject does now appear to be attracting greater and more balanced interest. Yet despite this being an immense subject, as it covered thousands of kilometres and years, there appeared to be no general survey putting all these barriers into context. For whatever reason no professional military – or indeed other – historian has comprehensively reviewed the subject of linear barriers. But military indifference and dubious morality should always inspire curiosity.

Defining subject matter

As a general starting point the basic assumption is that people in the past were not stupid and they did what appeared rational in the light of experience at the time. However it might not be possible to fully recreate the context now that gave rise to such rational decisions. Thus, linear barriers were built because people expected them to work and experience had taught them that they did. Generally, states and polities did not have the resources to indulge in posturing or grand-scale landscaping: therefore, linear barriers were probably built as a response to present and real dangers. Also, the success of linear barriers should be judged carefully in terms of the objectives and survival of the actual builders and their immediate and direct successors.

At first the subject matter of this book might seem to be walls with distinct ends and solid vertical structures, but what really is being discussed is a range of linear barriers. While a wall is a type of linear barrier not all linear barriers are walls. Linear barriers tended to be made out of the most easily available local resource – which could be earth, wood or channelled water which might, for obvious reasons, not be suitable for making vertical barriers. A linear barrier is basically a long obstruction and can be above or below ground level, respectively a rampart or a ditch. Often it is a combination of both (indeed the word dyke can describe both the dug out and the elevated part.)

Most walls of stone and brick are associated with point defences – that is cities, towns, fortresses and castles. It might seem easy to make a distinction that defences which denied access to open land were linear while defences surrounding densely built up areas, occupied by urban dwellers and garrisons, were circular. But oases, for example in Central Asia, appeared to have circular walls that protected not just human habitations but also large areas of surrounding irrigated land. Western German cities like Frankfurt had not only city walls but also, at some distance, boundary perimeters of earthwork and dense hedge, enclosing fields. Linear barriers did not always seem to be built to meet a continuous threat but to counter some one-off challenge – some examples being, Julius Caesar's earthwork blocking the path of the Helvetii in 58 BC or Athanaric the Goth's effort to stop the Huns in AD 376.

Although the net will be cast wide in the search of strategic linear barriers, a definition is needed of what barriers specifically might or might not be covered in the main part of this study. The suggested definition is:

Linear barriers of any material, built in anticipation of, rather than in immediate response to, a continuous rather than a single threat, blocking access to largely open land.

The essential quality is that the barrier presents a substantially unbroken face to the threat that it is intended to block or channel.

Sources of evidence

The challenge of researching linear barriers was daunting because no general survey, or even accepted methodology, could be found on which to draw. While many more general history books and academic papers could be consulted, this is the internet age and the web transforms the researching of perhaps hitherto obscure subjects. Much of the material might fail academic peer review but often it is a great deal better than nothing – and occasionally it is extremely illuminating.

Websites unexpectedly offered up images of linear barriers which would otherwise exist only in disembodied, often fragmentary, written descriptions. For example, the first visions of the Ukraine's Zmievi Vali and Romania's Brazda lui Novac came from the internet. A website traced its creators' journey along the Valul lui Traian, in the Romanian Dobrogea[16], giving real insights into its length and location. Articles by Danish antiquaries, trawled in Danish from the web, revealed the existence of several dozen Folkevolde, literally people's ramparts, in Denmark.[17] On the internet were found old maps containing barriers seemingly unknown to modern scholarship, for example, a sixty-kilometre barrier in Moldavia along the river Prut.[18]

The translation function on the Google search engine opened up a huge amount of new material. Many local people are intrigued by the linear barriers around them and post documents, images and ideas. The translations which result are confusing, fragmentary and occasionally hilarious (or downright rude) but sometimes a new direction for research – or even a new barrier – emerged.

Tackling the evidence

As more evidence was considered, its fragmentary and complex character became increasingly obvious. It seemed unlikely that any surviving wall had been continuously known from its construction up to the present by its original name. Even where there were long standing names, they seemed obviously not original: unless devils, dragons, and worms really stalked the earth, and heroes, real and mythological, laid aside appropriately heroic tasks and laboured mundanely on barrier building. There were walls that existed in literary sources that could not be traced with any certainty on the ground. Equally there were walls on the ground that had no description in contemporary literature. Who built the Brazda lui Novac de Nord or de Sud across Romania's Wallachian Plain? Did anything remain of the Sumerian king Shu-Sin's wall called *Muriq Tidnim*?

Given the fragmentary and contradictory nature of the evidence, how could it be confronted and the problems resolved? Certain approaches can be suggested:

- The judgement of contemporaries should be respected as to whether a linear barrier would be a rational response to a perceived threat. There often seems to be a modern prejudice against linear barrier construction, but contemporaries may have made entirely rational decisions based on their own actual experience when building linear barriers. Therefore, their judgement of the situation that led to the building of linear barriers should not lightly be discounted as irrational.
- Occam's razor should be applied: the simplest explanation might be the best. Historians appear to over-elaborate motivation. This is particularly the case with China where there is surviving literary material in which emperors, generals and bureaucrats debate the merits of wall building. At different times, possibly responding to more intense frontier pressures at times of military weakness, the wall-builders appear to win the arguments. But the motives ascribed are not so much to do with the need to keep dangerous nomads out but rather to protect a notion of 'Chineseness' that refused to engage with an outside world that did not accept its superiority. The most likely explanation is that the Chinese simply built a barrier for military reasons in response to a perceived threat at the time.
- Contemporary literary and surviving physical evidence should be considered equally valid. It is unlikely that contemporary sources would have completely invented a linear barrier. Therefore, the fact that it has not survived, or may have survived but has not been clearly identified, does not mean it should not be covered here – particularly if it contributes to an overall pattern. Equally, if there is a surviving linear barrier which has a name that is obviously not an accurate identification of the builder – unless devils and dragons are countenanced as barrier builders – this does not mean it should be excluded. It might again contribute to clarifying a broader pattern.
- Consideration of individual linear barriers should not be excluded because they are 'difficult'. Many linear barriers, particularly earthworks, are mute. There are thousands of kilometres of linear barriers in Hungary, Romania, Moldavia and the Ukraine, whose builders are not certain. The fact that they are there, and may be

part of a broader pattern, means that they should be included as part of the overall analysis.

- Broader context should be considered. Sometimes linear barriers seem isolated and *sui generis*. But, if considered – in the context of similar situations, in different times and places – they might fit into a broader pattern. Equally, on this basis, some linear barriers that might have been treated as archetypal (like Hadrian's Wall or the Ming Great Wall of China) could, on a broader consideration, be atypical.

Book outline

Having described the problems approaching linear barriers and suggested approaches to resolving them, the book will follow this general plan.

- **Introductory** – since the relationship between nomads and settled states seems particularly important in terms of understanding why so many linear barriers were built, a special effort should also be made to understand the characteristics of nomads, as perceived by settled states, which might have caused this.
- **Survey** – this section looks at linear barriers in different geographical areas in roughly chronological order.
- **Questions and issues** – certain broad questions regarding patterns and motivation are considered. This part will review matters of functioning, construction and operation. It will also consider certain issues emerging in the survey which might merit further attention.
- **Aftermath** – lastly, the subsequent treatment and interpretation of linear barriers after their period of first use, is considered.

Nomads

It might seem odd to precede a survey of linear barriers with an introductory section on nomads. It was, however, the peoples who came first, and the linear barriers built in response to the threat they were perceived to pose which came second. Therefore, it is actually relevant to start by looking at how nomads were viewed if the reasons which gave rise to linear barrier building are to be understood. (Readers are anyway free to skip this chapter and move straight to the Survey Section and the walls.)

Outside north-western Europe, linear barrier building almost always appeared to involve nomads – both on their own and as the result of forcing other non-nomadic people to migrate. Looking back, it might be difficult to understand why nomadic peoples posed – or were perceived to pose – such a threat, given they now seem so marginalised. This chapter considers the perceptions of nomads, the threat they posed, and the problems in dealing with them – using contemporary descriptions where possible – that might mean that the construction of linear barriers was an entirely rational solution to problems as perceived at the time.

The interaction of the nomad and the agriculturalist, of the steppe and the sown, the mobile and static, is one of the great and enduring dramas of history. This chapter focuses on how nomads were viewed as their relationship with settled states and local barbarian peoples was often the driver of unstable situations which gave rise to linear barrier building. In short, any migration or popular movement, it may be argued, created a situation of uncertainty which might be resolved through the construction of such barriers.

Nomadic pastoralism and transhumance

The nomad's character and relationship with his geographical and political setting explain why, at certain times, he could dominate not only his environment but also threaten and sometimes destroy surrounding states. Equally, this character and relationship contained inherent weaknesses which meant that nomads could not conquer, and hold for long, the land of settled states without changing so fundamentally that they ceased to be nomads.

Nomadic pastoralism is the life of tent dwelling peoples who move between lands usually incapable of sustaining settled agriculture. The agriculturalist, by definition, stays in one place. The situation, as is usual, is somewhat more complex because both nomads and settled peoples practice transhumance – the seasonal movement of herds between winter and summer pastures. The distinction is that, in the case of nomads, whole peoples move on wagons with the herds. With settled agriculturalists most of the people stay put, while specialist shepherds and other herders move away, in particular seasons, from the village with the animals. (This is significant because linear barriers might be built not only to deal with whole groups of nomads in or adjacent to steppe regions, but even in non-steppe regions settled states might have to make provision for the controlled movement of animals by otherwise mostly sedentary peoples.) Also, not all nomads followed regular annual patterns of transhumance, as some lived in areas of uniformly poor grazing and moved only when regions became exhausted regions to those offering less depleted resources.

Generally, nomadic peoples were not entirely self-sufficient but relied on settled peoples for certain necessities and luxuries. When trading was denied, when starvation threatened, or when raiding opportunities were too tempting, then there may have been nomad attacks. The threat, usually continuous but relatively low level, was generally a nuisance rather than overwhelming.

Names and ethnicity

For anyone other than a nomad aficionado, trying to make sense of the development of nomadic peoples is a daunting task. The sheer number of names that stream across the pages can be utterly bewildering. The Amorites, Scythians, Huns, Magyars, Mongols, Tatars and Turks are well known, and possibly the Xiongnu, Avars, Bulgars, and Polovtsians. But what of the Getae and Massagetae, Onogurs and Kotrigurs, Xanbei, Yuezhi, and Juan Juan – and there are many more.

Also, nomads transmogrify into other nomads, for example, Xianyun into Xiongnu, or split, for example, Donghu into Xianbei and Wuhuan. Some divisions are colourful: there were Red, Black and, possibly, White Huns. The Blue Khaganate Turks split into a Western and Eastern Khaganate. Further (debatable) connections have been made from China into Europe between the Xiongnu and the Huns, and the Rouran and the Avars.

There is the question of ethnicity on the Eurasian Steppe as there appear largely to be Mongol, Turkic and Indo-European groups. Looking at the issue of ethnicity from the viewpoint of the sedentarist, the nomadic condition was almost a disorder – a restless reluctance to accept normal responsibilities of settled existence. Particular peoples were afflicted by this disorder – for example, Asiatics, Huns, Mongols, and Tatars. Thus, the nomadic existence could be seen as the product of a certain ethnicity. Only particular ethnic types – those deficient in the skills necessary for civilised existence – would become nomads. Really, however, the question of ethnicity is something of a red herring: nomadism can be seen as the product of environment not ethnicity. Any peoples living in an environment that could not sustain sedentary agriculture – but could support herding and transhumance – became nomads. These could, in theory, be Mongolian, Turkic, Caucasian, Semitic and North African. In practice, after the melting pot of confederating and migrating, ethnicity was more probably a group political construct than a representation of individual DNA.

Development of nomadic way of life

Nomadism probably did not evolve directly from hunter gathering. A period of settled agriculturalism may have been required in order for the animals, necessary for pastoral nomadism, to be domesticated. Initially, also, the horse was not necessary for a nomadic way of life – indeed Ancient Egypt and Sumer were tormented by footslogging, tent dwelling, Asiatics and Martu. Horses first emerged in recorded history just over four millennia ago in use by both settled states and those polities threatening them. Bitted horses appeared in western Iran in the regions of the Elamites and the Shimashki confederation in the period 2100 to 2000 BC.[1] Also, horses were recorded in Mesopotamian cities at this time when the word for horse, ass of the mountain, was first written. Horses presented defences with difficult challenges as speed facilitated movement to where defending forces were sparse: equally, however, their progress could be blocked relatively easily by physical obstacles and it may have been necessary to dismount in order to traverse them.

The second millennia BC may have seen the perfection of the short composite bow of glue-bonded horn, wood and sinew, resulting in a weapon capable of long range and rapid rate of fire, with which a skilled horseman could shoot arrows in all directions at speed. A weakness of the bow was that it took a long time to construct – up to a year for the glue to cure – but the real deficiency was that the glue could fail in consistently humid conditions and the bow deconstruct if immersed. This might be a problem if trying to occupy wet regions away from the steppe for protracted periods – southern Chinese paddy fields and north-western European forests come to mind. Paddies and forests are not ideal cavalry country anyway. Thus there were regions to which it was possible to escape from nomads and recover.

The first half of the first millennium BC saw great changes in the capabilities of nomads. Stronger horses were bred, capable of carrying a warrior long distances. Improved saddles and harness enhanced manoeuvrability and flexibility. Historical reports began to emphasise the speed and irresistible force of the nomad with his invincible combination of compact yet powerful composite bow and inexhaustible small horse. Climate change around 800 BC reduced the steppe range but conferred a relative advantage on those nomad groups able to shift long distances. At this time history records nomadic peoples moving outside their local ranges. In what is now China, the Wei state nearly collapsed under attack from the semi-nomadic Di people. As seen, nomadic peoples weakened the Assyrians and assisted the Medes and Babylonians in sacking Nineveh in 612 BC. Eventually, in the late fourth century BC, the northern Chinese states of Qin, Zhao and Yan eliminated the northern semi-nomads, building walls to consolidate the hold on the ground taken, and were confronted by the far more dangerous true steppe nomad. In the mid-first millennium AD the stirrup and the tree saddle added to the nomads' power.

Politics, leaders and confederations

Most of the time nomads live in fairly small, mobile groups. Therefore, what political organisation there was must usually have been highly devolved. From time to time however, nomad peoples have been galvanised into confederations – a process often identified with a charismatic individual: Attila, Mohammed, Ghenghiz Khan or Tamerlane are well known. Others perhaps less familiar are Maodun, Shetu, Esen and Altan, but they maybe more important in terms of provoking wall construction. Behind the emergence of leaders and confederations may have been some underlying factor, like climate change or expansion by settled states, which reduced the nomad range and forced a response if the nomads' relative position was not to be fundamentally weakened.

Operating in small groups, nomads could usually only be an irritant, albeit a serious and disruptive one; but when united by exceptional leadership in confederations, they confronted surrounding settled states and, in the process, found they could dominate them. Such confederations were however difficult to maintain, being dependent on the leaders' ability to extract tribute from settled states in order to distribute to, and secure loyalty from, confederates. Inherently unstable, confederations often collapsed after the death of the leader or the weakening of his authority. Also, there was the question of what a nomad confederation should do if it proved able to dominate an adjacent state? Given the nomads' lower numbers, should it assimilate with the settled state and lose its identity; or destroy it, killing its citizens, razing its cities, and returning its fields to pastures, but ending up with nothing to prey on?

Main regions of state and nomad interaction

There are two areas where nomads were found on a grand scale in the Old World: a strip running from Mesopotamia through North Africa to the Atlantic; and the Eurasian Steppe from Mongolia to Hungary. As will be seen, walls are found all around these regions.

The first area is the belt of arid and semi-arid land extending from the Atlantic in the west to the Persian plateau in the east across North Africa and Mesopotamia. This would be continuous were it not for the great rivers of the Nile, Euphrates and Tigris where irrigation resulted in land of exceptional fertility and vulnerability. Along the southern and eastern Mediterranean and in southern Anatolia there are fertile lands. In the semi-arid northern borders of the Arabian and Saharan deserts – with the Negev and Sinai deserts in between – there were nomadic peoples, mainly Berber and Bedouin and their predecessors. There also is a land corridor between Africa and Asia which is narrowed by the Gulf of Aqaba and the Red Sea.

The second area is the Eurasian Steppe. It might initially seem as though a region of grassland extended from Mongolia to Hungary, along which highly mobile nomads were free to travel, stopping off for plunder and mayhem as the spirit moved them. In fact the picture is rather more complicated and the Eurasian Steppe, while easier to traverse than mountains or deserts, is hardly the steppe nomad superhighway to which it is sometimes likened. Indeed, it can be broken down into four units which reduce in the scale and size of nomad forces they can sustain, moving from east to west.

The largest unit, the Mongolian and Manchurian Steppe, lies north of China's Yellow River. It is vast in scale and was able to sustain great steppe nomad confederations. The Central Asian Steppe lies largely in the modern countries of Kazakhstan, Kyrgyzstan, Tajikistan, Turkmenistan, and Uzbekistan. It is linked to the Mongolian Steppe by routes passing north or south of the Tian Shan Mountains. To the west, across the Volga, is the Caspian and Pontic Steppe which runs between the Black and Caspian Sea to the south, and the forest steppe to the north. The last area of broad grassland is the Great Hungarian Plain or Alföld which is separated from the Pontic Steppe by the Carpathian Mountains.

Linking together the Eurasian Steppe was a slow process and the first true travellers across its length did not make the journey until the Roman and Han Empires period. Also, the four units existed through much of history as discrete parts – and, even when linked up, mass movement between the units was often explosive rather than continuous. The constricted points, linking the various units, meant pressure could build up within one until it reached such a level that whole peoples burst out into adjacent units. The violence of this process could produce shock waves that reverberated further along the Eurasian Steppe from China to Europe.

Nomads as seen through the prism of sedentarists' texts

Nomads seldom left written records. Thus knowledge of them comes partly through archaeology but mostly through the written descriptions of sedentary states and assessment of their impact on the course of history. Therefore, nomads are largely seen through the prism of the sedentarists' viewpoint – either their contemporary written records or the studies of modern historians and archaeologists. The sources are very one-sided but there is remarkable consistency in them between descriptions composed thousands of years and miles apart. The overarching image of the nomad, as seen by the sedentarist, was one associated with restlessness and disorder, creating uncertainty and the urge for clarity.

Uncertainty brought fear – perhaps not untinged with envy. The farmer and the town dweller, tied to the plough or trapped at his desk or shop counter, unable to escape his hen-pecking wife, might inwardly have longed for the liberty of the nomad to indulge in some wanton destruction and plunder and then ride off into the sunset with loot and slaves in tow – while fearing that his family, farm or business would be the next target. Perhaps in part it was in this perception – on the part of the sedentarist – of the unpredictability and scariness of the nomad and the need for order and clear boundaries, that an explanation of linear building might be sought.

Restlessness

The literary records are engrossing: four millennia ago already the civilised states' compelling mixture of fascination with and repulsion towards nomads emerged. Around the end of the twenty-first century BC, a Pharaoh called Kheti gave his son Merikare some paternal advice, known as the Instructions to Merikare. The Asiatics, who sound like the same people as the Bedouin, were obviously a curse even though, at this date, they were not mounted:

> As for the wretched Asiatic … He does not dwell in one place, being driven hither and yon through want, going about (the desert) on foot. He has been fighting since the time of Horus; he never conquers, yet he is not conquered, and he does not announce a day of fighting, like a thief (short of) water, he does not dwell in one place … Do not worry about him, for the Asiatic is a crocodile on his riverbank; he snatches a lonely serf, but he will never rob in the vicinity of a populous town.[2]

Herodotus in the fifth century BC described the prowess of the Scythian nomads, now mounted archers, who were much more dangerous:

> Having neither cities or forts, and carrying their dwellings with them wherever they go; accustomed, moreover, one and all of them, to shoot from horseback; living not by husbandry but on their cattle; their wagons the only houses they possess, how can they fail of being unconquerable, and unassailable even?[3]

The Chinese *Shi Ji*, or Grand History, written by Sima Qian in the late second and early first century BC, described the nomads:

> Mountain Barbarians, Hsien-yün (Xianyun), (are) living in the region of the northern barbarians and wandering from place to place pasturing their animals. The animals they raise consist mainly of horses, cows, and sheep, but include such rare beasts as camels, asses, mules, and the wild horses. They move about in search of water and pasture and have no walled cities or fixed dwellings, nor do they engage in any kind of agriculture.[4]

In the fourth century Ammianus Marcellinus talked similarly of the Huns – although later in the same passage (quoted below) he demonstrated far greater hostility:

> No one in their country ever plows a field or touches a plow-handle. They are all without fixed abode, without hearth, or law, or settled mode of life, and keep roaming from place to place, like fugitives ... They are never protected by any buildings ... But roaming at large amid the mountains and woods, they learn from the cradle to endure cold, hunger, and thirst.[5]

But when Ammianus Marcellinus described – in the ambivalent way of sedentary peoples that could veer from fascination to horror – the more familiar Alans, who roam over vast tracts as nomads do, he depicted an enviable almost idyllic existence:

> In that land the fields are always green, and here and there are places set thick with fruit trees. Hence, wherever they go, they lack neither food for themselves nor fodder for their cattle, because of the moist soil and the numerous courses of rivers that flow hard by them.[6]

Appearance and character

Throughout pre-classical and classical history settled peoples rubbed up against nomads and, while often uncomplimentary, they did recognise them as fellow human beings with good as well as bad qualities – at least until the Huns appeared. Ammianus Marcellinus found the Alans comely:

Moreover, almost all the Halani are tall and handsome, their hair inclines to blond, by the ferocity of their glance they inspire dread, subdued though it is. They are light and active in the use of arms.[7]

But the Huns he sees as something quite new, different and horrible. Perhaps this is because it was the first confrontation with an eastern Asiatic people:

The people of the Huns exceed every degree of savagery ... The cheeks of the children are deeply furrowed with the steel from their very birth, in order that the growth of hair, when it appears at the proper time, may be checked by the wrinkled scars, they grow old without beards and without any beauty, like eunuchs. They all have compact, strong limbs and thick necks, and are so monstrously ugly and misshapen, that one might take them for two-legged beasts.[8]

Danger to sedentarists' women

The sedentarist, leading his humdrum life, must have feared the nomad not just because he would take the women but also because they might go by choice. A poem describes the despair of a civilised Sumerian at the strange attractions for women of the god Martu who shares the unpleasing customs of the eponymous people better known as the semi-nomadic Ammonites. Martu proposed marriage to Adg~ar-kidug the daughter of the City god Numushda. Excerpts give the civilised Sumerian's horrified description of Martu. Adg~ar-kidug's girlfriend told her:

They never stop roaming ... they are an abomination to the gods' dwellings. Their ideas are confused; they cause only disturbance. He is clothed in sack-leather ..., lives in a tent, exposed to wind and rain, and cannot properly recite prayers. He lives in the mountains and ignores the places of gods, digs up truffles in the foothills, does not know how to bend the knee, and eats raw flesh. He has no house during his life, and when he dies he will not be carried to a burial-place. My girlfriend, why would you marry Martu?[9]

Thus, perhaps, speaks the authentic voice of the sedentarist genuinely baffled by the attractions of the roaming nomad for women. Adg~ar-kidug's response is simple: 'I will marry Martu'. A Russian princess is reported as having run away to the steppe to marry a Kipchak Khan.[10] Fastidious high born Chinese ladies, however, did not appreciate being handed over to nomads, as well as bolts of silk and other luxuries, in pursuit of peace and friendship policies – and much poetry is devoted to lamentations of their sad lot.

Mobility

The descriptions of nomads focus on their mode of movement – particularly the life on horseback and their ability as cavalry. The Shi Ji says:

The little boys start out by learning to ride sheep and shoot birds and rats with a bow and arrow, and when they get a little older they shoot foxes and hares, which are used for food. Thus all the young men are able to use a bow and act as armed cavalry in time of war.[11]

Here is one explanation of the nomads' ability to take on Empires with vastly greater populations: every male nomad was potentially a warrior while a settled state could only support a limited proportion of effective professional soldiers. Ammianus Marcellinus described how the Huns could live day and night on their horses:

They are almost glued to their horses, which are hardy, it is true, but ugly, and sometimes they sit on them woman-fashion and thus perform their ordinary tasks. From their horses by night or day every one of that nation buys and sells, eats and drinks, and bowed over the narrow neck of the animal relaxes into a sleep so deep as to be accompanied by many dreams.[12]

He describes too how the Alans despised going around on foot:

The young men grow up in the habit of riding from their earliest boyhood and regard it as contemptible to go on foot; and by various forms of training they are all skilled warriors.[13]

But almost as noteworthy as the horses are the wagons. If the word 'bark' were substituted with 'canvas', in the following passage where Ammianus Marcellinus describes the Alans, then it might equally apply to nineteenth century migrants across the veldte or wild-west:

They (the Alans) dwell in wagons, which they cover with rounded canopies of bark and drive over the boundless wastes. And when they come to a place rich in grass, they place their carts in a circle.[14]

But the passage continues and perhaps describes a different world:

(They) feed like wild beasts. As soon as the fodder is used up, they place their cities … on the wagons and so convey them: in the wagons the males have intercourse with the women, and in the wagons their babes are born and reared; wagons form their permanent dwellings, and wherever they come, that place they look upon as their natural home.[15]

Decentralised politics

Government such as it was among nomads was highly devolved. Most of the time the nomadic lifestyle meant it was necessary to function in small groups. Even when united in confederations, for some greater purpose, the fact of operating on horseback and without bureaucracy, or even often literacy, made it difficult to enforce agreements among themselves and adjacent states. The *Shi Ji* says:

> Their lands, however, are divided into regions under the control of various leaders. They have no writing, and even promises and agreements are only verbal.[16]

Ammianus Marcellinus described the 'irregular government' of the Huns and their horseback councils:

> And when deliberation is called for about weighty matters, they all consult as a common body in that fashion. They are subject to no royal restraint, but they are content with the disorderly government of their important men, and led by them they force their way through every obstacle.[17]

All this might seem quaint and rather charming: people living without kings, central government and bureaucratic paperwork. But it is actually helpful in understanding the dilemma facing settled states trying to deal with nomads. How can agreements that stick be made with a whole people when they have no compelling central authority and no written agreements. If even only some parts of nomad groups feel unbound by or are even unaware of agreements, and persist in raiding, what strategy can be adopted to control the situation? The construction of linear barriers might seem explicable as a response.

> In truces they are faithless and unreliable, strongly inclined to sway to the motion of every breeze of new hope that presents itself, and sacrificing every feeling to the mad impulse of the moment.[18]

In his deathbed testament to his sons Grand Prince Vladimir Monomakh (the Great, 1113–1125) of the Kievan Rus described how:

> I concluded nineteen peace treaties with the Polovtsians ... and dispensed much of my cattle and my garments.[19]

This implies that treaties with the Polovtsians did not hold for long (and admits that, apart from campaigning against the nomads, they were in practice often bought off with cattle and royal garments). Earlier, it was seen how the Pharaoh Kheti, in his advice to his son, said of the nomad Asiatic, 'he does not announce a day of fighting, like a thief'. Both Vladimir and Kheti were strong rulers who knew what they were talking about when dispensing advice to their progeny. They understood they were dealing with peoples who attacked without warning and did not keep treaties. In these circumstances, continuous barriers brought clarity and a line of defence against an unpredictable and unreliable enemy.

Reasons for migration

Migrations were the result of the push from overpopulation and the encroachments of other peoples and the pull towards more attractive, hopefully less threatened, lands. The Huns, chasing a doe across the Sea of Azov, saw the desirable land of the Scythians:

> While hunters of their tribe were as usual seeking for game on the farthest edge of Maeotis, they saw a doe... The hunters followed... Presently the unknown land of Scythia disclosed itself and the doe disappeared.... And the Huns ... were now filled with admiration for the Scythian land.... They returned to their tribe ... praised Scythia and persuaded the people to hasten thither.[20]

Later the migrating Huns pushed the Goths out of Scythia:

> When the Getae (Goths) beheld this active race (the Huns) ..., they took fright and consulted with their king (Hermanaric) how they might escape from such a foe.... Balamber, king of the Huns, took advantage of his (Hermanaric's) ill health to move an army into the country of the Ostrogoths.[21]

At times the situation became particularly confusing when there was a mix of migrating and non-migrating nomads and barbarians. Thus, barbarian Goths were migrating into the territory of the nomadic Scythians:

> But when the number of the people increased greatly and Filimer, son of Gadaric, reigned as king ... he decided that the army of the Goths with their families should move from that region. In search of suitable homes and pleasant places they came to the land of Scythia.... Here they were delighted with the great richness of the country.[22]

Sometimes the situation involved solely the migrations of non-nomadic peoples. For example, Tacitus, with considerable irritation, described how Gauls, driven by poverty, occupied the wedge of land between the Rhine and the Danube called the *Agri Decumates*, seemingly forcing the Romans to follow:

> By several worthless and vagabond Gauls, and such as poverty rendered daring, that region was seized as one belonging to no certain possessor: afterwards it became ... part of a province, upon the ... extending of our garrisons and frontier.[23]

Propensity to warfare – and its horrendous consequences
The *Shi Ji* says of the Xiongnu:

> It is their custom to herd their flocks in times of peace and make their living by hunting, but in periods of crisis they take up arms and go off on plundering and marauding expeditions. This seems to be their inborn nature. For long-range weapons they use bows and arrows, and swords and spears at close range. If the

battle is going well for them they will advance, but if not, they will retreat, for they do not consider it a disgrace to run away. Their only concern is self-advantage, and they know nothing of propriety or righteousness.[24]

The most revealing description is that 'plundering and marauding' was their 'inborn nature'. While it is possible for contemporaries occasionally to romanticise the life of the nomad, with the clear exception of the vile Huns; from the point of view of the sedentarist the nomad was usually someone at best disruptive and often downright dangerous. Four millennia ago the sage Neferti, gave the Pharaoh Sneferu a vision of a disordered Egypt where Asiatics loomed large:

When the Asiatics would move about with their strong arms, (they) would disturb the hearts (of) those at the harvest, and would take away the spans of cattle at the plowing.[25]

Also:

Everything good is disappeared, and the land is prostrate because of the woes from those feeders, the Asiatics who are throughout the land. Foes have arisen in the east, and Asiatics have come down into Egypt ... no protector will listen.[26]

The Chinese *Book of Songs* (during the reign of King Xuan, 827–782 BC) carries the lament of the victims of the Xianyun:

We have no house, no home
Because of the Hsien-yün (*Xianyun*).
We cannot rest or bide
Because of the Hsien-yün (*Xianyun*).
...
Yes, we must be always on our guard;
The Hsien-yün (*Xianyun*) are very swift.[27]

The consequences of defeat could be horrible. Ghenghiz Khan is reputed to have said, with characteristic brutality, the greatest happiness is to scatter your enemy, to drive him before you, to see his cities reduced to ashes, to see those who love him shrouded in tears, and to gather into your bosom his wives and daughters.

The leaders of the nomads' enemies could look forward to having their skulls used as drinking cups – a custom consistently reported of nomads from the north of China to the Byzantine Empire. The Xiongnu made a receptacle from the skull of the defeated king of the Yuezhi in 161 BC. The Bulgar Khan Krum worked a jewelled cup from the skull of Byzantine emperor Nicephoras I in 811 BC after the Battle of Pliska. The Pechenegs' Khan made a chalice from the skull of Prince Sviatoslav I of Kiev in 972.

The cost for the people generally could be unspeakably terrible. Procopius recounts how in 539 a great calamity befell the Byzantine Empire when the Huns attacked:

A mighty Hunnic army crossing the Danube River fell as a scourge upon all Europe, a thing which had happened many times before, but which had never brought such a multitude of woes nor such dreadful ones to the people of that land.... And taking with them the money and leading away one hundred and twenty thousand captives, they all retired homeward without encountering any opposition.[28]

The Persian historian al-Juvayni, writing a generation after the destruction of Merv in 1221 by the Mongols, reported:

The Mongols ordered that, apart from 400 artisans, the whole population, including the women and children, should be killed, and no one, whether woman or man, be spared. To each Mongol soldier was allotted the execution of 300 or 400 Persians. So many had been killed by nightfall that the mountains became hillocks, and the plain was soaked with the blood of the mighty.[29]

Estimates of deaths range from six to seven figures. As al-Juvayni lamented generally of the impact of the Mongols:

With one stroke a world which billowed with fertility was laid desolate, and the regions thereof became a desert, and the greater part of the living, dead, and their skin and bones crumbling dust, and the mighty were humbled and immersed in the calamities of perdition.[30]

Nomads in eschatology and legend

Eschatology is the science of the end of the world: of death, judgement, heaven and hell. So terrible was the destruction wreaked by nomads that it became absorbed into apocalyptical literature. Ezekiel called Gog, the leader of the Magog, from:

the north parts, (from whence comes) thou, and many people with thee, all of them riding upon horses, a great company, and a mighty army.[31]

(Josephus identified Magog with the Scythians.) The *Book of Revelation* says:

When the thousand years are over, Satan will be released from his prison and will go out to deceive the nations in the four corners of the Earth – Gog and Magog – and to gather them for battle. In number they are like the sand on the seashore.[32]

The Koran describes how Dhu'lkarnein, identified possibly with Alexander the Great, dealt with Gog and Magog, forces of chaos who laid waste the land, by walling them in:

(Dhu'lkarnein) came between the two mountains, beneath which he found certain people ... And they said: O Dhu'lkarnein, verily Gog and Magog waste the land; shall we therefore pay thee tribute, on condition that thou build a rampart between us and them? The power wherewith my Lord had strengthened me is better than your tribute; but assist me strenuously, and I will set a strong wall between you and them ... Wherefore, when this wall was finished, Gog and Magog could not scale it, neither could they dig through it. And Dhu'lkarnein said,... when the prediction of my Lord shall come to be fulfilled, he shall reduce the wall to dust.[33]

In the *Alexander Romance*, the hero who walled in Gog and Magog is definitely the great Alexander. Later, after 395, the Huns were likened to Gog and Magog and various legends of Alexander described how he blocked them out. For example, Pseudo-Callisthenes:

And immediately the mountains approached each other, leaving a gap of ten cubits, mountains that had stood fixed before. And when Alexander beheld what had happened, he glorified the power of God, and he built gates of brass, and made secure the narrow space between the two mountains.

... (Alexander) drove 22 kings and their peoples, and there, at the extremities of the North, he shut them in, and the gates he called Caspian and the mountains Breasts. And the names of the nations were these: Goth, Magoth, Anougoi ... And since he feared that these nations might come forth upon the civilised world, he confined them.[34]

So terrible were the irruptions of the nomads from their dread fastnesses beyond the mountains that for civilisation to survive they must be walled in by heroes – and when they did break out the end of the world was presaged.

Conclusion – nomads as seen through the sedentarists' prism

The basic conflict between settled states and nomads stemmed from two factors.

The first was the unequal relationship between the nomad and the sedentarist which meant that it could never be stable. The nomad was strong in military capability but weak in material resources and the ability to preserve and store them – while the situation of the sedentary state tended to be the reverse. The challenge then was to work out some strategy to manage such an unequal relationship.

The second factor was the inability of the nomad to deliver reliably on explicit or implicit agreements for organising the relationship. As seen earlier Vladimir Monomakh concluded nineteen peace treaties with the Polovtsians which does not say much for their longevity. The nomad posed a constant threat but one where the time of an actual attack could not be predicted ('he does not announce a day of fighting, like a thief'). When agreements were made with sedentary states, usually involving tribute, it may have been difficult for nomadic leaders to control all members of the tribe or confederation. Gradually demands increased – as did free-lance raiding. Eventually, the sedentary polity may have decided the benefits from paying protection money were not worth the costs and attempted a different strategy, involving counter-attack, or imposing clarity and exclusion using linear barriers.

In the last resort, however, it appears the conflict could only be resolved by the destruction of one side or the other as an independent political power. Sometimes, the nomads annihilated all – particularly the Mongols in some regions – but eventually it was the settled Russian and Chinese Empires who agreed, at the Treaty of Nerchinsk in 1689, that the steppe should be totally subordinate to the sown.

Before this final resolution however, there were millennia of conflict between settled states and nomads. In order to understand the conditions which gave rise to linear barrier building, a starting point was the settled states' common perception, as reflected in the texts selected in this chapter, of the turbulent character of nomads who were peoples in most ways different: unstable, unpredictable, unreliable, untrustworthy, and uncivilised. They were hard to resist militarily and nearly impossible to form reliable agreements with. Also, even if it were possible to reach a working relationship with local nomads, another unfamiliar and more dangerous horde might appear over the horizon. The costs of mismanaging the relationship could be intolerably high, given the military effectiveness of the nomad and his proven record of murder and mayhem when on the rampage.

Therefore, it was essential for survival to find successful strategies for dealing with nomads – other than relying on usually unenforceable accords – one of which was the construction of a physical line that even an illiterate nomad would understand as a border, which would challenge the rapidity of his horse, provide a barrier to hide from his stinging arrows, and the opportunity on the retreat to cut him down and retrieve booty. While covering other aspects of the nomad relationship with settled states, the objective of this book is to discuss the particular importance of linear barriers in the strategic mix developed to contain nomads, until the military technological balance tipped decisively, after two millennia, in favour of the settled states.

Non-nomadic peoples provoking wall building – barbarians and migrants

Writing this book might have been easier if Hadrian's Wall did not exist and the construction of linear barriers could be ascribed solely to the interaction of states and nomads. Unfortunately things are never so simple and there are many linear barriers which were obviously not built by states to deal with the nomad threat.

One such group of wall builders was the warring states who built linear barriers to keep each other out. Another consisted of states who sought to keep out barbarians. (Here, barbarian simply means a polity deemed, by the settled state, to be at a lower stage of development.)

A further group was migrating peoples who could be nomads or normally sedentary barbarians. Both groups could move outside their established tribal localities and ranges of transhumance – thereby becoming migrants and demanding some kind of strategy from the settled polities whose own territories might be threatened with uncontrolled migrant invasion. (Examples of this were the barbarian Helvetii's efforts to move into Gaul at the time of Julius Caesar in 58 BC, or the barbarian Goths attempt to enter the Roman Empire, fleeing the nomadic Huns, in 376.) It was difficult for settled states to evolve satisfactory cost effective strategies to deal with long distance migrations due to sheer uncertainty as to when they might threaten. But when they did – if there were no strategy in place – the consequences could be shattering.

Particularly serious disruption could come when many peoples, both nomad and non-nomad, started moving and knocking into other peoples who had no desire to move. This was particularly intense in the period between about 400 and 800, called the Age of Great Migrations. Such situations might give rise to the construction of linear barriers – both by the incumbent polities but also sometimes by the migrant invaders who equally wished to pre-empt counter-attacks and stabilise new borders.

As a starting point, a settled state may have on its borders basically three types of polities: another settled state, nomads or barbarians. If it were another settled state then relations would generally be managed through negotiated agreements or treaties where there was a justified expectation that they would be observed. This obviated the need for linear barriers which were likely anyway to be ineffective against the type of major armies – combining infantry, cavalry and siege engines – that only the settled state or possibly the great nomad horde could put into the field. Dealing with both nomads and barbarians, where negotiated agreements did not stick, often required imposing clarity through the construction of a physical object, a linear barrier, that made it absolutely obvious where the border was and clear that incursions would be resisted and result in reprisals.

This book largely explores the relationship between settled states and nomads because it was this condition that gave rise to most linear barrier building. As, however, Hadrian's Wall and over 500 kilometres of Roman linear barriers in Germany demonstrate, the relationship between states and barbarians cannot be ignored – particularly as barbarians, as well as nomads, could become long distance migrants.

Part II

Survey

Chapter One

Egypt, Mesopotamia and China – Early Riverine Empires and Irrigation Defence

In the Prologue the seventh century BC adventures of the mounted, bow-armed, Eurasian Steppe nomads were recounted, as they careered into the empires of the Hither East. But what of earlier empires – what about going back to the great riverine civilisations like the Nile, the Tigris and the Euphrates, the Indus, and the Yellow River? The civilisations based around the first three rivers flourished and grew in the period up to 2200 BC when climate conditions were benign. Developing at a time of relative plenty, from a low base with sufficient for all, the surrounding, less advanced nomadic peoples were not a fundamental threat, and had no particular reason to be. At the end of the third millennium BC the climate became much drier for several centuries leading to more incursions from nomads. This suggested focusing on the later third millennium, in Egypt first and then Mesopotamia, in the search for earlier linear barriers. China will be looked at separately later. (Searches revealed no linear barriers around the Indus civilisations and, as the issue of the absence of walls in itself is revealing, this will be discussed later.)

1. Egypt and the River Nile

Footslogging nomads emerged early as a major pest for the ancient Egyptians. So what strategies did the Egyptians evolve to deal with them?

Egypt was created by the Nile which defined its long thin shape. Its annual flood fertilises a narrow strip on both river banks which is able to sustain intensive agriculture in what would otherwise be desert. The north-eastern border area is somewhat less infertile – allowing a pastoral nomadic existence from the Delta to Palestine where there is a land corridor between the Mediterranean Sea and the Red Sea. Also, the Nile itself is an aquatic corridor that flows through the desert where movement is restricted in its upper reaches by natural obstacles in the form of the cataracts where the flow is obstructed by boulders.

Egypt most certainly has valued land, indeed in many ways the most valuable and vulnerable of all: that which is irrigated. Intruders can quickly damage or destroy water channels, threatening the high populations that intense irrigation can sustain. (Such intrusion can be borne of desperation. The animals of pastoral nomads need water and in times of drought, nomads and their herds will be compelled to go to irrigated areas and their water sources, resulting in an uncomfortable collision of pastoralist and agriculturalist.)

The great fertility of the land, once irrigation techniques were mastered, meant the early development of a civilisation whose dynastic period started in the late fourth millennium BC and whose Old Kingdom survived until the later third millennium BC. After 2200 BC there is literary and archaeological evidence for the onset of much drier conditions, after a time when populations – after good times – had risen sharply. The Prophecy of Neferti – supposedly made by the sage Neferti during the reign the Pharaoh Sneferu during the Old Kingdom fourth dynasty in the twenty sixth century BC – foresaw a time when: 'The rivers of Egypt are empty, so that the water is crossed on foot.'[1]

The Egyptian Old Kingdom collapsed internally with the ending of the sixth dynasty (2181 BC), leading to the First Intermediate Period seventh to eleventh (2181–2060 BC) dynasty pharaohs. During this Intermediate era, between the Old and the Middle Kingdoms, much was heard of displeasing nomads, for Egypt was troubled by 'Asiatics'. Powerful Pharaohs emerged mid-way through the eleventh dynasty, reunited the state and pursued an aggressive nomad control policy and took Egypt into the Middle Kingdom period.

Neferti gave Sneferu a vision of a disordered drought-smitten Egypt: 'When the Asiatics would move about with their strong arms, would disturb the hearts (of) those who are at the harvest, and would take away the spans of cattle at the plowing.'[2] In this most early of periods, shifting sands and disruptions of later irrigation projects means dependence largely on literary texts in the search for linear barriers, where interpretation must of necessity be subjective and inconclusive.

Egyptian linear barriers

The Walls of the Ruler[*] – Starting with the land corridor through the Isthmus of Suez, searches revealed the presumed existence of a rather enigmatic early linear barrier, translated as the Walls of the Ruler. These appeared by name in two literary sources – the Story of Sinuhe and the Prophecy of Neferti. Another source, the Wisdom for Merikare, although it does not specifically refer to the Walls by name, did give a clue as to what kind of barrier might be sought. Putting together these three sources, what kind of picture emerges?

The Story of Sinuhe recounted how an official who feared being framed for complicity in a plot to murder the Pharaoh, possibly Amenemhet I (who was assassinated in 1962 BC), fled Egypt past the Walls of the Ruler: 'I attained the Wall of the Ruler, which was made to repel the Setiu (Asiatics) and to crush the Sandfarers. I bowed me down in a thicket through fear lest the watcher on the wall for the day might see.'[3] Amenemhet I was the first ruler of the Middle Kingdom twelfth dynasty, who reasserted authority over a united Egypt.

The earliest reference to the Walls of the Ruler in terms of chronology however, was the Prophecy of Neferti. Neferti presented the pharaoh Sneferu with a vision of a disordered Egypt overrun by Asiatics. But there would come a ruler, Ameny, and: 'The Asiatics will fall at the dread of him. Men will build the Walls of the Ruler, and there will be no letting the Asiatics go down

---

[*] Sometimes 'Walls of the Ruler' is translated as 'Walls of the Prince'. The translation is standardised here using the former.

into Egypt, that they may beg water after their accustomed fashion to let their herds drink. Then order will return to its seat, while chaos is driven away.'[4]

The reference is almost certainly again to Amenemhet. Unless it is accepted that this really was a prophecy then it must be presumed that the Prophecy of Neferti was written following the reign of Amenemhet – as it could only then have been known that something called the Wall of the Ruler had been built. This would place the construction of the Walls between 1991 and 1962 BC, during the reign of Amenemhet. The Walls meant the Asiatics could no longer get into Egypt to beg. This implies that the Walls were some kind a physical linear barrier which could not be readily crossed by nomads and their herds.

The Wisdom for Merikare was advice given by First Intermediate Period Pharaoh Kheti III to his son, the future Pharaoh Merikare, in the tenth dynasty of First Intermediate Period. If the date of Merikare's succession was 2066 BC then the idea for some kind of construction, to deal with the problem of Asiatics, would first have appeared in the twenty-first century BC. After denouncing the Asiatics, in the passage cited above, Kheti paternally advised Merikare to: 'Dig a moat and flood the half of it at the Bitter Lakes, for see, it is the navel-string of the desert dwellers. Its walls are warlike.'[5] This passage indicated that some form of canal should be dug. (A canal can be a form of linear barrier.) Also, the term 'navel-string', as translated here, perhaps implied an umbilical cord through which the necessities of life – of which the most basic is water – could be provided to the desert dwellers. Rather than creating a barrier to keep out Asiatics from the Nile delta, perhaps fresh water was to be brought to them, and their herds, to enable them to stay away.

A prophecy, some paternal advice, and a story: really can anything very serious be read into all this? The Prophecy of Neferti said the Asiatics go down into Egypt to beg for water after their accustomed fashion to let their herds drink. This sounds as though the occurrence was regular either because of annual transhumance or due to frequent water shortages. The strong Pharaohs of the twelfth dynasty were certainly known to have been great builders with canals and fortresses to their credit. It seems likely that a linear barrier of some form, called the Walls of the Ruler, had been built by the end of the reigns of Amenembat I (1991– 1962 BC) and Senusret I (197 –1962 BC) because there was something there that Sinahe had passed by on his travels. Overall, however, it is difficult not to conclude that the term Walls of the Ruler might be somewhat misleading. The evidence makes it difficult to interpret this as any form of continuous, above ground, construction of stone or brick. There is, however, the possibility that it was a canal, built either for transportation purposes or to take water to the Asiatics so they did not have to come to the Nile, and it may have had a defensive function to stop raiding.

The Eastern Frontier Canal – When Israel occupied Sinai for a period after the 1967 Six-Day War Israeli archaeologists examined three traces of lines of displaced earth along the eastern delta border.[6] They conjectured that these were the remnants of a canal which joined the Nile to the Mediterranean which ran west to east from the Nile, along the Wadi Tumilat depression, and then north-east to the coast at Pelusium. This was 'clearly a man-made feature' whose width was about seventy metres at the surface and about sixty metres wide at the bottom at a depth of about two to three metres.[*] The purpose and dating of the Eastern Frontier Canal, as it is prosaically

---

[*] This is wider than the modern Suez canal which, to deal with modern shipping, is about three times deeper.

known, is uncertain. The archaeologists had identified three functions: defence, irrigation and navigation – of which the first was the most important.[7] The presence of: 'A wide body of water too deep to be forded, would have been as effective in keeping out both foraging herds and mounted hordes of any kind as well.'[8]

Southern Nile Cataract Walls – Ancient Egypt had a threatened southern border across which the Nubians raided. There is a narrow land corridor of irrigated land along the Nile which suggests that there might have been a linear barrier across it marking the frontier. Two long walls have been found at the first and second cataracts but their configuration might seem somewhat unexpected. They do not run at right angles to the river but rather roughly parallel to it.

During the Old Kingdom the Egyptian frontier lay on the first cataract. In the Middle Kingdom, under the very strong Pharaohs of the twelfth dynasty, Egypt expanded further into Lower Nubia, down to the second cataract. Control of the river and surrounding land was managed by a number of huge forts built out of mud brick. If a boat were to proceed past the cataracts, either a channel had to be cut through them, which needed constant maintenance, or the cargo or the boat itself had to be dragged overland on a portage route. In the Old Kingdom the general Weni became governor of Upper Egypt. He pierced the rocks of the first cataract making it possible for the Egptian army to control Nubia – the source of raids on Upper Egypt. But soon portage was seen as a better option than maintaining a passage through the cataracts. In a border area, a ship or its valuable cargo would be particularly vulnerable while being dragged overland. (A vivid description of the encounter between nomads and those practising portage is provided by the Byzantine Emperor Constantine VII Porphyrogenitus (913–959). He wrote that the Russians could not come to Constantinople 'unless they are at peace with the Pechenegs, because when the Russians come with their ships to the barrages of the river ... they ... carry them past by portaging them on their shoulders, then ... the Pechenegs set upon them, and, as they cannot do two things at once, they are easily routed and cut to pieces.'[9]) The protection of the Nile overland portage route seems to have produced an original solution – that is, building a wall on the landward side of the portage route, leaving the river itself to provide protection for the other side.

At the first cataract, the wall from Aswan to Philae is 7.5 kilometres long. It was about five metres at the base and tapered up to an estimated height of about ten metres. Every six to ten layers of mud brick the structure was reinforced with reed mats. The Wall below the second cataract from Semna to Uronarte has been traced for about five kilometres, and could be longer. The Semna wall is about 2.5 metres thick.

The dating of these walls seems unresolved although the timing of expansion into the area and the similarity to the construction of the forts indicate a Middle Kingdom date. If this dating were correct then these could be among the oldest mud brick walls which constituted a linear defence. That said, they are not frontier barriers – rather they are an early solution to the specific problem created by the cataracts and were built because of the vulnerability of transportation routes around them. Sections of the lower levels of the walls survive, possibly making them the earliest surviving long walls built of coursed material.

Pharaoh Seti I returns from Asia in a relief in Ammon's Temple at Karnak which may show the crocodile filled Eastern Frontier Canal. *(Drawing of relief by Emma Spring)*

Analysis – Egyptian linear barriers

The most obvious features of Egypt's border control strategy were forts along the Nile to the south and along the eastern border, guarding the major routes. That there was some form of canal linking some of the lakes between the north and south coasts of the Sinai Isthmus, seems incontrovertible. These also played a key role in keeping the Asiatics and their herds out of Egypt.* In the south there were two major linear barriers at the first and second cataracts, but they were not frontier barriers – as any intruder could have skirted around them – rather they appear to have protected portage routes. Thus, these barriers might be seen as emanating from the tense conditions arising when settled states were confronted by more nomadic peoples although they constitute a somewhat specialised solution.

2. Mesopotamia and the Rivers Tigris and the Euphrates

Egypt shows that the conjunction of irrigated lands and nomads produced linear barriers – even if the evidence might seem elusive and inconclusive. Therefore, might also then Mesopotamia, with the similarly intensely irrigated Tigris and Euphrates Rivers, produce evidence of walls in the presence of nomads?

---

* There is actually a clear example of a fortified canal in the Sinai region to guard the frontier between Egypt and Sinai. After the 1967 War, between Israelis and the Arabs, the Bar Lev Line, built by the former, incorporated the Suez Canal. The east canal bank was raised to form a sand rampart, which the Egyptians reduced at the beginning of the Yom Kippur War in 1973 with high pressure hoses, an option not available to earlier invaders.

In Mesopotamia, the area of irrigated lands runs along the flood plains of the Tigris and the Euphrates up to, and somewhat beyond, the convergence points of the rivers between ancient Babylon and modern Baghdad. Above that point the alluvial plain peters out and the land becomes too hilly to allow for intense irrigation. From the north-east flows the Diyala River which passes through the Zagros Mountains to join the Tigris, linking the high Persian plateau to Mesopotamia. Around the river was especially valued irrigated land. The area of convergence of the Tigris and Euphrates constituted a constricted land corridor. Local nomads and semi-nomads would have been expected to press particularly hard on the rich and productive irrigated lands of Mesopotamia.

As in Egypt, civilisation, sustained by the irrigated lands of Mesopotamia, came early, in the fourth millennia BC, with the Sumerians. Again, as with Egypt, there is evidence of climate change. In the last century of the third millennium BC the stream flow of the Euphrates and the Tigris was very low, according to analysis of sediments in the Persian Gulf. The end of the Akkadian era, due to defeat by the hated Gutian peoples from the mountainous east in the twenty-second century BC, coincided with a few decades of intense drought which was followed by two to three centuries of dry weather. Ur revived and under Ur-Nammu defeated the Gutians and established the third dynasty of Ur, commonly abbreviated to Ur III, in 2112 BC. The Sumerians initiated a short period of cultural renaissance in a time of constant conflict with the semi-nomadic Martu – more familiar as the biblical Amorites.

Indeed, Ur III may have faced two reasonably distinct threats. From the north-west there was the Martu whose aim may in part have been to gain sustenance for their herds in times of drought. The direction of the threat that they posed would have been through the relatively flat lands between and to both sides of the convergence point of the Euphrates and the Tigris. To the north-east were the Elamites and Shimashki confederation in the highlands to the east of the Tigris. Their lines of attack would have been more focused down river valleys – perhaps the Diyala River flowing through the Zagros Mountains to the Tigris.

Mesopotamian linear barriers

In this early period there is only textual evidence for linear barriers, based on letters that remarkably survive from the third dynasty of Ur. These writings between Sumerian kings and their often disobedient generals and officials, are called the Royal Correspondence of Ur (abbreviated to the RCU).* Much of the correspondence in the twenty-two or so surviving letters was about defence against the Martu. There was also information about linear barriers in the year names of Sumerian king lists (Mesopotamian kings named each year of their reigns after some major event).

---

* After the fall of Ur III, a Semitic language, Akkadian, replaced Sumerian as the dominant regional tongue but the latter survived as a medium for religious, administrative and cultivated discourse. Sumerian was taught by copying texts which included administrative letters found in excavated school rooms of the eighteenth century BC.

1.1: Mesopotamia

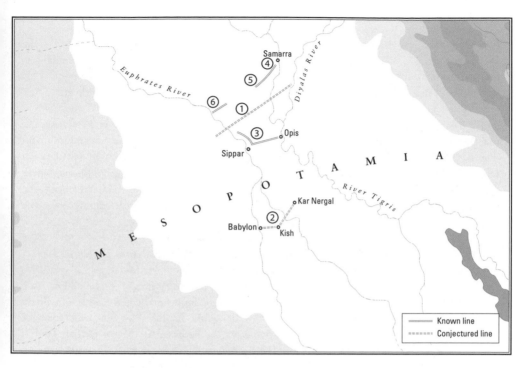

Sumerian
1. Muriq Tidnim (conjectural)

Babylonian Line 1
2. Nebuchadnezzar's Babylon to Kish Wall (conjectural)

Babylonian Line 2
3. Habl es-Sakhar (Nebuchadnezzar's Sippar to Opis Wall, Median Wall)

Line 3 (uncertain)
4. El-Mutabbaq
5. Sadd Nimrud (also called El-Jalu)
6. Umm Raus Wall (site of Macepracta Wall(?), Artaxerxes' Trench(?))

Sasanian
Khandaq-i-Shapur (see Map and linear barrier list 3)

The Sumerian kings Shulgi (2094–2047 BC), Shu-Sin (2037–2029 BC) and Ibbi-Sin (2028–2004 BC) were mentioned in the context of three walls:

bad-mada/**Wall of the Land** – The Wall of the Land is known only from one reference in the king lists: 'Year 37: Nanna (the god) and Shulgi the king built the Wall of the land.'[10] Shulgi was on the throne for forty-seven years so the wall belongs to the last quarter of his long reign. This was a time of increasing pressure on central and southern Mesopotamia from the Martu.

bad-igi-hur-sag-ga/**Wall Facing the Highlands** – In the RCU there are several references to *bad-igi-hur-sag-ga* – both during Shulgi's reign and that of his successors, Shu-Sin and Ibbi-Sin. The *bad-igi-hur-sag-ga* has been variously translated as the Wall, Fortress, or the Fortification facing the highlands or mountains – making it uncertain whether this was a continuous linear barrier. If, however, Shulgi really did build a long wall then he has the distinction of being the first known builder of such a barrier. This obstacle possibly faced a threat coming down the Diyala River as it faced the Highlands, presumably the Zagros Mountains.

Muriq Tidnim/**Fender off of the Tidnim** – There are three references to *Muriq Tidnim*, or fender (off) of the Tidnim and Shu-Sin. First, the king lists of his fourth regnal year said: 'Shu-Sin the king of Ur built the amurru (Amorite) wall (called) '*Muriq Tidnim*/holding back the Tidanum''[11] Second, there is an inscription in a temple built for the god Shara: 'For Shara Shu-Sin built the Eshagepada, his (Shara's) beloved temple, for his (Shu-Sin's) life when he built the Martu wall *Muriq Tidnim* (and) turned back the paths of the Martu to their land.'[12] Third, the most informative reference to the *Muriq Tidnim* is in a letter from Sharrum-bani, an official of Shu-Sin. 'You sent me a message ordering me to work on the construction of the great fortification *Muriq Tidnim* … announcing: "The Martu have invaded the land." You instructed me to build the fortification, so as to cut off their route; also, that no breaches of the Tigris or the Euphrates should cover the fields with water … from the bank of the Ab-gal watercourse to the province of Zimudar. When I was constructing this fortification to the length of 26 danna, and had reached the area between the two mountain ranges, I was informed of the Martu camping within the mountain ranges because of my building work.'[13]

In this letter, the construction is described as 'great'. Whatever the uncertainties about Shulgi's earlier edifices, it is difficult not to interpret this passage as describing a major continuous linear barrier. In the west the Ab-gal canal is associated with an earlier western course of the Euphrates and to the east the province of Zimudar is identified as being on the east side of Tigris in the region of the Diyala river. A danna is about two hours march so 26 dannas may be over 150 kilometres. Therefore, the edifice appeared to extend from the Euphrates to the other side of the Tigris because its length was much greater than the distance between the two rivers. The instructions to build the walls specifically cite stopping the semi-nomadic Martu from overwhelming the fields by a breach between the Tigris and the Euphrates, showing that irrigated land was perceived as particularly vulnerable.

Analysis – Ur III

In the hillier east controlling access down the Diyala river area there may have been a single fortification, the *bad-igi-hur-sag-ga* or the Wall/Fortress facing the Highlands, first built by Shulgi, which might or might not have been part of another system *bad-mada* (the Wall of the Land) built in the flatter west. During the reign of Shu-Sin it seems more likely that a linear barrier called *Muriq Tidnim* was built from new, or it consisted of earlier lines that were linked and much reinforced including Shulgi's Wall of the land. This is all speculation but there is good if circumstantial literary evidence that Ur III's strategy for defence against the Martu involved the construction of what would be the first recorded long continuous non-aquatic linear barriers.

There does seem to be a fairly general academic acceptance that under Shulgi and Shu-Sin long walls were built and their purpose was to keep out nomads. For example: 'Even as early as year 35 of Shulgi, the (nomad) problem was becoming so grave that Shulgi constructed a wall to keep them (pastoral and semi-nomadic Amorites) out, and Shu-Sin built another barrier, called "fender off of Tidnim," 200 kilometres long, stretching between the Tigris and the Euphrates across the northern edge of the alluvial plain.'[14] Also: 'Yet despite Shulgi's talents, within a few years of his death in 2047 BC his Empire, too, imploded. In the 2030s raiding became such a problem that Ur built a hundred-mile wall to keep the Amorites out.'[15]

Later Mesopotamia

Looking at later Mesopotamia, after the fall of Ur III, how did it defend itself in times of necessity? What emerges is three intense periods of barrier building: firstly, that already discussed, during the short lived Ur III period; secondly, in the neo-Babylonian period associated with Nebuchadnezzar in the sixth century BC; and thirdly, later in the fourth century, aquatic linear barriers were built by the Sasanians. There are also a number of major but little studied walls, discussed below, north of the Tigris and Euphrates convergence point, which are not clearly dated.

After Ur III fell to the Elamites and the Shimaskhi confederation, the so-called Amorite dynasty of Isin completed its breakaway. Given that lower Mesopotamia had fallen to peoples from outside the region there was no reason for a barrier between the north and southern Mesopotamia. Also, Martu or Amorite semi-nomads were becoming increasingly sedentarised. Subsequently, the Babylonians of the era of Hammurabi were able to project their power well to the north of Babylon. The Assyrians, coming from the north, had no need for walls around 700 BC to defend Babylon in this region as they controlled the regions to its north and south. (The Assyrians may have built walls on their northern border, an issue which is discussed later.)

The neo-Babylonians recovered control of their city in the sixth century BC and made it the capital of the region. The second period of major barrier building materialised in this later Babylonian period, associated with Nebuchadnezzar and textually with Queens Semiramis and Nitocris. Nebuchadnezzar II ruled for forty-three years from 604 to 562 BC. The Medes' conquest of Lydia made Nebuchadnezzar suspicious of their intentions and this led him to strengthen his northern border. Behind the Medes loomed the Persians. This was clearly seen, rightly as it turned out, as a real, unpredictable threat – and one that prompted the construction of a comprehensive linear barrier system. Notwithstanding this attempt, in 539 BC Cyrus the Great led the Medes and the Persians into Babylonia which was absorbed into the Achaemenid Empire.

Linear barriers – survey

There were three lines of barriers at and above Babylon looked at here, starting in the south and going to the north.

Babylon to Kish – Line 1

Two walls of Nebuchadnezzar (604–562 BC) are known from a clay cylinder, dated to 590 BC when relations between the Babylonians and the Medes had deteriorated. (These compose Line 1 and Line 2 in this and the next section.)

Nebuchadnezzar's Wall from near Babylon to Kish – This cylinder is inscribed: 'In the district of Babylon from the chau(s)sée on the Euphrates bank to Kish, 4 2/3 bēru long, I heaped up on the level of the ground an earth-wall and surrounded the City with mighty waters. That no crack should appear in it, I plastered its slope with asphalt and bricks.'[16] A bēru is the distance which could be travelled in two hours so is variable according to terrain. At five kilometres an hour this barrier would be about 47 kilometres long. The problem is that this is considerably longer than the distance between Babylon and Kish – which is little more than 10 kilometres – unless the barrier followed a particularly circuitous route. Also, it would seem a fairly pointless military exercise building a barrier from Babylon to Kish leaving the flood plain open to the east from Kish to the Tigris. Using up the surplus kilometres would take the wall further east to Kar-Nargal, near an earlier channel of the Tigris, hence blocking the land corridor between the Euphrates and the Tigris. No physical evidence of this wall has been identified.

Opis to Sippar – Line 2

The second line ran between the cities of Sippar, above Babylon on the Euphrates, and Opis on the Tigris, the precise position of which has been lost. A number of walls are associated with this location in texts and there is a surviving wall called Habl-es-Sakhar.

Nebuchadnezzar's Wall from Sippar to Opis – Nebuchadnezzar's inscribed cylinder described the second wall as follows: 'To strengthen the fortification of Babylon, I continued, and from Opis upstream to the middle of Sippar, from Tigris bank to Euphrates bank, 5 bēru, I heaped up a mighty earth-wall and surrounded the city for 20 bēru like the fullness of the sea. That the pressure of the water should not harm the dike, I plastered its slope with asphalt and bricks.'[17] This Opis to Sippar wall would have been about 50 kilometres long. Both the Babylon to Kish and the Opis to Sippar walls were water-proofed by asphalt so they must have been built in proximity to water – possibly water-courses like canals or in flatlands prone to flooding or swamping.

Wall of Semiramis – The geographer Strabo, citing Eratosthenes, when describing Mesopotamia, said the Tigris, 'goes to Opis, and to the wall of Semiramis, as it is called.'[18] Therefore, this wall was in the region of the Tigris and the Euphrates' convergence point. (Herodotus mentioned Semiramis' works but did not specify a wall. Rather he described levees which controlled flooding.)

Wall of Nitrocris – Herodotus also described a Babylonian queen called Nitocris – possibly the daughter of Nebuchadnezzar and the mother of the *Book of Daniel*'s King Belshazzar brought down by Cyrus – whose constructions in Babylon were mainly connected with diverting the Euphrates. Nitocris built works in the entrance of the country (which is clearly a description of a land corridor) against the threat of the Medes. 'Nitocris ... observing the great power and restless enterprise of the Medes, ... and expecting to be attacked in her turn, made all possible exertions to increase the defences of her empire.'[19]

Wall of Media – In the *Anabasis*, Xenophon described how he led the 10,000 Greeks back from Mesopotamia. In it he encountered the Wall of Media twice. Here what is described is the second occasion when Xenophon actually crossed the wall itself following the battle of Cunaxa in 401 BC. 'They reached the so called Wall of Media and passed within it. It was built of baked bricks, laid in asphalt, and was twenty feet wide and a hundred feet high; its length was said to be twenty parasangs, and it is not far distant from Babylon.'[20] Assuming that a parasang is the same as a bēru or a danna, that is a two hours march, then the wall was about 100 kilometres long.

Habl-es-Sakhar – There is a surviving wall in the vicinity of Sippar. In 1867 one Captain Bewsher described the ruins of a wall then called Habl-es-Sakhar – which translates from the Arabic as a line of stones or bricks. 'The ruins of this wall may now be traced for about 10½ miles and are about 6 feet above the level of the soil. It was irregularly built, the longest side running E.S.E. for 5½ miles; it then turns to N.N.E. for another mile and a half. An extensive swamp to the northward has done much towards reducing the wall.... There is a considerable quantity of bitumen scattered about, and it was probably made of bricks set in bitumen. I can see nothing in Xenophon which would show this was not the wall the Greeks passed, for what he says of its length was merely what he was told him.'[21] The description of the 'baked bricks laid upon bitumen' is like Nebuchadnezzar's description of his wall between Opis and Sippar: plastered with asphalt and bricks.

In 1983 a joint team of Belgian and British Archaeological Expeditions to Iraq investigated the ruins of Habl-es-Sakhar. This confirmed that Habl-es-Sakhar was built by Nebuchadnezzar, for bricks marked with his name were found during its excavation. The team reported that Habl-es-Sakhar is the name of 'a levee 30 metres wide and 1 metre high which could be followed for about 15 kilometres. A trench across the levee to the north of the site of Sippar revealed baked brick walls (largely robbed) on either side of an earth embankment. The earth core was about 3.2m wide and the brick walls about 1.75m in width. Between the brick courses was a skin of bitumen. On the bottom of each brick was a stamp of Nebuchadnezzar. If the wall extended to the ancient line of the Tigris it would have been nearly 40k long.'[22]

The wall stood astride the northern approaches to Babylon itself. The wall's function appeared primarily to have been military as it was not well situated to protect land against the flooding of the Euphrates which lay to the south. It is 'beyond reasonable doubt' that Habl-es-Sakhar is Nebuchadnezzar's wall and Xenophon's Wall of Media due to the location north of Sippar, the details of the construction, and the stamped bricks set in bitumen. This is rather satisfying because a surviving wall has been matched up with literary text.

Umm Raus to Samarra – Line 3

A third line of walls runs from Samarra on the Tigris to Ramadi on the Euphrates which delineated the upper limits of the alluvial plain where intense irrigation was possible. Here the fertile plain is not continuous between the Tigris and the Euphrates but the regions close to the rivers fit the description of valued irrigated land. As the rivers have diverged already significantly in the area of the third uppermost line, compared to the lower two lines, a wall that extended the whole distance would have had to have been much longer. Central sections might also have been purposeless as there was little valued, highly irrigated, land to protect and attackers would not have wanted to stray too far into less fertile land. This area is the site of two walls described in ancient texts and three surviving linear barriers.

Trench of Artaxerxes – In the *Anabasis* Xenophon described the march along the Euphrates, at the point where canals began, thereby indicating intense irrigation: 'Cyrus … expected the king to give battle the same day, for in the middle of this day's march a deep sunk trench was reached, thirty feet broad, and eighteen feet deep.… The trench itself had been constructed by the great king upon hearing of Cyrus's approach, to serve as a line of defence.'[23] The trench does not appear to have survived but the site might have been reused to build later walls – the first being the Wall of Macepracta, discussed next, and second the surviving wall at Umm Raus.[24]

Wall of Macepracta – Ammianus Marcellinus, describing the assault in AD 362 by the apostate Emperor Julian on the Sasasian Empire of Shapur II, wrote: 'our soldiers came to the village of Macepracta, where the half-destroyed traces of walls were seen; these in early times had a wide extent, it was said, and protected Assyria from hostile inroads.'[25]

There is a surviving belt of linear barriers which extends – with long gaps – between the Euphrates and the Tigris.[26] The three walls mark the line where the fertile Babylonian plain peters out. There is the rampart starting at Umm-Raus which extends east from the Euphrates; El-Mutabbaq is a burnt brick wall with towers running west from the Tigris; and between them is a dyke named Sadd Nimrud (also called El-Jalu). Their dating is very uncertain.

Wall at Umm Raus – The wall, running east from the Euphrates, has been described: 'From Umm Raus we see the wall running inland for a distance of about 7 miles, with rounded bastions at intervals for 2½ miles.… The wall appeared to be about 35–45 ft broad, with bastions projecting about 20ft. to 25ft., set at a distance of about 190 feet axis to axis. At its highest point the mound made by the wall is about 7 to 8 feet high. From the air it can be seen that there are about forty buttresses in all.'[27]

The line may follow that of Artaxerxes' trench. It is not a brick wall but an earth rampart. It was 'never defensible, perhaps never finished'.[28] Also: 'This wall must have been designed … to protect the suddenly broadening area of fertile irrigated land to its south from raids and infiltration; large armies entering Iraq by the Euphrates would not have found it a serious obstacle.'[29]

Again, there is the explicit mention of defending irrigated land. The Umm Raus rampart must date between 401 BC, as it is not mentioned by Xenophon, and AD 363, when a ruined wall was described at Macepracta by Ammianus Marcellinus.

El-Mutabbaq – The modern name, El-Mutabbaq, means built in layers or courses of bricks. This is a massive rampart lying at the boundary of the irrigatel alluvium of the widening Tigris valley south of Samarra and the desert to the north-west. It is about forty kilometres long and 'has traces of turrets and moat on the north-west side and follows … the natural contours of the land. The rampart was four to six metres high, thirty metres wide at the bottom.'[30] It is, 'a mud-brick wall three and a half bricks wide behind which is 10.5m of gravel-packing held in by a small mud-wall. The gravel packing was compartmented by mud-brick cross walls. There are projecting towers at regular intervals and a ditch about 20 to 30m. wide which is now about 2m. deep.'[31]

The following description shows El-Mutabbaq as being designed to protect valued land against a nomad threat: 'Herzfeld (a German explorer and historian) attributed construction to the threat of the Bedouin invading the fertile area along the Tigris by the river Dujail.'[32] These walls were seen as intended to stop nomads thereby affirming their ineffectiveness against great armies: 'Cross-country walls of this type are notoriously inefficient at stopping great armies; this particular example could be outflanked without any difficulty at all. A stronger objection to any theory that it was designed to stop a great army is that it blocks the one route into southern Mesopotamia which, because of natural obstacles north of Samarra, invading armies have preferred never to use.'[33] The walls were intended to defend irrigated land: 'El-Mutabbaq was more probably intended to help protect the irrigated land from unwanted settlers and raiding parties coming from the desert.'[34] There is no consensus as to the builder although they are described as Sasanian.[35] Basically, these linear barriers do not seem to have been examined since the 1960s and remain effectively undated.

Sadd Nimrud – A dyke called Sadd Nimrud or El-Jalu, which is about forty kilometres long, that lies to the west of El-Muttabaq. This linear barrier does not extend the full distance between El-Muttabaq and the Wall at Umm Raus: 'The fortification in the central area peters out in the direction of Falluja – perhaps as a considerable gap did not need to be defended – as armies could not advance far into the desert away from water.'[36] No date, other than this possibly being pre-Islamic, has been suggested.[37]

Analysis – three lines at the Euphrates and Tigris convergence point

These three barriers between the Tigris and the Euphrates present a very baffling picture. They follow roughly the line where intense irrigation ceases. Rather than being a single response, however, they seem to be three discrete ad hoc reactions to separate threats to irrigated lands near the rivers Tigris and Euphrates. They can lay claim to being among the longest and oldest walls outside China, excepting certain Roman and Sasanian walls, yet there appears to have been no very detailed study of them. The attribution is generally vague – with comparisons made to features on Sumerian to Sasanian walls, in other words millennia apart. Generally commentators do regard them as forming part of a local response to the need to protect valued irrigated land in the immediate vicinity, rather than as having any strategic purpose to block routes into central and southern Mesopotamia.

Sasanian aquatic barriers

In the early fourth century AD a semi-nomadic people, the Lakhmid Arabs, who were originally from the Yemen, emerged as a serious threat to Sasanian Mesopotamia.

Khandaq-i-Shapur – Arab tradition associates Shapur II (AD 309–379) with a defensive dyke that reputedly ran west of the Euphrates, from Hit to Basra. This barrier is looked at again later when Sasanian barriers are discussed. It is clear however that the linear barrier was built to hinder the nomadic Arab people from the desert. Although this Khandaq is much later than the Egyptian Walls of the Ruler, it throws an interesting perspective on it. Firstly, there is neat symmetry. In the face of a threat from nomadic Asiatics, the response to both the east and the west of the Arabian Desert was to build a moat or canal. Secondly, the historian Yāqūt, writing later in the Islamic period, said that Anushirvan (531–579) who rebuilt Shapur's earlier work, 'built on it (the moat) towers and pavilions and he joined it together with fortified points.'[38] Therefore, this was a continuous fortified aquatic linear barrier. The fact that such a barrier was constructed by the Sasanians perhaps meant that Egypt's early Walls of the Ruler were also a continuous aquatic barrier, strengthened by forts.

Conclusion – Egypt and Mesopotamia

When these two areas of early riverine civilisation, Eygpt and Mesopotamia, were first researched it was without knowledge of any linear barriers within them. By now it would appear that there were many barriers in these regions although some of the evidence for them is rather circumstantial. If this evidence from varied sources, however, is considered together, then certain patterns do emerge. Both Ancient Egypt and Mesopotamia have areas of land corridors and valued irrigated land protected by walls or fortified canals. There are multiple linear barriers where the Tigris and the Euphrates converge, separating lower and upper Mesopotamia. Where nomads threatened the irrigated areas from semi-arid or arid desert regions, fortified canals appear to have developed as a response; in Egypt, possibly as early as two millennia BC, and again later to the east under the Sasanian Empire in the third century AD.

The argument for early linear barriers in Egypt and Sumer is based on literary texts but the solution is quite consistent. For example: 'There were repeated attempts on the part of semi-nomadic tribes to penetrate the fertile river-valleys of the Nile and the Tigris-Euphrates regions. These infiltrations were of great concern to the urban rulers, and brought about offensive military responses, as well as the construction of defensive lines. The latter consisted of networks of fortresses – to forestall the unwanted incursions. Two such networks are attested in 20th century BC, at opposite ends of the Fertile Crescent. At the eastern frontiers of Egypt, the Pharaohs constructed the "Walls of the Ruler" to keep out nomads whom they designated as "sand-dwellers." At the other end, in Sumer, … King Shu-Sin of the Ur III dynasty, established (c. 1975 B.C.) a defensive border called *Muriq Tidnim* "The Repeller of the Amorites."'[39] This passage describes a 'network' of fortresses but probably the *Muriq Tidnim* and possibly the Walls of the Ruler were continuous systems.

Research for this book started with the assumption that linear barriers would be found along the Eurasian Steppe. That so much could be discovered where intensely irrigated Egypt and Mesopotamia bordered with arid and semi-arid lands in which nomads roamed was unexpected but encouraging as civilisations separated by millennia and thousands of miles arrived at similar 'solutions'. There appears clearly an early link between Empires, nomads and linear barriers even if the evidence is hardly overwhelming in quantity or quality. That said a case can be made that – from the earliest times in regions where developed literate civilisation encountered nomads – linear barrier building arose as one solution to problems posed by nomads. And such building was part of the *condition humaine*.

3. China's Warring States and the Yellow River

If challenged with the question 'When was the greatest period of wall building in history?' – excluding the construction of the Great Wall of China itself in its various forms – the answer might surprise most people; as it was during the period when China was disunited between the seventh and third century BC. This epoch was poetically known as the Spring and Autumn period, up to the fifth century BC, and then more prosaically as the Warring States period.

The walls of this Eastern Zhou period (770–221 BC) are remarkable both in terms of length and function. They dwarf in length most non-Chinese walls. For example, the Qi Wall, started in around 685 BC, grew to an estimated 620 kilometres and the Hexi or West Wall of Wei of 361 BC to an estimated 700 kilometres. Also, the majority of these walls were built not to keep out nomads but other warring states in China.

Much simplified, China looks like a homogeneous mass with the Pacific to the east, the Himalayas to the west, Indo-China to the south and a great mass of open steppe to the north. It is bisected by two great rivers running very roughly west to east, the Yangtze River to the south and the Yellow River to the north.

Northern China, around the Yellow River, was the font of Chinese civilisations. It was later that occupation extended into the wetter south around and below the Yangtse. The clue to the question why this region was developed so early might be in the word 'yellow'. The land and river is that colour because of the friable loess soil. Loess is wind-blown silt that can form uniform pale yellow strata over a hundred metres deep. With appropriate agricultural techniques it can be extremely fertile. The Chinese loess plateau is bisected by the upper and middle Yellow River largely running west to east in the modern Gansu province, the Ningxia Hui Autonomous region, and the Shaanxi and Shanxi provinces. This soil was – and is – highly erodible, indicating special protection might be required to render sustained large scale agriculture viable. Although the loess soil is fertile its ecological context in China is extremely hostile. There is very little rainfall outside of summer and there needs to be careful irrigation for the land to be productive.

When looking at riverine civilisations, those of Egypt and Mesopotamia developed earlier than China. China's history – as opposed to pre-history – goes back to the Shang of about 1700 to 1025 BC who built great bronze cauldrons, walled cities, and whose writing has been found inscribed as oracles on animal shoulder blades which were burnt and the cracks divined for meaning. There were great Shang walls but these were built around cities. For example, the recently discovered Huanbei Shang City in Henan province had four rammed or tamped earth walls, each 2,150 metres long. These walls provided a technique for building long walls with tamped earth.

The Western Zhou period ran from 1025 BC and saw a decentralised system of government that finally collapsed in 771 BC. The Eastern Zhou era from 770 to 221 BC is divided into two parts: the Spring and Autumn periods which lasted to 476 BC; and the subsequent Warring States period which was brought to an end with the unification of China under the first Emperor Qin Shi Huang in 221 BC.

The Eastern Zhou era started with the break-up of the Zhou Kingdom into many states – supposedly 148. The period is partly known from the chronicles of the small state of Lu which were recorded biennially in Spring and Autumn, hence the name. (It was during the Spring and Autumn period that Confucius travelled from state to state seeking a suitably enlightened but conservative ruler willing to apply his philosophical system.) Apart from Lu, the chronicles recounted the history of Qi, Qin, Chu and Jin states, the last one of which broke up into Wei, Zhao, Yan and Han States. By the end of the Spring and Autumn period in 476 BC, the number of States had consolidated to seven or eight major Warring States.

It might help to try to clarify the geographical relationship between the major warring states of the Western Zhou period. There were three major states with northern borders: Yan by the Yellow Sea; Zhao in the centre; and Qin, to the west, largely within the Yellow River loop and somewhat to the south-west of Zhao. The small Zhongshan state was squeezed between the Yan and Zhao states. There was a central belt of states with Qi by the Yellow Sea and then Wei to its west which extended across the Yellow River where it flowed north to south. To the west of the Wei state laid the above mentioned Qin. To the south of the Yellow River were the Zeng and Han states with the major Chu state further the south again. To the south of Qi and the east of Chu there were a number of small states including Song and Lu.

With seven or eight relatively equal sized major states there was more potential for greater armies who were less able immediately to dominate each other – a recipe for a sustained period of warring states. Indeed from 476 to 296 BC, when the comparatively small Zhongshan state fell to central northern state of Zhao, the states warred constantly without any reasonably large sized state succumbing.

Warfare in the Western Zhou, and particularly in the Warring States period became vast in terms of scale and ferociously savage. Also during this period warfare was evolving, and these changes had a profound effect on the design of linear barriers. During the Western Zhou period even quite small states could bring into the field armies of hundreds of chariots. Chariots have the merit of speed, giving the attacker more opportunity to focus his forces on less well defended areas. (Julius Caesar commented on the use of chariots in Britain, also a region of warring polities and rich in linear barriers.) The aristocratic charioteer, with weapons of bronze, was increasingly replaced by professional cavalry and infantry. Iron and bronze armour, and weapons of exceptional sharpness, became more common. New weapons, like the halberd and the trigger crossbow, heightened lethality. Armies became much larger. Professional warfare on a heroic scale – if less than heroically conducted – required exceptional economic efficiency from states who had to extract the highest yields from their agricultural resource base. The consequences of defeat became more horrible, often followed by massacre of defeated armies. Basically, the stakes had become much higher – requiring consideration of all possible survival strategies including linear barriers.

During the fourth century the Wei, Zhao and Qi states attempted to assume leadership, but eventually it was the relatively backward Qin state that rolled up the other states over the third century BC. Qin, it should be stated, had the advantage of relatively defensible borders as it only faced other states to its east, while being able to absorb manpower from the west.

In the mid-fifth century BC agricultural yields rose as grants of title were exchanged for military service and taxes. Also, to sustain large populations irrigation was developed. China dates the introduction of irrigation systems unusually precisely. Ximen Bao was a Wei state general who became a magistrate of Ye, now in Heibei Province. Ye was afflicted with floods, and around 430 BC Bao built twelve irrigation canals along the Zhangshui River and is credited as the founder of China's irrigation systems. Other warring states followed Wei's example and raised output and, in turn, the size of armies that could be put into the field. As Egypt and Mesopotamia showed, irrigated land is particularly valuable, yet also because of that, vulnerable. Thus the development of irrigation may have contributed to the acceleration in the construction of linear barriers during the time of the Warring States.

Chinese linear barriers evolved out of the very materials which they also protected. First, town walls were made of rammed or tamped earth which made possible vertical walls of solid earth. Loess or clay was pounded solid between parallel planks which were raised as the wall increased in height. Sometimes branches or mats were added between the layers to add stability (it might be recalled that the Egyptian cataract walls were similarly reinforced.) Such walls could be built relatively quickly and cheaply using *corvée*, or forced labour and the result, if maintained, was very durable. In fact, stretches of tamped earth wall are still being found in China's western desert areas. During the Western Zhou period a wider range of building practice developed and many walls were built of stone – often without a bonding agent like mortar – in a rather utilitarian manner. Later adobe wall was developed where sun dried clay bricks were bonded with clay mortar.

Early antecedents

Before looking at walls built between Chinese states at war a couple of precocious antecedents might be considered.

Survey of walls

1.2: Chinese Warring States

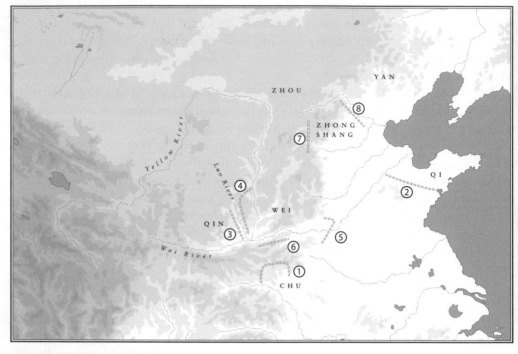

Spring and Autumn Period
1. Chu Wall
2. Qi Wall
   Jin Wall (not shown)
   Lu Wall (not shown)

Warring States Period
3. Qin East (Anti-Wei) Wall
4. Wei Hexi (West) Wall
5. Wei South Wall
6. Zhenghan Wall
7. Zhongshan Wall
8. Yan South Wall
   Zhao South Wall (not shown)

Some walls are not shown as their location is not clear. Other walls are marked with broken lines as even such maps as are available can be hard to interpret.

Nan-Zhong's anti-Xianyun Wall – The Book of Songs, dating from the tenth to the seventh century BC, described how:

The king has ordered Nan-chung (*Nan-Zhong*)
To go and build a fort (*wall*) on the frontier.
To bring out the great concourse of chariots,
With dragon banners and standards so bright.
The Son of Heaven has ordered us
To build a fort (*wall*) on that frontier.
Terrible is Nan-chung;
The Hsien-yün (*Xianyun*) are undone.[40]

The king or the Sun of Heaven was Xuan whose reign is placed 827 to 782 BC – in other words, predating surviving Chinese walls by several centuries. Sometimes the word 'wall' is translated as 'fort' but a later history described how Nan-Zhong was ordered to build a wall in the same passage, describing how Emperors Qin Shi Huang and Han Wu also built long walls.[41] As these two Emperors certainly did build long walls, later Chinese historians also understood Nan-Zhong to have built a wall.

Yiqu anti-Qin Wall – Also, according to some translations, the semi-nomadic Yiqu people built a double wall after 453 BC against the Qin state. Unusually it was the nomads, supposedly the more barbarous people, who built a wall to keep out a more developed state. That said, most other Chinese states saw the Qin as pretty barbarous.

Spring and Autumn period walls

The Chu and Qi states built the two major walls in the Spring and Autumn period. The location of these and other known walls of this period appears to indicate that, during this earlier period of the Western Zhou, the 'hot spots' were located to the east and south of later wall building. While these two walls were started in the Spring and Autumn period they were extended in the Warring States period.

Qi Wall – This may be the oldest long wall in Chinese history – dates of 685 to 645 BC being given – of which there are physically surviving elements and some solid historical information. The Qi state lay in eastern China and bordered the Yellow Sea. It was one of the most powerful of the period but was threatened by the growing power of states to the west. The state responded by building a wall along the sacred Taishan Mountain in modern Shandong province where it bordered the Jin and the Lu states.

Building continued into the Warring States period for three centuries, extending the wall to 600 kilometres. The walls were gradually consolidated until there was a comprehensive defensive system from the Yellow Sea to the Yellow River. 'On flat lands the wall was built of tamped loess earth and on mountains out of stone. Reports describe the Wall as in two lanes, 5 metres in height and 25 metres in thickness, with an inner galloping runway upon the wall, which is 4 metres in height and 2 metres in width.'[42] Some of the wall survives in the Dafeng Mountain Tourist Area where: 'Stretching and undulating for more than 1,500 metres on top of the Dafeng Mountain, with 200-plus barracks rooms straggled aside, the Great Wall of Qi has become a tourist attraction.'[43]

The wall was part of a comprehensive defence system: 'Apart from the walls, there are remains of fortified passes, wall fortresses and beacon platforms. To conserve resources in mountainous areas, builders constructed the walls on the top or southern side of ridges, integrating cliffs and strategic features into the walls themselves. Across level ground, they used local materials: slabs of timber, quarried rock or a mixture of earth and stone.... These walls are the best and most extensively preserved of all the Warring States Great Walls.'[44]

Chu Wall – This wall protected the Chu state from more northerly states. The Man had been a southern barbarian people who were absorbed by the expanding Yellow River states. By the mid-650s BC the Man re-emerged as the Chu, one of the most powerful states of the Western Zhou period, which expanded through conquest during the Spring and Autumn period. In the mid-seventh century BC Chu's territory reached its maximum and to consolidate and protect its borders it began to build fortresses along its border against the Jin and Qi states. These were linked by walls which were about 250 kilometres long. The wall gradually assumed the shape of three sides of a rectangle, like an inverted U, hence its name the Rectangle Wall. Some 1400 metres have been excavated.[45] During the Warring States Period, the Chu extended the wall, and in total the walls ran for around 400 kilometres.

Recently, attention was drawn to the Chu Wall as one section, which had survived in relatively good condition, was brutally destroyed in an afforestation project. At least the destruction provoked a useful modern description of the wall. 'The Chu Great Wall relics were distinguished by three features. First, construction materials were used from local sources. If there was earth, earth was used to construct the wall; when there was no soil, stones were stacked up. Second, earth and stones on the southern side of the wall were dug up to construct a wall along the steep northern side of the hills so as to strengthen the boldness and abruptness on the northern side. Third, a wall would be constructed along the site that allowed people to pass through, while no wall was built along the dangerously steep sites, such as trenches and cliffs.'[46] Thus, wall-building was essentially utilitarian, pragmatic, flexible and, to summarise, functional.

Jin and Lu Walls – Textual sources and archaeology have added to the list of Spring and Autumn period walls. The Jin state in 571 BC built a wall at Hulao in Henan facing the Chu-backed Zheng state. In 2009 a section wall was found in Shandong Province which was attributed to the Lu, one of several quite small states which lay between the larger Qi and Chu states. The section found is thirty kilometres long, between 1.2 and 2.8 metres thick and up to two metres high.[47]

Warring States period

Most intra-state wall building took place in the Warring States period when the number of states had reduced to relatively few in number but nearly all were now of significant size. Exploitation of the loess plateau, using irrigation and terracing, raised Wei state food production, and its example was then copied by other states. An intense period of wall-building followed.

Qin East (Anti-Wei) Wall – In the early part of the Warring State period the eventually dominant Qin state was still then weaker than the powerful central Wei state which had been the first to exploit the agricultural potential of the loess plateau with extensive irrigation projects. The result may have been the construction of the first great wall by a northern state. The Qin built a wall about 300 kilometres long between it and the Wei state to the west of the Yellow River and the Luo River dated to 461 BC. This wall was subsequently extended towards the end of the fourth century BC.

Zhongshan Wall – The relatively small Zhongshan state was founded by a group from the semi-nomadic Di people who had become sedentarised. It was initially a powerful state able to field 400 chariots and had a peaceful relationship with the Yan and the Qin to the east. Its south-western neighbours, the Wei and the Zhao, however, considered the Zhongshan state a danger and it had a particularly unhappy relationship with its larger Zhao neighbour. It built a wall in 369 BC of about 250 kilometres along its western border. In 307 BC the Zhao attacked what it called the barbarian state of Zhongshan and, notwithstanding the presence of this wall, the Zhao finally absorbed the Zhongshan state in 296 BC.

Wei Hexi (West) Wall – By the fourth century BC the earlier dominant Wei state was coming under pressure from states to the west and south-east. In the west the relative strength of the Wei and Qin states reversed and it was the Wei who fortified their western border against the Qin in the first half of the fourth century BC. This appears to be dated to between 361 and 352 BC. It extended more than 500 kilometres roughly north to south.

Wei South Wall – As Wei lost wars to Qin, Chu, and Qi, it built a wall in about 325 BC about 200 kilometres long on their south border in what is now the province of Henan. The aim was to resist the Qi across the Yellow River in the south-east of the Wei kingdom.

Zhenghan Wall – Zheng and Han were two states south of the Yellow River that consolidated, and this resulted in a wall named after the newly combined states. The Zheng built a wall in the mid-fourth century BC which was extended after they were absorbed by the Han – hence the 300 kilometre long Zhenghan Wall. It was in what is now Henan Province and runs south from the Yellow River.

Yan South Wall – The Yan state built this wall on its south border, along the Yishui River, in the second half of the fourth century because, having earlier attacked the Qi state, the Yan anticipated retaliation. This barrier was constructed between 334 and 311 BC and was about 250 kilometres long.

Zhao South Wall – At roughly the same time as the Yan, the Zhao built a wall to the south against the Wei and later the Qin in 333 BC. It was constructed along the Zhangshui River and stretched to about 200 kilometres in length.

Analysis – Warring States Walls

Looking back over the walls of the Western Zhou period, the sheer extent of wall-building is quite astonishing. Indeed, apart possibly from the later Han and Ming periods, the building is unrivalled in history and, in terms of wall building against other states, it is completely unrivalled (except in the twentieth century inter-war period).

The Warring States period saw a reducing number of increasingly well-resourced states competing in an area where there were limits to the size of areas of high land fertility. More efficient political and agricultural systems resulted in rising populations with little space to expand – either at the expense of weaker Chinese states or non-Chinese semi-nomads. The situation of Warring States might therefore be expected to prove conducive to linear barrier building. A 'factor that may have favoured the building of long walls among the Chinese states was reduced space for territorial expansion. Whereas during the Spring and Autumn period the stronger states could expand relatively easily at the expense of non-Chou (Zhou) communities and weaker Chou (Zhou) states, by the fourth century BC the competition had become limited to a few powerful states, thus increasing the pressure to improve both defensive and offensive capabilities.'[48]

Also, while wall building went on before the commencement of intense irrigation projects by the Wei, it does appear that the construction of large scale irrigation systems provoked an acceleration of construction. By making valuable land even more so it was necessary to build even more walls. 'Rulers did everything possible to increase revenues, and the best practices spread quickly, since the alternative was destruction. Around 430 BC the state of Wei had begun rounding up labourers and digging vast irrigation channels to raise farm output; the other states, including (eventually) Qin, followed suit. Zhao and Wei built walls to protect their valuable irrigated land; as did others.'[49] The use of the word 'valuable' is of note – coming before 'irrigated land' for, as land is irrigated, it becomes even more valuable and vulnerable. The consequences of ravaging were so detrimental to easily damaged irrigations systems that it was necessary to use all means possible to block access to irrigated lands.

All this wall-building did not stop the relentless march of Qin – but then the Qin absorption of the other states largely took place over a limited period between the middle of the third century and 221 BC, and mostly in the last decade under the exceptionally ruthless Qin Shi Huang. The individual states may have survived longer due to their walls, and if a wall's success is measured by the lifetime of its constructor then these walls enjoyed success. Certainly, from the Qin point of view, its walls might be judged a success as they may have stopped the earlier Qin falling to the more economically developed Wei and then militarily advanced Zhao states.

Also, the development of internal warring state walls seems critical to the later development of northern walls. 'The states of Yen (Yan), Chao (Zhao), and Ch'in (Qin) … adopted a defensive technology developed among the Central States to expand into the lands of nomadic and semi-nomadic peoples.'[50] And without the anti-nomad walls, China might not have survived at all as a robust empire in the face of constant nomad depredations. Thus it might be argued that the experimentation and development of the Warring States period gave China the wall building skills necessary to deal with the challenge of the northern nomads – when these became a real threat under the Xiongnu – but this was fortuitous and not a consideration in their original planning.

Conclusion – Early Riverine Civilisations Considered Together

Three early riverine civilisations in the areas of the Nile, the Tigris and Euphrates, and the Yellow River have been considered in this chapter.* The key threats were different. In the case of Egypt and Mesopotamia the dangerous relationship was between states and nomads; whereas with China it was states at war with each other. A common factor appears to have been irrigation. All managed and needed to sustain very high levels of agricultural productivity. It was considered absolutely essential to keep intruders – both human and animal – out of irrigated areas. Therefore, it was necessary to put a physical linear barrier around much or all of the irrigated area.

---

* Walls were also sought in the Indus Valley but none were found – an issue which will be considered later.

Chapter Two

Greek World and Roman Empire – Barbarians and Local Nomads

T he search now moves away from inland regions into the maritime world around the Mediterranean and the Black Sea. Given that the circumstances of the Greek and Roman world were very different to the riverine empires and states covered in the previous chapter, with their highly developed irrigation systems, any linear barriers might be expected to be quite unlike those discovered in the previous chapter.

1. The Greek and Hellenistic World

Did the Greeks build long walls? There were the Long Walls of Athens but these linked the city of Athens to its harbour of Piraeaus. Thus they were not the usual type of linear barrier which obstructs passage from one open area to another. The Phocian Wall at Thermopylae was famously the site of the last stand of Leonidas and his 300 Spartans in 480 BC. There was a Delphic reference to Zeus granting that the 'wooden wall only shall not fail' which Themistocles interpreted as meaning the Athenian fleet and therefore not a land wall at all. Thus the Greek world might not seem fertile territory for the search for long walls. There were the heroic duals of the Iliad, the shield walls of the hoplites, the phalanxes of the Macedonians, the cavalry companions of Alexander, even great sieges like Syracuse, but not linear barriers. Yet in the Greek world land corridors and warring states abounded, so a systematic search might produce results.

Four fifths of modern Greece is mountainous – circling and separating relatively small plains – with a jagged coastline dotted with small bays and harbours. Often the small coastal plains have rocky protrusions which would provide suitable sites for cities which could dominate the local land. The Aegean Sea has a highly irregular coastline that is replete with land corridors in the form of peninsulas. On the western side of the Aegean Sea, the Corinthian isthmus provides a short land corridor to the Peloponnese. To the north there are the three fingers of the Chalcidike off the Macedonian coast, from west to east, the Pallene Peninsula, Sithonia and Agion Oros. On the eastern side of the Aegean is the Gallipoli Peninsula, jutting off what is still Europe, which was previously known as the Thracian Chersonesos. And on the south-west corner of the Ionian coast is the Reşidaye Peninsula.

The Black Sea initially looks as though it has a smoother coastline than the Mediterranean. But the Crimea itself is a large, narrow necked peninsula with several smaller peninsulas along its south-western coastline on the Heraclean Peninsula. Its eastern end is the Kerch Peninsula. The Cimmerian Bosphorus links the Sea of Azov and the Black Sea. There are small narrow necked peninsulas and headlands at

Kazantip on the north of the Kerch Peninsula, at Sinope on the Black Sea south coast, and Kaliakra on the west coast off modern Bulgaria.

The mountainous character of Greece means that there are a number of land corridors in the form of narrow passes which provide the mainland passageways into the region. On the eastern coast there is a narrow land corridor between mountains and sea on the west side of the Gulf of Malia which passes by Thermopylae. Access to the Attic Peninsula from the west is through the Parnes and Aigaleo mountains.

Greece and the Greek world, at least until it expanded into the southern Pontic Steppe and central Asia, had almost nothing in the way of large expanses of fertile land. Such packets of reasonably fertile land, often rock-strewn and hard won, thus were particularly valued. On the Greek mainland, in the vulnerable area above the Corinthian isthmus, there are fertile areas on the Attic Peninsula, the Boeotian plain around Thebes, and the Salganeos plain behind Chalkis. The Pallene Peninsula is distinct from Sithonia and Agion Oros in being substantially a fertile plain. The Thracian Chersonesos is a long fertile peninsula. In southern Anatolia there is the rich Pamphylian plain. Much of the Crimea is an extension of the Pontic Steppe but there is very fertile land on the Heraclean peninsula and the southern part of the Kerch peninsula. In Central Asia, first conquered by Alexander, oases and inland river deltas provide land that could be rendered fertile through irrigation.

Starting with mainland Greece, before Philip of Macedon imposed unity in mid-fourth century BC, this was most definitely a land of warring states where ethnically and culturally similar people fought in an area of increasingly constrained physical resources. The cities were located on high points and an associated harbour would be developed by the sea. Life in such a resource-constrained area – with localised, discrete states – invited war. Indeed, it was a region where conflict was so frequent that war was the regular default relationship between states.

As agricultural land and other resources were limited, the cities established colonies around the Mediterranean and Black Sea to which surplus people could be sent and food and resources returned. The first Greek colonies were founded around 800 BC and, up to the fifth century, about thirty city states founded colonies. Some were purely trading, fishing and manufacturing bases; others, however, were agricultural, raising issues as to how to deal with native 'barbarian' peoples who may not have been overjoyed by the arrival of new land-grabbing neighbours. Such colonies may have disrupted local agricultural and trade patterns. In Central Asia the growth of irrigation around oases and inland deltas would have blocked access to water and fodder for local nomadic peoples.

The Greek mainland was also subject to foreign attacks. Perhaps most famously in 490 and 480 BC the armies of Darius and Xerxes invaded Greece. Greece, however, was also invaded by Celtic, Scythian and Germanic peoples.

Survey of Greek walls

The Greeks were nothing if not inventive and, as will be seen, developed a wide range of linear barriers. Therefore, the survey of Greek linear barriers will focus on types rather than locations.

2.1: Greek World

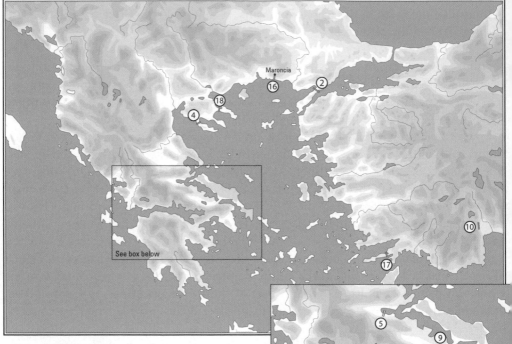

Major Peninsula Walls

1. Corinth Isthmus (Mycenaean, Anti-Xerxes, Anti-Epameinondas, Anti-Gaul, Valerian)
2. Thracian Chersonesos (Miltiades, Pericles, Dercylidas)
3. Kerch Peninsula (Akmonai Wall, Uzunlar Wall, Beskrovnyi Wall, Tyritkate Wall) (See Map and linear barrier list 5.3)

Minor Peninsular and Headland Walls

4. Pallene Pensinsula Wall
   Sinope Isthmus Wall (Black Sea – not shown)
   Kaliakra Headland Wall (Black Sea – not shown)
   Mayak Peninsula Wall (See Map and linear barrier list 5.3)
   Heraclean Peninsula Wall (See Map and linear barrier list 5.3)
   Cape Kazantip Wall (See Map and linear barrier list 5.3)

Pass Walls

5. Thermopylae (Phocian, Anti-Xerxes, Antiochus)
6. Dema Wall
7. Mount Oneion Walls
   Derbent Wall (see Map and linear barrier list 9)

Field Walls

8. Theban Stockade
9. Antiforitas Wall

10. Termessos Wall
    Parpač Ridge Earthwork, Crimea (See Map and linear barrier list 5.3)
    Margiana, Central Asia (see Map and linear barrier list 8)

Long Walls

11. Argos
12. Athens
13. Corinth
14. Megara
15. Patras
16. Maroneia

Other

17. Reşidiye Peninsula Canal
18. Xerxes' Canal

Isthmuses and headlands

Isthmuses can be divided into major and minor. The major isthmuses are at Corinth and Gallipoli, historically named the Thracian Chersonesos. These all offered obvious locations for man-made linear barriers.

Isthmus of Corinth

The Corinthian isthmus presented an obvious point where a relatively short linear barrier could block access to a large part of the Greek mainland land mass. Not unsurprisingly it proves to be the site of many linear barriers.

Mycenaean Cyclopean Wall – A section of Mycenaean Cylopean Wall has been found across the isthmus.[1] It is hard to say whether it was planned as a full trans-isthmian linear barrier and, if it were so planned, whether it was completed. It might date back to about 1200 BC to stem the recurrent waves of Dorian invaders at the end of the Mycenaean period. It was possibly unfinished when the decisive invasion took place. (Leaving aside the question of the Greekness of the Mycenaeans, this might lay claim to being the first long European stone wall.)

Anti-Xerxes Wall – The next line of defence, built in haste in 480 BC against an expected Persian attack that never materialised here, has left no traces. But Herodotus' description tells us that this was a serious effort for he says that 'battlements had begun to be placed on it.'[2]

Anti-Epameinondas Wall – By the fourth century BC Thebes rose under the leadership of Epameinondas. After defeat, at the battle of Leuctra in 371, the Spartans tried to hold the line at the Isthmus of Corinth. 'When the Lacedaemonians and other allies arrived at Corinth.... They decided to fortify the approaches and prevent the Boeotians from invading the Peloponnese. From Cenchreae to Lechaeum they fenced off the area with palisades and deep trenches.'[3] The successful assault of the trench and palisade by Epameinondas was seen as an achievement matching his victory at Leuctra.

Hellenistic Wall – There are remains of a fortification, built possibly in 279 BC, when the Gauls, led by Brennus, having overrun the north of Greece, threatened invasion of the Peloponnese.[4]

Later Walls – As will be seen, when Roman walls are discussed, there are references to a wall built in the reign of Valerian (253–60) to keep out the nomad Scythians and the Germanic Marcomanni. Also, the Byzantines later built the Hexamilion Wall on this site.

Thracian Chersonesos

The Thracian Chersonesos is now better known as the Gallipoli Peninsula. The narrowest point, about 6.5 kilometres, is nearly eighty kilometres from Cape Mastusia to the west. In the seventh century BC the peninsula was colonised by Greeks who founded twelve cities.

Miltiades' Wall – Miltiades was credited with developing the winning tactics at Marathon. He became ruler of the Greek colonies on the Thracian Chersonesos around 516 BC, after being invited by the Thracian Doloncian tribe to bring a colony and protect it against the warlike Apsinthians. Herodotus said: 'His first act was to build a wall across the neck of the Chersonese from the city of Cardia to Pactya, to protect the country from the incursions and ravages of the Apsinthians. The breadth of the isthmus at this part is thirty-six furlongs (about 7.2 kilometres), the whole length of the peninsula within the isthmus being four hundred and twenty furlongs (about 84 kilometres).'[5] Basically, the length of the peninsula was nearly twelve times that of the wall – making it a good investment to protect a fertile area.

Pericles' Wall – It does not sound as though Miltiades' wall lasted long, as another was built by the Athenian leader Pericles in the fifth century BC. Plutarch describes how, 'by belting the neck of land, which joins the peninsula to the continent, with bulwarks and forts from sea to sea, Pericles put a stop to the inroads of the Thracians, who lay all about the Chersonese, and closed the door against a continual and grievous war, with which that country had been long harassed, lying exposed to the encroachments and influx of barbarous neighbours.'[6]

Dercylidas' Wall – Dercylidas was a Spartan commander during the fourth century BC with a reputation for inventiveness and cunning. In the early fourth century BC he led the Spartans plundering through Thrace to the west coast of Asia. According to an embassy from the people of the Chersonesos, 'it was impossible for them to till their land nowadays, so perpetually were they robbed and plundered by the Thracians; whereas the peninsula needed only to be walled across from sea to sea, and there would be abundance of good land to cultivate – enough for themselves and as many others from Lacedaemon as cared to come.'[7] Also: 'This district, he soon discovered, but was singularly fertile ... Accordingly, having measured and found the breadth of the isthmus barely four miles, he no longer hesitated.... The whole wall begun in spring was finished before autumn. Within these lines he established eleven cities, with numerous harbours, abundance of good arable land, and plenty of land under plantation, besides magnificent grazing grounds for sheep and cattle of every kind.'[8]

Later walls – As will be seen later, the sixth century Byzantine Emperor Justinian rebuilt the Thracian Chersonesos walls in the sixth century.

Certain themes re-emerge consistently in the sixth to fourth centuries BC descriptions of walling the Thracian Chersonesos: this was highly fertile and hence valued land; constant harassment by non-Greek locals made it impossible to realise its value; building a wall was presented as a relatively small investment which would produce a large return; and there was a very convenient narrow land corridor on which to site the wall.

Perhaps it is not unexpected that the Greek writers did not consider the views of the barbarians and nomads who their cities displaced. These peoples' customs were undoubtedly seen as barbaric. But they were there first. Any of the earlier barriers constructed in the region cannot be seen as wholly defensive: they were there to enforce the displacement of pre-existing peoples.

Smaller peninsula walls

Pallene Peninsula Wall – The Pallene Peninsula is the western of the three fingers of the Chalcidike. It was the most fertile and defensible of the three peninsulas, having an extremely narrow neck and the northern half is a fertile plain: Sithonia and Mount Athos are more mountainous. Across the neck of the Pallene Peninsula lay the town of Potidaea which was a sixth century BC colony of Corinth. Potidaea appeared to have had a north and a south wall which protected the town and the fertile region on the peninsula against attacks from the mainland north. These walls also offered defence from aggressors landing on the peninsula who might seek to use it as a base for broader operations in the region. Potidaea revolted against the First Delian League and the Athenian leader Pericles demanded that the south wall be destroyed – presumably because this would leave the town open to control by the Athenian fleet landing on the peninsula itself below the narrow neck. After Potidaea was destroyed by the Philip II of Macedon in 356 BC it was reconstructed by Cassander in 316 BC and was renamed Cassandreia.

Sinope Cape Wall – The Sinope Cape on the southern Black Sea coast is a land nodule with a very small neck. As with the Pallene Peninsula a walled Greek city was built across the full width of the very narrow isthmus cutting off the rest of the peninsula from mainland Anatolia. Behind the city the peninsula broadens out providing a protected agricultural zone.

Crimea west – Mayak Peninsula

Strabo described the fertility of the Crimea and, therefore, its attractions to colonising agriculturalists. 'The Chersonesus, except for the mountainous district that extends along the sea as far as Theodosia, is everywhere level and fertile, and in the production of grain it is extremely fortunate. At any rate, it yields thirty-fold if furrowed by any sort of a digging-instrument.'[9] This, however, was not an empty space. There were local barbarian Tauric peoples in the coastal regions and Scythian nomads in the areas which were a continuation of the Pontic Steppe. These peoples might be described essentially as predatory threats by the hard working Greek colonisers with their highly organised farms. But this is to forget who was there first.

The Heraclean Peninsula, or Heracleotic Chersonesos, juts out on the south-west coast of the Crimea. It may not sound familiar until a modern map is examined and one finds located there the places made famous during the Crimean War – for the peninsula is the triangle formed by *Ctenus*/Inkerman, *Symbolon Limen*/Balaklava and *Parthenium*/Cape Cherson. The Gulf of Ctenus is now the Gulf of Sebastopol. The Heraclean Peninsula, on the south-west tip of the Crimea, has itself a number of mini-peninsulas from its western tip along its north coast. These could provide suitable bases for a colony until it was strong enough to occupy the whole peninsula.

The date of the foundation of the colony on the Heraclean Peninsula is not known but a colony was there by the fifth century BC. The Thracian and Heraclean Chersonese linear barriers show how Greek colonists used walls to protect land taken from local savages or barbarians. Therefore these were walls securing expropriation, keeping out of rich grazing or farm land the peoples who previously lived on it.

Mayak Peninsula Double Wall – The most westerly inlet on the north coast of the Mayak Peninsula extends to near the south coast and the Greeks constructed a double wall there, from the inlet to the coast across the neck of the Mayak Peninsula, protecting a core of intensely farmed land.*

Inkerman-Balaklava Wall – From the Mayak Peninsula core, the farms were extended east up to the escarpment line between modern *Cternus*/Inkerman on the north coast and *Symbolon Limen*/Balaklava on the south. A second later wall runs roughly north to south, along this line defending the whole Heraclean Peninsula. In the early nineteenth century this wall was traced from *Ctenus* to *Portus Symbolorum* about forty stadia sea to sea – about twenty-two kilometres. The stone had been mostly robbed but there was a mound and vestiges of turrets were still visible.[10]

---

* Until quite recently this was possibly the best preserved agricultural landscape from the Greek period – across which it was possible to identify the fields and farms of an entire region.

Crimea east – Kerch Peninsula

The Kerch Peninsula constitutes the eastern end of the Crimea and was clearly an attractive area for building a mini-state whose capital lay at Panticapaeum on the north-eastern tip. There was water to the north, east and south. To the west there was the defensible narrow Akmonai isthmus. In Hellenistic times this was the site of the Bosphoran Kingdom which was defended by several linear barriers running north to south across the Kerch Peninsula of which 'There can be no real doubt that (they) were strategic structures designed to control lateral movement across the eastern Crimea, not least by pastoralist Scythians.'[11] They are generally attributed to the first century BC and particularly the reign of Asander (44–17 BC). These linear barriers appear almost unresearched in any English language texts but were quite complex affairs involving ramparts, ditches, some parts using stone, and with towers, which might be later additions, at intervals. Two ran to lakes at the southern ends which reduced the length of man–made structures. In total they were about a hundred kilometres long with over fifty fortified towers and farmsteads.

Akmonai Dyke – The most obvious place to build a linear barrier was the narrowest point of the Kerch Peninsula – that is the Akmonai Isthmus and this is the site of the Akmonai Dyke about eighty kilometres from the peninsula's eastern tip. The barrier was less than twenty kilometres long and may have been supported by fortresses.

Uzunlar Dyke – The main outer defence was about forty kilometres from the Kerch Peninsula's eastern tip and ran across what is nearly the broadest point of the Peninsula but is located so that, by incorporating Kazantip Bay to the north and the long thin Uzunlar Lake to the south, the length of the linear barrier itself could be considerably reduced to just over twenty kilometres.

The Uzunlar Dyke was a ditch and embankment construction, reinforced by about fifteen fortified strong points, built in the first century BC by King Asander who 'walled off the isthmus of the Chersonesus which is near Lake Maeotis and is three hundred and sixty stadia in width, and set up ten towers for every stadium.'[12] This barrier seems to have been a very substantial affair incorporating a stone wall along the embankment. Unlike the other Crimean linear barriers it is clearly marked on modern maps, although this might be the result of modern reworking as this area was the site of ferocious fighting in the Second World War.

Beskrovnyi Dyke – Next, to the east, came the Bestrovnyi dyke, between twenty and thirty kilometres from the Kerch Peninsula's eastern tip. This was shortened by Lake Chokratske at its northern end and Lake Tobechytscke at its southern end – so it was roughly the same length as the Uzunlar Dyke and had about six fortresses.

Tyritake Dyke – The most easterly dyke is usually termed the Tyritake Dyke, having the town of Tyritake at its southern end and is about fifteen kilometres long and had about ten forts.

Later Byzantine defences – As so often with sites walled earlier in Greek and Hellenistic periods, the Byzantine Emperor Justinian, as described by Procopius, returned to the site when 'he strengthened the defences of Bosphorus'.[13]

Black Sea Headlands

There are a couple of headlands, perhaps mini-peninsulas, in the Black Sea which were walled off by Greek colonies.

Kaliakra Headland Wall – Kaliakra is a long, narrow headland in the southern Dobrogea region of the northern Bulgarian Black Sea coast about sixty kilometres north-east of Varna. The Black Sea colony of Kaliakra on the headland was clearly marked off by walls.

Cape Kazantip Dyke – There is a short linear barrier controlling access to Cape Kazantip which projects into the Sea of Azov off the Kerch Peninsula.

Mountain Passes

The mountainous nature of Greece meant that access to it generally – and particularly to fertile areas within it – can often be controlled by passes.

Thermopylae

The eastern route to Greece runs inland through the Vale of Tempe onto the Thessalian plain and then back to the sea coast around the Gulf of Malia. The narrow gap between mountain and sea on the east side of Greece at Thermopylae is a key strategic point on the land corridor that provides the main land route into Greece from the east. As such it has been the site of many battles and invasions and occasions of wall building. In the fifth century BC the pass here, between mountain and sea, was very narrow but has now broadened due to silting.

Phocian Wall – The Greeks, led by Leonidas, rebuilt the Phocian Wall* at Thermopylae in anticipation of attack by Xerxes' Persians. Therefore, if there was a wall to rebuild, someone must have previously built a wall. Some time in the early fifth century the Phocians built a wall to resist the Malians[14] who, setting the example exploited by nearly everyone subsequently, used the Anopea route through the mountains to defeat the Phocians. Later the Phocians reversed the defeat and liberated themselves. Thus, the wall was originally built as a defensive measure in a war between two Greek states and therefore fits the warring states model. Interestingly, the waters of the Thermopylae springs were diverted to make the route more difficult to pass. 'As the Thessalian strove to reduce Phocis, the Phocians raised the wall to protect themselves, and likewise turned the hot springs upon the pass, that so the ground might be broken up watercourses, using thus all means to hinder the Thessalians from invading their country.'[15]

Anti-Xerxes Wall – Herodotus said that the Greeks decided to block the Persians at Thermopylae which was nearer and narrower than the Vale of Tempe and controlled access to the Thessalian plain. The Phocian wall was rebuilt and carefully guarded. When the Greeks were outflanked through the mountains, their leader Leonidas sent back the major force and remained with his 300 Spartans and 700 Thespians. Eventually Leonidas and his troops advanced beyond the wall to win immortality.

Antiochus of Syria's Wall – In 192 BC the Seleucid king Antiochus III invaded Greece and was confronted by its new Roman rulers. In this case it was the invader rather than the defender who built the wall. The Romans, under Marcus Porcius Cato, like many others, got round behind Antiochus using the mountain path, forcing the foreign king to withdraw.

Byzantine Walls – Procopius described how Justinian reinforced the walls across the mountain pass at Thermopylae and this is discussed later.

---

* There is confirmation this wall was actually called the Phocian Wall from an obscure poem by an even obscurer third century poet called Lycophron which refers to 'Amphissa's Phocian Wall'. Amphissa was a major city of Phocis. Thermopylae is some forty kilometres from Amphissa so the wall was a strategic barrier to stop access to a broader territorial area.

Other passes

Aigaleo-Parnes or Aigaleo-Parnes or Dema Wall – There is a wall about 4.4 kilometres long that traverses the pass between the Aigaleo Mountain to the north and the Parnes Mountain to the south. It controls access to the Athenian plain from the Eleusinian plain – the direction from which attacks from the Peloponnese would come. Although short it is very distinctive with regular sally points designed for use against soldiers bearing shields on their left sides.

The wall faces west away from Attica and Athens. It appears intended for active defence only at times of direct confrontation for there are no visible signs of provision for continuous occupation by troops. This indicates that it was only manned when it was expected to be needed. Its date is uncertain, although the fourth century BC appears most likely. It may have been designed by the Athenian general Chabrias to ward off the Spartans under Agesilaus. If this were so then it would be paralleled by the Theban Stockade, discussed below, as this was built against the same Spartan threat by Athens' then ally Thebes.

Mount Oneion Walls – Mount Oneion lies in the north-western Peloponnese, to the south of the Gulf of Corinth, and runs from east to west for about nine kilometres with two passes running from north to south. There are a number of small north-facing walls on Mount Oneion at the Stanotopi Pass to the east and the Maritsa Pass to the west. They are made of rubble and the main walls in each group do not exceed a kilometre long. They are generally identified with the fourth and third century BC – the period of the very different Theban and Celtic threats to the Peloponnese. (The site was reused by the Venetians at the end of the seventeenth centuries.)

Central Asia – Derbent Iron Gates* There is a very narrow and easily defended gorge, known as the 'Iron Gates', through a spur of the southern part of the Hissar Mountain chain. In the third century BC the Graeco–Bactrians abandoned Samarkand and much of Central Asia under pressure from the Scythians and a wall was built near Derbent to protect the northern border. In the second century, under King Eucratides, the Graeco–Bactrians recovered Samarkand and the wall fell into disuse – although, as seen below in the Chapter on Central Asia, it was subsequently rebuilt by the Kushans.

---

* Derbent, sometimes Derbend, means a narrow way. There are two Derbents with walls, one extending from the town of that name on the west Caspian and the other in a pass through the Hissar Range between the ancient Bactrian and Sogdian States. Both have 'iron gates' those by the Caspian also being known as the 'Gates of Alexander.'

Field walls

The total land mass of Greece, the areas it colonised, and the Hellenistic states, contained a relatively small proportion of fertile land which was commensurately highly valued. Initially city states at war followed certain conventions and siege work was barely developed so city walls were largely impregnable. Hoplite warriors ravaged agricultural land, forcing the attacked state either to fight or settle terms – while non-combatants, livestock and portable goods were gathered behind the city walls. The rugged land of Greece was resilient so it could be abandoned until the enemy eventually went away or the conflict was resolved by the shove of hoplite shields. In earlier periods, attacking the social and economic system was effectively banned by the accepted conventions of war, but in the late fourth century BC these relatively reassuring conventions were increasingly abandoned.[16] There was a greater variety of troops, more mercenaries and resources to keep armies in the field longer, and fortifications could now be more effectively garrisoned.

The break down of conventions meant war could never return to pure hoplite battles, and this resulted in exploration of other ways of defending agricultural land against a determined and ruthless attacker. Also, the improvement in siege technology meant that it was possible to break down city walls – so simply shutting oneself up inside them was a less attractive option. Overall, it became more necessary to defend agricultural land from continuous devastating attack. The consequence was the development of linear barriers intended to block access to outlying fields and not to people who could be protected within city walls.

Theban Stockade – Xenophon described how in 379 to 378 BC the Spartan king Agesilaus was frustrated in his efforts to ravage the Asopos basin around Thebes for, 'the most valuable portions of their territory had been surrounded by a protecting trench and stockade.'[17] Like the Dema Wall, the stockade was equipped with sally ports and Theban cavalry would dash out when Agesilaus' peltasts, or light infantry, were going to dinner and strike them down. The crafty Agesilaus, however, noted that the Thebans always appeared after breakfast and he broke through the stockade by the cunning plan of attacking before breakfast and duly burnt the region right up to the city walls of Thebes. The stockade is estimated to have been about twenty kilometres long which for a Greek linear barrier was quite a length. The interest lies in its new specific purpose of defending valuable crop land. 'Although passes had long been defended and blocked by walls, an extensive cross-country fieldwork of this sort was a novelty.'[18]

Salganeos Plain – Antiforitas Wall – There is an extensive system of walls around the Salganeos plain, close to Aulis and opposite Chalkis. The main barrier, called the Antiforitis Wall, ran along the mountains of Salganeos and separated the Boeotian coastal plain from the inland plains of Boeotia. The wall is dry rubble and originally stood only about 1.5m high. In total it is about eleven kilometres long. It defended the Salganeos plain from attacks from Thebes and Tanagra to the west. It closed all the mountain passes of which the most important was Antiforitis. It would also have constituted a patrolling and rallying line and still provides the most convenient route over the mountain slopes. Constructed out of crude dry stone masonry, it was possibly built by Polemaios Diodorus Pollernaios in 313 BC in order to defend a base for military operations.[19]

Termessos in Pisidia – Kapikaya Wall – In south-eastern Anatolia there is a linear barrier on the borders of the states of Termessos and Pergamon on the western edge of the Pamphylian plain. The barrier is short and well built with proper walls and towers but it could not have withstood siege engines. It has been dated to the reign of Attalos II (160–138 BC). At first, its location looks curious as usually linear barriers were built facing down from higher land. This wall was built across where a valley narrows, facing up to the higher land with the Pamphylian plain below behind. 'It seems clear … that the Kapikaya wall must have been built by the masters of the plain to the east, probably Pergamon, as a protection against attack from the direction of Termessos, and not as a Termessian defensive work.'[20]

Kerch Peninsula – Parpač Ridge – There is a linear barrier facing north that was intended to defend the agricultural territory of the Crimean south coast town of Theodosia. It runs from the Uzunlar Dyke to the village of Novopokrovka for nearly seventy kilometres along the Parpač

Ridge. The area to the north which runs down to the Sea of Azov is a steppe-like plain which would have been the main land corridor along the Kerch Peninsula used by nomads. The Parpač Ridge bank would have kept the nomads out of the more agriculturally amenable land facing south towards the Black Sea.

Margiana (Merv) Oasis – The conquests of Alexander the Great took the Greeks into Central Asia. At what later became the great city of Merv, the Greeks established the Hellenistic city of *Alexandria Margiana* on the deltaic oasis of the river Margus. Strabo described how the region was surrounded by mountains occupied by 'tent-dwellers'[21] which was a descriptor for nomads. 'Admiring its fertility, Antiochus Soter (281–261 BC) enclosed a circuit of fifteen hundred stades (about twenty-eight kilometres) with a wall and founded a city, Antiochia. The soil of the country is well suited to the vine.'[22] The combination of fertile oasis land and a region of tent-dwelling nomads was an obvious recipe for the construction of a linear barrier. Also, given that the threat could come from all around, the wall might be expected to be circular – as described by Strabo. The problem is that the linear barrier now called the Antiochus wall is not a full circuit and faces only north. Probably Antiochus built an inner full circuit, now largely lost, the remains of which are called the Giliakin-Chilburj Wall. (The northern Antiochus wall is probably Sasanian and is discussed again in the chapters on the Sasanians and on Central Asia.[23]) The walled oasis and city had a distinct broader defensive purpose: it protected the Seleucid Empire against the nomadic Parni – unsuccessfully, it proved, as they displaced the Seleucids and set up the Parthian Empire.

Long Walls

In the Peloponnesian War the Athenians did not fight a hoplite war against Sparta but a maritime one. This resulted in the construction of long city walls linking polis and harbour.

Paradoxically the only Greek walls which are explicitly called long walls are not at all what would generally be identified as such in any other context. These are the Long Walls of Athens which connected the city of Athens based around its Acropolis with the ports of Piraeus and Phalerum. One way of anticipating and avoiding siege by *periteichismos*, or encirclement during a siege, was to link the town to a harbour with a linear barrier – providing, of course, there was a convenient nearby harbour. The town became, in effect, a land island which could not be surrounded by a full circumvallation; it could be resupplied and reinforced from the sea – as long as control of the water was not lost. There were two main phases of long wall construction.

In the first phase Athens built walls about 5.5 kilometres long to Piraeus and to Phalerum in 461 BC enclosing a triangular area of land. Later in 445 BC Athens built a second inner parallel north wall for uncertain reasons. Athens induced or coerced its ally Megara to build long walls to Nissaea and Minoa on the coast, enclosing a rectangular area of land as the walls were some distance apart. Athens' enemy Corinth responded in the later 450s BC by building its own long walls to its port of Lechaion. These, like those of Megara, were some distance apart. In the second phase Argos and Patras built long walls at the instigation of the Athenian Alcibiades in early 410s BC.

All these long walls are concentrated relatively near Athens, and the Gulf of Corinth and the Saronic Gulf. The long walls of Maronia in Thrace were unusual in their relative isolation. Maronia's walls were over ten kilometres long to its harbour at Aghios.

Other unusual structures

There are some curiosities which might also be mentioned.

Cnidus' Reşidiye Peninsula Canal – There is a rather nice story about the efforts to build a linear barrier across the long narrow Reşadiye Peninsula which extends about eighty kilometres out to sea from the south-west corner of Anatolia. The city of Cnidus, a Dorian colony (later famous for snapping up the Cnidian Venus of Praxiteles), stood at the tip of the long, narrow Reşadiye Peninsula. Hypagus, a general of Cyrus the Great, invaded Ionia in the mid-sixth century BC. The Cnidians started to excavate a canal between Bencik and Kucukcati on the eastern end of the peninsula with the intention of turning it into an island. Herodotus said an oracle was consulted and advised that, 'Fence not off the isthmus nor dig it through – Jove would have made an island, had he wished.'[24] Cnidus submitted to the Persians but was well treated.

Xerxes' Canal – Building a canal across the narrow neck of an Aegean Sea peninsula, as at Reşadiye, was not a unique idea: later Xerxes did complete the excavation of such a canal across the Mount Athos Peninsula in the Chalcidike. Although Xerxes' Canal was not a linear barrier, the issue of motivation is interesting. It was supposedly intended to provide a safer passage for his fleet than going around the peninsula – which had caused the destruction in a storm of his father Darius' fleet ten years earlier. Herodotus doubted the Persian explanation for the canal and thought Xerxes' objective was to cow the Greeks into submission by the construction of so mighty a work (an issue which will be discussed below).

Wall of Alexander Jannaeus – The colourful and murderous Hellenistic king of Judea, Alexander Jannaeus (103–76 BC) tried to block the advance through his territory of the Seleucid army, led by Antiochus XII Dionysus en route to campaign against the Nabateans in 88 or 87 BC. 'Alexander was afraid of him (Antiochus XII), when he was marching against the Arabians; so he cut a deep trench between Antipatris, which was near the mountains, and the shores of Joppa; he also erected a high wall before the trench, and built wooden towers, in order to hinder any sudden approaches.'[25] Remains of this barrier have actually been found along the River Yarkon and in Tel Aviv.

Analysis – Greek Walls

Having reviewed Greek walls certain overall points might be made. The Greeks were unusual in that they built many stone walls. This was largely a reflection of the materials available. The Greek world had much stone and little good fertile earth. Therefore, it was worth protecting what little earth there was with copiously available stone. Building walls of stone, however, is a particularly laborious process demanding oversight and skill. They were, therefore, carefully sited in order to maximise their impact. This meant construction across passes between mountains and isthmuses on peninsulas.

As with their inventiveness and diversity in the arts, politics, philosophy and waging war, so the Greeks and Hellenistic peoples pioneered a whole range of wall types, including isthmian walls, pass walls, field walls and oasis walls. The result is that Greek walls might have a surprisingly extensive legacy. Sites selected by the Greeks provided the locations for four walls which were later rebuilt, often by the Byzantine Emperor Justinian I (527–565) – these were the Thracian Chersonesos, the Corinth Isthmus, the Pallene Peninsula and the passes at Thermopylae. Arguably, the Greeks introduced some wall types into Central Asia, where they went on to have a long history, for Hellenistic states built oasis walls at *Margiana* and the pass walls at Derbent. Certainly they were copied, at or near these locations, when later non-Hellenistic rulers built more walls. The Roman Emperor Hadrian was an avid Graecophile. As will be seen in the next section, Roman linear barriers were very substantially the work of Hadrian. Also, his eponymous Hadrian's Wall in northern England and the Borders region with Scotland (and the later Antonine Wall in the Scottish Lowlands, which was perhaps intended to surpass it) was very much *sui generis* but not unlike a great unfurled Greek circuit wall.*

2. The Roman Empire

The bracing air of northern Britain has had a remarkable effect on invading peoples – resulting in three quite special stone structures built between the second and thirteenth centuries. Caernarfon Castle, which consolidated the English conquest of North Wales in the early thirteenth century, has polygonal towers and bands of different coloured stones, consciously modelled on the Theodosian Walls of Constantinople. The eleventh century Norman Durham Cathedral, with its high ribbed vaults, was the most advanced Romanesque structure of its age. And earliest and largest of all is Hadrian's Wall, with its multiple towered gates and forts, first started by the Roman Emperor of that name in the early second century. Hadrian's Wall is what one might expect a wall should be: built of regular squared stone with lots of towers – rather like a straightened out city wall. And it may have conditioned modern expectations as to what a Roman linear barrier should look like, and created the belief that long wall building, to defend Roman frontiers, was fairly general practice. This section looks at Roman barriers and questions whether man-made continuous linear obstacles did play a significant role in defending

---

* There is a beautiful surviving – albeit much later – example of a wall traversing a long narrow peninsula, which was a common ancient Greek type of linear barrier. It is found on the west side of the Balkans, is of medieval date, and shows how a wall can cut off a long thin peninsula like the walls across the Thracian Chersonesos. This Wall of Ston traverses a narrow point at the start of the Peljesac Peninsula on the Croatian coast. It encloses a built-up area as well as unoccupied land and has a circumference of five kilometres. (In the positioning of a walled town on the neck of a peninsula, it is similar to Potidaea on the Pallene Peninsula and to Sinope.) It is dated to the fourteenth century when in 1334 the Republic of Dubrovnik took control of Ston and of the Peljesac Peninsula and built defences against the Venetians and Ottomans. Another objective was to protect valuable salt works. The walls were completed in the fifteenth century in the shape of a pentagon with forty towers and five fortresses.

the Empire – something which might be expected given the perhaps strong popular association between Imperial frontier defence and Hadrian's Wall.

A base starting point, when examining the possible role of linear barriers in defending the Roman Empire, is that the Empire attempted to tightly control its perimeter borders and determine who could and could not enter and on what terms. Therefore, the entire length of the frontier needed to have some form of obstacle to control the flow of peoples. (By contrast other empires and states appeared to recognise that absolute perimeter control was impracticable or impossible and, therefore, inner defence lines were developed.)

Given Rome's determination to maintain a strong perimeter frontier, a brief review of the patterns or hunches set out in the introduction may give some guidance as to where Roman linear barriers could be expected to be found. The sheer size of the Roman Empire might indicate that natural obstacles would be used as much as possible. Therefore, the search of linear barriers might focus on land corridors between natural obstacles. For example, Hadrian filled gaps with linear barriers: 'In many areas where the barbarians are separated not by rivers but by land-boundaries he (Hadrian) shut them off with high stakes planted deep in the earth and fastened together so as to form a palisade.'[26]

In Europe, moving from north-west to south-east, land corridors, where linear barriers might be sought, were the following natural features: the isthmuses between the Firth of Forth and Clyde and between the lower Firth of Solway and the river Tyne; between the headwaters of the Rhine and Danube; the gap between Lake Geneva and the Jura Mountains along the Rhone which led into Gaul from Helvetia; the ancient salt road that went south into Transylvania between where the eastern and western arms of the Carpathian Mountains converge; and the route from the Pontic Steppe to the Wallachian Plain between the Carpathian Mountains and the Black Sea. In Asia, the main routes passed the Caucasus Mountains were the Darial Pass, which runs through the centre of the mountains, and the pass at Derbent, between the Caucasus and the Caspian Sea. In Africa, between the coastal plain and the Sahara, there was much high ground and mountain, traversed by passes and saddles, in what is now modern Libya, Tunisia and Algeria; and in north-west Africa there was a land corridor between the Atlantic and the higher, drier land to the east in modern Morocco.

The temperate climate of most of the Roman Empire meant that land was not particularly differentiated in terms of a clear division between highly fertile land (often the result of irrigation) and less fertile land like desert. Given that threats were anyway supposedly stopped at the border, there should have been no need to protect any particularly valued land other than that which might lie on the border. But two areas particularly stand out as likely areas where linear barriers might be sought. Firstly, there was an area of rich irrigated land in modern Algeria along both banks of the Oued Djebi which flowed from west to east. Secondly, the modern Budjak, which lies to the north of the Danube where the river flowed east to the Black Sea – a region where freshwater lakes extend north like fine fingers.

Turning to political patterns, the Roman Empire did not face another comparably developed state except on its eastern border where it encountered the Parthians and then the Sasanians. Generally, building linear barriers is pointless against similarly developed powers, as such barriers seldom hold against great armies and relationships can be reasonably reliably regulated by written treaties. The unpredictable threat to Rome came largely from barbarian people along its northern borders. Also, while Rome was not to face the full force of distant steppe nomad invasions until the appearance of the Huns in the later fourth century, there were however areas where it had to evolve strategies for dealing with peoples, nomad and non-nomad, who practiced transhumance. In North Africa nomadic tribes moved between the mountains and coastal plain. There were also nomads practicing transhumance between the Carpathians and the Pontic Steppe – probably passing by lakes along the north side of the Danube.*

Also, migration was a constant pressing issue as adjacent lands became overpopulated and resources depleted. Famously, the barbarian Helvetii attempted to move into Gaul in 58 BC. During the time of Nero (AD 54–68) Sarmatian nomadic Iazyges and Roxolani appeared on the lower Danube. In AD 376 the Goths from the Ukraine, fleeing from the Huns, crossed the Danube – heralding a new era as their flight was driven by the nomads from Asia – initiating the Age of Migrations.

To sum up, the search for Roman linear barriers should focus particularly on two types of areas along frontiers. That is, land corridors between natural obstacles; and the relatively few regions of valued vulnerable land in frontier regions where the Empire encountered barbarian and nomadic peoples.

Survey of linear barriers

For the purposes of this brief survey Roman linear barriers are divided up into a number of geographical zones. First, however, a few pre-Imperial antecedents are considered.

Pre-Imperial Rome

In central Italy warring states as Romans, Etruscans, Sabines, Oscans, and Albians fought for dominance – with Rome eventually triumphing. The origins of Roman frontier strategic linear barriers might be found in the earthworks built by Roman legionaries for short term tactical purposes. After the military reforms of Gaius Marius at the end of the second century BC, the Roman legionary was not just a formidable fighting machine, he was a mighty digger too. For Marius' 'mules' digging was part of the route to victory and entrenching tools were some of the massive panoply of equipment carried by each legionary. The skills attained while digging nightly camps could easily be extended into

---

* In comparatively modern times there has been transhumance – as practiced by sedentary peoples living in villages where there are specialist herders – from the Carpathians to wintering grounds in the Crimea, North Caucasus, Bohemia, Istria, Bosnia and the Danube. Villages each sent about 100,000 sheep.

2.2: Roman Empire

Early Republican Warring States (not shown)
Fossa Cluilia (Rome)
Fossa Quiritium (Rome)

Legionary Earthworks
1. Crassus' Anti-Spartacus Wall
2. Caesar's Anti-Helvetii Wall

Britain and Germany (Zone 1)
3. Hadrian's Wall
4. Antonine Wall
5. Lautertal Limes
6. Odenwald-Neckar Limes
7. Upper German Limes
8. Vorderer Limes
9. Raetian Limes

Lower Danube (Zone 2) Roman Walls and Earthworks
10. Limes Porolissensis
11. Limes Transalutanus

Conjectured Foederati Earthworks (See Map and linear barrier list 5.1)
    Csörszárok
    Crasna to Zalău River Entrenchment
    Brazda lui Novac de Sud
    Brazda lui Novac de Nord

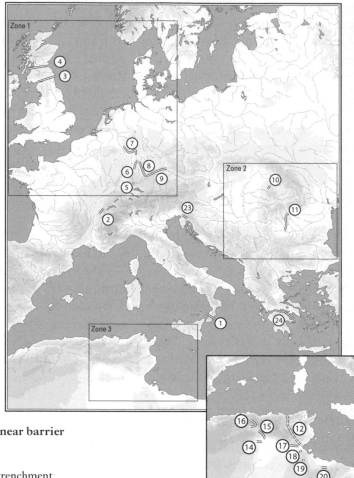

Earthworks with Possible Roman Elements (highly conjectural – see Map and linear barrier list 5.2)
    Valul lui Traian de Sus
    Valul lui Traian de Jos
    Valul Ploscuțeni – Stoicani
    Trayanovi Vali Podnestrovya

Africa and Asia (Zone 3)
12. *Fossa Regia*
13. Sala Wall

Fossata Africae
14. Seguia Bent el Krass section
15. Mesarfelta to Thubunae section
16. Hodna Mountains section

Tunisia and Libya
17. Djebel Cherb Clausurae (12 in Tunisia)
18. Djebel Tebaga Clausura (Tunisia)
19. Djebel Demmer Clausurae (Tunisia)
20. Hadd Hajar Wall (Libya)

Asia
21. Khabar River to Djebel Sinjar Wall (see Map and linear barrier list 8)
22. Darial Pass Wall (see Map and linear barrier list 8)

Interior Walls
23. *Claustra Alpium Iuliarum*
24. Corinth Isthmus Valerian Wall

constructing forts, encirclements, then longer tactical barriers and eventually strategic linear barriers.

Atavistic antecedents

A couple of linear barriers have been found which might be registered as presaging later Roman linear barrier building. There seems, however, to be little in the way of linear barriers between central Italian warring states.

Fossa Quiritium – The fourth King of Rome Ancus Marcius (640–616 BC) was a great builder in and around Rome. Livy said, 'The *Fossa Quiritium*, no inconsiderable defence against the easy access to the city from the low grounds, is the work of King Ancus.'[27] The Fossa lay in the valley between the Aventine and the Palatine Hills. (The Quirites were the citizens of ancient Rome considered in their civil as opposed to military capacity.)

Fossa Cluilia – The *Fossa Cluilia* was a trench built by the Alban leader Cluilius during the war between Rome and Alba Longa in the seventh century BC. It formed the boundary between Rome and Alba to the south, which was where the brothers Horatii and Curiatii fought. It was clearly a sufficiently substantial and durable structure to be recorded as the site where Hannibal camped in the third century BC about eight kilometres away from Rome.

Frontier marker

Fossa Regia – The first substantial Roman linear barrier in terms of length might have been the *Fossa Regia*, built in 146 BC by Scipio Aemilius after the capture of Carthage. It cut off the right-angled corner of North Africa at the apex of which lay Carthage, and it separated the Roman Province of Carthage from Numidia. Its course is known from stone markers put up in 75 and 74 BC. The name *Fossia Regia* may indicate that the king of Numidia was meant to remain to the west of the trench. The barrier was about 150 kilometres long and, while it does not seem to have presented much of an obstacle, its presence would have provided clarity.

Legionary earthworks

Two legionary earthworks are worth considering even though they do not strictly meet the definition of linear barriers covered in this book in the introduction. That is because they were built in immediate anticipation of a one-time threat. They are, however, of note because of their size and respectively their anti-migrant role and the geographical isthmian position.

Caesar's Anti-Helvetii Wall – In 58 BC Julius Caesar built a genuine linear barrier to stop the movement of a migrating people, not just an army. 'He (Caesar) carries along for nineteen miles a wall, to the height of sixteen feet, and a trench, from the Lake of Geneva, which flows into the river Rhone, to Mount Jura, which separates the territories of the Sequani from those of the Helvetii. When that work was finished, he distributes garrisons, and closely fortifies redoubts, in order that he may the more easily intercept them.'[28] This is a clear description of the construction of an anti-migrant wall intended to block a land corridor giving access to valued land, for 'He saw that it would be attended with great danger to the Province to have warlike men, enemies of the Roman people, bordering upon an open and very fertile tract of country.'[29]

Crassus' Anti-Spartacus Wall – In 71 BC Crassus built a wall about sixty kilometres long across the toe of Italy intended to contain Spartacus and his rebellious slave army: 'from sea to sea, across the neck of the land, for a length of three hundred stades (around sixty kilometres), above the ditch he raised a wall of astonishing height and solidity.'[30] Although Spartacus broke through the barrier, the cost was great and Spartacus' loss of 10,000 men might have partly explained his eventual defeat.

There are several other famous examples of very substantial tactical linear earthworks. In 67 BC Pompey attempted to encircle Mithridates in Asia Minor with earthworks twenty-seven kilometres in length and joining together a string of forts. And in 49 BC Caesar and Pompey both built walls – Caesar's being nearly thirty kilometres long – in prosecution of their mutual extended battle of Dyrrhachium, in what is today Albania.

Main Zones of Roman Linear Barrier Construction

The bulk of Roman linear barriers and barriers were built in three areas: firstly, the Lower Rhine and Britain; secondly, the lower Danube; and thirdly, North Africa. Therefore, these are treated as separate zones.

Lower Rhine and Britain (Zone 1)

Given the power of the Roman war machine, expansion over the Rhine probably seemed like business as usual until Augustus' legions, led by Varus, were ambushed (ironically from behind an earthern rampart) and massacred by the Germans under Arminius in AD 9. Augustus then determined that the borders of the Empire should be consolidated. Expansion across the Channel was subsequently driven, at least initially, by imperial need to give the lame Claudius (41–54) soldierly credibility.

In the mid-70s, while Vespasian (69–79) was Emperor, expansion into Germany began again, driven by border 'creep' under the impulsion of local peoples to expand into the wedge-shaped area between the Rhine and the Danube – into the area called the *Agri Decumates*.

Under Domitian (81–96) in the early 80s there was a push from Mainz on the Rhine forward to where the fort of Saalburg had been built earlier above the river Main. Roman expansion in Britain reached its high water mark in Scotland with the Inchuthil Line in the mid-80s. This was followed by a gradual retreat to the Gask Ridge and Newstead lines. Here forts and towers were built but these were not linked to form a continuous barrier. In the early second century under Trajan (98–117) it is possible that the first section of a linear barrier was built with the construction of the Lautertal Limes (a modern use of Latin to denote a frontier) south-east from the Necker between the forts of *Grinaria*/Köngen and Ursprung. To the north the line bulged northwards, to form the Wetterau Limes, into the Taunus.

Hadrian (117–138) sought to consolidate the Empire, if necessary withdrawing from recent conquests. In Britain he built the first continuous stone wall along the Stanegate line between the Firth of Solway and the Tyne. In Germany there were linear barriers now called the Odenwald Limes, east of the Rhine, which linked the two rivers, Main and Neckar, and the Raetian Limes which extended west from the Danube.

Hadrian's successor Antoninus Pius (138–160) advanced the frontier in both Britain and Germany. In the former he shifted it north to the gap between the Firth of Forth and the Firth of Clyde. In the latter the line moved east to form a largely non-riverine border starting at the Rhine and incorporating a length of the Main. By now the German border consisted of the Upper German Limes going roughly south from the Rhine, and the Raetian Limes which moved roughly west from the Danube. They almost but not quite joined and, together, incorporated the *Agri Decumates* region and a fair amount of western and southern Germany into the Empire.

In Britain the border appears to have moved several times between the Antonine Wall and Hadrian's Wall to its south. The former was possibly the border for two periods, first in the reign of Antoninus Pius and then again under Septimus Severus (193–211) and Caracalla (198–211). By 260 the Antonine Wall appears to have been conclusively abandoned with the border settling on Hadrian's Wall. By the 280s Rome's German border seems to have settled on the much less ambitious Rhine-Iller-Danube Limes, thus effectively abandoning most land east and north of the Rhine and the Danube. Whereas in Germany the border line could be returned to great rivers (the Rhine and Danube) in Britain there was no suitable riverine line and Hadrian's Wall had to be made fit for purpose. By the late fourth century, Rome began its withdrawal from northern England, abandoning the walls and then quickly all of Britain.

First Roman linear barrier construction

Lautertal Limes – The first Roman linear barrier in north-west Europe was probably the Lautertal Limes between *Grinario*/Köngen and Ursprung which was just over twenty kilometres long and may have been built during the reign of Trajan (98–117). Thus it bridged the gap between the forts of the Rhine and the Danube defence systems. It consisted of a palisade fronted by two trenches. It may have been constructed at the very end of the first century. Samian ware finds in the trench dated the last use of the Lautertal Limes to 120–130. Its function might have been to close the land corridor between the border lines that were advancing eastwards from the Rhine and northwards from the Danube. It also served to protect the Roman Road between *Grinario*/Köngen and Ursprung which was part of the major road from *Mogontiacum*/Mainz to *Augusta Vindelicorum*/Augsburg.

Hadrianic consolidation in Britain and Germany

Hadrian appears to have been the first Roman to build long linear barriers in north-western Europe.

Hadrian's Wall – Hadrian's Wall is the most iconic of linear barriers outside China, and has been comprehensively covered in many other books. It was also one of the most elaborate – indeed, besides the Great Wall of China, only the Sadd-i-Iskandar, near Gorgan, north-eastern Iran, seems comparable in terms of the complexity of supporting structures and the intensity of manning, as well as being a true wall. At its simplest it consisted of three lines of defence: a ditch to the north; the main stone wall with associated forts and towers; and a further earthwork was added to the south that, when combined with the stone wall, probably delineated a militarised zone. There was an associated protected road behind the wall. With the possible exception of the African walls it was the longest functioning of the unambiguously Roman walls.

Upper German Limes – Expansion east of the Rhine resumed before the reign of Hadrian and the borders were marked by lines of watchtowers and forts, and possible earthworks. It was probably Hadrian who added continuous features in the form of palisades and stone walls. At the start of his reign the German Frontier could be divided into a number of sections. Working down from the north, first there was the Lower Rhine riverine frontier. Then there followed a land border from the Rhine to the Main, including the north-facing bulge called the Wetterau Limes. After that the border reverted to a length of riverine frontier along the Main. Then there was a land border which was the site of the Neckar-Odenwald Limes (forty kilometres long) which filled the gap between the Main and the Neckar Rivers. It consisted of an earthwork and palisade with a ditch before it. Dendrochronology, or tree-ring dating, suggests a Hadrianic date of 119/120 for the continuous palisade. (It was later rendered superfluous when Antoninus Pius moved the border about thirty kilometres east to create the Vorderer Limes.) Lastly, there was a length of land border below the Neckar River in the south-western state of Baden-Württemberg.

Raetian Limes – The Raetian Limes ran east from the town of Lorch, eventually joining the Danube at Eining. Hadrian may have built a palisade onto a line of forts and watchtowers. Antoninus Pius might have given the line its final position. The stone wall, which accounts for about 170 kilometres of its length, may be the later work of Marcus Aurelius (161–180).

Antonine expansion in Britain and Germany

Antoninus Pius pushed forward the area enclosed by walls in both Britain and Germany.

Antonine Wall – Expected to be no more than a caretaker emperor, the comparatively elderly Antoninus may have wished to burnish his military credentials by expanding the Empire in a clearly defined area and, given recent activity in the region, outdoing Hadrian in north Britain might have seemed an obvious challenge. In terms of its shorter length the location of the Antonine Wall might seem more logical than that of Hadrian's Wall. Yet the former wall did not prove stable and it appears to have been abandoned three times. It is a turf wall built on a stone foundation, with multiple forts, behind a substantial ditch.

Vorderer Limes – It was probably Antoninus Pius who pushed the border east – building a section that runs completely straight for fifty kilometres. His work starts further east along the Main from the Neckar-Odenwald Limes and joins the Raetian Limes at Lorch. This brought the total length of the Upper German Limes to 330 kilometres. It represents the furthest point of expansion into Germany as defined by linear barriers.

Analysis – Britain and Germany

Once across the Channel and in Britain the Romans found there no suitable riverine frontier line. Therefore, some form of man-made frontier line became necessary – if conquering all of what is now Scotland were not possible. Initially these lines were composed of forts and watchtowers. Before they might have been linked, the more northerly lines were abandoned, and the first continuous line was formed near the Stanegate line – the most conservative in being the furthest south – which later provided the location for Hadrian's Wall.

The border was pushed forward to the narrow point between the Firths of Forth and Clyde, the site of the Antonine Wall. It then shifted back and forward between Hadrian's Wall and the Antonine Wall before finally settling on Hadrian's Wall. Given the lack of major British rivers, which might have provided defensible borders, the choice was basically either to hold Hadrian's Wall or to abandon the whole country. Due to their relative proximity there was a tension between the Antonine Wall and Hadrian's Wall as a location for a frontier. The Antonine Wall extended across a shorter isthmus and included all the territory of the Brigantes. But it also brought into the Empire much rather barren land and greatly extended supply lines. So, on the basis of a rational cost benefit analysis, it was probably not worth holding.

In Germany there was a clear riverine frontier provided by the Rhine and the Danube. Even when Rome extended beyond the Rhine, other rivers like the Neckar shortened the German Limes and later the Upper German/Raetian Limes. The non-Rhine German Limes lasted for less than two centuries – and as a continuous line for about one and a half centuries. Basically, the expansion beyond the Rhine and Upper Danube was relatively short lived in the context of Roman history and the linear barriers here cannot be seen as particularly successful, if their long term intention was to stabilise the holding of land.

Lower Danube (Zone 2)

The story of Roman linear barriers would be a lot simpler if the Romans had stopped at the Rhine and the Upper Danube. But at least with the Rhine there is no question that it was the Romans who built and used linear barriers. With the Lower Danube the question becomes a lot more complex. The issue is that there are three types of linear barrier: those definitely built by the Romans; those possibly constructed by tribes allied to Rome; and those generally seen as largely non-Roman but which might have had Roman elements in them.

In future sections, the linear barriers of Hungary, Romania, Moldavia and the Ukraine will be described in more detail in the context of their geographical position since this is often about the only thing that is certain about them. This section will briefly review whether these linear barriers might have been entirely, or in part, built by the Romans, or whether they might have been constructed by tribes allied to Rome.

It is the interaction of the Romans, nomads from the Pontic Steppe, and migrating German and Slav people which makes the region so complicated. In the mid-first century AD the Romans moved across the Danube into the region called the Budjak. This area lies on the coast of the Black Sea between the Danube and the Dniester rivers in what are now modern Romania, Moldavia and the Ukraine. They might have also occupied territory further west on the Wallachian Plain. During the first century AD the Romans effected major movements of local trans-Danubian peoples from the north to the south of the Danube. In year 2 or 3 Aelius Catus shifted 50,000 Getae from Muntenia, the eastern part of the Wallachian Plain, to Moesia, south of the Danube. Around AD 60 the Governor of Moesia, Tiberius Plautius Silvanus Aelianus, brought across more than 100,000 trans-Danubians into Moesia.[31] These movements might have required defensible trans-Danubian zones possibly protected by linear barriers.

In the early second century the Emperor Trajan conquered the Wallachian Plain and Transylvania, thus creating the province of Dacia. He expanded territory north of the already romanised Budjak which remained part of Moesia. (There are Ukrainian claims that this expansion went as far north as trans-Dniestrian Ukraine and was consolidated by linear barriers.) In around 120 Hadrian withdrew from most of the conquests north of the Danube and east of the Olt River – except possibly from the Budjak, again possibly resulting in linear barriers along the Budjak's northern border and along Dacia's new eastern border on the Wallachian Plain. Sometime in the mid-third century there was a general withdrawal from all the conquests north of the Danube with the possible exception of the Budjak.

During the reign of Constantine (306–337) Roman authority was restored across the Danube in the Wallachian Plain and in Barbaricum (the region to the east and north of the Danube on the Great Hungarian Plain). Allied tribes may have been encouraged to build linear barriers to defend the trans-Danubian Hungarian and Wallachian Plains. After Constantine died Rome ceased to try to exert control across the Danube – except possibly in the Budjak region which may have remained under Roman and then Byzantine authority until the arrival of the Bulgars in the seventh century.

Linear earthworks which are definitely Roman

Limes Porolissensis – The Limes Porolissensis run along the north-western border of Trajan's Dacian conquests in Transylvania in the Meseş Mountains. Only a short length is composed of a continuous linear barrier. This lies near the fort of Porolissum and is about four kilometres long. It ran close to a much longer line of watchtowers that was strung along a watershed line. The positioning of this short length of linear barrier may be related to the land corridor between the eastern and western Carpathian Mountains. (This was a salt road from Transylvanian salt mines via Zalău – west of Porolissensis – to the markets of central Europe.) In the mid-third century the Romans withdrew from the Dacia and abandoned the Limes Porolissensis.

Limes Transalutanus – When Hadrian withdrew from the trans-Danubian region east of the *Alutanus*/Olt River the border then alternated between the fortified road along the Olt, the so-called Limes Alutanus, and the more easterly Limes Transalutanus. The precise sequence of alternations is not clear. The Limes Transalutanus was a fortified linear earthwork that extended, with riverine sections, from the Danube to the Carpathians. It was composed of a road with associated forts, a three metre high vallum about ten to twelve metres wide, reinforced with wood palisades and a ditch. In total the Limes Transalutanus was about 235 kilometres long from the Danube across the Wallachian Plain and up the River Olt Valley into the Carpathians; but not all of it was a continuous linear barrier. In the mid-third century the Romans withdrew from the trans-Danubian region, abandoning the Limes Transalutanus and Limes Alutanus.

Linear barriers possibly built by allied peoples

The Romans reached agreements with peoples living on their borders whereby they would not raid Roman land and would prevent others from doing so too. Although they were termed *tributarii*, the direction of any payments tended to be from and not to the Empire. These *tributarii* may have constructed linear barriers to strengthen the defence of their lands and by proxy those of Rome.

Csörszárok – This great skein of earthworks which runs along the east and north-eastern borders of Barbaricum, might have been first dug as a western defence of trans-Danubian Roman Dacia. 'The several lines of the system, which sometimes cross each other, may be interpreted to mean that they are not contemporary. For example, it has been suggested that one or more of the earthwork lines in the Banat could have already been constructed in the early empire as the western frontier of Dacia.'[32] Therefore, in this first phase it would have faced west (like the Crasna and Zalău rivers line described below). Only later was its direction reversed, after Dacia was abandoned by the Romans, so that it faced east to defend Barbaricum.

Brazda lui Novac de Nord – This earthwork runs roughly west to east along the Wallachian Plain. Under Constantine in the 330s the trans-Danubian region was briefly reconquered. The construction or reconstruction of the Brazda lui Novac de Nord has been associated with this time, the earthwork having been built and manned by tribes, possibly Goths, allied to Rome, who served as a buffer people.

Valul Proscuțeni-Stoicani – Lying between the Prut and Seret Rivers and facing south-west, the Valul Proscuțeni-Stoicani, in conjunction with the Limes Transalutanus and Limes Alutanus, might have enclosed a clear zone of occupation for Sarmatian Roxolani nomads, an Iranian group, who acted as a buffer people for the Romans. The function of the earthwork would have been to keep the Roxolani from ranging too far away from the Roman frontier.

Crasna and Zalău Rivers Line – Recently an earthwork with a west-facing ditch was discovered in Barbaricum, about fifty kilometres west of the Limes Porolissensis, at the exit of the valley of the river Crasna which runs into the Tisza River, now situated in the Satu Mare county of north-western Romania.[33] It was possibly a demarcation line built by barbarian tribes allied to Rome against those attacking the Empire. This earthwork has been traced for about five kilometres and its limits have not been identified. The ditch is approximately 2–2.5 metres deep, and 3 to 4.5 metres wide.

Linear barriers which might have had Roman elements in them

Many of the region's linear barriers lie close to the frontiers of the Roman Empire and might have Roman elements within them, although this is highly speculative.

Valul lui Traian de Jos – The northern border of the Budjak is still defined by the Valul lui Traian de Jos (described in more detail below). This region was under Roman authority before Trajan's Dacian conquests and may have continued as such after the Roman withdrawal from Dacia. The Valul is composed of three sections and some of it, particularly in the more westerly area, might have a Roman core. The Romans had a strong interest in maintaining control of the northern, left bank of the Danube as it approached the delta, both as a bridgehead and to protect the Danube transport route. As seen above, Tiberius Plautius Silvanus Aelianus, in around AD 60, had brought across the Danube in Moesia 'more than 100,000 of those living across the Danube, with their wives, children, chiefs and kings to pay tribute'.[34] The Valul lui Traian de Jos might have served to protect his bridgeheads across the Danube. Later it might have provided a forward defence of the Danube waterway and controlled access to valuable fresh water lakes.

Valul lui Traian de Sus – The linear earthwork cuts roughly across the middle of Moldavia from the Prut to the Seret. It might have been partly built by Romans in the first or second century to protect expansion into what was briefly eastern Dacia.

Valul Traian–Tuluceşti – This earthwork starts on the Prut River on its marshy west side and runs south-west till it joins the Seret River. It covers the approaches to the modern city of Galatz and the older Roman fortified camp at Barbosi. It might have provided a forward defence for the camp.

Trayanov Vali Podnestrovya – Some Ukrainians insist that the Romans were in Podillya under Trajan at Kamyanets Podilsky. 'The Romans left traces of their rule in Trajan's Wall, which stretches through the modern districts of Kamianets-Podiliskyi, Nova Ushytsia and Khelnytskyi.'[35]

Analysis – Lower Danube linear barriers

The linear barriers of the Lower Danube are a complex and still rather unresolved area. If the few kilometres of the linear earthwork in the Limes Porolissensis are excluded then the Limes Transalutanus is the only clearly Roman linear barrier in the region. However, given the level of activity involving Roman expansion and barbarian and nomad invasion and migration, in a region with a long history of transhumance, this seems a very meagre haul compared to north-western Europe. The problem is that the nomad and migrant incursions, which might have given rise to linear barriers in the

Roman period, persisted on an amplified basis throughout the Age of Migrations and beyond with continuing Bulgar, Pecheneg, Polovtsian and other movements. Therefore, even if there *were* Roman cores to any of the earthworks outlined above, there is very good reason why they would subsequently have been heavily reworked and rebuilt.

Africa (Zone 3)

North Africa was not a difficult area to control and only one legion and 10,000 to 15,000 auxiliaries were located there. (By contrast three legions were based in Britain.) Trajan expanded Roman Africa to include the Aurès Mountains, and brought within the boundaries of the Empire nomads who practised transhumance. With the Romans' arrival, however, came the question of how to regulate nomad movement. This was a challenge, like many, that especially concerned Hadrian. There are long walls in Algeria which go by the collective modern name, the Fossatum Africae, which were first surveyed by the Frenchman Jean Baradez in the 1940s.[36] His dating to the time of Hadrian, the first reigning Emperor to visit Africa, is broadly accepted. Basically the walls of North Africa break down into four groups: there are three long walls in modern Algeria called the Fossatum Africae; multiple '*clausurae*' (short walls in passes) across passes in Tunisia; one wall in Libya; and a wall in Morroco.

Fossatum Africae

Seguia Bent el Krass Section – This is the most southerly part of the Fossatum Africae and runs about sixty kilometres east to west, both beginning and ending near, and running roughly parallel to, the Oued Djebi. The south-facing wall is of mud brick with a V-shaped ditch and towers and gates. The major Roman military establishment of Gemellae lies to the north of the centre of the wall. It is south and south-west of *Vescera*/Biskra in the centre of the Zab group of oases located in the depression between the Aurès Massif and the Tell Atlas Mountains. 'The purpose of this barrier must have been to cover a region of comparatively abundant water sources and palm groves around Ourella and Oumach and stretching from west of Tolga as far east as Biskra.'[37] The wall marks the end of the irrigable area (with the Oued Djebi as source) and the beginning of the Sahara desert. Therefore, the wall appears to fit into the type of barriers that protected valuable irrigated land rather than blocking a land corridor to another region.

Mesarfelta to Thubunae Section – This section is north-west of the Seguia Bent el Krass section and runs roughly north to south for about forty-five kilometres. It consists of a wall with ditch and towers. It lies south-west of the Aurès mountains and controls access to them between Mesarfelta and Thuburnia. Its function may have been to control transhumance going north to the Plains of Constantine. Therefore, it fits into the land corridor pattern of linear earthworks.

Hodna Mountains Section – This is the most northerly section and runs about 150 kilometres in semi-circle around the eastern end of the Hodna Mountains, possibly warding off an uncertain threat from the Aurès Mountains to the east. It faces north, east and south.

Despite their relative proximity and the fact they are collectively called the Fossatum Africae the three linear barriers could have had different functions. The Seguia Bent el Krass section protected valued irrigated land along the Oued Djebi, the Seguia Bent el Krass section controlled transhumance, through a land corridor, and the Hodna Mountains section had an uncertain function around the mountain area.

Tunisia and Libya

In Tunisia the linear barriers take the form of *clausurae*, that is short barriers blocking passes, and can be divided into northern, central and southern groups. In Libya there is a single wall quite close, in regional terms, to the Tunisian walls.

Tunisia – northern group (Djebel Cherb region) – There is a northern group of about twelve *clausurae* in a cluster that runs roughly east to west in the Djebel Cherb. These are the Djebel Taferma, Djebel Zitouna, Gorge de l'oued Halfaya, Djebel Sif el Laham, Khanget Oum Ali, Oued Kerma, Oued Batoum, Djebel Batoum, Kanghet Lefaia, and Kandiat Soukra. To the west there is a single *clausura*, Dejbel Asker, which traverses the Roman way from Capsa to Turris Tamallani.

Tunisia – central area (Djebel Tebaga region) – The west-facing Djebel Tebaga *clausura* runs about seventeen kilometres, much longer than the other *clausurae*, across the plain between Djebel Tebaga and Djebel Matmata. It is a stone bank fronted by ditch with watchtowers with single gate near the south-east end. It blocks a land corridor between two mountain ranges.

Tunisia – southern group (Djebel Demmer region) – There is a southern group of *clausurae* in the Djebel Demmer mountain range which runs roughly north to south. This includes: Oued Skiffa (one kilometre long), Oued Zraïa (400 metres), a short wall south of the Oued Skiffa (200–300 metres), and Oued Chenini (500 metres).

Libya – Hadd Hajar Wall – In eastern Libya there is a wall with a ditch to the south at Hadd Hajar which runs east to west about six kilometres long across road north to Tripoli.

Morroco – Atlantic coastal area

Morocco – Sala Wall – About six kilometres to the south of Sala on the Atlantic coast there is an eleven kilometre ditch, reinforced in places by a wall that is probably second century. It is uncertain whether it was intended to defend a border or just the town. It does, however, block access along the coastal plain land corridor.

Africa Analysis – Transhumance

The reason for the walls of North Africa probably lie in the protection of irrigated riverine borders and in stemming the flow of nomad pastoralists practicing transhumance. As seen earlier, the Egyptians were greatly concerned about controlling the movement of nomadic herds and the function of the Walls of the Ruler was in part to restrict the movement of herds. Transhumance survived in Algeria until quite recently. For example, the Hizia (or nomadic journey) of the Dhouaouda tribe meant wintering near southern oases near Sidi Khaled; in the summer they moved north to the plains of Constantine. The caravans moved about thirty to forty kilometres a day – a distance called a 'rihla' – and the total distance was about fifteen rihla.[38]

Whatever, their precise function – which must remain debatable – the answer in Roman North Africa to the broader question as to whether linear barriers were built where empires and nomads interacted would appear to be a qualified yes. 'The discovery of several new *clausurae* walls in the UNESCO Libyan Valleys Survey – now twelve separate sections, at least – confirms the judgement that they were never military barriers that divided the desert from the sown but were internal controls on shepherds and herdsmen who traditionally traversed them.'[39]

Asia

The fact the Roman frontier largely faced the great Parthian and then Sasanian Empires meant that walls were rather less likely to be found in Asia than in Europe or Africa, as such linear barriers generally proved to be futile defences against other powerful states. Therefore, the haul in Asia is rather meagre.

Khabar River to Djebel Sinjar Wall – A double ditch and wall of nearly twenty-five kilometres ran westwards from the Djebel Sinjar Mountains, which themselves extend roughly westward from the Tigris above Mosul, to the Khabar River which runs south to the Euphrates. Therefore, the barrier blocks a land corridor between river and mountain although its purpose is not clear. The barrier consisted of a mix of double ditch, dry stone wall, and wall and ditch combined. In itself it was not a very formidable construction and must have clarified a border line rather than enforced it. There is no obvious date for this barrier but it might have predated a treaty between the Roman Jovian and the Persian Shapur II in AD 363. After the death of the Emperor Julian during his campaign against the Sasanians – mentioned above in the context of the Wall at Macepracta as described by Ammianus Marcellinus – Jovian made a humiliating peace with Shapur which saw the border move to the Khabar River. This pact rendered redundant any barrier between the river and the mountains to the east.

Darial Pass – In the later Roman Empire the Darial Pass through the Caucasus was controlled by the Sasanians. Earlier in the first century the Romans supported allies by building walls for them. 'At Harmozica Vespasian constructed a defensive wall for the Iberian king Mithridates, and his son Iamasaspus. It was completed in the latter half of AD 75 – the work, ultimately, of Pompeius Collega – in a unique position to block the southern exit of the Darial Pass (the Caucasian Gates) before it widens into the Plain of Tiflis.'[40]

Interior walls

The Romans generally tried to maintain tightly controlled frontier lines. When during the third century, however, outer frontiers began to buckle under barbarian and semi-nomad pressure, interior walls were needed particularly to defend valuable core areas.

Claustra Alpium Iuliarum – As control over the Danube provinces of Dalmatia, Noricum and Pannonia weakened in the third century it became necessary to create a defence system closer to the north-east of Italy. The result was a system of stone walls and forts based around the major fortress at *Ad Pirum* (modern Hrušica) across passes, largely in modern Slovenia, controlling access from Italy through to the Julian Alps. The construction of the barrier walls across valleys, reinforcing the forts, might date to the time of Constantine. The system is mentioned by Ammianus Marcellinus as the *Claustra Alpium Iuliarum*[41] and therefore was in place by the later fourth century. (Thus it constitutes one of the comparatively rare examples of a surviving linear barrier system whose original name is known.) The lengths of barrier wall extended between a few hundreds of kilometres and a length of nearly ten kilometres.

Corinth Trans-Isthmian Wall – There are references to the refortification of the Corinthian Isthmus in the reign of Valerian (253–260) as the result of depredations of the nomadic Scythians and the barbarian Marcomanni: 'The excursions of the Scythians, and of the Marcomanni, who made an inroad into all the countries adjacent to the empire, reduced Thessalonica to extreme danger; and … all Greece was in alarm. The Athenians repaired their walls … The Peloponnesians likewise fortified the Isthmus, and all Greece put itself upon its guard for the general security.'[42]

Roman linear barriers – questions

The subject of Roman frontiers has been very comprehensively covered in major books and papers. Yet certain new questions might be considered in this review of Roman linear barriers, some of which relate to broader themes covered in this book. For instance, there is the role of irrigation and transhumance, and aggressive not defensive motivations, in giving rise to the construction of such barriers.

Did animal management play a significant role in the decision to construction linear barriers?

While Roman borders are not generally identified with the issues of animal control and the protection of irrigated land – might these not have been factors shaping linear barrier construction in Africa, in what is now Romania, and even in Britain?

The two areas where transhumance was practiced until recently on the borders of the Roman Empire are in modern Algeria, Tunisia and Libya; and in Romania, Moldavia and the western Ukraine. These regions are full of linear barriers. In North Africa the various walls, that constitute the Fossatum Africae and the *clausurae*, may have had differences, but overall their function appears related to control over the movement of animals. The Mesarfelta to Thubunae section of the Fossatum Africae looks as though it was intended primarily to channel transhumance. The Seguia Bent el Krass section may have been built to stop animals getting to the irrigated areas along the Oued Djebi. The *clausurae* appear primarily intended to control seasonal movement of people and animals.

The following passage about specialist herders from certain Carpathian villages makes clear what problems herds on the move could create for stationary agriculturalists – a theme since time immemorial. 'There is an antipathy towards transhumance on the part of arable farmers which results from the damage caused to crops along the routes taken by flocks as they travelled.'[43] A function of linear barriers to the east of the Carpathians might have been to prevent damage to crops. Many nomadic peoples have practised nomadic pastoralism in the region. During the time of the Roman Empire these included the nomadic Sarmatian peoples.

Even in Britain there appears to be evidence that transhumance was an element in the shaping of Hadrian's Wall. At Knag Burn Gateway on Hadrian's Wall to the east of Housesteads Fort the sign reads: 'Hadrian's Wall obviously caused considerable inconvenience to local traders, and particularly people who relied on feeding their flocks and herds between lowland feeding grounds in winter, and those of the uplands in summer.' The gate was built later than the fort and it sounds as though the occupants of the fort got frustrated with herds of animals being moved through the fort itself where the main gate was located. It appears that they constructed a purpose-built gate through the wall to keep the noisy and destructive herds away.

Are there motivations other than defence?

Given the grandiloquent character of Hadrian's and Antoninus' Walls, could there be motivations other than pure defence involved in the construction of Roman walls? Were they intended to have any assertive or aggressive purpose? Were they, to use modern public relations parlance, playing to internal or external audiences?

In the case of these two great northern walls, the view that these were an assertion of power and status might be pressed too far. Most Roman linear barriers look functional. The two walls that seem particularly elaborate are in north Britain. While Hadrian's Wall is regarded as a response to the need to stabilise a region recently in revolt, the Antonine Wall has been seen as an act of imperial statement-making. 'Unlike Hadrian's Wall, the Antonine Wall was an offensive, aggressive declaration of intent; it was not simply a means of securing the frontier, but a springboard for advance.'[44]

It is hard, however, to see which Romans these walls would have impressed, given their sheer distance from any normal itinerary likely to have been travelled by most of the Romans an emperor might have wanted to dazzle. Hadrian might have enjoyed making an aesthetic statement – being an avid Graecophile – and may have wanted to surpass anything in the eastern Empire by reproducing what was essentially an unfurled great Greek city wall with towers and gates. But above all his task was to stabilise and consolidate Roman borders. Short of retreating to the Channel he might have made his wall particularly substantial in order to announce that the issue of the fixing of the border was permanently resolved. (Functionally it needed lots of gates and towers as it was placed right in the middle of the Brigantes' territory. So in order not to stir people into constant rebellion, it needed to be able to breathe by having plenty of protected gaps.) Antoninus Pius' attempt to cap Hadrian with a further more northerly wall – perhaps in search of some *gloire* – only proved Hadrian right as the more northern Antonine wall was unsustainable.

Is too simple a picture drawn of Roman Lower Danube linear barriers?
In the lower trans-Danubian region, attention is focused on forts and roads and only the Limes Transalutanus is admitted as a significant Roman linear barrier. The area, however, has thousands of kilometres of linear earthworks. Some of these are identified as having been built by peoples allied to Rome – particularly at sites such as the Csörszárok and the Brazda lui Novac de Nord. Are they then linear barriers constructed by proxy, and might they be considered at least as part of Roman frontier systems? Also, if the Romans encouraged allied peoples to construct linear earthworks on the Great Hungarian and the Wallachian Plains, is it impossible that they may also have encouraged such construction in what are now eastern Romania, Moldavia and the Ukraine?

The other question is whether the Romans themselves built parts of the linear earthworks now collectively called the Valurile lui Traian in the Dobrogea, Romania, Moldavia and the Ukraine. Here, it would perhaps be surprising if some part of some of them did not have any Roman origins. The Valul lui Traian de Jos demarcates the Budjak which corresponds to the trans-Danubian Moesia. A Roman attribution to part of it does not seem entirely unreasonable. It was an area of Roman and Byzantine occupation for over half a millenium.

Would Rome be seen as a linear barrier builder if it had not crossed the Channel, Rhine or Danube?
Following from the iconic status of Hadrian's Wall: how might one regard Romans as wall builders if Claudius had not decided to invade Britain in 43? Or if the Romans had not re-crossed the Rhine after Augustus' withdrawal after the defeat in 9 at Teutoburg Forest? Or if Rome had not conquered Dacia under Trajan? Or, indeed, if Antoninus had not decided that advancing further into Scotland might enhance his imperial status?

The answer perhaps is there would have been a much simpler picture of Roman frontiers, certainly in Europe, and one almost without linear barriers. Essentially Roman frontiers would be riverine: the walls of North Africa basically have a local function only; and the Asian Khabar River to Djebel Sinjar Wall was really a highly local solution to an uncertain problem.

So the Romans built walls in Europe largely in what proved to be a rather futile bid to consolidate its advances beyond riverine defence lines. The sheer presence of Hadrian's Wall in Britain, an area where interest in Latin history and culture has been intense, may have served to distort expectations about what Roman frontiers should look like. Arguably it was only for a comparatively brief period that Rome had frontiers which consisted of substantial lengths of linear barriers. This era lasted for roughly one and a half centuries in Germany and Dacia. That the period was longer in Britain might have been because there was no riverine border to fall back on, thus leaving the choice either to hold the line at Hadrian's Wall or retreat beyond the Channel – which is what the Romans did between 383 and 410.

Analysis – Roman linear barriers

This section started by pointing out that there were three quite extraordinary stone structures built by invaders in north England and Wales: the Norman Romanesque Durham Cathedral with its proto-Gothic high ribbed vaults; the Edwardian Caernarfon Castle with stone bands modelled on the Theodosian Walls of Constantinople; and biggest and earliest of all, the Roman Hadrian's Wall. This wall might have had two general if misleading impacts on the non-specialist's understanding of Roman linear barriers – firstly, it may have given the impression that the Romans were frontier wall builders in the same class as the Chinese, seeing as the Great Wall of China and Hadrian's Wall are the best known of all long walls. Secondly, it may have given the general impression that wall building was a common Roman practice.

In fact, it appears that the Romans' use of frontier linear barriers was quite limited both in terms of location and duration. Mainly, it was the result of trying to consolidate aggressive and relatively quickly unsustainable over-expansion across the Rhine and the Upper Danube. Its duration was restricted to barely 150 years in Germany. Expansion was perhaps longer only in Britain as there was no riverine border on which to fall back. Therefore, in the greater scheme of things – given the longevity of the Roman Empire and the area conquered – linear barrier building possibly appeared as a somewhat peripheral activity largely concentrated in the north-western regions and, with the exception of England, lasting less than two centuries.

The previous section on the Greeks showed there was quite of lot of textual information on the construction of linear barriers. There seems, however, to have been remarkably little Roman writing on the same subject. Such descriptions of linear barriers as there are tended to be short, almost laconic, and restricted to north-western Europe. There is some specific information on Hadrian's Wall: 'And so, having reformed the army quite in the manner of a monarch, he set out for Britain; there he corrected many abuses and was the first to construct a wall, eighty miles in length, which was to separate the barbarians from the Romans.'[45] Sources show Antoninus Pius built the wall that is attributed to him: 'He waged a number of wars, but all of them through his legates. For Lollius Urbicus, his legate, overcame the Britons and built a second wall, one of turf, after driving back the barbarians.'[46] Overall, however, it is easy to take the view that the Romans were not particularly interested in linear barriers *per se* and they simply formed part of the mix of frontier strategies where and when appropriate.

The motivation for Roman linear barrier building seems quite atypical in terms of broader global patterns where linear barrier building appears to be linked to the presence of steppe nomads. For Rome it was largely due to the presence of barbarians and local nomads in Europe and in North Africa. Roman linear barriers might, therefore, be seen as temporary and not very successful solutions to the problems created by over-expansion across the Danube, Rhine and Channel. In North Africa, however, they appear to have been part of the successful management of local nomads. In the one area the Roman Empire did come up against nomadic Sarmatian, Iazyges and Roxolani, in eastern Europe, there are many linear barriers but the extent to which any of them are Roman is very uncertain.

Any temptation, therefore, to put the Roman Empire in the same class as the Chinese Empire in terms of great wall builders might be resisted. But then the Romans never faced the full fury of the steppe nomads until the arrival of the Huns who – although they were not the ultimate gainers – possibly did more than any other people to break down the resistance of Western Roman Empire.

Roman linear barrier building is generally associated with frontiers. Yet it is questionable to what extent Roman linear barriers were really general frontier defence systems. Mostly Roman barriers are associated with blocking specific land corridors. Perhaps the only really long frontier line was the German Limes of Hadrian and Antoninus Pius and that was short lived. Conceivably without Hadrian, and the example he set to Antoninus Pius, the Roman Empire would hardly be associated with linear barriers at all.

By the fifth century the Roman Empire had split and both the Eastern and Western Empires were largely dependent on riverine frontiers on their northern European frontiers. While rivers have many good qualities as frontiers they also freeze over and dry out. In 406 the barbarians crossed the Rhine when it froze and could not be expelled. (Perhaps if Rome had been able to retain its north-western linear barriers it might not have proved vulnerable to this threat?)

Conclusion – the Greek world and the Roman Empire

The classical world of Greece and Rome is interesting because it does not conform with the pattern that linear barriers were generally built in order to deal with a nomad threat. With the Greeks the purpose of linear barriers was mainly to further war between city states and to protect against highly localised non-Greek threats, largely in areas of colonisation. The purpose of Roman linear barriers was more strategic – because there was a unified Empire: to block land corridors along frontiers. But the threats still remained largely local until the later fourth century. Rome's defence systems were adequate until the whole context changed with the onset of the Age of Migrations. Then the Western Empire could not hold when faced with the onslaught of mass migrations, involving both barbarian and nomadic peoples. Would the Western Empire have survived longer had it chosen or been able to retain its third century system of linear barriers in advance of the Rhine? This can only be a subject of speculation.

Chapter Three

North African and Middle-Eastern Semi-arid Belt – Unification by Nomads Transcends Walls

T he search for linear barriers seemed most promising where barbarians and particularly nomads met settled states, particularly in areas of land corridors or highly valued land. Originally it was expected that linear barriers would largely be discovered along the borders of the Eurasian Steppe. But, if the evidence found so far is put together, then another extended area with multiple linear barriers appears to exist. This is the semi-arid zone to the north of the deserts of Africa and the Middle East.

Semi-arid belt

There is a desert zone that stretches across North Africa extending from the Sahara, through Sinai, the Negev, and to Arabia. To the north of the zone there is a fertile strip along much of the Mediterranean coast of Africa, and then in Asia there is the Fertile Crescent itself. The zone is traversed by the Nile, the Red Sea, the Gulf of Aqaba and the Euphrates and Tigris, covered in the earlier chapter about riverine empires.

On reflection it is perhaps hardly surprising that multiple linear barriers have been found here due to the interaction of nomadic peoples and the occupants of fertile irrigated areas. An added factor was transhumance moving from the semi-arid southern area to the coastal plain in what are now the nation states of Algeria, Tunisia and Libya. There was possibly transhumance from Sinai to the Nile delta too, judging from the descriptions of nomads seeking water in the earlier chapter on riverine civilisations. In Mesopotamia there were the depredations of the semi-nomadic Martu before they sedentarised. From time to time nomads like the Scythians, Cimmerians and the Huns from the Eurasian Steppe burst through to Hither Asia. Lastly, the Sasanians had to deal with semi-nomad Arabs.

So far linear barriers have been found in: Africa in Morocco, Algeria, Tunisia, Libya, and Egypt; Mesopotamia at the Tigris and Euphrates convergence points, along the west side of the Euphrates; and in northern modern Iraq.

Possible other sites for walls in the region

The linear barriers discovered in the belt between the Atlantic Ocean and the Zagros Mountains have been discovered, largely as the result of looking at early riverine Empires and the Roman Empire. By focusing on the belt it might be possible to find more linear barriers.

Syrian Early Bronze Age Wall – In Syria there is a wall that is apparently about 220 kilometres long which can lay claim to being the world's earliest long wall, indeed, one of the longest of all stone walls built in any era. It was not very substantial – being low and only about a metre thick and made of dry stone – which means that it must have done little more than indicate to potential intruders the line they should not cross without fear of retaliation. Therefore, it is hardly comparable to later Mesopotamian Walls of brick and asphalt. Notwithstanding its limited dimensions, its length would have made it a major enterprise in terms of planning, execution and operation, indicating a polity of no little authority and power.[1] It was discovered as part of researching the Syrian steppe in the process of promoting this region for inclusion in the World Heritage list of agro-pastoral cultural landscapes. The wall is dated to the Early Bronze Age, from about 2,400 to 2,000 BC[2] on the basis of an Early Bronze fort at its northern end. In the south it finishes in the hills overlooking the Bekaa Valley. 'The frontier separated two worlds, that of sedentary agriculturalists and nomadic herders.'[3] It protected early sedentary agriculturalists from nomadic pastoralist peoples – possibly the Martu who proved so troublesome to Ur III.

Cappadocian Assyrian/Hittite Frontier Wall – There is a stone wall about fifty kilometres south of modern Sivas in Anatolia at an altitude of about 2000 metres.[4] About twenty kilometres has been identified to the south-east of ancient *Sarissa*/Kuşakh but it might have extended a hundred kilometres. It may have marked the northern border of Assyria following the campaign in Anatolia by the Assyrian King Sargon II and protected the sources of the Euphrates. In the late eighth and early seventh centuries BC the Cimmerians and Scythians burst into Hither Asia and in 705 the Cimmerians killed Sargon.

Sur Umm al-Khawashij – The stone wall of Sur Umm al-Khawashij cuts off a loop of the Euphrates about a hundred kilometres north-west of the Wall at Umm Raus discussed earlier. The wall itself is about 1.5 metres wide, in places stands more than 2 metres high, and is about 3 kilometres long.

Taif Oasis Wall – Already it has been seen how the oasis at the Hellenistic state of *Margiana*, later Merv, was surrounded by walls. In the Arabian Desert the city of Taif was also encircled by a wall. Taif was named after the Thaqif tribe who, having taken over the oasis in the pre-Islamic period, built a wall around it to prevent their being forced out.[5] This wall 'enclosed a large area in which different tribal groups inhabited separate hamlets, leaving plenty of open ground where flocks could graze'.[6] Therefore the wall included not just built-up areas but also protected herds, as here the valued agricultural commodity was grazing for animals rather than crops.

Conclusion – North African and Middle Eastern semi-arid belt

On a smaller scale than the Eurasian Steppe, there was another long border zone between desert and semi-arid desert; and the fertile and intensely irrigated lands in Africa and the Middle East. All along this zone linear barriers have been found. This is an area of local solutions occurring in different locations at different times. Looked at collectively there is, however, an impressive number of linear barriers, located in the regions of irrigated land and transhumance where nomads and settled states had potentially dangerous encounters. These linear barriers largely seem to fall out of use

3.1: North African and Middle Eastern border lands

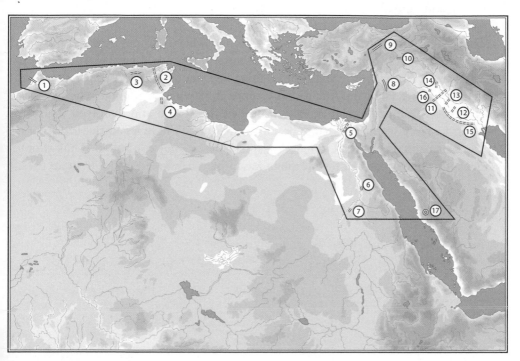

Africa
1. Sala Wall
2. *Fossa Regia*
3. Fossata Africae (Seguia Bent el Krass section, Mesarfelta to Thubunae section, Hodna Mountains section)
4. Clausurae (Djebel Cherb (12 in Tunisia), Djebel Tebaga (Tunisia), Djebel Demmer (Tunisia), Hadd Hajar (Libya, a wall))
5. Walls of the Ruler, Eastern Frontier Canal
6. Nile First Cataract Wall (Aswan to Philae)
7. Nile Second Cataract Wall (Semna to Uronarte)

Asia
8. Syrian Early Bronze Wall
9. Assyrian Era Cappadocian Wall
10. Khabar River to Djebel Sinjar Wall
11. Muriq Tidnim
12. Nebuchadnezzar's Wall from Babylon to Kish
13. Nebuchadnezzar's Wall from Opis to Sippar
14. Umm Raus Wall, Sadd Nimrud, El-Mutabbaq
15. Khandaq-i-Shapur
16. Sur Umm al Khawashij
17. Taif Oasis Wall

by the seventh century. The obvious solution for ending the hostile interaction between sedentary and nomadic polities was to unite them all under one authority – which is what the Arabs, energised by Islam, did.

History focuses on the Eurasian steppe nomad where, although in the thirteenth century the Mongols conquered the greatest empire the world has known, the steppe nomads were eventually crushed. The Arabian semi-nomad, however, conquered and created an empire from the Atlantic to Central Asia with a common religion, Islam, and language, Arabic. Nomad expansion unified the region and dissolved the reason for linear barriers – which ceased to be a major feature. 'There was little reason for the Muslims to maintain elaborate defences against a desert they controlled. Thus after the conquest this line of Persian fortifications was either abandoned or put to other uses.'[7]

Chapter Four

Northern Europe –
Barbarians and Ancient Roads

Northern Europe starts at the English Channel and the Danevirke – the great mix of earthworks and later brick wall built across the southern Jutland Peninsula. This was, before the fifth to eighth centuries, largely a non-literate world, comprising Great Britain and Scandinavia, where only what is now England spent a sustained period under Roman domination and was drawn into continental Europe.

This region can be viewed as a series of discrete land masses defined by the waters of the Irish Sea, the English Channel, the North Sea and the Baltic which both separated and linked them. The sea was important as a transport route for both raiders and migrants and offered a choice of landing points where existing land masses could be skirted. For example, a Viking did not need to travel across Britain to get to Ireland. Also, it greatly increased the border area under threat – and the direction from which attacks could come to places inland, particularly where the rivers were navigable.

The island land masses, viewed from west to east, are modern Ireland, Britain, and the Danish Islands in the Baltic. The mainland masses, the Jutland Peninsula and southern Sweden or Götland, are land extrusions into the sea but in the context here have some of the characteristics of islands. These areas are largely defined by coastlines and fertile lands. Mountains, by continental standards, are low. Rivers are plentiful but, again by mainland Eurasian standards, they are relatively easily crossed. In other words, once on land, nature provided relatively few obdurate barriers, and these could mostly be avoided by reverting to sea or river transport.

There are two obvious isthmus areas on the land masses of Britain and Jutland, respectively, between the Firths of Forth and Clyde, and the Eider River and Schlei inlet.

The extensive coastline provided another factor. Trading, raiding and migrating peoples needed safe landing points. The coastline itself provides headlands, which can be cut off by linear barriers, and pairs of inlets, which can be linked, in order to provide closed off regions for the purpose of securing landing points.

Given the absence of great mountains or rivers there are few obvious major natural land corridors. Roads are a form of easy-to-travel, artificial land corridor between harder to traverse ground. Such routes must be guarded at frontiers and the peoples passing along them need to be monitored.

The region is generally fertile, so specific areas of land are unlikely to be valued for solely agricultural reasons. Polities might however have defined significant regions that were not built over, as being especially valued for strategic, military, political or religious reasons.

So far, in this survey, many of the regions and periods covered have involved the interaction of settled literate states with nomads and barbarians. In this chapter, one literate empire,

Rome, only played a brief role in a limited area, largely comprised of what is now England. Therefore, the polities and peoples covered are mostly barbarian and migrant. Migration was a significant factor, although the medium for movement was seas and rivers, not the grassland steppe, and the means of conveyance, the flat-bottomed boat not the horse and wagon. There were significant migrations by the Belgae and possibly Parisii and later the Goths, Gaels, Danes, Angles, Saxons and Jutes. The annual movements of sea people, going 'a-viking', might be interpreted economically as a form of aggressive seasonal search for the means of sustenance – either by extortion or expropriation – comparable to the movement of nomads practicing transhumance. Doubtless the people could be described as barbarians and migrants, excepting the Romans and the Romanised. But they were not nomads in the sense of the whole people collectively practising transhumance. Therefore, looking at this region allows the opportunity to explore broader reasons as to why linear barriers might be built where there are neither great states nor nomads.

Throughout the region there was violent warring of tribes as growing populations fought over increasingly resource-constrained areas. In Britain this warfare was temporarily stopped by the period of *Pax Romana*, and later, after another onset of infighting, it ebbed in the ninth and tenth centuries; in Denmark it was ended by unification possibly in the early seventh century.

Any linear barriers found in northern Europe are likely to be rather different to those across Eurasia and Africa, given the absence of great settled states and nomad hordes, and of land corridors defined by mountains and seas. Once searched the region proves rich in linear earthworks, which are indeed of a rather different character to those discussed both before and after this chapter. Generally, linear barriers tend to be located on land corridors; but given the relatively low relief of Northern Europe those found here are, as might be expected, quite modest in scale. An important feature in North Europe is the impact of roads. If roads are regarded as man-made land corridors – their position partly determined by natural features – then the search for Northern Europe's linear barriers might be facilitated.

1. Britain

Using a combination of sources – both books and on-line maps – it was not difficult to find over a hundred linear barriers in England and near the Welsh and Scottish borders. Most of these are mute and their constructors and purpose can only be speculated at. Given the lack of contemporary or near contemporary texts and comprehensive modern exegesis, perhaps the best approach is to simply consider what is known – which is basically three things: the actual linear earthworks which survive or are reliably attested in old maps or documents; the geography of the area in which they are found and other structures nearby; and the main phases of the area's history. By focusing on clearly discernible patterns in the location of linear barriers and their relationship with geographical features and certain man-made constructions, it may be possible to build a sound, if incomplete, framework; and only then to try to place, by analogy, existing linear barriers, whose date and purpose are otherwise unclear, within it.

Given its relatively low relief, land corridors might seem rare in Britain but they do exist and their importance lies not in their scale but the way they determine the siting of ancient roads. By continental standards, the Pennines are low, yet even so east-west corridors run through or between the Peak District, the Yorkshire Dales, and the Cheviot Hills. There is a passage of low ground from Cambridgeshire up to the Vale of York to the east of the Pennines leading to the Scottish borders. Southern England has a number of chalk uplands separated by vales and it is the uplands not the vales that become the locations of roads. (These uplands, rather than being obstacles, were often easier to travel along in all weathers than the lower, wetter vales.) The main chalk upland line runs through the Chilterns in Bedfordshire, Buckinghamshire, Hertfordshire, Oxfordshire, the Berkshire Downs, Salisbury Plain and Cranbourne Chase in Dorsetshire, Wiltshire and Hampshire. There are important passageways and links through and between the various chalk uplands. At the Goring Gap the Thames divides the Chilterns and the Berkshire Downs. There is a saddle which separates the valley of the Kennet, which feeds into the Thames, from Vale of Pewsey and the Salisbury Avon valley.

While the natural landscape of Britain is relatively undifferentiated, man has played an important role in creating semi-artificial land corridors which might be the location of linear barriers. To some extent the location of roads tended to reflect and amplify the natural situation, in terms of land corridors, as old road systems followed lines of ground that were firmer all year round. Such ground tended to be higher along watershed lines or ridgeways, as all-weather use was easier and the sight lines for identifying dangers were clearer. (Non-Roman roads should not be seen as consisting of a single well-built track – rather there was a skein of routes, the choice of which would depend on weather, wear, the time of year, and the changing proximity of the nearest threat.)

Once constructed, a road becomes a land corridor of more easily traversable and safer land between less easily crossed and probably more dangerous land. Land corridors, as seen in earlier chapters, are good places to look for linear barriers. In England there are three sets of road system to consider: the ancient route systems; the Roman roads; and the Anglo-Saxon army ways.

Firstly, England has a remarkable ancient route system going far back in time before the Romans following the Greater Ridgeway from Norfolk to Dorset, with a split near the Goring Gap where the Ridgeway bifurcates west to Avebury, while the line of the Portway continues south-west. Much of this is chalk upland, chosen as it allows all-weather travel. For simplicity, the part to the north-west of the Goring Gap will be called here the Icknield Way and the part to the west of the Goring Gap the Ridgeway. The way to Dorset follows the Roman Portway but the route is more ancient.

Secondly, whereas ancient routeways often consisted of many intertwining paths, the Romans stuck to one route whose straightness, to some extent, disregarded local natural features. Notwithstanding this characteristic, the overall shape of the Roman road system appears to be related to the earlier systems – except that London became the main nodal point when Roman military roads to southern Scotland and Wales were constructed. A number of Roman roads were particularly strategic: Ermine Street and Dere Street, running to the east of the Pennines, linked London to Scotland; the Portway going from London to Dorchester near the south coast; and Ashwell Street and the Peddar's Way linking London to Norfolk.

Thirdly, in the post-Roman period, Anglo-Saxon war bands and armies tended to revert to the older Ridgeway road systems due to their more certain all-weather capability and lesser maintenance requirements. Gradually some such routeways were rationalised and recognised as *herepaths* or *herewegs*.

Raiders, invaders and migrants would have used routeways to penetrate the country. Therefore, local polities would have wanted to monitor and control those passing along them. In many situations the most realistic course of action was to hope that the threat stayed on the road and, if harm were to be inflicted, it would be on people literally further down the road. Thus while some linear barriers *do* cross the routeways, others block exit roads from the routeways, or run parallel to them.*

Another particular feature of the late Iron Age English landscape, the territorial oppidum, could also be surrounded by discontinuous linear barriers of considerable length. This is an area of land enclosed by earthworks that is only very partially, if at all, built over. It is often not entirely clear why the land they covered was determined as being more valuable than surrounding land. But, given the general homogeneity of the landscape, some means of clearly defining the selected area became necessary, which took the form of a discontinous circuit of often rather straight, linear barriers.

Survey of linear barriers

The first stage in surveying Britain was quite simply to mark linear barriers on the Ordinance Survey Historical Map of Roman Britain. Certain earthworks are well known, like Offa's Dyke – and others are reasonably familiar to those interested in early English history and landscape, like Wansdyke in Wiltshire and Somerset, and the Cambridgeshire Devil's Dyke. Putting Devil's Dyke or Grim's Dyke into search engines brought up many results. A remarkable number could be located or found on streetmap. co.uk simply by following ancient ways and Roman roads. Many are just marked as 'Earthwork'. Quickly certain zones stood out on the map.

There is not enough space here to analyse in any detail all the British linear barriers and it would unbalance this book to do so, as most are shorter than the linear barriers covered in other sections. Therefore, the linear barriers of Britain are summarised in tabular form. To try to clarify the situation, England is divided into zones and linear barriers tend to be found in clusters within those zones.

The Greater Ridgeway and southern England (Zone 1)

When all the linear barriers are plotted on a map of Britain, the most obvious pattern is a zone of linear barriers close to the Greater Ridgeway. At first this runs from just east of The Wash, on the English east coast, covering parts of East Anglia, Norfolk and Lincolnshire. It then runs over heath and farm land until the chalk escarpment of the

---

* A recent discovery might underline the danger that loomed close to routeways. In 2009, fifty-four decapitated Scandinavian bodies were found near Weymouth at a site called, appropriately, Ridgeway Hill. These are thought to have been captured and executed Viking raiders.

4.1: Britain

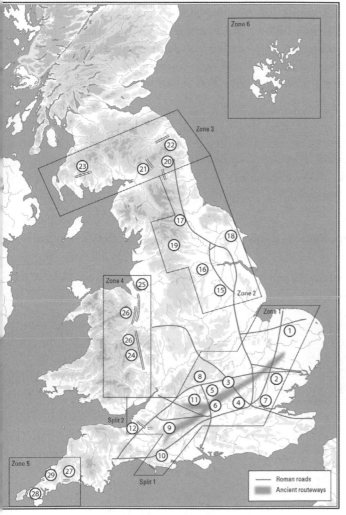

The Greater Ridgeway and Southern England (Zone 1)

1. Norfolk Dykes cluster
2. Cambridgeshire Dykes cluster
3. Drays Ditch (Bedfordshire)
4. St. Albans / Verulamium and Wheathamstead cluster
5. Chilterns Grim's Dyke
6. Goring Gap cluster
7. Watling Street (Faesten Ditch, Harrow Grim's Ditch)
8. Akemen Street (North Oxfordshire Grim's Ditch, Ave's Ditch)

The Portway (Split 1)

9. Wilton (Grovely Grim's Dyke)
10. Portway group (Bokerley Dyke, Coombs Ditch, Battery Banks)

The Greater Ridgeway (Split 2)

11. Berkshire Grim's Dyke
12. West Wansdyke, East Wansdyke

North of England (Zone 2)
Ermine Street, Dere Street

15. Roman Rig
16. Aberford Entrenchments
17. Scots Dyke
18. East Yorkshire cluster

Pennines

19. Pennines cluster – Grinton Fremington Dykes, Tor Dyke, Black Dyke

Scottish Borders (Zone 3)

20. Black Dyke, 21. Catrail, 22. Heriot's Dyke, 23. Deil's Dyke

Welsh Borders (Zone 4)

24. Offa's Dyke
25. Wat's Dyke
26. Central section clusters (not individually shown)

Cornwall (Zone 5)

27. Giant's Hedge (Looe to Fowey), 28. Giant's Hedge (Lelant to Long Rock), 29. Bolster Bank

Orkneys (Zone 6)

Chiltern Hills and then onto the Goring Gap where the Thames cuts through the chalk hills. For simplicity this is called the Icknield Way section.

After the Goring Gap there is a split into two lines. One line follows the Dorchester to Silchester Roman Road and then follows the Portway to Dorset, named here the Portway section. The other post-split line, called the Ridgeway section, goes east along the Berkshire and Marlborough Downs and then south along the Roman Road – through Swindon to Winchester – to Mildenhall where it shifts west, crossing the Fosse Way south of Bath.

Table 4.1: The Icknield Way

Norfolk Dykes cluster – Bichanditch, Fossditch, Launditch, Panworth Ditch

Norfolk other – Bunn's Bank, Devil's Ditch, Grim's Ditch

Cambridgeshire Dykes cluster – Black Ditches, Devil's Dyke, Fleam Dyke, War Banks, Brant Ditch

Bedfordshire – Dray's Ditch

St Albans/ *Verulamium* and Wheathamstead cluster – Beech Bottom Dyke, Devil's Dyke, the Slad

Chilterns – Grim's Dyke

Goring Gap cluster – South Oxfordshire Grim's Bank, Aldworth-Streatley Grim's Bank, Devil's Ditch

---

Devil's Dyke – The Cambridgeshire Devil's Dyke is such a substantial system as to merit separate discussion. It is possibly the best preserved English linear earthwork which runs straight for over twelve kilometres traversing both the Roman Peddar's Way and the pre-Roman Icknield Way. It has been dated to the late sixth and early seventh century, which means that it is probably Anglian, given its south-west-facing direction. It is part of a complex cluster of linear barriers.

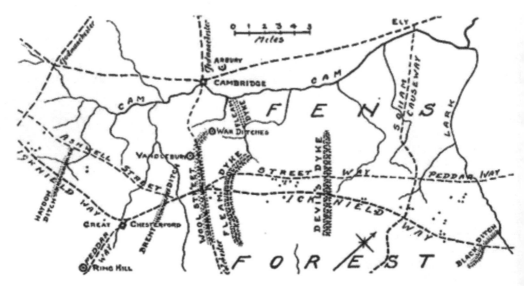

The Cambridgeshire Dykes – showing a cluster of dykes intersecting ancient routeways and Roman roads, lying on land corridor between fen and forest. *(Earthwork of England, Allen Alcroft, p. 507)*

Split 1 – The Portway – Hampshire, Dorset

At the Goring Gap the first Zone splits. One split goes south down the Dorchester to Silchester Road to the Portway and then along it to Salisbury and on to Badbury and Dorchester.

Table 4.2: The Portway

Silchester/*Calleva Atrebatum* – Padworth Grim's Bank

Andover Region cluster – St Mary Bourne, Devil's Ditch, Hurstbourne Tarrant, Grim's Dyke Linkenhalt

Wilton – Grovely Grim's Dyke

Portway group – Bokerley Dyke, Grim's Ditch, Coombs Ditch

Other – Battery Banks, Winchester Earthwork, Froxfield Entrenchments

Coastal – Hengistbury Head Double Dykes

Split 2 – The Ridgeway – Berkshire, Wiltshire, Somerset to Bristol Avon

The second split follows an easterly course along the northern edge of the Berkshire Downs to the Marlborough Downs and on to the Bristol Avon.

Table 4.3: The Greater Ridgeway

Berkshire Grim's Ditch
Bedwyn Dyke
East Wansdyke
West Wansdyke

Wansdyke – This consists of two sections: East Wansdyke (about nineteen kilometres) along the Marlborough Downs; and the West Wansdyke (about fourteen kilometres) which runs below Bath where it crosses the Fosse Way. There is an unresolved question of the extent to which a Roman Road from Mildenhall to Bath may have formed part of a middle section. Also, there is the question whether Bedwyn Dyke, to the east, might have been part of a broader Wansdyke system. Could it or constituent sections mark a border between sub-Roman or Anglo-Saxon polities; or might they constitute a mixture of both? What does seem clear is that by crossing the Fosse Way, West Wansdyke conforms to the pattern of a post-Roman linear barrier built across a Roman Road. Overall, by British standards, the two Wansdykes are substantial systems in their own right. Yet whether there is a more comprehensive system remains an open and still unresolved question.[1]

Other south-east roads

The remaining linear barriers in the south-east appear related to the Roman Roads, Watling Street and Akeman Street.

Table 4.4: South-east England Roads

Watling Street
Faesten Ditch, Harrow Grim's Ditch
Akeman Street Group
North Oxfordshire Grim's Ditch, Ave's Ditch

North of England (Zone 2)

The Midlands of England seem remarkably free of linear barriers with the exception of the western border with Wales. The journey up to Scotland can go either side of the Pennine Spine. There are a number of linear barriers in land corridors and passes running through the central Pennine spine which control access east and west. Most of the linear barriers lie to the east of the Pennines and to the west of the Humber Basin and the North Yorkshire Moors.

Table 4.5: North of England

Ermine Street, Dere Street

King Lud's Entrenchments

Roman Rig

Aberford Entrenchments Cluster – Becca Banks, the Rein, South Banks, South Dyke, Grim's Ditch
East Yorkshire Cluster – Dane's Dyke, Scamridge Dykes, Cleave Dyke, Double Dykes, Great Givendale earthwork, Queen's Dyke

Scots Dyke
Pennines and West of Pennines
Grey Ditch

Black Dyke

Grinton Fremington Dykes

Nico's Ditch

Scottish Borders (Zone 3)

There are four substantial linear barriers to the north of Hadrian's Wall.

Table 4.6: Scottish and Borders linear barriers

Black Dyke
Catrail
Heriot's Dyke
Deil's Dyke

Welsh Borders (Zone 4)

The Welsh Borders provide a somewhat different picture to the zones already discussed as here Roman roads are sparse. Besides the Kerry Ridgeway, other ancient roads seem rare too, at least in the border area. Generally, the border zone is connected to one major linear earthwork, Offa's Dyke. There are several other dykes along the border area, including the long Wat's Dyke. There are also much shorter earthworks on both sides of the Dyke. Those in Wales appear to be close to the Dyke and to the border but this might be because the only research that seems available is that done in the Welsh county of Powys.

Table 4.7: Welsh Borders

Border dykes

Offa's Dyke

Wat's Dyke

Whitford Dyke

Wye and Redbrook Dyke

Herefordshire cluster – Rowe Ditch, Scutch Ditch, Lyonshall Bank, Cowland Dyke, Redcross Dyke, Shepherds Well Dyke

Kerry Ridgeway cluster – Crugyn Banks, Wantyn Dyke, Giant's Grave, Upper Short Ditch, Lower Short Ditch

Cantref of Merchain area cluster – Clawd Mawr Dyke, Clawd Llesg Dyke, Ty Newdd Dyke, Abernaint Dyke, Bwlch y Cibau Dyke

Other

Shire Ditch (possibly Bronze Age)

Offa's Dyke – There is a broken series of linear barriers which extend from the River Wye in the south to the River Dee in the north – a distance of about 240 kilometres. The north central section over one hundred kilometres long is definitively associated with King Offa of Mercia (757–796) and lay on or close to the frontier of his Kingdom and Welsh Powys. Regardless of whether a maximalist or minimalist approach is taken to Offa's Dyke it is hard to avoid the judgement that it is *sui generis* in the context of British linear barriers. Indeed, in terms of length, the only non-Roman linear barrier that comes close in length is Wat's Dyke (see next) which runs parallel to it. Offa's Dyke is one of the very few which appears to have a near contemporary attribution. 'There was in Mercia, in recent times, a certain valiant king, who was feared by all the kings and neighbouring states around. His name was Offa, and it was he who had the great rampart made from sea to sea between Britain and Mercia.'[2]

Wat's Dyke – To the east of but close to Offa's Dyke lies Wat's Dyke which is over sixty kilometres long and runs from the River Dee's estuary south to Shropshire. Its dating is uncertain with the fifth to the ninth centuries suggested.

There are a couple of unrelated fringe areas which are worth looking at but barely merit being considered as full zones due to their limited size.

Cornwall (Zone 5)

There are three linear barriers in Cornwall which all involve linking together bodies of seawater in different forms, thereby creating discrete defensive areas.

Table 4.8: Cornish Hedges

Giant's Hedge (Looe to Fowey)
Giant's Hedge (Lelant to Long Rock)
Bolster Bank

Orkneys (Zone 6)

Finally, there are several linear barriers on the Orkney Islands.

Table 4.9: The Orkneys

North Ronaldsay
Muckle Gairsty
Matches Dyke
Mainland
Dyke o'Sean

British linear barriers

A number of summarised points about distribution, size and function can be made without going too far into the thorny issue of dating and attribution.

Linear barriers are not distributed randomly across Britain but exist in zones. These zones largely run along route systems. Even within the zones, linear barriers are not distributed evenly but appear to exist in clusters. Some clusters are strung along the routeway but others surround nodal points where different routes converge. Mostly the zones and clusters lie south of or close to the Greater Ridgeway. The exceptions are Yorkshire, Northumberland and the Borders. There are smaller 'hot spots' in east Yorkshire, the Welsh Borders, and, on a smaller scale, Cornwall. The concentration is probably explained by faster population growth in the south-east leading to greater pressure on resources, possibly exacerbated by Belgae intrusion. A similar situation appears to have occurred in south-east Yorkshire in the area identified with the Parisii tribe. In the post-Roman period pressure from Anglo-Saxon invaders was greatest in the south-east.

Although linear earthworks are generally located in zones along routeways their relationship to the particular routeway varies. Some lie across the routeway, some appear to run at right angles to one side only, and some are parallel. The great majority of linear earthworks are quite short and cross or are in the vicinity of Roman roads. In part this may be because Roman roads often followed ancient routes – while nevertheless straightening and rationalising them into one line.

Many earthworks run parallel to the routeway indicating that their function was not to impede traffic going along routes but to monitor and stop that traffic coming off the routes. The fact that the majority of linear barriers were relatively short, route-related earthworks may have been because these were quite cheap to build and operate when individual tribes and kingdoms lacked the resources to make and man longer frontier barriers. As long as traffic came down the routeway itself it would have had to stop at, or decide to make a detour around, the linear barrier. Offa's Dyke and Wat's Dyke appear *sui generis* in terms of length and most linear barriers in Britain are usually less than ten, even five, kilometres long and are generally focused on a natural or, more usually, man-made feature.

With the exception of the systems centred on Offa's Dyke, and possibly Wansdyke, there do not appear to be comprehensive frontier systems. Most dykes which were situated on frontiers bisect ancient routeways that crossed over the frontier and the dyke's function was to control the road rather than whole frontier. Therefore, if there are frontier systems in Britain they must largely be sought in putting together separate sections of linear barriers.

The following might be speculated as possible pre and post-Roman frontier systems:

- The Aves Ditch, the North Oxfordshire Grim's Ditch and the South Oxfordshire Grim's Ditch, in conjunction with the Cherwell and the Thames, might have been a boundary system of the iron age Catuvellauni facing the Dobunni.[3]
- The linear earthworks in south-east Yorkshire might have marked the border between the iron-age Brigantes and the Parisii tribes.
- The west-facing Launditch (on the Fen Causeway) and Panworth Ditch, the south-west-facing Cambridgeshire Dykes across the Icknield Way and the Peddar's Way, and the south-facing linear earthworks across the Roman roads from Norwich to Colchester and Ipswich, may have delineated the borders of an Anglian kingdom.[4] (Possibly, in the pre-Roman era they may have marked the frontiers of the Iceni.)
- The north-facing East and West Wansdykes and Bedwyn Dyke might be a frontier of post-Roman kingdoms or the Saxons against the Mercians.[5]
- Offa's dyke and other west-facing linear earthworks could have been a border system against the Welsh kingdom of Powys.

In England there are many linear barriers which create 'bounded' spaces which are not fully built up. These fall into two broad types, the first of which consist of linear barriers blocking off coastal areas and particularly headlands. Examples are the Cornish hedges, Hengistbury Head and Flamborough Head. The second is territorial oppida where substantial areas of largely open land are bounded by discontinuous earthworks. At Camulodunum (Colchester) the bounded area is around thirty square kilometres with nearly twenty-four kilometres of linear barriers. The dykes around Chichester enclose up to 150 square kilometres.

Table 4.10: Territorial Oppida

Zone 1: The Greater Ridgeway and southern England
Colchester or Camulodunum (Essex), Verulamium and Wheathampstead (Hertfordshire)

Split 1: the Portway
Silchester (Hampshire)

Nadder-Wyle (Wiltshire)
Chichester (Sussex)

Split 2: to Bristol Avon
Bagendon (Gloucestershire)
Akeman Street
North Oxfordshire Grim's Ditch (Oxfordshire)
Watling Street
Canterbury and Bigbury (Kent)

Zone 2 – North of England
Stanwick (Yorkshire)

Clearly the bounded area constituted valued land which needed to be differentiated from surrounding and often otherwise agriculturally similar land. As with oases, where the threat comes from all directions land is protected by a circular linear barrier providing all-round defence.

Curiously unlike oases, territorial oppida do not quite form continuous circular barriers. The surprising mix of irregularity and straight lines implies some egregious factor which meant that the linear barriers of British territorial oppida were formed of many discrete overlapping but not interlocking lengths, sometimes with outliers spinning off like the arms of an irregular galaxy. The explanation may lie in chariots. Julius Caesar was particularly struck by the British charioteers. Chariots need horses and horses need pasture. In emergencies, reserve areas of pastures could be contained within linear earthworks. Outlying earthworks could disrupt the approach of chariots and their ability to circle the barriers. On the interior it is far easier to drive a chariot at speed along a straight line with occasional changes of direction than to gallop around in circles (hence the long narrow shape of the hippodrome). Sally areas would also need to be larger with chariots than for infantry or cavalry.

Attribution of linear barriers to particular historical phases

Most British linear barriers appear to have been constructed in the pre-Roman later Iron Age and in the post-Roman period. There are, however, a number of outliers which can be quickly explained. These are the Stone Age Orkney dykes and the Bronze Age Shire Ditch in Herefordshire. The Chilterns and Berkshire Grim's Dykes that run along the chalk escarpment on either side of the Goring Gap are generally attributed to a time before the late Iron Age. Also, the cross-route Dray's Ditch outside Luton on Icknield Way is dated to 500 BC. Grim's Dyke in Cranborne Chase may also date to this period. This seems to indicate quite a lot of activity in the central southern chalk uplands in the mid-first millennium BC. It is possible that King Lud's Entrenchments also belongs to this period. In the period of *Pax Romana* there was a lacuna in linear barrier building except for Hadrian's and the Antonine Wall. Basically, however, there are two main periods – lasting two to three centuries on either side of the Roman occupation – that seemed to account for most linear barrier construction.

The late Iron Age was a period of growing population pressure – exacerbated by invasion or cultural differentiation. This trend resulted in intensification of tribal border control. These pressures were more intense in the south-east side of England and south-eastern Yorkshire. In part these might be attributed to the invasion of the Belgae from the continent which drove a wedge up through central southern England centred on Winchester or *Venta Belgarum*. But the use of linear barrier along frontiers appears to have been developing already in the south among British tribes.

The Iceni may have used linear barriers. Launsditch and Panworth Ditch have been dated in part to the pre-Roman period. The Cavenham Black Ditches might an anti-Iceni barrier. A border between the Dobunni and the Catuvallauni has been identified along the Cherwell and the Thames. This comprises the North and South Oxfordshire Grim's Ditch and Ave's Ditch. There are also hill forts along the Cherwell. The intensity of linear barrier construction to the west and north-west of the headland Dane's Dyke of Flamborough Head in east Yorkshire is quite unique outside south-eastern England. This might be associated with the emergence of a tribal Parisii identity differentiating itself from the Brigantes. The Northumberland Black Dyke and the Catrail (Roxburghshire) might have been a response to invasions from Ireland. In none of these situations was a comprehensive linear barrier system built along a whole frontier. Rather, the linear barriers guarded routeways and specific bulges into neighbouring tribal territories.

The withdrawal of Roman authority was followed by the break-up of Roman Britain into sub-Roman kingdoms possibly based on the Roman division of Britain into *civitas* for governmental purposes. (These *civitas* were based upon pre-Roman tribal areas). In such a situation a clearly defined road, which was an artificial man-made land corridor, became a source of danger rather than a benefit. An obvious response was to place a linear earthwork across – or at least near – the road, so as to monitor, regulate, tax and, if necessary, obstruct the flow of traffic.

The survey above showed that many Roman roads were crossed by linear earthworks. To cite a few, the Norfolk, Cambridgeshire and Suffolk dykes cross the Peddar's Way, the Fen Causeway and the roads from Norwich to Ipswich and Colchester. The Portway is crossed by dykes near Saint Mary Bourne and Quarley, and by Bokerley Dyke and Coombs Ditch. Faesten Dyke and the Harrow Grim's Dyke lie at right angles to Watling Street. The West Wansdyke crosses the Fosse Way. Tor Dyke traverses the road from Buxton towards Doncaster road. The Aberford Entrenchments cross the Roman Ridge Road.

In the post-Roman period there are several combination of polities which might have resulted in linear barrier building: sub-Roman kingdom versus sub-Roman kingdom; sub-Roman kingdom versus Anglo-Saxon invader; Anglo-Saxon invader versus sub-Roman kingdom; and Anglo-Saxon versus Anglo-Saxon. It is hard to identify any individual linear earthwork with borders between particular sub-Roman kingdoms, although it is possible that Wansdyke, at least in its early stages, might have been such a border. A mid-fifth century date for Wat's Dyke might mean this was a border between two British sub-Roman kingdoms before the split between the Mercian and Welsh polities. Given their location in the extreme south-west of Britain it appears unlikely that the two Great Hedges and Bolster Bank in Cornwall were defences against Anglo-Saxon invaders. Rather it seems more likely that they secured local kingdom heartlands against other local British threats. Bokerley Dyke, which lies across the Ackling Dyke section of the Portway between Salisbury and Dorchester, is generally identified with a sub-Roman defence against Saxon encroachment. After this line was defeated a new one may have been established on the Portway west of Dorchester at Coombs Ditch. The Cambridgeshire dykes might have been part of the borders of an Anglian Wuffing kingdom against local sub-Roman kingdoms or against Anglian Mercians. The Welsh border dykes appear largely to be have been built by Anglian Mercians to counter a British threat. The Norfolk and Cambridgeshire Dykes might have been built by Anglian Wuffing kings against an Anglian Mercian danger. Also, a greater Wansdyke system might have been a Wessex Saxon border ranged against an Anglian Mercia.

Analysis – British linear barriers

It is almost pointless trying to date with any precision many British linear barriers as, so often, they either lack dating evidence or they have been rebuilt at different times. Also, it is often a matter of speculation when it comes to identifying who built a particular barrier and why. Generally, the only solid evidence is the simple presence of a linear barrier in a particular location. It is of note, however, that most of the linear barriers found are not randomly distributed across Britain but tend to be located in certain distinct zones. These zones appear largely related to the country's ancient and originally pre-Roman transport routes. Therefore, it is perhaps roads rather than frontiers that hold the key to understanding British linear barriers.

2. Ireland

A History of Ulster describes the Dane's Cast and the Black Pig's Dyke earthworks:

> Described on maps as the Dane's Cast, it begins in the east near Scarva on the Down-Armagh border; the next section, known as the Dorsey, stands at Drummill Bridge in south Armagh; it continues into Monaghan near Muckno Lake, where it is known either as the Worm Ditch or as the Black Pig's Dyke; and further short stretches extend through Cavan and Fermanagh to Donegal Bay. A tradition survives that it was ploughed up by the tusks of an enchanted black boar; archaeologists, however, have proved this great linear earthwork to have been a series of massive defences, not continuous, but guarding the routeways into Ulster between the bogs, loughs and drumlins.[6]

In Ireland the weight of history is heavy and analysis of the linear barriers of Northern Ireland can become bogged down in subsequent events. Thus, the division of Ireland into north and south goes back more than two millennia and was defined by a great linear earthwork. As usual, the truth, to the extent that it can be discerned, must be more complex for there are many earthworks in Ireland and their precise functions do not appear fully resolved.

The separate identity of Ulster and the Six Counties seems to have been determined deep in Ireland's history and the linear barriers of Northern Ireland could have been part of this process. Is it, however, possible to look at the issue with a fresh perspective and use the lessons of Britain determined in the previous section? In Britain, in the absence of extremely large natural obstacles, the linear barriers were generally associated with ancient and Roman routeways. Could the lessons which were learned from Britain, that man-made routeways determined the location of linear barriers, help to understand Irish linear barriers; with the obvious proviso that there are no Roman roads? Ireland is more similar to mainland Britain and northern Europe, than to eastern and southern Europe, in its lack of mountains and great rivers. In addition there are no great extremes of verticality for mountains and breadth for rivers when defining land corridors and frontiers. As in England, man-made land corridors may have provided the key to understanding Irish linear barriers.

Looking briefly at history, the Irish Iron Age began around the seventh century BC and continued until the Christian era in Ireland, which brought full literacy in the fifth century. There may have been several invasions of Ireland. It is possible that the people in the north-east – who might have been the same as the Picts – had a distinct ethnic identity which accentuated a sense of separateness. They may have fought hard to maintain this identity – a factor that increased the propensity to construct linear barriers as part of an overall defence strategy. Anyway, to the north of a line of loughs and bogs lay the ancient kingdom of Ulster and to the south, Connacht, Meath, Leinster, and Munster. Thus, there was a northern kingdom that was driven back by the southern kingdoms to its stronghold, Emain Macha, which was destroyed in AD 331. Its last king was slain by kings from the south, thus bringing to an end six hundred years as a royal centre. Therefore, in Ireland there was a warring states environment.

Ancient Ireland had a distinct road system, possibly centred on the Hill of Tara in County Meath near the River Boyne. Traditionally, this was the seat of the High King of Ireland and, whether or not there was such a recognised central kingly authority, it was a sacral royal ritual site. Five ancient roads, possibly really only in myth, went out from Tara. The interest here is in the Slighe Midluachra which ran to the north Antrim coast. It divided into two branches, the main eastern one of which went to the east of Amagh's high point, the Slieve Gullion, through the Moyry Pass (or 'Gap of the North') to Newry and then to Scarva on the border of Counties Amagh and Down. From Scarva it continued under the name, Slighe Midluachra ta Dunseverick, through County Antrim. The western branch of the Slighe Midluachra ran over Marry Pass to the west of the Slieve Gullion and on to Emain Macha, the ancient power centre of Ulidia (Ulster) near Navan, to the south of the modern city of Amagh.

Linear Barrier Zones

4.2: Ireland

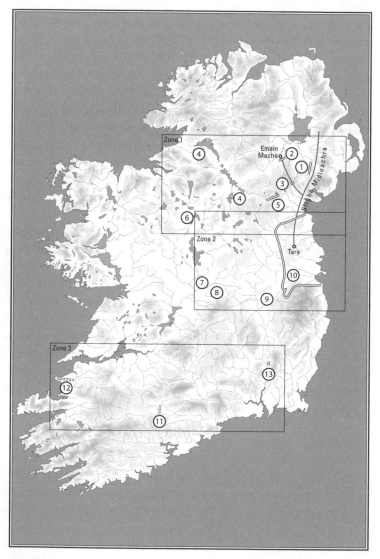

Northern Ireland (Zone 1)
1. Dane's Cast (north to south)
2. Dane's Cast (east to west)
3. The Dorsey
4. Black Pig's Dyke
5. Duncla (Black Pig's Race)
6. Doon of Drumsa

Central Ireland (Zone 2)
7. Split Hill – nr. Clonmacnoise (location)
8. Killurin – Blueball to Mucklagh (location)
9. Black Pig's Race (location)
10. Irish Pale

Southern Ireland (Zone 3)
11. An Claidh Dubh (Black Ditch)
12. An Claidh Ruadh (Red Ditch)
13. Rathduff Dyke

Northern Ireland (Zone 1)

In the north–east there are two great linear barriers. To the east there is the Dane's Cast which covered part of the gap between Lough Neagh to the north and Carlingford Lough, on the Irish Sea, to the south. To the west the Worm's Ditch may have linked Donegal Bay on the Atlantic Coast to Carlingford Lough. The short but intensively fortified Dorsey blocked the saddle on the road north leading to Emain Macha, the ancient capital of Ulster, and lies between the Dane's Cast and the Worm's Ditch.

The Dorsey and shorter Dane's Cast (cross-route barriers between Tara and Emain Macha) – The Slighe Midluachra ran from Tara to Emain Macha linking the all-Irish Tara to the ancient Ulster royal centres. Such a strategic road might have been expected to have cross-route linear barriers controlling it and indeed there are two.

- There is a major barrier at the Marry Pass to the west of the Slieve Gullion Mountain, at the Dorsey which may have been close to the frontier of Ulida or Ulster.
- There is also a second barrier, the shorter of the two Dane's Casts, which runs east to west just to the south of Emain Macha.

Thus there seems to have been a major forward frontier barrier and an interior second line of defence. The Dorsey was the more substantial construction, consisting of two large if discontinuous lines between two rivers. In itself it may have bounded an area of regnal or sacral significance.

The Dane's Cast (parallel barrier shielding off the Slighe Midluachra) – The eastward split of the Slighe Midluachra runs within ten kilometres of Emain Macha and the core of the Ulster Kingdom. There would have been compelling arguments in favour of screening the Ulster Kingdom from movement along the Slighe Midluachra. Indeed, this second and longer, north to south, Dane's Cast does just that. It runs close and parallel to the ancient road for possibly around twenty kilometres, starting in the south near the Gap of the North.

The Worm's Ditch/Black Pig's Dyke (possible frontier barrier) – The Worm's Ditch or Black Pig' Dyke might cover a length of well over a hundred kilometres, from the east to west coasts, but most of it is lost and, anyway, much of its length was definitely formed by loughs and it may also have made use of forests and bogs. The Black Pig's Race earthworks generally consist of a bank with a ditch on either side. The bank is usually about nine metres wide and the ditches are about six metres deep. Excavation of a stretch in County Monaghan revealed that the original construction had a substantial timber palisade with an external ditch. Behind the palisade was a double bank with an intervening ditch. The timber structure has been radiocarbon dated to 390–370 BC. This is seven centuries before the fall of Emain Macha. Therefore, it is questionable whether it was part of a systematic frontier system of a proto–Ulster. The Black Pig's Race may instead have been a series of ad hoc responses to endemic cattle raiding. The large gaps between the earthworks might have been there because such linear barriers were simply built across trackways used by raiders between loughs – or perhaps the gaps were once heavily wooded or very boggy, obviating the need to build a defence.[*]

---

* There is another intriguing interpretation of these earthworks in a thesis by Peter Wise (see Bibliography) which postulates 'a new hypothesis that the linear earthworks known as "travelling

The Duncla (forward barrier) – The Duncla lies to the south of the Worm's Cast and runs about ten kilometres between Loughs Gowra and Sheelin to the south of the Worm's Cast in County Longford. It might be part of an earlier frontier system from which the Ulster kingdom retreated, or a forward frontier marker of a comprehensive three-stage in-depth system. Or again it might have a purely local significance. The Duncla has also been named Granard Dyke and the Black Pig's Race.

Doon of Drumsa (controls fords on road to Rathcroghan) – There is an intriguing outlier in the northern part of Ireland in County Roscommon. This is the splendidly named Doon of Drumsa. It connects two sides of a loop of the River Shannon but in an unexpected way. Usually, barriers faced away from the loop, thereby creating a defensible zone protected by the loop and the barrier. The Doon, however, faces towards the river loop. The explanation is that the Shannon is easily fordable in the area of the loop. Therefore, the Doon provided a more secure line of defence. It blocked the road to Rathcroghan about twenty kilometres to the south which was the seat of the kings of Connacht.

It was therefore essentially a cross dyke, linking the same river. (This is similar to the South Oxfordshire Grim's Ditch which faces the loop of the Thames and crosses the Ichnield Way.) The Doon must have been huge. It was about 1,600 metres long and surviving sections are six metres high and thirty metres wide. On the northern side there are double banks about four metres in front of the main rampart and on the southern, inner, side there is another pair of banks at a distance of about forty metres.[7] The rampart has been dated to between 338 and 44 BC using carbon dating. 'This symbol of the centralised authority from the Celtic 'Dark Age' sheds light on the heroic era which finds echoes in the text of the Táin. Here is recorded an ancient conflict between the forces of Connacht under Queen Maeve and the forces of the ancient kingdom of Ulster.'[8] In other words this sounds like a warring states environment.

---

linear earthworks" were built to facilitate a river-trading network by providing "portage" from one river or lake to another'. ('Travelling linear earthworks' are those used for portage as opposed to those which might have a 'ritual purpose'.)

Central Ireland (Zone 2)

The counties west of Dublin contain a number of basically unrelated linear earthworks.

Black Pig's Race (Curragh) – In County Kildare to the south-west of Dublin there is an earthwork, possibly a raised roadway, across the Curragh Plains which are an extensive tract of semi-natural grassland.

Offaly Earthworks – There are a number of linear earthworks in County Offaly which are mentioned in *A History of Offaly Through its Monuments*.[9] All that can be gleaned is that there are 'the split hills near Clonmacnoise, the ancient entrenchments at Killurin or Cromwell's lines, a linear earthwork between the Blueball and Mucklagh.' Little remains of them.

Irish Pale – This is dealt with in a further section below but it should be recorded as a substantial Irish linear earthwork around Dublin in central Ireland – albeit of a rather later date.

Southern Ireland (Zone 3)

In the southern part there are some linear earthworks which appear linked to inter-tribal rivalry and conflict.

Black Ditch (Claidh Dubh) – In counties Cork and Limerick there is a twenty-two kilometre long Black Ditch across the Blackwater Valley which is a land corridor, between the Ballyhoura Hills and Nagle Mountains. It was clearly a substantial affair for there were two parallel ditches on either side of earthen mound. There was also a palisade and a cobbled road. Peat that has grown over the road was dated to around AD 140 indicating an earlier date for construction. The discovery created such excitement that it made it into *The Times* under the gushing title, 'Archaeologists discover Irish Hadrian's Wall'.[10] This article says of the Irish linear earthworks, indicating a warring states condition that, generally 'All have been dated to around 100 BC, when, according to early chroniclers, there were great battles between emerging Celtic kingdoms.'[11] Archaeologists 'believe the ditch was a frontier earthwork'[12] and the road may have been used to patrol the defences on the eastern side, implying a threat to the west.

Red Ditch (Clee Ruadh) – This is a linear earthwork of unknown length that starts at Caher Carbery near to Kerry Head on the coast of County Kerry. It extends east to the Cashen River to the Knockanure Mountain and into County Limerick.

Rathduff Dyke or Gripe of the Pig – Rathduff Dyke is about five to ten kilometres long running from the River Barrow at Duninga to the Sliahb Margy or Castlecomer Plateau. As such this might be a valley land corridor between river and hill. It marks part of the border between the modern Counties Carlow and Kilkenny and might be the border of the ancient territories of Idrone and Gabhran.[13]

Analysis – Irish linear barriers

Ireland might now be another country but in practice its linear barriers appear to fit into the model of the rest of Great Britain. There are many quite short dykes between natural obstacles, and lakes are common in the northern half of the country. They are related to land corridors, particularly in the north where there are man-made roads. There is also possibly a frontier earthwork in the various Black Pig's earthworks linking the line of loughs between the east and west coasts. Unlike Offa's Dyke, however, which might have delineated the frontier created by aggressive expansion, the Black Pig's works might track the receding borders of a kingdom in retreat.

3. Denmark and Sweden

The Danevirke is a system of Danish fortifications in German Schleswig-Holstein, and both it and the English Channel mark the point where northern Europe begins. Despite its size, initial attempts to locate the Danevirke on maps failed until the discovery that it now lies about forty kilometres south of the Danish border in Germany, as the result of territory lost in the Schleswig-Holstein war of 1864. Thus are the Danes separated from one of their most resonant national monuments, although in the Danevirke Centre exhibits are labelled in both Danish and German. Near the Centre is a massive redoubt built in preparation for the nineteenth century German assault and absorbing a good deal of the earth from the linear barrier. The Danevirke, a symbol of Danish national unity, was to be reused against the Germans after many centuries as the main line of the country's defence.*

The Danevirke raises the question: could there be other linear barriers on the Jutland peninsula or in Scandinavia more generally? Also, the Angles came from southern Jutland and may have built several great linear earthworks in England. Could they have drawn on experience derived in Jutland before they migrated? While this section will obviously cover the Danevirke it will also investigate any other linear barriers found in southern Scandinavia.

The Danevirke lies in southern Jutland, a peninsula which was known in classical times as the Cimbrian Chersonesos. (In AD 5 the Cimbri still existed as a recognisable people – Pliny reported that they sent ambassadors to Rome.) Both the Cimmerian Chersonesos (Crimea) and the Thracian Chersonesos (Gallipoli) had many linear earthworks built across their isthmuses over the centuries and the word Chersonesos must alert any searcher of the possibility of linear barriers at narrow points.

Jutland is a peninsula with a relatively narrow southern neck, which makes it an obvious location for a linear barrier. Yet despite having a remarkably low highest point – less than 200 metres – it also boasts a central spine or ridgeway with a wide diversity of moor, forest and farmland, and with pronounced ridges and valleys.† This spinal ridge provides the watershed line from which rivers flow to either the North Sea or the Baltic. Given the absence of obstructing rivers on the ridge line itself, and its freedom from the risk of flooding in wet weather, it was clearly a convenient route for a road system linking all of Jutland to the mainland continent. This is called the Hærvejen. As seen in the British Isles, ancient routes along ridgeways are good places to look for both cross-route and parallel linear barriers.‡ Jutland narrows as it approaches the Continental mainland. It is pierced here by inlets that run quite far towards the central ridge line, of which the Schlei on the east side is the most important. At the Schlei's inland end is the port and commercial centre of Hedeby and to its south lies the Schansen peninsula. It is hardly surprising this is the site of Denmark's major linear barrier, the Danevirke.

---

* But it was then abandoned for fear that the intense cold would mean that the rivers to the west – that otherwise provided a defensive obstacle – having frozen over would be more easily crossed in an outflanking movement. (Freezing over is the flaw in the use of the water as a barrier in northerly climes. In 406 the Rhine froze and the barbarians who got into the Roman Empire then were never ejected.)

† The importance of control of the Hærvejen is reflected in the damage that could be done when ravaging forces were not blocked. Jutland suffered horribly from the assault of the Swedes under Field Marshal Lennart Torstensson in the Thirty Years War in 1642.

‡ A useful point to bear in mind is that Jutland has little stone. (This is reflected in the way the early cathedrals incorporate the local granite at load bearing points but the stone parts are otherwise imported tufa.) Early on, brick was extensively used.

Danes appear inordinately proud of their Viking inheritance – even quite small towns have their Viking museum or outdoor centre. The Viking period of raiding extended from the eighth to the eleventh century and involved people not just from modern Denmark but also from Norway and Sweden. The history of Denmark is, of course, much longer than the Viking period and the search for linear barriers is perhaps more likely to be productive at times when the peoples faced each other inwards, when there were warring polities, rather than releasing their energies abroad.

For Scandinavia literacy and written history started quite late, in the first millennium AD. What is known comes largely from archaeology and some rather second-hand ancient texts on geography. The following is much simplified and probably debatable:

The late Iron Age was a time of troubles. From about 200 modern Denmark was divided into tribal areas where groups of tribes federated under some regional authority. Danish archaeologists have identified a period of inter-tribal conflict which continued until unification more than four centuries later. A rising population resulted in a shortage of arable land and hence food. Such situations of increasing population pressure, within a constricted area, often resulted in war between polities. The pressure was only relieved or controlled by migration and ultimately via unification.

The Harudes occupied the west coast of Jutland. The Jutes occupied the northern and eastern coasts. The Angles lived in southern Jutland. The Frisians lived on the south-west coast, extending into what is now Germany and the Netherlands. In the fifth century the Danes, a Gothic-Germanic tribe, migrated from southern Sweden into Jutland. The Jutes mostly went to Kent in England – if Bede is to be relied on – and the Angles to eastern Britain. The Harudes migrated to what is now Norway to become the Horder of Horderland. Any remaining peoples were incorporated into the now Danish population.

By around 600 the peoples of Jutland were collectively known as Danes. Some time in the early eighth century Denmark was unified under one king, possibly Angantyr. In the late eighth and early ninth century the southern border was vulnerable to the expanding Empire of Charlemagne and then his Germanic imperial successors. To the south-east there was a strong Slav presence and West Slavs frequently raided south-eastern Jutland. Under Harald Bluetooth (958–986) Denmark became Christian.[*]

Linear barriers

In the earlier sections on Britain and Ireland searches became focused on ancient routeways and also on Roman Roads in what is now England. Additionally, linear barriers were found not to be scattered randomly but typically appear in zones and

---

[*] It was in the thirteenth century that the beginnings of the Schleswig-Holstein question first arose which ultimately ended up with the Danevirke now lying in Germany. While not resolved until the after the end of the First World War with a plebiscite, which saw the return of North Schleswig to Denmark, the fact is the German language line moved up Jutland and this caused a conflict between political authority and linguistic allegiance. A significant part of historic Denmark, including the Danevirke and the adjacent trading city of Hedeby, now lies in Germany.

4.3: Denmark

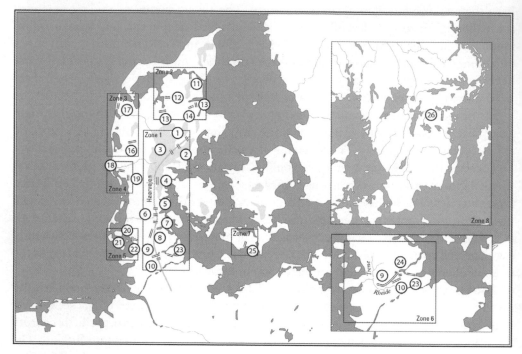

The Hærwejen (Zone 1)
1. Kong Knaps Dige
2. Isen Dige
3. Margrethe Dige
4. Trældiget
5. Margrethevolden
6. Volden
7. Vendersvold (or Æ Vold)
8. Olmerdiget
9. Danevirke
10. Kovirke

Northern Jutland (Zone 2)
11. Molles Dige
12. Vejspæring without name in Aggersund–Viborg
13. Trediget
14. Dandiget
15. Margrathes grav

North western Jutland (Zone 3)
16. Bardedige
17. Rammedige
    Fandensdiget, Vendeldiget (not shown)

West Jutland (Zone 4)
18. Gellerup
19. Kamdiget

South West Jutland (Zone 5)
20. Danmarksgraven
21. Kuugswall
22. Dannervirkenvolden

South East [Schwansen] Peninsula (Zone 6)
23. Østervolden
24. Slispærringen OR Stegsvig

The Islands (Zone 7)
25. Hejrede Vold

Sweden (Zone 8)
26. Götavirke

clusters. Using these lessons, what sense can be made of the linear barriers of Denmark? Examination of their location on the map indicates that, as in Britain, the linear barriers can be found in groups or zones. This is the case even along the ancient road system called the Hærvejen. Basically the survey can start with the Hærvejen as this runs nearly the entire length of Jutland. It would be expected that when Jutland was broken up into warring tribes, these divisions might be reflected in the construction of linear barriers across its way.

As with Britain these linear barriers are numerous, mostly short, and there is not space here to discuss them in any detail.

The Hærvejen (Zone 1)

The Hærvejen runs almost due south from Viborg in northern Jutland all the way to the Danevirke. It then continues on to Hamburg. It is easiest quite simply to set out the linear barriers on the Hærvejen running from north to south. These are called *vejspærringen* or road blockers. Most are quite short but have been carefully located to link natural obstacles on either side of the way. A few are quite substantial like the Olmerdiget. If they were intended to stop a threat from continental Europe then they would all face to the south, yet some face north. Therefore, it appears that the threat came not from the continent but from other polities on the Jutland Peninsula. There are very roughly three clusters of barriers which traverse the Hærvejen which may correspond to divisions between tribes or peoples and there are other linear barriers closely associated with this roadway system.

Table 4.12: Jutland – Hærvejen (from south to north)

Southern cluster – Danevirke, Kovirke, Østervolden, Slispærringen (or Stegsvig)

Central cluster – Margrethevolden, Volden, Vendersvold (or Æ Vold), Olgerdiget (or Olmerdiget)

Hærvejen – Trældiget (lies parallel and to the east)

Northern cluster – Kong Knaps Dige, Isen Dige, Margrethe Dige

North-eastern cluster – Trediget, Dandiget

Olmediget – There is a central group of more substantial barriers: the Olmediget (7.5 kilometres); the Vendersvold or Æ Vold (3 kilometres); and the Margrethevolden (1.6 kilometres). The first two faced north and the last may face south. They have been associated with the border of the Angles to the south and the Jutes to the north. Wood extracted from the Olgerdiget has been dated to 219 and 278. The Olgerdiget is the longest linear barrier in Jutland after the Danevirke. While the earthwork itself was not remarkably large it was preceded by three oak palisades estimated to have incorporated up to 90,000 tree trunks. The barrier was not continuous as its length covered marshy ground.

Northern Jutland belt (Zone 2)

There appears to be a distribution of linear barriers very roughly in a line from in the east around Hobro and Randers, through the vicinity of Viborg, Holstebro, Ikast and Herning and on west to the North Sea coast at Husby. (This appears to be similar to the line between what are coyly called 'archaeologically defined regional groupings' – which basically means different peoples might have lived next to each other.)

Table 4.13: Jutland – Northern Jutland belt

Northern central cluster – Molles Dige, unnamed earthwork near Aggersund-Viborg, Margrathes grav

North-western cluster – Bardedige, Fandensdiget, Rammedige[1], Vendeldiget

---

Other Jutland Zones

West Jutland (Zone 3) – There are two short dykes in the central west, the Gellerup and the Kamdiget.

South-west Jutland (Zone 4) – There are three dykes in the south-west – which might correspond to the northern area of Frisian territory, the Danmarksgraven, Kuugswall, Dannervirkenvolden.

The Danevirke – This great and complex set of linear barriers adds a new dimension to the issues surrounding such barriers in Denmark and Sweden. Of course, it seems tremendously big when actually encountered. But it is not just a question of dimension but also of the length of time it was used. It may first have been constructed in the seventh or eighth century but it continued to be rebuilt and reused all the way through to the thirteenth century. Not only that – excavation shows changes in technology from a simple earthwork to a larger more complex earthwork, then to an earthwork with a wooden framework, to one faced by rubble, and finally a fired brick wall. Perhaps no other linear barrier demonstrates such development over such a long period of time. Also, perhaps no other earthwork has been so comprehensively examined, so there are some dates for the individual phases of construction which can be related to the course of history.

If the Danevirke were not there it might have been necessary to invent it. There are two very obvious reasons for its existence: firstly, there is the narrow isthmus of a large peninsula; and secondly, there is a man-made land corridor running down that peninsula through the isthmus along the watershed line or ridgeway. It is logical to construct any linear barrier across the narrowest point of any land corridor. In the case of the southern Jutland Peninsula there are two inlets on the east and west sides, respectively the Schlei inlet and the Eider River, which halve the seventy-five kilometre gap between their mouths. If one adds the Trene River, the major tributary of the Eider, then the gap to the Schlei is further reduced. The Trene to Schlei gap is the location of the Danevirke. If one includes the tributary of the Trene, the Rheide River, then the distance is again reduced. The Rheide to Schlei gap is the location of another barrier to the south of the Danevirke, the Kovirke. The Hærvejen follows the watershed line between the Rheide River and the Schlei inlet. Thus, it is intersected by both the Danevirke and the Kovirke.

The central Hovevolden section, which crosses the which crosses the Hærvejen, is the most worked and reworked part and therefore gives the most clues as to the stages of construction and the threats faced. There are eight stages in the Hovevolden between the seventh and twelfth centuries. Unfortunately only one can be precisely dated and it proves to be unexpectedly early. That is 737 for the fourth stage when a palisade was built. Three archaeological phases therefore pre-date 737; this means that the earliest parts probably dated to the seventh century.

The written evidence however, puts the construction of the Danevirke in the early ninth century. In terms of texts there is a well-known reference in the Frankish Royal Annals for 808 which says Godfred, 'decided to protect the frontier-area of his kingdom facing Saxony with a rampart in such a way that a protective bulwark, broken by a single gateway through which wagons and horsemen could be let out and admitted, would form a border from the gulf on the eastern seaboard which they call Ostersalt (the Baltic) along the entire length of the northern bank of the river Eider as far as the western ocean.'[14] This is both informative and confusing because, as seen, archaeology shows the Danevirke possibly dates from the late seventh century and certainly from the early eighth century. Also, no known work extended along the Eider River as opposed to the Rheide River. (The annalist is at this point possibly referring to the border and not necessarily the linear barrier.) Reric, on the southern Baltic Sea, was destroyed and moved to Sliesthorp – or Hedeby – the success of which move required reconfiguring the whole barrier in order to protect the trading city.

The chronicler Saxo Grammaticus (1150–1220) mentions the 'rampart of Jutland' (*Clutiae moenia*) in his *Gesta Danorum* as having been once more extended by Valdemar the Great (1157–82).[15] This is identified with the brick facing given to part of the Hovevolden. Also, on a lead scroll found in Valdemar's tomb, the scribe wrote: 'also a wall to the defence of the Kingdom, Danevirke he raised with baked stones'.

The Danevirke had a remarkable long life from the seventh to the thirteenth century. It controlled the main land route into Jutland up the Hærvejen and faced a continuous threat from Franks, Saxons, Abodrites, and the Holy Roman Empire. It was almost certainly as old as unified Denmark and its construction might have marked the end of Jutland's warring polities period. It appears to fit the pattern of the construction of a frontier linear barrier *after* unification, with the result that linear barriers remaining on the interior were suddenly rendered superfluous.

Baltic Zones – islands and southern Sweden

On both the island of Østlolland in the Danish Baltic Sea and in Østergötland in modern Sweden are two pairs of parallel linear barriers running between lakes and wetlands.

Østlige Vold and Vestlige Vold – On the island of Østlolland there are two barriers, one facing east and one west, called respectively the Østlige Vold (1300 metres) and the Vestlige Vold (300 metres) about 3.5 kilometres apart. They link lakes and wetlands to create a defensible sanctuary area and are dated to the mid–sixth century. There appears to have been an internal wooden framework in some of the barrier structure.

Götavirke – About 125 kilometres south-east of Stockholm are barriers called the Götavirke. Effectively it controlled access to inner Østergötland by managing the route from the sea. As so often in northern Europe, there may be an association with an old road. The lines of the

Table 4.14: Phases of construction of the Danevirke

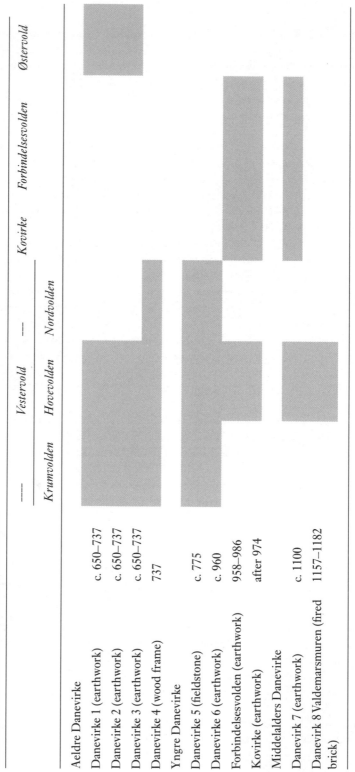

Column headers: Krumvolden | Vestervold (Hovevolden) | Nordvolden | — | Kovirke | Forbindelsesvolden | Østervold

Aeldre Danevirke

Danevirke 1 (earthwork)	c. 650–737
Danevirke 2 (earthwork)	c. 650–737
Danevirke 3 (earthwork)	c. 650–737
Danevirke 4 (wood frame)	737

Yngre Danevirke

Danevirke 5 (fieldstone)	c. 775
Danevirke 6 (earthwork)	c. 960
Forbindelsesvolden (earthwork)	958–986
Kovirke (earthwork)	after 974

Middelalders Danevirke

Danevirk 7 (earthwork)	c. 1100
Danevirk 8 Valdemarsmuren (fired brick)	1157–1182

Götavirke may run south, at right angles, to the Royal Road from Söderköping to Linköping. These barriers consist of parallel rubble walls with earth infilling. There are two parallel linear barriers, running north to south, the longest of which is about 3.5 kilometres long. It is generally dated to about 800 but earlier dates may be possible. Central Østergötland is protected by great forests to the north and south and Lake Vättern to the west. It is close to an inlet which runs about forty kilometres inland from the Baltic Sea. These lie between lakes Asplangen and Lilisjon. North of Asplangen there stand hill forts which may have been part of the same defensive system. To the south the ground is difficult to negotiate.

Analysis – Denmark and Sweden linear barriers

With the exception of the Olmerdiget and, of course, the Danevirke, most of these barriers are quite short. They are dated to some time after 200 and appear to mark tribal boundaries and possibly different Germanic sub-groups. It is arguable that the tensions and pressures, resulting in linear barrier construction, were caused by the Danish invasion of Jutland, followed by the exodus of many Harudes to Norway, and Jutes and Angles to England with the absorption of those remaining. These Danish linear barriers run largely across or roughly parallel and close to ancient routeways and, with the possible exception of the Olmerdiget, do not appear to be frontier systems. Although short, they are carefully sited to make the best possible use of natural features – forests, rivers, marshes and lakes. Overall, they appear similar to the linear barriers found in Great Britain in that they are largely related to routeways.

Perhaps it is no accident to say that the Danevirke and the Channel mark the start of Northern Europe. Maybe, without the Danevirke what is now Denmark would have been absorbed into the Holy Roman Empire in the earlier Middle Ages. The Danevirke effectively made Denmark an island off Europe like Great Britain and, in practice, separate from Europe, like Sweden and Norway. Denmark was separated long enough to consolidate a separate Danish and northern European identity rather than being absorbed into mainland Europe. The Danevirke helped establish the concept of Danish independence and Denmark as part of the Scandinavian world.

4. Germanic peoples

Linear barriers appear remarkably frequently in the history of German speaking peoples as they established or tried to fix frontiers. This section provides an opportunity to look at the continuity of Germanic linear barrier building. It also provides an opportunity to introduce some linear barriers which may be unfamiliar, like the *Landwehren* of western Germany, and the *Letzimauern* of German-speaking Switzerland, in the High and Late Middle Ages.

Early period

Nervii abatis – Tacitus, in his book *Germania*, wrote that in his time the Nervii believed that their Germanic ancestry distinguished them from the weaker Gauls. Julius Caesar wrote that in 57 BC, 'The Nervii... because they were weak in cavalry, ... in order that they might the more easily obstruct the cavalry of their neighbors ... cut young trees, and bent them, by means of their numerous branches (extending) on to the sides, and the quick-briars and thorns springing up between them, had made these hedges present a fortification like a wall, through which it was not only impossible to enter, but even to penetrate with the eye.'[16]

Teutoburg Forest Wall – Although this was not intended as a permanent linear barrier it may be worth mentioning the role a wall played in ending Rome's first phase of trans-Rhine expansion. The story begins when at the battle of Teutoburg Forest Publius Quintilius Varus' three legions were completely destroyed in AD 9. The German leader Arminius had served under the Romans. It was not until the battlefield was discovered and excavated in the 1980s that it was revealed that the Germans had built a wall and concealed themselves behind it, at the base of Kalkriese Hill near Osnabrück. Excavation showed that a trench blocked the road. Furthermore, they had constructed a giant earthwork, about 600 metres long, nearly 5 metres wide and 2 metres high with a palisade on top. The Germans placed this structure along the road from which they could attack the Romans, and when counter-attacked they could negate the advantages of heavier Roman armour and weaponry.

Treveri Rampart – From around 150 BC the Treveri, who according to Tacitus claimed German descent, occupied the lower valley of the Moselle centered on *Augusta Treverorum*/Trier. Tacitus says that when the first, fourth and eigthteenth legions attacked the Chatti, Usipii, and Mattiaci, the Treveri defended themselves with a linear barrier for, 'The Treveri had constructed a breastwork and rampart across their territory.'[17]

Angrivarii and Cherusci Boundary Earthwork – Tacitus described the revenge the Romans took for the destruction of Varus' legions – led by Augustus' great-nephew Germanicus. The Germans' last stand took place by a linear earthwork which divided the Angrivarii from the Cherusci[18] somewhere to the west of modern Hanover, between the Steinhuder See and the Weser. Tacitus mentioned: 'The woods too were surrounded by a bottomless morass, only on one side of it the Angrivarii had raised a broad earthwork, as a boundary between themselves and the Cherusci. Here their infantry was ranged.'[19]

Greuthungi Rampart – Ammianus Marcellinus described how the Thervingi, or forest Goths, fled before the Huns in 376. The Goths 'established his camp near the banks of the Danastius ... conveniently at some distance from the stockade of the Greuthungi (*Greuthungorum vallem*)'[20] but they were outflanked by the Huns and forced to retreat.

Thervingi Rampart – Taking up the story of Athanaric's flight from above: 'Athanaricus, troubled by this unexpected attack and still more through fear of what might come, had walls built high, skirting the lands of the Taifali from the banks of the river Gerasus as far as the Danube, thinking that by this hastily but diligently constructed barrier his security and safety would be assured. But while this well-planned work was being pushed on, the Huns swiftly fell upon him.'[21]

Brazda lui Novac de Nord – This earthwork runs west to east across the Wallachian Plain and is discussed in more detail below. It might have formed part of the defences of a Gothic state in the fourth century.

Middle Period

Frankish expansion

Limes Saxoniae and Limes Sorabicus – The eastern boundary of Frankish expansion under Charlemagne was marked by the Limes Saxonia and Limes Sorabicus from the Danish Mark (or border regions as in the English word 'marches)' to the Mark of Avaria.

- The location of the Limes Saxoniae was described by Adam of Bremen in around 1075.[22] It was not a linear earthwork but appeared to have incorporated marsh and forest. In the latter it might have taken the form of a lost abatis whose presence might be indicated by place names like Mannhagen.[23]
- In 805 there was a *Dux Sorabici limitis*, or duke of the Sorb border. Again toponyms in the region, like Mannhagen or Zasek, might have indicated the presence of abatis.

Anti-Avar Earthwork – When the Franks and the Bulgarians crushed the Avars at the turn of eighth and ninth centuries, Widukind reported that Charlemagne built earthworks to contain them. 'And then Charlemagne defeated them (the Avars), ousted them across the Danube, and fenced them in with earthwork, and this prevented them to raid the folks in their familiar way.'[24]

Northern Europe

Götavirke – In southern Sweden, as seen above, the Goths built the Götavirke which ran beside the Royal Road from Söderköping to Linköping.

Angle and Saxon linear earthworks – The Angles almost certainly constructed linear earthworks in the central band of the Jutland peninsula. In England they were probably responsible for the dykes in East Anglia and Cambridgeshire. Anglian Mercians built Offa's Dyke. Wansdyke might be a long Saxon frontier.

Dane's Dyke and Hogue Dyke – The Vikings were sea-borne migrants to Great Britain and Continental Europe. As such they needed secure beaching places and if they were trying to establish themselves in contested areas, defensible bases. At Flamborough Head in Yorkshire the coastal headland is traversed by a linear earthwork called Dane's Dyke. This is probably originally a pre-Roman structure but there is speculation that it might have been the base in 548 for the Anglian King Ida who created the Kingdom of Northumbria. At the north-west of Cotentin peninsula is the Cap de la Hague. The Cap is traversed by Hogue Dyke which was reused by the Viking settlers after the 880s.

Late period

There are some later linear barriers which seem to be largely uncovered in the English language.

Western Holy Roman Empire (Landwehren)

In the introduction a pattern was outlined where linear barriers were constructed by ethnically or culturally similar states existing in an increasingly resource-constrained area. The western part of the Holy Roman Empire, in the later Middle Ages, might be considered in this context. As Voltaire said, it was 'neither holy, nor Roman nor an empire'. Certainly by the High and Late Middle Ages the area to the east of the Rhine was a disunified patchwork of bishoprics, imperial cities, princedoms, duchies and other petty states, usually centred around one or a few, often cathedral, cities. Between the fourteenth and the sixteenth century, hundreds if not thousands of kilometres of linear earthworks were built upon, or dense thickets were grown, to defend the borders of many of these polities.

The story of Charlemagne's Frankish Empire after his death in 814 is one of increasing fragmentation under the titular authority of the Holy Roman Emperor. In 1220 and 1232 the Emperor Frederick, who preferred to live in Sicily and who was embroiled in wars in Italy, removed many powers to ecclesiastical and secular authorities, including the right of fortification.

In the fourteenth and fifteenth century Imperial power declined further as the emperors became increasingly removed from the old German core areas, while multiple papacies and Hussite wars divided and drained ecclesiastical authority. The result in the west, where states were often tiny, was endemic feuding. The Diet of Worms in 1495 resulted in imperial reform which produced somewhat more stable structures in the form of Imperial Circles. These were regional grouping of territories of the Holy Roman Empire, which organised common defensive structures and supervised the collection of imperial taxes. The regions that became the Upper Rhenish Circle and especially the Swabian Circle, however, remained very fragmented. Searches here reveal a large number of linear barriers called *Landwehren*: here, for example, around the Duchy of Berg, the Imperial Cities of Schwabisch Hall and Rothenburg, and the Bishopric of Spire.

Conflicts between rulers were seldom fought with massive troop deployments on open battle fields. It was more usual for smaller groups, moving rapidly, to invade the border areas, pillaging farms, stealing cattle and destroying crops. Such ravaging undermined the states' economic bases. It was the duty of the ruler to provide for peasants while losses of livestock and agricultural land and infrastructure were made good.'[25]

Given the frequency of feuding during this period, the unpredictability of attack, and the cost of damage, it was not practicable or sufficient to gather people and livestock into city walls. This situation made frontier defence the necessary solution. As a result princes, dukes, counts and bishops constructed *Landwehren* along their borders which obstructed raiders, or at least prevented their return with livestock and booty. They also stopped animals from straying and controlled flows of goods on which customs dues could be charged.

Landwehren – The *Landwehren* combined earthwork ramparts and ditches. The main obstacles used, however, were trees, usually beech, where the tip was bent back into the earth where it formed new roots. Into the skeleton of doubled-over beeches, the builders introduced thorny bushes, like wild roses, blackberries and hawthorn, thereby forming a dense thicket up to twenty metres deep. Constructing a living barrier took time and required constant maintenance. Farmers had to plant and tend barriers which would take a decade to mature.

Apart from protecting frontiers *Landwehren* were planted alongside roads, both to protect travellers and to guide the paths away from potentially vulnerable settlements. As seen with the Hærvejen and the Ridgeway, roads often followed the higher ground watershed line. If the road had to descend into a valley before joining another such line then it might be protected by *Landwehren*.

Cities might also be surrounded not only by stone city walls but also by an outer ring in the form of a *Landwehr* – for example the city of Hagen. Maps of seventeenth century Frankfurt show that it was once surrounded at a distance by a full hedge circuit.

Switzerland

Another region where both warring of states and state building were combined was the early cantons of Switzerland.

Letzimauern – Many Swiss cities had *Letzimauern* which were walls built several kilometres ahead of the main city defence circuit; these controlled valleys where access was narrow and sides steep so the walls could be short. There were also palisades built along lake waterfronts where access could be blocked to communications routes. There were often stone towers that frequently survive as isolated reminders of the existence of such walls which have mostly been robbed but whose foundations can be traced.

Letzimauern played a key part in the battles through which the Swiss won their independence. In 1291, the three German speaking cantons of Uri, Schwyz, and Unterwalden united to defend the peace upon the death of Emperor Rudolf I of Habsburg. Schwyz was strongly defended with strategically placed *Letzimauern*. The single route open for the Duke Leopold of Austria and his knights was past Äegeri and onto the defile or narrow gorge at Mortgarten (1315) where they were ambushed by the Swiss defenders and largely slaughtered. Leopold only just escaped.

By 1353, the three original cantons had been joined by the cantons of Glarus and Zug and the city states of Lucerne, Zürich, and Bern, forming the 'Old Federation' of eight states. In the mid-fourteenth century the Canton of Glarus built a *Letzimauer* at Näfels, in 1388 the site of the Battle of Näfels. In 1389, a seven-year peace left the Swiss Confederation in control of all the territory they had acquired in the recent war. Again a *Letzimauer* was the site of the Battle of Stoss Pass in 1405 in the Appenzell Wars between 1401 and 1429 which resulted in the defeat of the Hapsburgs.

When not at war with the Holy Roman Empire the Swiss cantons fought against each other, and more *Letzimauern* were built. This recalls the now familiar warring states scenario of ethnically similar peoples, fighting in a resource-constrained area, resulting in the construction of linear barriers.

Analysis – Germanic peoples

There is no intention here to divine some particular genetic proclivity of Germans or Goths to build linear barriers. It is more likely that the migrations of such peoples took them to locations where the situation and readily available materials, particularly earth and forest, made linear barrier construction a logical solution to strategic problems. It remains however a fact that Germanic peoples, as they expanded from Saxony and around the Baltic, left a trail of linear barriers which may have helped secure their hold on certain locations.

5. The English overseas

This section includes some linear barriers in what are now France, Ireland and the Anglo–Scottish Borders which have a common thread in that they are all associated with monarchs of England.

Les Fossés-le-Roy (or Fossés Royaux) – Southern Normandy was a highly contentious border between the Anglo–Normans and Angevins, who were both Kings of England and Dukes of Normandy, and the Kings of France. According to the chronicler Robert Torigny it was after the troops of Louis VII took Chennebrun, in the French region of Haute-Normandie, in 1169, that 'Henry II ordered the digging of wide and deep ditches between France and Normandy in order to repel brigands.'[26] The Les Fossés-le-Roy complemented the already existing line of castles reinforced during the reign of Henry I Beauclerc and consisted of a rampart as well as a ditch and hedges between five and ten metres wide and five metres deep, behind the l'Avre River, about 130 kilometres long, between Perche and Normandy and from Dreux to Mêle-sur-Sarthe. This does not sound like a frontier barrier which was intended to stop armies. That would have been the task of the castles of Henry I which such armies would have had to take or, at great risk, leave in their wake. Rather, as Robert Torigny says, the Les Fossés-le-Roy's function was to 'repel brigands'.

Calais Pale – The defences of the Calais Pale are something of a mystery. The Pale included an area of about 310 square kilometres – heavily fortified against incursions from France. (The Field of the Cloth of Gold took place within the Pale but outside the city itself.) A Pale, generally interpreted as a palisade, was first mentioned in 1494 when Sir Edward Poynings was deputy lieutenant at Calais. The word pale derives from the Latin 'palus', or stake used to support a fence. The Calais Pale might have been a palisade of fully cut down dead wood or an abatis of living wood. As seen, the city states of the western Holy Roman Empire protected their frontiers with *Landwehren* or linear earthworks which incorporated living forest. (Poynings had travelled in north-east Europe, for in 1493 he was sent on a mission to Archduke Philip to gain the pretender to Henry VII's throne Perkin Warbeck's expulsion from Burgundy.)

Irish Pale – Sir Edward Poynings was appointed governor of Ireland in 1494 after leaving Calais. The Irish Pale was constructed under an act of Poyning's Parliament in 1494 to defend the dwindling Anglo–Irish territory, about thirty kilometres around Dublin in the medieval counties of Louth, Meath, Dublin and Kildare, against the Gaelic Irish. Its purpose was to protect those within, 'from attack and plunder from English rebels and Irish enemies, and also to prevent cattle being driven from the Pale to Irish areas.'[27] Poynings may have imitated the defensive circuit around the Calais territories and applied the same name.[28]

A late nineteenth century description of the Irish Pale is informative – particularly because it says the barrier included a living hedge. 'This barrier consisted of a ditch, raised some ten or twelve feet from the ground, with a hedge of thorn on the outer side. It was constructed, not so much to keep out the Irish, as to form an obstacle in the way on return from raids with cattle, and thus give time for a rescue.'[29] Parts of the Pale 'double ditch' have survived in an area north of Rathcoffey at Graiguepottle and in two areas on either side of Clongowes wood. Possible sections may also have survived at Baltracey and Painstown.[30] The Pale might be regarded as a success – depending on one's point of view – for it survived to serve as the launching area for the Tudor reconquest of Ireland.

Scots' Dyke – This dyke was constructed by the English and the Scots in 1552 across the so-called Debatable Lands in the western borders region. This area measured fourteen kilometres from north to south and five kilometres from east to west. The dyke itself was a 5.25 kilometres long linear earthwork; it served an overtly political function in that it established the exact boundary between the Kingdoms of Scotland and England, following an agreement reached under the arbitration of the French Ambassador.

Analysis – British overseas

Mostly, this section finds a home for linear barriers which are hard to place. The fact however that the English appear to be associated with linear barriers in areas abroad which otherwise seem to be devoid of them, at least in the broad medieval period, does seem to affirm that linear barrier construction is a particularly northern and – as will be seen next eastern – European tradition.

Conclusion – Northern Europe

There are certainly a lot of linear barriers in Jutland, England and Northern Ireland. Also, they appear to have common features. Mostly they are quite short, less than ten kilometres in length. They seem to be associated with old road systems, the Ichnield Way and the Ridgeway in England, the Hærvejen in Jutland, the Slighe Midluachre in Ireland, and the Royal Road in Sweden. They include cross-route dykes and earthworks which run parallel to routeways. Indeed, the idea of linear barrier building, at least in northern Europe, might have developed specifically from the early emergence of strategic routeways.

There may be some frontier systems although they probably seldom functioned as continually patrolled borders. It is hard to believe there were the necessary resources to build and permanently man a full frontier-length linear barrier. They may have been intended to impede raiding, particularly of livestock, by gaining time for counter-attack and by making it harder to return driving herds and flocks of animals. Such systems might include Offa's Dyke, Wansdyke, and the Dane's Cast and Black Pig Dykes. The Danevirke and Offa's Dyke might have been intended to be more than purely defensive.

4.4: English overseas expansion

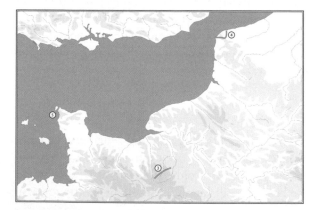

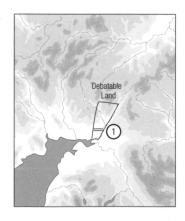

England and Scotland Border
1.   Scots' Dyke (Debatable Land)

Ireland
2.   Irish Pale

France
3.   Fossés-le-Roy
4.   Calais Pale (possibly a linear barrier)

Also shows
5.   Hogue Dyke

One may even go as far as to say that they represented a political statement of sorts, as they marked the culmination of the unification of Denmark under the Danes and the final line of Mercian expansion in the English Midlands.

The areas the Anglians occupied, both in Jutland and in England, appear to have been particularly rich in linear earthworks. Indeed, it might be speculated that Anglians brought a particular propensity to build such barriers from Jutland to England.

Very often the barriers consist not just of earth, formed into ditch and rampart, but also of living hedge and trees. This would hardly seem to be surprising given their ease of growth in the wet temperate climate of north Europe. Given, however, the inevitable tendency of linear barriers of living wood to disappear, the extent of linear barriers that once existed in Northern Europe might be much underestimated.

Chapter Five

Eastern Europe – Multiple Barriers where Steppe and Europe Collide

In the early eighteenth century the scholarly Prince Dimitrie Cantemir, the ruler of the principality of Moldavia, wrote a study of the region called the *Descriptio Moldaviae* in which he described a massive linear earthwork which extended from the River Tisza in modern Serbia to the River Don in Russia.

> This ditch, as I myself saw with my eyes, begins in the Hungarian country at Petrovaradin (now Novi-Sad in Serbia) in the shape of two waves. Then it descends and enters in the Romanian-country at the Iron Gates, and from here continues as a single wave over all the Romanian-country, crosses the Seret River at the village called Traian and the Botna River at the village called Causiani (Basarabia), then goes along the whole of Tataria and ends at the River Tanais (Don).[1]

While almost certainly no such fully continuous ditch existed, there remain many linear earthworks, along much of the route he described, spread across eastern Europe from Hungary to the eastern Ukraine. In Serbia near Novi-Sad are the Römerschanzen. The Brazda lui Novac de Nord runs across the Wallachian Plain north of the Danube – possibly as far as the Seret River. The Valul Traian–Tuluceşti links the Seret and the Prut Rivers. There is a linear barrier running up the east bank of the Prut to the Valul lui Trajan de Sus which runs across Moldova to the Dniester River. In the western Ukraine there are several Zmievi Vali earthworks along Cantemir's route, first crossing the Southern Bug, then in central Ukraine around the Dnieper, and lastly in eastern Ukraine running close to the Don.

Prince Cantemir was well placed centrally in Moldavia to hear reports of linear barriers, both to the east and west, and possibly elaborated on these reports to create a continuous barrier. What is not in dispute however, is the fact that very substantial linear barriers were spread over all Eastern Europe from the Hungarian and Wallachian Plains to across the Pontic Steppe. In Hungary and the Ukraine there are, if combined, 2,000 kilometres of the Csörzárok and the Zmievi Vali respectively. From the Dobrogea, in eastern Romania north to the Galicia in western Ukraine, there are four great lines of earthworks – each called the Valul or Valurile lui Traian. On the Wallachian Plain there are two great barriers – the Brazda lui Novac du Nord and the Brazda lui Novac du Sud. In southern Bulgaria, the Erkesia separated the Bulgarian and Byzantine Empires. Poland has several earthworks, probably linked to its emergence as a separate state. The Crimea has many linear barriers.

These barriers are, individually or collectively, among the longest in the region but there are many more. Indeed certain regions are – or were – densely filled with long earthworks. Examples include the area between the Danube and the western Carpathians, the eastern Carpathians and the Dniester, south of Kiev on both sides of the Dnieper, or the Crimea's Kerch Peninsula. Perhaps this might not be surprising: after all, the Pontic Steppe is where the Eurasian Steppe narrows before colliding with Europe.

Although the presence of a great number and length of linear barriers is incontrovertible, there is little consensus both as to when and by whom they were built. The situation is complicated because linear barriers were often remade, reversed and reused and, therefore, two or more builders and sets of dates frequently apply.

Basically the linear barriers will be divided into three geographical groups: first, the Hungarian and Wallachian plains (modern Hungary and Romania); second, the Pontic Steppe exits (eastern Romania, Moldavia, western Ukraine); and third, the Pontic Steppe itself (eastern Ukraine and Crimea). There is another group – where it is fairly clear who was likely to have built at least some of the linear barriers and that such construction had something to do with state formation – which will be looked at in the next chapter on Bulgaria, Poland and the Kievan Rus.

1. Lower Danube

The lower Danube runs through both the Hungarian and Wallachian Plains which poses challenging questions as to where to place and how to manage frontiers. The river is an obvious location but what happens if there is equally attractive land on the other side? The Roman Empire might have decided that it was not cost effective to fully control and occupy land across the Danube. But it might have needed to exert some form of authority over a sensitive and desirable area. Also, other polities were likely to try to contest that authority. In this section about these two Plains, the question is asked: what role might man–made barriers play in controlling a contested zone created by a natural linear barrier? In this instance, the quandary is posed by a major river which divides an essentially similar region into two halves, where one is considered to be within and the other outside a more advanced polity?

Great Hungarian Plain

The Great Hungarian Plain or Apföld is the last stop on the Asian Eurasian Steppe. It provided a final home from home for nomadic peoples from Asia who were looking for pasture and a base for further raids into the richer Mediterranean and western parts of Europe. The trans-Danubian area, of interest here, was known as 'Barbaricum'. It was bounded to the west and south by the Danube and to the east, and to a lesser extent to the north, where it is more open, by the Carpathian Mountains. The Tisza River runs north-south, down the centre of Barbaricum, with important tributaries on the eastern side, the Maros to the north and the Koros to the south.

Before the First World War the entire region lay in the Austro-Hungarian Empire but after the war Transylvania and a wedge of the Apföld were handed over to what is now Romania and Serbia – a slight largely forgotten elsewhere but bitterly remembered in Hungary. Serbia, in the south, has lands north of the Danube, where it flows eastwards, on both sides of the River Tisza. This includes the Bačka region between the Danube and the west of the Tisza.

In eastern Hungary, western Romania and northern Serbia, there is a huge complex of earthworks, generally called the Csörszárok and the Ördögárok, which lie across the eastern part of the Great Hungarian Plain. In the north, the earthworks run west to east, from the Danube to the Tisza, and then from the Tisza north to south, ending again in the vicinity of the Danube. (For simplicity here, the northern part is called the Csörszárok and the eastern section the Ördögárok. For the collective works the former name is used.)

Much of the Csörszárok and the Ördögárok has been lost to modern agriculture but it was sufficiently mapped in the eighteenth and nineteenth centuries for it to be clear that the total length of earthworks exceeded 1,200 kilometres. Therefore, these can lay claim to being the greatest combined group of earthworks in Europe. In the region to the west of the confluence of the Tisza and the Danube, called the Bačka, in modern Serbia, there lies a group of earthworks called the Römerschanzen.

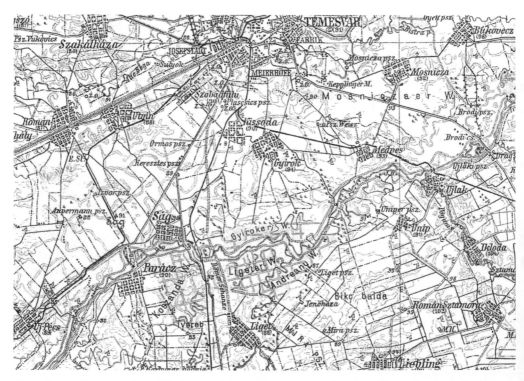

Csörszárok – Temesvar (now Timişoara) dyke, in Banat region of western Romania, marked as Römer Schanze. *(3rd Military Mapping Survey of Austria-Hungary (1910))*

5.1: The Carpathian Basin and the Wallachian Plain

Carpathian Basin
Danube to Tizla River (Hungary) (Zone 1)
1. Csörszárok
2. Petit Fossé

Tizra to Danube (Zone 2)
3. Ördögárok (multiple lines)
4. Crasna to Zalău River Entrenchment (not shown)

Koros River (Zone 3)
5. Koros River Earthwork

Danube, Tizra confluence, Bačka (Serbia, Hungary) (Zone 4)
6. Groß Römerschanze (Novi Sad to Csurog)
7. Römerschanze (Kulpin to Csurog)

8. Kleine Römerschanze (Gospodince to Bacs-Petrovoszelo)
9. Römerschanze (Apatin to Rac–Militics)

Wallachian Plain
10. Brazda lui Novac de Nord
11. Brazda lui Novac de Sud
12. Limes Transalutanus (see Map 2.2)

Linear barriers on the Great Hungarian Plain

There are two main groups of surviving linear barriers. To facilitate describing them, they are divided into zones: Zones 1 to 2 include the Csörszárok and Ördögárok which border the north and east of Barbaricum. Zone 3 is the Koros River earthwork. Zone 4 consists of the Römerschanzen that lies largely between the confluence of the Danube and the Tisza. There are also earthworks known from texts: the Avar Hrings, and Charlemagne's anti-Avar earthworks.

Csörszárok (Zone 1) – The first zone consists of the linear barriers which lie within the Hungarian part of the Alföld. There are two roughly parallel and continuous earthworks which run from the Danube, in the west, to the Tisza, in the east. The northern line is called the Csörszárok and the southern line the Petit Fossé. These two lines covered off the northern end of the region called Barbaricum.

Ördögárok (Zone 2) – The north-east and eastwards facing Ördögárok lies in Hungary, Romania and Serbia. There are up to four earthworks lines in certain places, which run roughly parallel at a distance of three to fifteen kilometres from each other. The shapes and sizes of the mounds and trenches varied considerably, with depths ranging from 1.5 to 3 metres, and widths from 3.4 to 10.4 metres. In Hungary, there are multiple lines between the River Tisza and the River Crişul Repede, itself a tributary of the Koros River which flows into the Tisza to face north-east. Within the Banat region of Romania there are two groups: those between the Rivers Crişul Repede and Maros; and those from the Maros to the border of Romania and Serbia near Versac. The third group of multiple lines, also collectively called the Ördögárok, lie in modern Serbia and run from the city of Versac to the Danube.

Koros River Line (Zone 3) – One earthwork of uncertain function runs roughly east to west, across central Barbaricum from the River Tisza along the north side of the Koros River with a ditch to the south. Its position indicates that it might have been a line to which its builders retreated having abandoned the section of the plain to its north.

Römerschanzen (Zone 4) – There are a number of linear barriers in the region to the west of the confluence of the Danube and the Tisza – running west towards the Danube – in a region of Serbia called the Bačka. These are quite complicated as mostly they face south-east and therefore might appear to be a continuation of the Ördögárok around the south-eastern border of the Alföld. One however, the Groß Römerschanze, faces north-west.

- **Groß Römerschanze** – There is an earthwork running about twenty-five kilometres north-east – from the Danube at Novi Sad to near the Tisza to the north-west of Csurog. It faces north-west. Therefore it was not built to defend the Hungarian Plain but to face a threat from peoples on the Plain.
- **Kleine Römerschanze** – This earthwork runs parallel to the Tisza on the east side – from just south-east of Csurog north to Bacs-Petrovoszelo. Its south end starts near the more northerly end of the previous earthwork, the Groß Römerschanze, and it runs about thirty kilometres to the river Csik-Völgy. It faces east whereas the Groß Römerschanze faces north-west.
- **Römerschanze – Kulpin to Csurog** – The longest earthwork follows a somewhat convoluted course from the town of Kulpin, which lies roughly half way between the Danube and the Tisza, and eastwards roughly parallel to the Danube till it crosses the Groß Römerschanze where it curves around facing east until it stops to the south-west of Csurog.
- **Römerschanze – Apatin and Rac-Militics** – This earthwork starts at the town of Apatin on the Danube and extends south-east about thirty-four kilometres to Rac-Militics. It is unclear from what direction the threat it was intended to face came from, as parts of the structure had ditches on both sides in some sections. (Some old maps show it as continuing to the meet the Römerschanze from Apatin to Rac-Militics, described before.)

There is literary evidence that the Avars used earthworks to defend core areas of their Empire.

Avar Hrings – In his *Life of Charlemagne*, the Monk of St Gall, Nokter, reported that an old soldier who accompanied Charlemagne said: 'The land of the Huns (meaning the Avars) ... was girdled with nine circles.... 'It was fortified with nine hedges.... One circle was as wide as the distance from Zurich to Constance (fifty-five kilometres): it was made of stems of oak, beech, or fir, twenty feet high, and twenty feet broad. All the hollow part (between the walls) was filled either with very hard stones, or with most tenacious chalk, and then the top of the structure was covered with strong turfs. In between the turfs were planted shrubs which were pruned and lopped, so as to make them shoot forth boughs and leaves.... From the second circle, which was constructed like the first, there was a distance of twenty Teutonic or forty Italian miles to the third, and so on to the ninth, though (of course), each successive circle was smaller than the one before it.'[2]

This passage is difficult to interpret as the description suggests concentric earthworks, which is hard to reconcile with what survives. The tale of a 'yarn-spinning old soldier' to a credulous monk might understandably be unreliable. But it does indicate the Avars built or rebuilt very substantial defensive barriers.

Analysis – Great Hungarian Plain

The linear earthworks of the Great Hungarian Plain to the east of the Danube are particularly complex and the phases of development can only be conjectured.

The Romans occupied the right bank of the river Danube during the reign of Augustus (27–14 BC). During the first century a group of nomadic Sarmatians, the Iazyges, moved across Dacia, within the loop of the Carpathian Mountains, into the region between the Danube to the west and the Tisza to the east. For over three centuries the relationship of the Romans with the Sarmatian Iazyges and the Germanic tribes, who pressed upon the Hungarian plain, determined the security of the central Danube area – the trans-Alpine area closest to Italy.

The Roman conquest of Dacia was completed by AD 106 under the Emperor Trajan. It meant that the Iazyges were from now on bounded in Barbaricum by the Romans to the west, south and east. Trajan suppressed the Iazyges to the west of Dacia and the Sarmatian Roxolani to the east. His successor Hadrian reduced and consolidated the Empire after 117 and gave the Iazyges and Roxolani their independence, after which they largely remained allies with Rome and became buffer peoples. During the reign of Marcus Aurelius (161–180) Rome was pressed by the German Marcomanni (or Marcher Men). Later came Huns, Gepids, Lombards, Avars and Magyars.

The next boxed section conjectures a chronology for the construction of Great Hungarian Plain's linear barriers.

While there might be a possible coherence in associating the linear barriers across the left bank of the Danube on the Hungarian Plain to various occupants of the area, this is all quite speculative.

- **West-facing linear barriers along the east of Barbaricum** – After the Romans conquered Dacia they or allied tribes built parts of the Ördögárok along the western border of Dacia and the eastern border of Barbaricum, at this time facing west. (Also, allied peoples might have built the recently discovered west-facing Crasna and Zalău rivers line at the exit of the valley of the Crasna which runs into the Tisza River.)
- **North-facing linear barriers along the north of Barbaricum** – The north of Barbaricum was open to intrusion by German peoples. There are two distinct lines of earthworks, the Csörszárok and the Petit Fossé running across the north of Barbaricum which might initially have been built as a northern border to Barbaricum to block out Germanic invaders. 'At certain parts of the Csörsz, for example between the rivers Danube and Tisza, it seems obvious that whenever it was built, it consolidated an older border line between the Sarmatians and the Germans.'[3] That was no later than the beginning of the early second century.
- **East-facing linear barriers along the east of Barbaricum** – In the mid-third century the Romans abandoned Dacia meaning the eastern border of Barbaricum was no longer protected. Diocletian (284–385) fought bitter wars with the Iazyges, as did Constantine (306–337). Constantine is generally described as making the Iazyges a buffer people throughout Barbaricum and as being the authority behind the completion of the earthworks to the north and to the east of the Great Hungarian Plain respectively called the Csörszárok and the Ördögárok. The Ördögárok may then have been rebuilt as a linear earthwork, possibly by the Iazyges, facing east. The lack of forts and irregular character of the earthworks – which, while generally roughly parallel, occasionally intersect – mean that they are not interpreted as directly Roman. There are lines which cross over each other, possibly because some were originally built to face west and then others to face east when the direction of the frontier reversed from west to east. The earthworks, west of the Tisza but facing east, in the area between the confluence of the Tisza and the Danube, called the Kleine Römerschanze and the Römerschanze – Kulpin to Csurog – might have been southern extensions of the Ördögárok.
- **Lower line of north-facing linear barriers** – Around 379 the Gepids broke through into Barbaricum. The linear earthwork along the right bank of the Koros river, which runs east to west till it joins the Tisza, might have been an effort by peoples, possibly the Iazyges, to hold back the advance of invaders in the northern, now lost, part of Barbaricum. In the fifth century Huns replaced such Iazyges as remained to the east of the Danube.
- **Linear barriers in disuse** – The vast, if fissiparous, character of the Hun Empire meant there was no need for a linear barrier around the north-east and east of the Hungarian Plain. The Huns were crushed by the Gepids and other German peoples at the Battle of Nedao in 454. The Gepids then fought intermittently over the region with the Lombards until they were defeated by a coalition of the nomadic Avars who had come from Central Asia and the Lombards.
- **Reconstruction of linear barriers around the eastern Hungarian Plain** – The Avars may have used, or reused, the Csörszárok, Ördögárok, and Römerschanzen earthworks, in order to defend their kingdom. The Avars dominated the Hungarian Plain until defeated from the west by Charlemagne and the east by the Bulgars between 791 and 795. The Avars are associated with the Hrings.
- **Linear barriers facing into the eastern Hungarian Plain** – Finally, it was the turn of the Avars, or what was left of them, to be walled in. Widukind of Corvey writes in the tenth century that: 'Charlemagne defeated them (the Avars) and fenced them in with earthworks, and this prevented them from raiding people in their usual way.'[4] The north-west-facing Groß Römerschanze has been claimed as Greater Bulgarian, following the defeat of the Avars by an alliance of Charlemagne and the Bulgars in the late eighth century. The destruction of the Avar kingdom enabled the Bulgars to annex eastern Pannonia and establish a border with the Frankish Empire now on the Tisza.

Wallachian Plain

The Wallachian Plain lies between the lower Danube and the Carpathian mountains. It is crossed by rivers running south from the Carpathians. The plain itself is something of a dead end, if the objective was entry into central Europe as opposed to the Balkans. The reason is that the Danube's Iron Gates gorge between the Wallachian Plain and the Great Hungarian Plain was effectively impassable, certainly for a large migrating people or barbarian army. Most invaders went through the Carpathians or the Dobrogea. Therefore, whatever linear earthworks crossed east to west across the Wallachian Plain, they were effectively protecting something which related to the plain itself rather than defending the route to somewhere further west beyond the Iron Gates.*

Linear barriers might have been to be found running north to south across the Wallachian Plain between the Danube and the Carpathians to control movement into Europe. Indeed such a barrier does exist in the form of the Roman Limes Transalutanus which was probably built after the Romans withdrew from part, if not all, of the Budjak region along the Black Sea, between the Danube and the Dniester, and from Muntenia which lay to the west of the Danube and the Dobrogea. On the Wallachian Plain there are, however, two other long, one of them very long, linear earthworks – which have already been met in the context of barriers possibly built by trans-Danubian tribal allies of Rome. These are the Brazda lui Novac de Nord and the Brazda lui Novac de Sud. There appears as yet to be no consensus about who built these barriers, or when and why they were built. They have been variously determined as being at least in part pre-Roman, Roman satellite and Greater Bulgarian.

Neither of these earthworks has forts, which indicates that if there were any Roman association it was likely to be the result of being constructed by peoples allied to Rome. Both run roughly east to west and cross the line of the Limes Transalutanus at points sixty kilometres apart.† Considering their length, remarkably little appears to be known about them; and that is suprising particularly as the former is a candidate for the longest single continuous earthwork in Europe.

Brazda lui Novac de Nord – The Brazda lui Novac de Nord starts near the 'Iron Gates' at Dobreta on the Danube and swings in a gentle arc, slightly to the south, and then, after it crosses the river Olt, it curves to the north ending near the most westerly point of the Carpathian Mountains. In the nineteenth century it was about three metres high and about two metres in depth. It is approximately 275 kilometres long (but might have been much longer when fully built, and may even have extended to the Seret River).

Brazda lui Novac de Sud – The Brazda lui Novac de Sud starts east of the Brazda lui Novac de Nord on the Danube. It ends on the west bank of the Olt about forty kilometres north of the Danube. It was up to two metres high and had a ditch about 1.50 metres deep. The Brazda lui Novac de Sud is about half as long as the Brazda lui Novac de Nord. Very little remains of this earthwork now.

---

* The plain itself is good land that used to be the bread basket of much of Europe in the 1920s and 1930s.
† Early archaeological evidence, now lost, indicates that the Limes Transalutanus may have been built over the Brazda lui Novac, arguing possibly for a date before the second century AD.

Analysis – Wallachian Plain

Given that the Wallachian Plain was fully incorporated into the Roman Empire between 102 and 106 when it was conquered by Trajan, partially abandoned by Hadrian after 117 and fully abandoned in the mid-third century, it seems quite unlikely that the Brazdas were first built in the century and a half after 100.

Looking at the period before 100 the Brazda lui Novacs might be associated with incursions and deportations that took place in the first century when Rome forced tens of thousands of people from north to south of the Danube. After the mid-third century when the Romans withdrew from north of the Danube the area was increasingly controlled by Goths. Constantine reconquered Dacia in the 320s and generally the construction, or reconstruction, of the Brazda lui Novac de Nord is associated with this event. As with the Csörszárok, it is seen as being built by Roman tributary peoples who in turn defended the outer border. After the reign of Constantine, the Romans abandoned the Wallachian Plain to the north of the Danube. The Goths, who had occupied the area, resumed control until the Huns destroyed their settlements in the later fourth century. The Brazda lui Novac de Nord might have marked a Gothic frontier.

In the later seventh century the Bulgars invaded Europe. The borders of Greater Bulgaria have been defined by the lines of surviving linear earthworks by the somewhat circular argument that, as the earthworks are physically there they might have been built or rebuilt by the Bulgars; so therefore, they mark the borders of Greater Bulgaria as part of the northern Bulgar border defences against the Turkic Khazars. Thus, the Bulgars reused the Brazda lui Novacs. They remained in control of the region to the north of the Danube until the tenth century when they were driven out by the Magyars who went on to establish modern Hungary and then by the Pechenegs.

Conclusion – the Great Hungarian and the Wallachian Plain

The lower Danube flows through two basins, the Great Hungarian Plain and the Wallachian Plain. The right bank is the more settled by states and empires, which expanded from the 'civilised' Mediterranean south. The left bank was regarded as being wilder, as it was occupied by the barbarian Germans and Slavs from the forests and the nomads from the steppes. The Danube itself formed a natural frontier but one that resulted in good land falling on the 'wrong side' of the great river. Therefore, it is not surprising that such land was protected by trans-Danubian linear barriers which have a varied character. The question is, who was it that built the Csörszárok, Ördögárok and the Römerschanzen around the eastern Great Hungarian Plain and the Brazda lui Novac de Nord and the Brazda lui Novac de Sud across the Wallachian Plain?

There may have been an effort to create a zone of stability over the trans-Danubian areas. It is almost irrelevant whether this was instigated by the Romans, who encouraged or coerced local peoples to define a linear zone, or by the peoples themselves who, facing a real threat, had plenty of incentive to build barriers themselves. It is possible that the intention was quite simply to protect the land for its own sake, on the part of whichever peoples were occupying it, and not through any pressure or guidance from the Romans. Invaders from the steppe traditionally marched through passes of the western Carpathians. Thus, the occupants of the plains that lie north and east of the Danube might quite simply have wanted such invaders to continue through those Carpathian passes and away from their land.

As to whom the builders were: in the case of the Great Hungarian Plain the most obvious candidates seem to be the Sarmatian Iazyges and the Avars; and regarding the Brazda lui Novac de Nord, the Goths and possibly the Bulgars. But there are still many niggles. In the case of both regions there is evidence of pre-fourth century construction so the question of who the constructors were remains very much open.

The presence of so many linear barriers across the Danube raises questions about the value of rivers as frontiers. As there was likely to be good agricultural land across the river there was always a temptation to move beyond the river to take possession of it.

2. Romanian/Moldova/Ukraine – the Valurile lui Traian and other barriers

The land corridor between the south-eastern Carpathians and the Black Sea was a busy region, channelled and obstructed by many lakes, marshes and rivers. There is the Danube with its Delta, the freshwater Lakes Lalpug, Katalbug, Sasâc, which extend north of the Danube like fine fingers. The smaller Lakes Cahul and Cartal lie between Lake Lalpug and the Prut River. As well as the River Danube there are also other major rivers, Prut, Seret and Dniester, with many areas of marshy banks. To the south and east of the Danube lies the Dobrogea, the northern area of which, until the Carasu Valley between *Tomis*/Constanța and *Axiopolis*/Cernavodă, is similar to the steppe.

Linear barriers

Such a complicated region and complex mix might be expected to be rich in linear barriers as it includes major land corridors, nomads, settled states, migrating barbarians, transhumance, and fresh-water lakes – and it does not disappoint. Quick researches revealed three roughly parallel sets of Walls of Trajan that run from south to north. The Valurile lui Traian in the Dobrogea descend from the Danube to the Black Sea along the Carasu Valley between Constanța and Cernavodă; the Valul lui Traian de Jos (Lower Wall of Trajan) in Moldova and the Ukraine extends from the River Prut across the top of the Budjak region; and lastly, the Valul lui Traian de Sus (Upper Wall of Trajan) in Moldova lies between the Prut and the Dniester. This looks fairly straightforward and the structures could be seen as systems intended to arrest and control the flow of peoples moving off the Pontic Steppe towards the Wallachian Plain and Thrace.

Further searches, however, showed that this picture is much too simple. The Valurile lui Traian in the Dobrogea, which runs from the Danube to the Black Sea, actually consists of three barriers, two of earth and one of stone. What is more, while two of the walls face north, as might perhaps be expected, one faces south. Also, they intersect in places.

The Valul lui Traian de Jos is composed of three lengths with varying quality of construction. There is also a Valul Lacul Cahul-Lacul Cartal, linking two lakes of those names. The Valul lui Traian de Sus remains a single line but its location is complicated by its relationship with the Prut River line (see below) which runs south from its western

5.2: The Walls of Trajan

Valurile lui Traian - Dobrogea (Zone 1)
1. Valul Mare de Pământ
2. Valul Mic de Pământ
3. Valul de Piatra

Valul lui Traian de Jos - Valul Vadul lui Isac - Lacul Sasâc (Zone 2)
4. Valul Vadul lui Isac- Lacul Lalpug (Bolgrad)
5. Valul Lacul Lalpug (Bolgrad) - Lacul Katalbug
6. Valul Lacul Katalbug - Lacul Sasâc

Inter-Lakes
7. Valul Lacul Cahul - Lacul Cartal (inter-lakes)

Dniester and Prut Rivers North South Lines
8. Odessa Line
9. Prut Entrenchment (Leova – Cahul)
10. Valul lui Traian de Sus (Zone 3)
11. Trayanovi Vali Podnestrovya (Zone 4)

Prut to Siret Rivers (Zone 5)
12 Valul Şerbeşti –Tuluceşti (before Galati)
13. Valul Ploscuţeni – Stoicani

end at Leova. There is a fourth rather elusive group, the Trayanovi Vali Podnestrovya in the Ukraine.

There are also linear barriers running north to south along the Prut and the Dniester Rivers. Further, between the Prut and the Seret rivers there are two linear barriers, the north-facing Valul Traian–Tuluceşti, and to its north, the south-facing Valul Ploscuţeni–Stoicani which connect the Prut to the Seret.

Valul lui Traian – Dobrogea (Zone 1)

The Dobrogea, the region of Romania bounded by the Danube to the west and north and the Black Sea to the east, is bisected by the Carasu Valley. It is open to Thrace, modern Bulgaria, in the south. It was inherently an unstable area: constantly posing the question, should it belong to the states to the south or to the north? And what ought its southern border be, the Carasu Valley or somewhere further to the south?

Valul Mic de Pământ – The Valul Mic de Pământ, or Little Earth Wall, is sixty-one kilometres long. It lies largely to the south of the other two walls and, unlike them, has no wooden or stone facing and no camps. It has a south-facing ditch. For virtually its entire length it runs some distance south of the other two barriers, converging or intersecting only at the ends.

Valul Mare de Pământ – Through much of its length the Valul Mare de Pământ, or Great Earthern Wall is the most northerly of the three linear barriers. It begins on the Danube, follows the Carasu Valley and ends at Palas, west of Constanţa. At its western end it runs parallel to the Valul Mic de Pământ for about three kilometres before shifting close to the Valul de Piatra and then, for more than a third of its length, it continues well to the north of both walls until it rejoins them a few kilometres west of the Black Sea coast near Constanţa. It is fifty-four kilometres long with an average height of 3.5 metres with ditches on both sides. It has sixty-three forts in total, of which thirty-five are larger and twenty-eight smaller. The average distance between fortifications is one kilometre. Reconstructions show it with a north-facing palisade.

Valul de Piatra – The Valul de Piatra, or stone wall, is the largest archeological monument in the Balkans. It is actually an earth rampart faced with stone with a ditch in front. It runs fifty-nine kilometres from the Danube, initially along the line Valul Mic de Pământ, and then goes close to the Valul Mare de Pământ to the north, before running between the two other walls until it reaches the Black Sea at Constanţa, at a point seventy-five metres south of the little earth wall. The rampart is about 1.5 metres in height, while the stone wall has an average height of two metres. It has a ditch on its northern side and twenty-six fortifications, the distance between them varying from one to four kilometres. Coins of Constantine VII Porphyrogenitus (913–959) and Romanus II (959–963) have been found in the forts.

Analysis – Dobrogea
The Dobrogea changed hands so frequently – even while the polities around it were relatively stable – that it becomes nearly impossible to create a coherent picture of the circumstances which resulted in the three linear barriers. The Valul de Piatra crosses both the Valul Mic de Pământ and the Valul Mare de Pământ, and more generally stone structures tend to replace

those of wood. This implies that the Valul de Piatra was the last to be built. As to whether the Valul Mic de Pământ or the Valul Mare de Pământ came first, there is no clear evidence, although there is a temptation to judge that the more complicated structure with forts would come later than a simpler structure without forts. But this might just be the result of the different intentions and functions of the two structures.

Collectively, the three linear barriers are known as the Valurile lui Traian, yet there is no obvious connection with the Emperor Trajan. It seems unlikely they were Roman given that the Romans had conquered all of the Dobrogea. They more probably date to the Byzantine era – although there is some debate as to whether they were all built by the Byzantines. The Bulgars are a candidate for the construction of the one south-facing barrier. They are, therefore, analysed in greater detail in the sections on the Byzantines and mentioned in that on the Bulgars.

Valul lui Traian de Jos and the Budjak region (Zone 2)

The Budjak region – which lies to the north of the Danube between the Prut and the Dniester – has a long history of attachment to the Danube and the regions to the river's south, rather than to what is now Moldavia to the north. It was part of the Roman province of Moesia from the first century and appeared to remain under Rome's authority even after Hadrian's withdrawal from eastern Dacia. The Byzantine Emperor Constantine VII Porphyrogenitus (913–959) described deserted cities in which there were distinctive traces of churches. So a Roman and Byzantine presence may have been fairly continuous up to the arrival of the Bulgars in the seventh century.[5] The strategic importance of the area was obvious, for it protected the left bank of the Lower Danube from the ebb and flow of peoples who were migrating and practising transhumance, from the Pontic Steppe to the Carpathians. (Even now the Budjak retains its separate identity as it is largely constituted of part of the Ukraine and not Moldavia.)

Valul lui Traian de Jos – The longest barrier in the region, collectively known as the Valul lui Traian de Jos, was that delineating roughly the northern border of the modern Budjak region. In the past it may have approximated to the frontier of the trans-Danubian Province of Moesia Inferior. The total length is about 126 kilometres. It was, however, not one entity, but rather a series of three north-facing linear earthworks starting at Vadul lui Isac (or Isaac's Ford) on the Prut in Moldavia, and moving through Moldavia to the Ukraine, ending near the top of Lacul Sasâc, a lagoon off the Black Sea. The path of the earthworks touches or passes near the northerly point of three of five finger-like lakes – east to west Lacul Cahul, Lacul Lalpug, Lacul Katalbug, Lacul Kytaj, and Lacul Sasâc – that extend from just above the Danube so that the earthworks to the north and the Danube to the south mark off freshwater lakes and the lands in between. It is composed of three sections.

- Valul Vadul lui Isac – Lacul Lalpug (at Bolgrad) – The first stretch of about thirty-eight kilometres extends from Vadul lui Isac (or Isaac's Ford) on the east bank of the Prut to Bolgrad at the north end of Lacul Lalpug. There is a well-built rampart and ditch with a berm, or gap, of about three metres between. The vertical distance from the ditch bottom to rampart top is about three metres.

- **Valul Lacul – Lalpug-Lacul Katalbug (at Suvorovo)** – The second stretch goes about twenty-four kilometres from Lacul Lalpug to Suvorovo at the north end of Lacul Katlabug. It has similar dimensions to the first instance except that it lacks a berm. (At Suvorovo remains of an early Greater Bulgarian fence have been excavated at the top of the wall.)
- **Valul Lacul Katalbug – Lacul Sasâc** – A third length, a less well finished section but of the same dimensions, runs parallel to the second section for about three kilometres and is sixty-eight kilometres long. It runs to Lacul Sasâc below the town of Tatar-Bunar which lies slightly below Lacul Sasâc's northern point. About a third of its way, from west to east, it crosses the top of Lacul Kytaj.

Valul Lacul Cahul – Lacul Cartal – This is a short wall, extending from the east side of Lacul Cahul, in an arc south-east to the small Lacul Cartal, whose purpose may have been to defend fortifications at Orlovka and fords on the Danube. (*Aliobrix*/Orklovka was a castrum where an auxiliary unit of the Moesia Inferior army had its civil settlement.)

North South Prut and Dniester Lines

There are two linear barriers which run north to south along the eastern and the western borders of the Budjak.

Prut Line – An earthwork runs along the east or left bank of the Prut and appears to face east. It starts above the town of Leova and runs over seventy kilometres to the Vadul lui Isac.

Odessa Line – There is a sixty kilometre long earthwork around the western side of the Dniester Liman where flow to the Black Sea is blocked by a bar of sediments, creating a body of water of low salinity over forty kilometres long and twelve kilometres wide. The City of Tyras stood near the south-west end of the Liman. In the first century it was a province of Lower Moesia. Some time in the mid-third century Tyras was sacked by the Goths – but it continued to have a Roman and then Byzantine presence as attested by Constantine VII Porphyrogenitus' description of deserted cities.

1827 Russian map showing linear barrier (no longer now shown) along Prut river between Valul lui Traian de Jos and Valul lui Traian de Sus. (*C. C. License - Kaptain Veltman*)

Analysis – Budjak region

Considered in largely local terms, the Valul lui Traian de Jos created a discrete area, to the north bounded by the Valul itself, to the south by the Danube and its Delta, to the west by the Prut River, and to the east by Lacul Sasâc. Anyone seeking to use the Danube as a transport route would have wanted to control the northern bank to protect shipping travelling along the river, in what was a region of high barbarian and nomad activity. The Budjak region is also full of valuable fresh water lakes: from west to east Lacul Lalpug, Lacul Katalbug, Lacul Kytaj, and Lacul Sasâc. Lacul Cahul and Lacul Cartal lie between the Prut River and Lacul Lalpug. Such lakes would have provided important watering points for nomads practicing transhumance across the region and would have been necessary stops for migrating peoples, both nomads and barbarians. Peoples and their animals moving across the region would have headed for the Vadul lui Isac or Isaac's Ford in order to cross the Prut River. Thus, there is a land corridor for migrating people to the north of the lakes and the south of the forest steppe which started roughly at the line of the Valul lui Traian de Sus. It is possible to speculate that one purpose of linear barriers in the region was to control and funnel the movement of peoples and animals to Isaac's Ford and away from the valued land between the Lakes, and stopping uncontrolled crossings elsewhere along the Prut River.

The Valul lui Traian de Jos might have performed a range of tasks. It protected the Danube transport route. It linked the northerly points of the freshwater lakes, thus controlling access to water and protecting valued land in between the lakes. It and the Prut Line might have channelled the flow of migrating peoples to the Vadul lui Isac. It blocked access to the Dobrogea. The three sections of the Valul lui Traian de Sus become progressively better built as they moved westward possibly as the threat which the polity faced became more dangerous.

Also, it has been seen how the Rhine and the Danube Rivers did not provide a straightforward frontier – as good quality land lay across the river – and linear barriers were built to protect the plains across the rivers. The Valul lui Traian de Jos fits into the pattern of the Upper German and Raetian Limes, of the Csörszárok and Ördögárok as all these run roughly parallel to and some distance from the river border. In the Budjak in what is now the western Ukraine, Rome and then Byzantium remained a trans-riverine power far longer than in Germany, or the Hungarian and Wallachian Plains. For example, the Roman province of Moesia extended north of the Danube to the Valul lui Traian de Jos and parts of the Valul might originally have been Roman. In addition, as described later in the section on the Byzantine Empire, there is a respectable argument that it remained Byzantine until the late seventh century and the arrival of the Bulgars. Thus, it seems quite probable that the Romans built parts of the Valul lui Traian de Jos to defend trans-Danubian Moesia and, therefore, to control the Danube. It might also have been intended as a defence against the Goths. It may have served the same purpose for the Byzantines until they were displaced by the Bulgars.

The Budjak was part of early medieval Greater Bulgaria and the earthwork might have been built or rebuilt as a defence against the Khazars in the seventh century. Excavations at Suvorovo in 1998 revealed at least two phases of construction of the Valul lui Traian de Jos and a Bulgarian fenced complex on top of the wide wall.[6] Constantine

Porphyrogenitus' (913–959) in *de Administrando Imperio*, when describing the route taken by the Kievan Rus annual trade convoy, said that the territory of Bulgaria is entered after the Dniester but before the Danube. Thus, in the mid-tenth century Bulgaria still extended across the Danube, meaning that there was a Bulgarian border in need of definition to the north of the Danube.

Valul lui Traian de Sus – Moldavia (Zone 3)

The Valul lui Traian de Sus – This appears a more straightforward affair in that it consists of one barrier that extends, within modern Moldova, all the way from the Prut, north of the town of Leova, to the Dneister, at Chitcani – a length of 138 kilometres. It faces north and marked the boundary of the forest and the grassland steppe. At Leova it meets the Prut Line which extends further to the north of the town.

Even though the Valul lui Traian de Sus is a unitary barrier, unlike the Valurile lui Traian in the Dobrogea and the Valul lui Traian de Jos, it still poses problems as to why and by whom it was built. There are several candidates. It might have marked a Roman frontier from the first or second century or played a similar role to that purported for the Csörszárok or the Brazda lui Novac de Nord – that is a barrier built by allied peoples to protect a buffer zone beyond to the Roman Empire frontier. It could have been a border between Gothic tribes. It has been identified as the Vallum of the Greuthungi after the description in Ammianus Marcellinus of the flight of the Thervingi.[7] Another claimant is Greater Bulgaria – this being another more northerly border to the Valul lui Traian de Sus. As with all the barriers in the region, however, it remains something of a mystery.

Trayanov Vali Podnestrovya – Ukraine, Romania's Bucovina (Zone 4)

If Змієві вали (Zmievi Vali) is put into Google, a Ukrainian Wikipedia site comes up. Using the translate function brings up a summary list of the Zmievi vali or Serpent's Walls (which will be looked at in a future section). The list includes another Traian's Wall, Траянові вали Подністров'я, or in direct translation from Ukrainian, Trayanov Vali Podnestrovya. The translation of the earthwork's description says there is 'a system of intermittent valla, located between the cities of Ternopil and Kamenets consisting of two main lines and randomly scattered valla, some of which are in Bukovina (northeastern Romania).'

Podnestrovya is the most westerly region of the Ukraine and corresponds to what was Galicia in the pre-Great War Austro–Hungarian Empire. Ternopil and Kamenets are cities in the region. Bukovina is the north-easterly region of Romania to the south of the Dniester.

Trayanov Vali Podnestrovya – There were two roughly parallel, if now somewhat discontinuous, lines. The longer extended from the river Dniester to near the city of Ternopil. The shorter runs from the river Prut and across the Dniester into Romanian Bukovina. There are some other lengths – one running between both the lines just described, north of the Dniester, as well as some short barriers between the Prut and the Dniester.

A website about the Heritage of Ukraine has an article on 'Kamyanets Podilsky, A Town at the Periphery of the Roman Empire'. This says, 'Authors of the seventeenth through the nineteenth centuries, considered that the Roman legionaries who conquered Dacia during the Trajanic wars, had crossed the Dniester and had founded a line of military settlements in Podillya (present-day south-western Ukraine). The remnants of the so-called Trajanic rampart lines, numerous hoards of Roman coins, and artifacts of the military Roman life found in Podillya support these references to a Roman presence on the left bank of the Dniester.'[8]

While the idea of Roman origins were generally discredited in the twentieth century, recent excavations have apparently supported a Roman foundation for the great castle at Kamyanets Podilsky. Further searches revealed a website setting out the villages of the Borshciv Rayon or administrative district. This included Hermakivka: 'What is remarkable about Hermakivka is that there is a Trayan wall, south of the village. It stretches from Hermakivka south via Zalissya and Kdryntis to the river Dniester. The Trayan wall was built by the Romans (under the emperor Trajan), as the north-eastern border of the Roman Empire (province of Dacia).'[9]

Here is confirmation that earthworks, now attributed to Trajan, did indeed extend to beyond the Dniester. Hermakivka can be found on maps and the broken line of a barrier is traceable along the river Zbruch to the Dniester. This barrier may originally have run about eighty kilometres from the Dniester to Teropil. About twenty-five to thirty kilometres to the south-west lay another shorter line which crossed the Dniester into Moldavia and Romania. The linear barriers appear to face east and north-east. Further east along the Dniester are three loops in the river which were cut off by earthworks. The two more easterly contain the villages of Voronovitsya and Slobidka.

It is very difficult to know quite what to make of these earthworks. They are clearly there and were substantial. They have been included in this section because they have been named after Trajan. Yet, while not discounting Ukrainian claims of a Roman presence in what is now the Ukraine, given that so many linear earthworks have been attributed to Trajan in modern times, which obviously were not built by him, there is not really enough evidence to make an exception in this case and attribute them to the Roman emperor. (Anyway, most constructions appear to have been attributed to Trajan within the last few centuries – the name having usually been changed from Troian who was possibly a Slav deity. In Ukrainian two versions of the name are given, Троянові вали Подністров'я and Траянові вали Подністров'я.)

But that leaves open the question who might have built these earthworks. If they are not Roman, then other candidates might include Germanic tribes and the Kievan Rus and their successor warring states. (The Kievan Rus will be considered in a later chapter.) The case for Germanic peoples might be made on the basis that they built other walls in the region but even this is not very clear. Although it is known from Ammianus Marcellinus that the Goths in the region built linear barriers, it is not really known with any certainty which barriers these were. This is clearly again an area which should be called 'work in progress'.

Prut-Seret barriers – Romania (Zone 5)

There are two linear barriers in the southern region between the Prut and the Seret.

Valul Traian–Tuluceşti – This barrier lies to the west of the Valul Vadul lui Isac – Sasac section of the Valul lui Traian de Jos and starts lower down the Prut on its marshy west side. It then runs south-west till it joins the Seret River. The Valul Traian covers the approaches to the modern city of Galaţi and the Roman Barbosi fortified camp. It consists of a roughly finished rampart and ditch without a berm or gap between. Some accounts suggest that it defended a Roman camp and dated originally from the second or third century. If this were the case, then it would be a true trans-Danubian, Moesian Roman barrier, and thus a strong counter-argument to the claim that the Romans did not build other barriers in the region.

Valul Stoicani – Ploscuteni – This is a most enigmatic wall. It extends from the Prut, starting between the Valul Vadul lui Isac – Lacul Lalpug to the north and the Valul Traian – Tuluceşti to the south, and proceeds north-west to the Seret. It is slighter and less well finished than the walls to the east. The Valul Stoicani-Ploscuteni completes the length of wall from the Black Sea to the Carpathians but, unlike the other linear barriers in the area which face north, this one points south-east. It may have had a wooden palisade which was burnt. This barrier has been improbably associated with the flight of the Thervingi Gothic leader Athanaric in 376. Also, it might have been constructed under Roman authority, in order to keep the Roxolani in the region between the Carpathians and the Black Sea where they could serve as a buffer people against invaders from the Pontic Steppe.

The Valul Stoicani – Ploscuteni blocked access to the region between the Seret and the Prut. To the west of the Prut are the Carpathians. The barrier therefore might have channelled peoples and animals on the move towards a crossing point at or below the Vadul lui Isac or Isaac's Ford. On the east side of the Prut, the Prut Line would have provided another protection to the region between the Seret and the Prut.

Conclusion – Danube, Seret, Prut, Dniester area

The Roman conquest moved north of the Danube, in the area between the Dniester and the Prut rivers, well before Trajan's conquest of Dacia. In the mid-first century during the reign of Nero, Tiberius Plautius Silvanus Aelianus extended Roman control to the Budjak along the Black Sea coast, between the rivers Prut and Dniester. He annexed the city of Tyras on the Dniester near the coast. The construction of parts of the Lower Wall of Trajan has been associated with this expansion of Roman authority. There is also a linear earthwork which runs along the western bank of the Dniester which might be associated with the defence of the Tyras area.

A Sarmatian group, the Roxolani, pushed south through the region between the Carpathians and the Black Sea to the Danube. Pre-Roman conquest Dacia was now weakened, being restricted to the area of the Carpathians, with the Iazyges to the west and the Roxolani to the east. An alliance of Dacians and Roxolani destroyed a Roman legion in AD 92 in the southern Dobrogea. Between 102 and 106 Trajan conquered a vast area extending from Dacia to the Dniester. The Sarmatians were a nomadic people and possibly an offshoot of the Alans. As seen in Egypt and in North Africa with the Fossatum

Africae, the movement of herds was seen as a threat by sedentary agriculturalists and linear barriers were constructed to control it. It could be speculated that some linear barrier construction in the region was intended to control local transhumance.*

The full area of Trajan's conquests included the region between Transylvania and the Budjak. The Valul lui Traian de Sus extends across Moldavia from the Prut to the Dniester and might have marked the northern border of Trajan's trans-Danubian conquests. Some Ukrainians think that Trajan's conquests extended as far as Kamyanets Podilsky in western Galicia and the linear earthworks to the north of the Dniester are his works.

After 117 Hadrian withdrew from north of the Danube, all the way back to the area of the River Olt which runs south across the Wallachian Plain. The south-facing linear earthwork, the Valul Stoicani-Ploscuteni, which runs between the Prut and Seret rivers, might have been constructed under Roman authority to keep the Roxolani in the region between the Carpathians and the Black Sea. There they could serve as a buffer people against invaders from the Pontic Steppe. There is a linear barrier running along the eastern bank of the Prut which may face east. These two barriers together could have been intended to channel migrating nomads and barbarians away from a polity between the Prut and the Seret. It would have forced them to move, south, towards a crossing point on the Prut at or below Vadul lui Isac or Isaac's Ford.

In the fourth century, frontier barriers may have been constructed on the trans-Danubian Hungarian and Wallachian plains. Parts of the Valul lui Traian de Jos and the Valul Traian–Tuluceşti, before the Galac fortified camp between the Prut and the Seret, might have served this purpose as a Roman protection of the Danube as a waterway and a defence against the Goths. The Valul lui Traian de Sus has been interpreted as a Goth defence line along the border between the forest and the grassland steppe and been given the name the Vallum of the Greuthungi. (The Valul lui Traian de Sus and the Valul lui Traian de Jas were later claimed as a northern border of Greater Bulgaria in the 660s.)

The basic point can be made that the area between the Carpathians and the Black Sea constituted a land corridor through which migrating nomads and barbarians moved between Europe and the Pontic Steppe. The Danube flowed across the region and was also the northern border of the Roman Empire. To complicate issues, there may have been nomadic peoples practicing transhumance who crossed the region in both directions. Therefore, linear barriers were likely to be constantly reused – so attributing their construction to any particular date is possibly a futile exercise. The result, however, is an exceptionally rich tangle of linear barriers, unravelling the sequence and purpose of which remains work in progress.

3. Ukraine and Crimea

This section briefly covers the Crimea and the Ukraine. In the case of the Crimea it largely summarises a number of linear barriers already encountered with the history of Greece. With the Ukraine the general context is discussed while the individual linear barriers are largely outlined later in the sections on the Kievan Rus and Russia.

---

* Until recently transhumance was practiced in the region, although the majority of people remained static and only the specialist herders moved.

Crimean Linear Barriers

5.3: Crimea

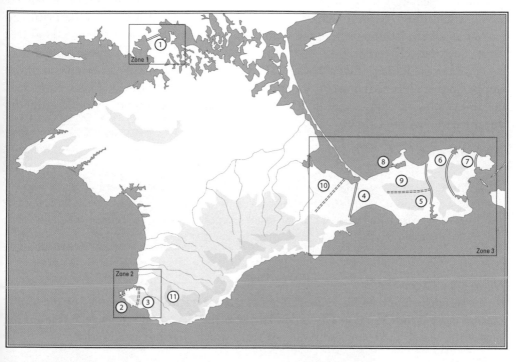

Perekop Isthmus (Zone 1)
  1. Perekop Wall (Turkish Wall)

Heraclian Peninsula (Zone 2)
  2. Mayak Peninsula Wall
  3. Heraclean Peninsula Wall

Kerch Peninsula (Zone 3)
  4. Akmonai Wall
  5. Uzunlar Wall

  6. Beskrovnyi Wall
  7. Tyritkate Wall
  8. Kazantip Wall
  9. Parpač Ridge Earthwork
  10. Blinded Slaves' Sons' Trench (conjectured location)

Other
  11. Dory Wall (location)

The Crimea

Given its comparatively small area, compared to the Eurasian Steppe, the Crimea includes a fascinating range of peninsula and field linear barriers. The one linear barrier which might most obviously have been expected to be found is that on the main and narrow northern isthmus where the Crimea is linked to the Pontic Steppe. However until comparatively recent, post-Medieval times, the evidence for a linear barrier here is very tenuous. Perhaps that is because the Crimea was essentially an extension of the steppe, so there was no requirement to protect it from a nomad threat. This section does not re-explore issues discussed in other sections but simply sets out systematically the linear barriers of the Crimea.

Early barriers

> **Cimmerian Walls** – Herodotus says that in the land of the Scythians there were still traces of the Cimmerians, including 'Cimmerian Walls'. That said, whether these were walls or forts, or whether they lay in the modern Ukraine or the Crimea (to whom the Cimmerians gave their name) is uncertain.

Heraclean Peninsula

By the second half of the fifth century colonists from Heraclea Pontica settled on the south-western coast of the Crimea in what is now known as the Heraclean Peninsula. It features the sites of the Mayak and Heraclean Peninsula Walls which were discussed earlier.

> **Blinded Slaves' Sons' Trench** – Herodotus noted that the Scythians blinded their slaves. When the Scythian men went on their great *chevauchée* around Hither Asia, their deserted wives set up home with the blinded slaves and later the sons of those blinded slaves resisted the return of the remnants of the Scythians after the latter were massacred by the Medes. Herodotus described how the slaves' sons built a trench: 'When therefore the children sprung from these slaves and the Scythian women grew to manhood, and understood the circumstances of their birth, they resolved to oppose the army which was returning from Media. And, first of all, they cut off a tract of the country from the rest of Scythia by digging a broad dyke from the Tauric Mountains to the vast lake of the Mæotis.'[10] The Scythians eventually re-stablished control after stout resistance by the slaves' sons through the stratagem of approaching the offspring with whips, the symbols of servitude, not swords.
>
> The Trench clearly existed as Herodotus mentions it twice again. Firstly, it came to mark the south-east border of the territory of the Royal Scythians. 'Its country reaches on the south to Taurica, on the east to the trench dug by the sons of the blind slaves.'[11] Secondly, from the Trench the Royal Scythians launched attacks across the Cimmerian Bosporos onto the Taman Peninsula. 'The sea freezes and the Cimmerian Bosphoros is frozen over. At that season the Scythians who dwell within the trench make warlike expeditions upon the ice.'[12] The Scythian linear barrier faced east, unlike the other Kerch Peninsula barriers which faced west.
>
> **Trans-peninsula west-facing barriers** – There are four linear barriers running from the Sea of Azov to the Black Sea across the Kerch Peninsula. They formed the outer defences of the Bosphoran Kingdom. To recapitulate, running west to east they are the following: the Akmonai Wall; the Uzunlar Wall; the Beskrovnyi Wall; and the Tyritake Wall.

Cape Kazantip wall – There is a short wall isolating Cape Kazantip which lies off the northern coast of the Kerch Peninsula in the Sea of Azov.*

Parpač Ridge or Latitudinal bank – There is a long field wall, also described earlier, which did not stop movement of nomads along the northern side of the Kerch peninsula but defended the intensively farmed southern side of the rampart.

---

* Cape Kazantip is now the location of an extremely popular jazz festival.

Kerch Peninsula and Bosphoran Kingdom

Main Crimean Isthmus

It is quite difficult to make sense of the linear barriers controlling the main isthmus. Given that the Crimea was called the Cimmerian Chersonesos a linear barrier would certainly be expected to be found there. (The Thracian Chersonesos and the Cimbrian Chersonesos, or Jutland, both have linear barriers.) The early evidence from classical writings, however, is tenuous.

There is an interesting description of the region dating back to the early nineteenth century. 'The fosse and wall are of considerable antiquity, having been formed by the inhabitants of Tauridia, to defend their peninsula against the incursions of the neighbouring Scythians. The *Taphros* of the more ancient geographers Pliny, and the New Wall, or *Neon Teichos*, of Ptolomy lie further south, about two versts (2.2 kilometres) within Perekop.'[13]

It has proved impossible to establish quite what the '*Taphros*' and '*Neon Teichos*' were but it does indicate that there was some kind of linear marker in the classical period. Constantine VII Porphyrogenitus said: 'This same gulf of Maeotis comes opposite to, and within about four miles of, the Nekropyla that are near the Dnieper River, and joins them where the ancients dug a ditch and carried the sea through, enclosing all the land of Cherson and of the Regions and the land of Bosphoros, which covers up to 1,000 miles or even rather more. In the course of many years this same ditch has silted up and become a great forest, and there are in it but two roads, along which the Pechenegs pass through to Cherson and Bosphorus and the Regions.'[14] Constantine did, however, refer to a ditch dug by the ancients, indicating the presence of some form of linear barrier.

Perekop Val – The Crimean Tatars constructed a very substantial linear barrier across the Isthmus in the fifteenth century and it was still very much operational in the eighteenth century when it was stormed by the Russians. In 1736 they found the Isthmus was traversed by a wall twenty metres high and a trench twenty-four metres wide and fourteen deep, which they succeeded in taking in two days. In part this was due to treachery by some Tatars and the carelessness of those meant to maintain it. By 1737 the Tatars had repaired the defences and fought the Russians off. In 1773 the Russians tried again to storm the Perekop and failed, but they succeeded in 1774.

Other

> **Dory Wall** – Procopius describes how Justinian built a wall for the Crimean Goths which is described in the section on Byzantine walls below.

Analysis – Crimea

The Crimea has a remarkable number of walls for its relatively small size, but perhaps this should not be surprising given the location by the Pontic Steppe and the Black Sea, both of which were routes of trade and migration. Politically, settled states had to interact with both nomads and barbarians. Also, its own geography meant that it was a peninsula with several sub-peninsulas where valuable, fertile land was located.

The Ukraine

The linear earthworks of the Ukraine will be largely covered in the chapter on state formation. (The exception is the Trayanov Vali Podnestrovya, already described.) The main threat to the Kievan Rus came from Turkic nomadic Pechenegs and Polovtsians, which resulted in the construction of much of the earth work structures in the Ukraine. There have, however, been strong arguments that many of the Ukrainian linear barriers, or at least parts of them, were built much earlier. Indeed, it would perhaps be surprising if this were not the case, given the number of nomadic peoples and migrant peoples associated with the Pontic Steppe. The following list cannot be regarded as exhaustive or the dates particularly certain:

    Cimmerians and Massagetae (pre-seventh century BC)
    Scythians (seventh century-fourth century BC)
    Sarmatians (first century-fourth century BC)
    Alans (fourth-eleventh centuries AD)
    Huns (fourth-eighth centuries)
    Bulgars (fifth-eighth centuries)
    Avars (sixth-eighth centuries)
    Khazars (seventh-ninth centuries)
    Pechenegs (eighth-tenth centuries)
    Polovtsians (tenth-thirteenth centuries)
    Mongols and Tatars (thirteenth-eighteenth centuries).

There are also non-nomadic migrating Germanic and Slavic people who moved south into the region in the early to mid-first millennium who could be quite the equals of the nomads – for example, the Goths displaced the Scythians from the Crimea and possibly other areas of the Pontic Steppe. Many of these peoples are explicitly associated with linear barrier construction elsewhere.

The dating of Ukrainian earthworks should have been more straightforward than in most places due to the presence of extensive woodwork structures within the earthworks. In fact this seems to have complicated and confused the issue. Carbon dating carried out in the 1960s appeared to place the linear barriers to the south of Kiev to between the second century BC and sixth century AD. This made the Goths, identified with the Chernyakhov archaeological culture which was broadly spread over eastern Europe, strong candidates as significant linear barrier builders in the Ukraine. It also encouraged conspiracy theories that the Goths had been written out of history due, perhaps understandably, to the poisonous legacy of Nazi irredentism. (Hitler's propaganda minister, Joseph Goebbels, claimed areas where the Chernyakhov culture was found, as German.)

In the 1980s, excavations and further dating demonstrated these earlier dates to be unreliable and placed the linear barriers below Kiev in the Kievan Rus period, showing them to have been built or rebuilt in the tenth or eleventh centuries. This does not, however, resolve the question of the barriers further to the west and east of Kiev. Nor does it remove the possibility that some parts of the barriers below Kiev predated the Rus. In the case of the Zmievi Vali in the east of Kiev there does seem to be some evidence for an earlier date. A horde of Roman coins from the first to third century AD was found in earthworks in the Poltava region. In the region of Kharkiv (the Ukrainian spelling of the Russian Kharkov) it is believed that in the Valkivsky Raion, the Perekopski earthwork had first been built way back in Scythian times. It was restored in the seventeenth century to block the Muravsky Shlyakh, or the trail used by the Crimean Tatars to raid the Muscovite Rus.

There also remain questions about whether the linear barriers to the south of Kiev may have incorporated earlier constructions. The fact remains that the Ukraine has vast lengths of linear earthworks which have yet to be comprehensively dated and their builders identified. This is discussed again in the next section on the Kievan Rus earthworks.

Conclusion – Eastern Europe

This chapter opened with the quotation from Prince Dimitrie Cantemir who described a great earthwork called the *Fossa Trajani Imperatoris*, one that extended from the River Tisza in Serbia to the River Don in Russia. And while it is fanciful to claim that a single continuous linear barrier extended all this distance, it is, in fact, possible to find great earthworks covering at least half, if not more, of its length. There are also many, many more earthworks in the region.

While the major trans-steppe nomads were important, particularly the Huns, Turks and Mongols, earlier more local nomads, like the Scythians and the Sarmatians, and the related Iazyges and Roxolanians, played a key role in the original process of linear barrier construction. At the same time Gothic and Slavic peoples were migrating into the region. Such a mix of empires and nomads, both settled within an established transhumance range, and migrating, and barbarians on the move, might be expected to produce a rich and complex haul of linear barriers. And it does. Sorting out who built what and when is a task that remains to be fully resolved.

Chapter Six

Bulgaria, Poland and the Kievan Rus –
Early State Formation

Any interpretation of history that involves peoples or ethnicity might be regarded with caution but certain groups do seem to be identified with linear barriers. For example, the Anglians, who in Britain also gave rise to the Mercians and the Northumbrians, appear to have left a string of linear earthworks behind them. These extended possibly from Jutland to East Anglia and onto the Welsh borders and maybe to Lancashire, Yorkshire and Northumberland. Generally, Gothic and Germanic peoples seem to have been prolific builders of earthworks.

Bulgaria, Poland and the Ukraine, despite long periods when they were conquered, annexed and even divided, are all independent states in the twenty first century. In the late first and early second millennia these states took root, and it is a valid question whether the construction of linear barriers could have played any part in this process. This could be: either in a stronger form by melding a sense of national identity through the actual joint venture of linear barrier building; or in a weaker form by simply keeping out enemies long enough for the idea and indeed the fact of national identity securely to be established.

Linear barrier building might be seen as aggressive not defensive – that is its purpose was strengthening the grip on expropriated territory and making the occupant more difficult to dislodge. For example, the occupation of Thrace by the Bulgars provides a useful study because there were no Bulgars in the region before the seventh century, but by the ninth century a Bulgarian Empire was well established and even now there is a country of Bulgaria.

1. Bulgaria

The Bulgarians see themselves as the unsung heroes of European history. They and perhaps the Magyars are among the few people, out of Central Asia, to build a distinct country within Europe, instead of disappearing off the map like the Sarmatians, the Alans, the Huns or the Avars. The Bulgarians claim they established the first European state based on national identity, rather than the principles of the universal state. They further claim that they developed an administrative system and religious rites using their own language and a script devised for them, Cyrillic, which went on to be that of the Orthodox east. The still pagan Bulgarians saved Constantinople from the Arabs in 717–718 when it was sorely pressed. The Bulgarians established an empire which saw itself as the equal of that of Charlemagne, with whom they combined to crush the Avars. On several occasions the Bulgarians defeated the Byzantine Empire.

So how did the Bulgars, from Central Asia, manage to establish themselves in Europe to the west of the Black Sea? What was their special skill which enabled them to hold ground as well as to take it? The area of modern Bulgaria and that of ancient greater Bulgaria – which extended to modern Romania, Moldavia and the Ukraine – is replete with linear barriers pointing north and north-east which could have defined the northern border of a consolidating state. There is also a major linear barrier to the south, and facing the south, called the Erkesia. There are other barriers on the eastern and western borders.

Modern Bulgaria extends east of the Black Sea and south of the Danube, with the exception of the Dobrogea region which is in modern Romania. To the south-west and to the west are the Vitosha, Rila, Pirin and Rhodope mountains. There is no access to the Mediterranean as Thrace, next the Byzantine Empire, and today Greece and Turkey, occupy the south-eastern Thracian Plain. The Stara Planina mountain range runs about 550 kilometres from the Timok River, a tributary of the Danube, eastwards to the Black Sea. Southern Bulgaria is traversed by the Maritsa River which, at 480 kilometres in length, is the longest to run solely through the Balkans. Its source is in the Rila Mountains and it empties into the Aegean Sea. Ancient Greater Bulgaria extended much further north to include the Wallachian Plain and southern Moldavia and the Ukrainian Budjak. Early Bulgaria's southern border was the Stara Planina Mountains.

There is access to Bulgaria along the full length of the Danube although some areas are easier to cross than others. To the north-west there is a land corridor to the Hungarian Plain which runs between the Danube and the Vitosha mountains which is traversed by many tributaries flowing north into the Danube. The Starina Planina has about twenty passes through it running roughly north to south. The Maritsa River is a natural border but this flowed into the Aegean, leaving a land corridor between the river and Black Sea which was open to the Byzantine Empire.

The Bulgar people emerge following the break-up of the Huns in the mid-fifth century. In AD 632 Khan Kubrat declared himself an independent ruler of old Greater Bulgaria and united the Bulgar tribes who settled in the northern Black Sea and Crimea. He built towns and forts of stone and developed heavy as well as light cavalry. The Turkic Khazars then conquered much of old Greater Bulgaria and one Bulgar group, under Kubrat's third son Asparukh, moved west. (Another group moved east, under Kubrat's second son Kotrag, to the Volga-Kama Rivers confluence area and founded a state called the Volga-Kama Bulgaria, which converted to Islam, and existed until the thirteenth century when it was conquered by the Mongols.)

The Bulgar Khan Asparukh travelled west at a time when the Byzantine Empire was under pressure through war with the Sasanian Persians and then the Arabs. He occupied the Danubian delta and settled in an unidentified stronghold called the Onglos. In the second half of the seventh century the Byzantines tried to recover ground; local Slavs and the incoming Bulgars made a treaty under which Slavs recognised the Khan who promised to defend them. (This was rather like Kievan Rus where the Slavs later asked the Varangians to rule over them.) In 680 Asparukh defeated the Byzantine Emperor Constantine IV and moved from the Danube Delta to the Stara Planina mountain range. The following year the Bulgars took the Dobrogea from the Byzantines. After the

Bulgars invaded Thrace, Constantine agreed to pay tribute and recognised the loss of Moesia, the Dobrogea and the Stara Planina and the establishment of the Bulgar state as a union of the Bulgars and the Seven Tribes of Slavs. Pliska, between the Danube and the Stara Planina, was established as the capital.

In 705 the Bulgar state's Khan Tervel took the Zagora Mountain area. Under the Treaty of 716 the southern boundary was fixed between the Bulgars and Byzantine. In 718 the Bulgarians, still under Tervel, came to the aid of the Byzantines and lifted the Arab siege of Constantinople. It was hard, however, for the Byzantines to accept the loss of a region that had been Roman since the first century BC to a pagan state. So Constantine V attempted to recover it between 756 and 775 with combined naval and land assaults respectively on the Danube and across Thrace. He also attacked the Black Sea coast – without success. Between 791 and 796 the Bulgars joined the Franks to destroy the Avar Khanate in central Europe. The Bulgars annexed eastern Pannonia and a border with the Franks was established along the Tisza River.

In 811 the Khan Krum defeated the Byzantines at the Vărbitsa Pass in the Stara Planina and killed the Emperor Nicephoras. In true nomad fashion Krum had a goblet crafted out of the Emperor's skull. In 816 a treaty between the Bulgars and the Byzantines established the border of the Bulgar state and the Byzantine Empire. This basically followed the 716 treaty border line and is generally associated with the construction of a great linear barrier called the Erkesia (although archaeology indicates that the Erkesia was started rather earlier in the eighth century).

The 850s saw the invention, by the monks Cyril and Methodius, of the earliest Bulgarian alphabet which became Cyrillic; and in 863 Khan Boris converted to Christianity. Bulgarian power rose to its peak after the Battle of Acheloi in 917 and during the reign of Simeon the Great (893–927) its remit extended over much of what is now modern Romania, Serbia, Bulgaria, Macedonia, Greece, Hungary, Bosnia and Turkey. In 968 the Kievan Rus Emperor Sviatoslav I annexed the Dobrogea, at the request of the Byzantine Emperor Nicephoras II.

Emperor John Tzimiskes (969–976) recovered some regions of eastern Bulgaria in 971 but between 976 and 986 the southern Dobrogea again became part of the Bulgarian Empire, then under the rule of Samuil. (The northern area may have continued to be Byzantine.) But in 1000 Emperor Basil's General Theodorokanos recovered all the Dobrogea for the Byzantines. Samuil died in 1014 – reputably out of shock when the Emperor Basil II *Bulgaroctonus* (Bulgar slayer) returned the remnants of the defeated Bulgar army, after the Battle of Kleidion Pass. The beaten troops were led by one man in fifty who was blinded in one eye, the rest being blinded in both. The First Bulgarian Empire then broke up.

Linear barriers

There is some literary evidence that the Bulgarians used well protected sites and linear barriers: 'Asparukh, after crossing the Dnieper and Dniester rivers and after capturing the Onglos, settled in the lands between it and the aforementioned rivers, because he noticed that that place was protected and difficult to attack from any side; being swampy in the front and from the other sides – surrounded by a ring of rivers, it offered great security against enemies.'[1] From this description, however, the barriers protecting the Onglos sound natural rather than man-made.

The Bulgarian Apocryphal Chronicle of the eleventh century recounts how Khan Asparukh built the city of Pliska and a 'great wall from Danube to the sea'.[2] This is often interpreted as meaning one of the three lines of the Valurile lui Traian which run across the Dobrogea from the Danube to the Black Sea, the obvious candidate being the south-facing Valul Mic de Pământ. There are, however, as will be seen, other candidates.

The Bulgar Byzantine peace treaty of AD 816 stated: 'Art.1: concerning the frontier, that it be fixed from Develtos and to the Castle – and between these places. Art.2: that they shall vacate the forts, which are numerous, which are between Balzena and Agathonike, and at Constantia and the Makre-Libas, and those which are towards Mount Haemus, until the setting of the frontier has been completed.'[3] The 'setting of the frontier' has been identified with the construction of the great linear barrier called the Erkesia, although it is not mentioned in the text and was started in the previous century. The Erkesia clearly existed in the 10th century for John Scylitzes wrote, 'In June of the fourth year of his reign (967), tenth year of the indiction, Nicephoras II Phocas set out to visit the towns in Thrace and when he came to the Great Dyke (as it is called) he wrote to Peter, the ruler of Bulgaria, to prevent the Turks (Magyars) from crossing the Danube to raid Roman land.'[4] Peter did not respond so Nicephoras invited the Kievan Rus to attack the Bulgars which they did in 968.

Bulgarian earthworks can be divided into groups, depending upon whether they are generally accepted as Bulgarian or whether there are claims to their being Bulgarian, which might be contested.

Modern Bulgaria

Lying within the borders of modern Bulgaria, and generally accepted as Bulgarian, are the following linear earthworks.

Southern frontier (Zone 1)

The main southern defence was the Erkesia which is a Turkish name and means cutting in the earth. The Byzantines called it the Great Dyke. As the Bulgarians moved south of the Stara Planina they came onto an open plain. The natural border was the Maritsa River but this flowed into the Aegean, leaving a land corridor between the Maritsa and the Black Sea which was open to the Byzantine Empire. Both Bulgars and Byzantines had a mutual interest in regulating the frontier between the Maritsa and the Black Sea which may have been determined in the Treaty of 816, mentioned above. This land corridor was blocked by the 164 kilometre long Erkesia which runs from the Maritsa River to the Black Sea.

6.1: Bulgaria

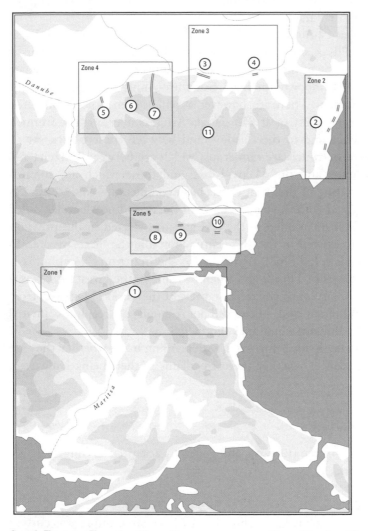

South Eastern Frontier (Zone 1)
1.   Erkesia

Eastern Frontier Black Sea (Zone 2)
2.   Black Sea Coast Dykes

Northern Danube Frontier (Zone 3)
3.   Tutrakan Dyke
4.   Belen Dyke

North Eastern Border (Zone 4)
5.   Lom Dyke
6.   Ostrov Dyke
7.   Khairedin Dyke

Stara Planina (Zone 5)
8.   Kotel Pass Wall (Kotlenski)
9.   Vărbitsa Pass Wall (Vărbitsa)
10.   Rish Pass Wall (Riški)

Fortified Enclosure
11.   Pliska Ramparts (location)

Greater Bulgarian Dykes (highly conjectural)
12.   Groß Römerschanze (see Map 5.1)
13.   Brazda lui Novac de Nord (see Map 5.1)
14.   Brazda lui Novac de North (see Map 5.1)
15.   Valul lui Traian de Jos (see Map 5.2)
16.   Valul lui Traian de Sus (see Map 5.2)

Erkesia – Although the Erkesia is often linked to the Treaty of 816, parts of it were started rather earlier and it is quite complex, being composed of several sections with different dates. The frontier set out in the Treaty of 816 was similar to that of 716, which first established the southern borders of early Greater Bulgaria, and the Erkesia was probably started in the intervening period. The barrier was built of two parallel lines of six metre high stakes filled by compacted earth from the ditch. (This sounds like the Avars Hrings on the Hungarian Plain, as described by the old soldier to Nokter.) There was an important gateway at Debeltos about twenty kilometres inland of the coastal city by Bourgas on the road from Pliska to Constantinople. Here, a customs post, dated to 816, has been recently excavated where for nearly two centuries the Byzantines paid an annual tribute to the Bulgarians. Seals have been discovered of the Byzantine ministers of roads and communications and for finance.

There are three main sections:

- **Western Erkesia** – This may be the earliest section, built following the Treaty of 716, and it runs sixty-four kilometres from Tenevo on the Tunja River to Simeonovgrad on Maritsa River.
- **Little Erkesia** – This runs about eleven kilometres from the Black Sea at Bourgos to Debelt. The Little and Eastern Erkesia, see next, may date from the time of the Treaty of 816 which established the southern borders of early Greater Bulgaria. Between 814 and 816 there were two short-lived Bulgar rulers. In 816 the Bulgars suffered a major defeat and were forced to accept peace.
- **Eastern Erkesia** – This extends sixty-seven kilometres from Debelt to the modern village of Tenevo. (There is a further section called the Gypsy Erkesia to the north of the Eastern Erkesia, where a supposed error in siting resulted in needless construction which was much later attributed to freelancing gypsies.)

Eastern Frontier Black Sea Coast Dykes (Zone 2)

Although the Bulgarians were able to displace the Byzantines on land they could not match them at sea. Along the Black Sea coast there are a number of linear earthworks, intended as Bulgarian defences against the Byzantine navy.

Varna Dyke – The greatest is the Dyke of Asparukh near Varna which has a stone core and which possibly represented the walls of the ancient city of Odessos.

Coastal Dykes – There are also five dykes between Kranevo and Obzor which overlooked beaches and may have been intended to stop surprise landings by sea.

Northern Danube Frontier (Zone 3)

There are linear earthworks which run along the right or south bank of the Danube which might have been built to counter a riverine Byzantine naval threat, or to counter Pecheneg or Magyar raids.

Tutrakan Dyke – The Tutrakan Dyke begins three kilometres west of the town of that name and reaches the village of Brashlen. It is sixteen kilometres long and has a ditch on its northern side. It is dated to the eighth and ninth centuries and is one of the most sophisticated earthworks in Early Bulgaria, being unique in having four fortresses.

Belene Dyke – The thirteen kilometre long Belene Dyke was about sixty kilometres east of the Tutrakan Dyke; it had no forts.

North-western Frontier (Zone 4)

In the north-west of the country there is a land corridor between the Danubian basins in modern Bulgaria and Serbia south of the river. Three west-facing dykes run from the Danube southwards to reach rivers on the northern slopes of the Stara Planina with ditches on the west side. These are ascribed to the second half of the eighth century due to finds in cemeteries and the historical context.

Ostrov Dyke – The longest earthwork and most easterly of this group is the Ostrov Dyke which is attributed to the Asparukh period (681–701). It is sixty-four kilometres long and starts at the village of Ostrov on the Danube and ends between the villages of Gabare and Tlachene to the south.

Lom Dyke – This dyke lies west of the Ostrov dyke and is twenty-five kilometres long.

Khairedin Dyke – This is the furthest west of the three and is twenty-one kilometres in length.

Stara Planina (Zone 5)

There are five major passes through the Stara Planina: the Iskar valley in the west, the Trojan and Skipka passes in the centre, and the Kotel and Riski passes in the east. The Bulgars and the Byzantines both had a history of battles in passes which blocked access to the plain south of the Danube. (These are outlined again below in the section on the use of linear barriers in pass battles.) These passes were strengthened with forts and walls.

Buiuk Konak Pass, Erkesiiata – There was a 0.8 kilometre long embankment called Erkesiiata near the Buiuk Konak Pass, not far from Rish Pass in the eastern Stara Planina.

Vărbitsa Pass – In 811 the Bulgars had built a wooden wall across the Vărbitsa Pass to block the Byzantine invaders who were soundly defeated alongside the wall.

Kleidion Pass – Khan Samuil constructed a wooden wall in 1014 across the pass at the village of Kleidion (meaning key) in south-eastern Bulgaria; but this time the Bulgars were beaten by the Byzantines under Basil II.

Fortified Enclosure

Pliska – This is the biggest fortification in Bulgaria. It encloses 5,681 acres and its rectangular linear earthworks surround rich alluvial soil. The north and south sides are respectively 3.9 and 2.7 kilometres long. The east and west sides are seven kilometres long. A ninth century stone fort lies at the centre but this is later than the perimeter barrier. The ground was clearly valuable but not because of the intrinsic worth of the earth, as this continued outside the boundaries set by the earthworks. The intention may have been to provide a safe haven where herds could have been protected from other raiders, and horses were quickly available for armed response. Also, the appearance of a tented nomadic existence could be maintained in safety within the boundaries. (The enclosure of unbuilt-up ground might be similar to the territorial oppida seen in Britain.)

Greater Bulgaria

Bulgarian historians argue that a number of linear earthworks to the north of the Danube were built or rebuilt by the Bulgarians and these defined the trans-Danubian borders of early Greater Bulgaria. The argument is essentially that the Bulgarians moved from north to south across the Danube. Therefore, at some time there would have been a northern border above the Danube's left bank. While one cannot discount the argument that some of the many linear barriers in this region are Greater Bulgarian, it does seem circular. The links of some of the following with Greater Bulgaria appear tenuous.

First refuge
An intriguing problem is the search for the Onglos which provided a refuge from which the Bulgars consolidated their hold on Danube region. It does not sound like a man-made barrier, judging from a description of its 'being swampy in the front and from the other sides – surrounded by a ring of rivers, it offered great security against enemies.'[5]

Valul Traian–Tuluceşti – If the location of the Onglos did involve a combination of rivers and a linear barrier then the position which might best fit the description is the Valul Traian–Tuluceşti which links the Prut and the Seret. Both these rivers are tributaries of the Danube; together with the Valul they provide a full circle combining earthworks and rivers. The Valul Traian–Tuluceşti covers off the open ground before the Roman camp at *Barbosi/*Galaţi.

Northern frontier
The northern border of Greater Bulgaria has been identified with the linear barriers running across the Wallachian Plain, the Budjak and Moldavia.

Valul lui Traian de Jos – On the southern side of the Valul lui Traian de Jos, excavations in 1986 to 1988 revealed a settlement with Slavic features that might have been occupied by workers on the dyke. These have been dated to the late sixth and early seventh century.[6] A later twelfth century text[7] says that Khan Asparuch (681–701) built a 'great wall from the Danube to the sea'.

If this were the case then the date would probably be the last twenty years of the seventh century. This 'great wall' is often identified with the south-facing Valul Mic de Pământ (see below) but it might equally describe the Valul lui Traian de Jos.

Valul lui Traian de Sus – This earthwork has also been suggested as Greater Bulgaria's furthest north-eastern frontier.

Brazda lui Novac de Nord – The Brazda lui Novac de Nord may have completed the frontier of Greater Bulgaria.

South-eastern frontier

The south-facing Valul Mic de Pământ has been suggested as a frontier in the Dobrogea.

Valul Mic de Pământ (Dobrogea) – The Valul has a ditch on the southern side unlike the other two Dobrogea earthworks which face northwards. This indicates that it might be the lower border of a northern Dobrogea territory. A later text says that Khan Asparuch (681–701) built a 'great wall from Danube to the sea'. If this were the case then the date would probably be the last twenty years of the seventh century. The south-facing Valul Mic de Pământ or Little Earth Wall does not, however, sound like a 'great wall from Danube to the sea'.[8] (Another possible interpretation might be that this was a reference to the Valul lui Traian de Jos – see above.)

North-western frontier

Between 791 and 795 Charlemagne and the Bulgars combined to destroy the Avar Khanate.

Groß Römerschanze – The north-west-facing Groß Römerschanze, between the Danube and the Tisza, might have been built at this date by the Bulgars. (Widukind said that Charlemagne built earthworks to prevent the defeated Avars from returning to old ways of raiding.)

If Greater Bulgaria was indeed defended by trans-Danubian linear barriers then such defences were not particularly successful as, by the ninth century, Bulgaria seems to have lost its trans-Danubian territories to other nomadic peoples.

Volga-Kama Bulgaria

For the record, the Bulgars who moved east have been associated with linear barrier building. When Khan Kubrat's third son Asparukh moved west, at the time when the Bulgars split under pressure from the Khazars in the early seventh century, his second son Kotrag and many other Bulgarians moved to the Volga-Kama area and founded a state called the Volga–Kama Bulgaria.

Volga-Kama earthwork – 'It is known that Bolgar, the capital of the Bulgarians settled along the River Volga, was also surrounded by earthworks; there still exists a linear earthwork, 400 kilometres long, extending from the Volga to the River Kama.'[9] Unfortunately, no other confirmation has been found of the existence this great earthwork. However, linking the two great rivers to create a large defensible region in new territory would seem like a logical action.

Analysis – Bulgaria

Although the early and modern state is named after the Bulgars, Bulgaria was based on a union with the Seven Tribes of Slavs. The modern language, although it has many words of Bulgar origin, is essentially Slavic. Also, Bulgaria does not have a continuous independent history, having been conquered by the Byzantines for much of the eleventh and twelfth century, and then by Ottomans between the fifteenth and nineteenth century. Notwithstanding these features, a sufficiently strong national identity was established during the first millennium for Bulgaria to eject both the Byzantines in the twelfth century and the Ottomans in the nineteenth century and to re-establish Bulgaria as an independent nation.

The use of fortified areas does appear important in the establishment of the Bulgars in the Danube area. Having entrenched themselves in the Onglos in the early seventh century they subsequently proved impossible to eject. Linear barriers in the east and the south were probably built by the Bulgars in the eighth and ninth century respectively. These barriers defended them against the Byzantine maritime threat and served to define and protect the land border. Their construction, particularly the Erkesia, might have been the culmination of a period of state-building similar to the roughly contemporary construction of Offa's Dyke and the Danevirke, or to the First Emperor Qin Shi Huang marking the end of China's 'Warring States' period.

The question of whether earthworks in Serbia, the Wallachian Plain, the Dobrogea and Moldavia, and the Ukraine have significant Bulgarian elements is almost insoluable as they appear largely to pre-date the early Greater Bulgaria Period. Or in the case of the Dobrogea Valurile lui Traian, some parts may have been reused by the Bulgarians. There is anyway sufficient evidence of linear barrier construction by the Bulgars to be fairly certain that they saw such structures as an important part of their strategic frontier management mix. It is not clear when the Bulgars withdrew south of the Danube but linear earthworks facing north on the right bank of the Danube might then have been important in resisting the Khazars, Magyars and Pechenegs.

Overall, it is difficult to reject the conclusion that the Bulgars' ability to establish themselves and sedentarise in Thrace was related to their use of linear barriers. Thus they avoided becoming just another one of the peoples on the great eastern European nomadic conveyor belt, a path along which other peoples moved and then disappeared.

2. Poland

Poland has, in some ways, been as much an idea as a country. Indeed at times – when it was divided between adjacent states – it existed only as an idea. But it was a remarkably tenacious one; so might this tenacity have something to do with the use of linear barriers? The main relevant work in English about Poland – The Archaeology of Early Medieval Poland: Discoveries, Hypotheses, Interpretations, indicates that linear barriers played a key role in state formation. 'In the times of Mieszko I (ca. 930–992) and Boleslaw the Brave (967–1025) Poland … was a country in which profound structural changes took place.… On the state frontiers, large investments were made to create the systems of permanent defence in the form of linear earthworks, traces of which survive in the landscapes of Silesia, Kuiavia and Mazovia and which survive in the toponyms such as brona (the term derives from bronić – to defend) in Little Poland.'[10] (Little Poland is a historical region of southern Poland.)

The entire northern European plain from Russia to Germany could itself be seen as a great land corridor traversed by rivers, of which the largest in Poland is the Vistula. To the north, Poland is bounded by the Baltic Sea and to the south by the Carpathian Mountains. Between the sea and the mountains the borders of Poland has shifted across the flat northern European plain, according to the dictates of politics as much as geography. In the north–eastern region of Mazovia there is a string of small lakes running roughly east west through dense forest that was occupied by Prussian tribes who remained pagan until the thirteenth century. This group of waters constituted a natural frontier in the early Middle-Ages. In the south–west the Bóbr River runs roughly from the south–east to the north–west below which the Sudetes Mountains form the border with the Czech Republic. To the south–west the Moravian Gate runs between the Sudetes and the Carpathian Mountains and is the main route between modern Poland and the Czech Republic. A land corridor from Poland to the modern Ukraine runs between the north-flowing Bug which joins the Vistula and the tributaries of the south-flowing Pripyat. It crosses the continental divide between northern and southern Europe in eastern Europe.

The first Slavs may have come from the upper and middle Dnieper region and settled in the upper Vistula area and in the south-eastern area of what is now Poland during the fifth and sixth centuries. This was after Germanic peoples moved south. By the mid-tenth century, the Polania tribe became dominant. The Piast dynasty was supposedly founded by the possibly legendary ninth century Chościsko and then Piast Kołodziej. The third Polish Duke Siemomysł, on his death in the mid-tenth century, left Greater Poland, now located in modern central south-western Poland, to his son Mieszko I, Poland's first historical ruler. In 966 Mieszko converted to Christianity, an event seen as the birth of the Polish nation. Mieszko incorporated Silesia into the Polish state and at his death the borders of the Piast state were similar to today's boundaries. The Piasts ruled Poland until 1370. The period of interest here however is the early Piast period.

On the western border the Piasts initially faced other western Slav peoples, and then increasingly Germanic peoples when the Ostsiedlung of the eleventh, twelfth and thirteenth centuries took hold. On the south-west border the Piasts and the Czech royal dynasty, the Přemyslids, were rivals in Silesia. On the north-east border the Poles clashed with pagan Prussian raiders. In the south-east, the expanding Kievan Rus, and then successor states to the Rus, confronted the Poles.

Polish – linear barriers

In practice searches for the actual remains of linear barriers in Poland does not provide a very rich haul. Most seem quite short and the dating is disputed. 'Another defensive element recognised in various parts of Polish lands is a number of linear earthworks. They have a number of common features. Most often these are earthern embankments sometimes having elements of wooden construction which are however often difficult to define. They have a linear form and are usually are quite long (several kilometres.) The archaeological material obtained from them is not very plentiful and for that reason it is difficult to date them precisely.'[11]

South-west – Silesia

Silesia was occupied in the south-west by Slavic tribes and incorporated into the Piast state in the tenth century.

Wały Śląskie or Dreigräben – There are earthworks in the south-west of the country running along the Bóbr River. In Polish these are the Wały Śląskie or Silesian Ramparts, and in German, the Dreigräben or Three Trenches. There are a number of sections of which about thirty kilometres are reasonably well preserved. The height is about 2.5 metres and the width between eighteen and forty-seven metres, depending on whether there are one or three parallel lines. A rather later fifteenth century date has been suggested, during the reign of Henry IX, for the Wały Śląskie. The possibility that they were earlier has not been excluded however, and these may have been built in pre-state times when the Dziadoszanie tribal confederation expanded towards Lusatia – a region now found on both sides of the Polish and German border. They were possibly constructed in the eighth or ninth century to block movements from the west; in which case they would initially have been built by Slav people before the area was controlled by the Piasts.

Przesieka Śląska (Schlesische Grenzwald)[12] – Another form of boundary that may have existed is in the type of abatis called the Przesieka Śląska or Silesian cuttings. These date to the eighth and ninth century, and blocked movement from the west. The Przesieka was a wide, uninhabited border forest, strengthened on the inside by cut-down trees whose branches were twisted together with thick bushes. Sometimes they also featured ramparts and trenches. Toponyms like Osiek, Ossig, Hag, and Hänchen may mark the location of Przesieka. As the *Ostsiedlung*, or German expansion east, gathered speed, the forests were cleared – and with them the Przesieka.

The area of Przesieka Śląska starts at Namysłów about fifty kilometres east of Wroclav (Breslau in German) and extends south-east to the Carpathians. It includes the Silesian and Lusatian border where the Wały Śląskie are located and covers the region of the Moravian Gate, which was the main route between the Carpathian and Sudetes mountains.

Piast frontiers

There appear to be two groups of early Piast linear barriers. The first ran along the north-eastern Mazovian-Prussian border. The second lay near to the south-eastern border en route to the Pontic Steppe between the Carpathian Mountains and Pripyat Marshes.

1. North Central 'Northern border'

Mazovia was the north-eastern region of Piast Poland and centred on the confluence of the Vistula and the Bug. Pagan Prussian tribes threatened the border region.

Swedish Wall – There is an earthwork called the Swedish Wall at Zimna Woda which may be part of the Mazovian-Prussian border. 'The neighbours were probably tiresome which seems to be suggested by the remains of linear barriers along the Mazovian-Prussian frontier.'[13]

Kuiavia – At Kuiavia, north of the Brda River, a tributary of the Vistula, there are linear barriers which might have been constructed by the western Slav Goplonie tribe or by the early Piasts to prevent Slavic Pomeranian incursions from the east.[14]

2. South-east 'Eastern Bulwark'

'Eastern Bulwark' – There is a linear earthwork at Czermno close to the south-east border of the modern country in the late eleventh and twelfth century. This might have provided protection against the Kievan Rus or the Pecheneg nomads.

Analysis – Poland

In the late twentieth century Poland re-emerged as an increasingly powerful eastern state despite the vicissitudes of many recent centuries. The foundations of Poland extend back to the tenth century when some linear barriers have possibly been identified along border regions. Given the use of use of linear barriers in comparatively nearby regions by the Danes, Swedish Goths, Bulgars and the Kievan Rus before and during this period, it would seem reasonable to expect that the Poles defined their frontiers with such barriers. The limited number of linear barriers found and the uncertainty of their dating means that Poland, however, remains work in progress. As Buko, who was quoted earlier, says: 'These structures which are such intriguing landmarks in the landscape of many parts of Poland will remain in the focus of interest of the next generation of historians and archaeologists'[15]

3. Kievan Rus

In 1008 the Holy Roman Emperor Henry II sent Bruno of Querfurt to convert the Pechenegs. Bruno had to pass through the land of the Rus, the medieval state that emerged in what is now the Ukraine and Russia in the ninth century. He converted thirty Pechenegs in five months, made peace between them and the Rus, and reported his story back to Henry. 'The lord of the Rus, a man great in his reign and wealth, ... argued with me, ... that I not go to such an irrational nation, where I would find no profit in souls, but only death... But when he was unable to convince me ... he himself along with his army took me two days journey to the farthest boundary of his kingdom, which he had enclosed on all sides with the longest and most solid of fences because of the roving enemy.'[16] Thus, by the early eleventh century, the Kievan Rus was apparently surrounded 'on all sides' by linear barriers against 'roving' nomads.

The grassland Pontic Steppe extends from Moldavia, Ukraine, Russia and north-western Kazakhstan to the Ural Mountains. It is bounded to the north by the forest steppe. This grassland steppe was potentially very fertile and included the Black Earth region of the Ukraine. But it needed extensive working and watering and during this period it supported nomadic pastoralism better than sedentary agriculture – as once an area had been exhausted the herds could be moved on.

The major rivers in between the Don and Danube are the Dnieper and the Southern Bug. These penetrate the forest steppe, and the Dnieper was the major Varangian or Baltic trade route from the Varangian or Baltic Sea to the Black Sea. Domination of that trade route conferred huge economic benefits which explained the rise of the City of Kiev and the burgeoning Kievan Rus state. To the south of Kiev the Dnieper runs through the Ukrainian uplifted hard rock Crystalline Shield resulting in a series of cataracts. Since the 1930s damming has eliminated these cataracts, and with it perhaps the archaeological evidence of linear barriers built to protect people moving onto land in order to circumvent the cataracts.

The Dnieper has many tributaries. On the west side, or right bank, going north along its length from Kiev, first the Irpen River and then the Teterev River flow north–east towards the Dnieper. This phenomenon created the opportunity to link the tributaries to the main river by linear barriers below Kiev. The rivers Stugna and then Ros flow roughly west to east before meeting the Dnieper below Kiev.

On the east side, or left bank, the tributaries tend to flow south-west into the Dnieper – meaning that the rivers themselves face south-east and can be reinforced as barriers against attack from the south. The most important below Kiev, going south, are the Trubezh, Sula, Vorskla and Horol. Above Kiev the River Desna flows roughly north; then its tributary, the Seim, shifts east, coming close to the Romen tributary of the Sula. Joining the Romen to the Seim by a linear barrier would create a fully bounded territory.

While the Pontic Steppe forms part of the Eurasian Steppe and of the land corridor that runs, with pinch points, from Mongolia to Hungary, it is considerably narrower than previous broad areas to the east. Also, it ends in a dense tangle of obstacles formed from the combination of the Dniester, the Prut, the Seret and the lower Danube.

The Pontic Steppe is itself a major land corridor. Trying to block something so wide, with migrating peoples passing through so frequently and forcefully, would be futile and counterproductive. Perhaps more of note, in terms of the search for linear barriers, are the land corridors leading off the Pontic Steppe. This is where such linear barriers might be more likely to be located. Basically, getting off the Pontic Steppe into Europe involved a choice of the following: going due west and traversing the Carpathian Mountains through to Transylvania and then on to the Hungarian Plain; traversing some combination of the Dniester, Prut, and Danube onto the Wallachian Plain and the Dobrogea; and negotiating the land corridor, north-west between the Pripyat Marshes and the Carpathian Mountains going on to what is now Poland and the Baltic region.

There are rivers that themselves form transport corridors up into the forest steppe and that connect to the Baltic area. The major river corridor is up the River Dnieper – this being the main trade route to the Baltic. Otherwise the Southern Bug is an important river.

The region has a number of significant watershed lines. As seen with the Hærvejen in Jutland and the Ridgeway in England, old roads often follow watershed lines and linear barriers sometimes cross or run parallel to such old roads. Rivers were all very well for trade but not much use for covering ground by nomad raiders or hordes, who instead tried to follow the all-weather land routes. There is also the continental divide watershed line itself from which rivers either go north or south, to the Baltic and to the Black and Caspian Seas.

The Dnieper formed the major part of the extremely important Varangian trade route which ran smack through Pecheneg territory and areas of the Rus that were subject to Pecheneg raids. To make life even more difficult the cataracts made a considerable length of the Dnieper to the south of Kiev impassable to fully laden ships. Constantine VII Porphyrogenitus' *De Administrando Imperio*, described how at the seventh barrage, 'the Pechenegs come down and attack the Russians.'[17] In 972 Prince Sviatoslav (964–972) was killed by the Pechenegs when he tried to negotiate the cataracts, and his skull was fashioned into a goblet in true nomad fashion. As seen in earlier sections, walls defended the portage routes along the Nile at the cataracts.

The emergence of Kievan Rus, while having its fair share of myth and mystery, offers a reasonably clear picture of state generation. Much simplified, Slavs appeared on the forest grassland steppe borders in the sixth and seventh centuries. The Vikings opened up the Varangian route to the Black Sea and Constantinople around the turn of the eighth and ninth centuries. In 862 the Kievan Primary Chronicle reported that the Slavs were so frustrated with their inability to organise a state that they asked the Varangians to rule them. The resulting Kievan Rus attacked Constantinople in 907 and afterwards a commercial treaty was signed between them. In 988 the Kievan Rus selected Christianity as their state religion – having been won over by the magnificence of the Cathedral of Hagia Sophia and the ritual of the Eastern Church which was judged superior to the offerings of Judaism and Islam.

The resulting Slavic speaking state grew rich through its control over the Varangian trade route. Every year trading parties were sent north to the Baltic region to gather slaves, and forest products, bringing them to Kiev from whence a great convoy set off into Pecheneg country to negotiate the cataracts and fight off the nomads. The Empire gradually extended far to the north with the successor warring Rus state of Novgorod eventually reaching the Baltic Sea. The Kievan Rus did not run all the way to the Black Sea, and so it left a land corridor across the Pontic Steppe which it would have been futile to block, given the tumult of nomadic peoples. Every year, however, the great flotilla had to fight its way down the Dnieper to the Black Sea and onto Constantinople.

The Golden Age of the Kievan Rus came to the fore with the reigns of Vladimir 'The Great' (980–1015) and Yaroslav 'The Wise' (1019–1054) who extended Kiev's rule over the whole of Rus by 1036. Vladimir constructed *grady*, or fortified towns, around Kiev; and he attracted occupants from the north to them with attractive concessions.

He also built or is associated with the building of great reinforced linear earthworks called Zmievi Vali.

In the twelfth century the Kievan Rus broke up into a number of warring states and Kiev ceased to be the dominant city. The Kievan Rus federation consisted of the Principality of Kiev, the Principality of Halych-Volin, the Principality of Pereyaslavl, and the Principality of Chernihiv. Other Rus states, not part of the federation, were the Lands of Vladimir-Suzdal, Polotsk and Novgorod. Wars between the Kievan states increased their vulnerability to outside attack and between 1236 and 1240 Kiev succumbed to the most ruthless and efficient of all nomadic hordes, the Mongols, who sacked the city and killed its inhabitants.

Nomads threatening the Kievan Rus

There is something rather intimate about the relationship between the Rus and the Pechenegs and then the Polovtsians, not unlike that between the Chinese and semi-nomadic Rong and the Di. Despite endless raids and wars, neither could destroy the other and a mutual history developed. The Polovtsians eventually combined with the Rus in a desperate and futile attempt to ward off the Mongols and in 1223 a joint Rus and Polovtsian force was destroyed by the Mongols.

The Pechenegs were a semi-nomadic Turkic people who began to emerge in the eighth and ninth century in the lower Volga, the Don, and the Ural Mountains. Eventually their territory extended as far as Seret River along the southern steppe passage between the Kievan Rus and the Black Sea and the Crimea. The area was a buffer zone between the Rus and the Byzantine Empire and the Pechenegs were employed by both groups in defence against the other when they were not actively engaged in attacking either Empire. They were defeated by Yaroslav the Wise (1019–1054).

A surprising amount can be learnt from Constantine VII Porphyrogenitus' *de Administrando Imperio* about the early relationship of Pechenegs and the Kievan Rus in the mid-tenth century before it became a Christian state. The Pechenegs do not now stand high in the list of fearsome nomads. But the very first instruction that Constantine gives to his son is to keep the peace with the Pechenegs. 'This nation of the Pechenegs is neighbour to the district of Cherson (the territory based around the Sevastopol and the Black Sea shore) and if they are not friendly disposed to us, they may make excursions and plundering raids against Cherson, and may ravage Cherson itself.'[18]

Bruno of Querfort called the Pechenegs, 'the cruellest of all pagans.' The *de Administrando Imperio* makes it quite clear that the Pechenegs are the alpha nomads of the age and the Bulgars and the Magyars are absolutely terrified of them. 'The tribe of the Turks (as the Magyars are somewhat confusingly called by Constantine) too, trembles greatly at fears of the said Pechenegs, because they have often been defeated by them and brought to the verge of complete annihilation.'[19] And, '(The Bulgarians) having frequently been crushingly defeated and plundered by them, they have learnt by experience the value and advantage of being always at peace with them.'[20]

Further, 'The Russians also are much concerned to keep the peace with the Pechenegs. For they buy off them horned cattle and horses and sheep, whereby they live more easily and comfortably, since none of the aforesaid animals is found in Russia. Moreover, the Russians are quite unable to set out for wars beyond their borders unless they are at peace with the Pechenegs, because while they are away from their homes, these may come upon them and destroy and outrage their property.'[21] The point about not being able to go to war elsewhere without being at peace with the Pechenegs is worth noting. Basically, until the Rus could secure its southern border against the Pechenegs – which it did with a combination of linear barriers and forts – it could not expand on other frontiers.

In 1055 the Kipchaks made their first appearance. Like the Pechenegs they were probably a Turkic people. The western Kipchak Turks were known as Cumans, and the eastern as Polovtsy or Polovtsians. The Kipchaks defeated the Khazars, drove the Alans south and overran the Pechenegs. By the mid-eleventh century the Rus trade had declined and farming became important. Kiev lost its dominance and new Rus centres emerged to the west and the north. The Polovtsians forced the border of the Rus to move north, thereby nearly pushing the lands of the principalities of Kiev, Chernigov and Pereyaslavl off the grassland steppe altogether.

The complex relationship between the nomads and the Rus is indicated in the Testament of Vladimir II Monomakh (1053–1125) on his deathbed to his children. (Incidentally, Vladimir was the grandfather of Valdemar the Great of Denmark who built the Valdemarsmuren section of the Danevirke). Like the Pechenegs, the Polovtsians are by turn enemies and allies of the Rus: 'I, supported by Polovtsians, marched against Odresk, carrying on constant warfare, and thence travelled to Chernigov.'[22] From then on the Polovtsians are largely enemies, as shown in this example: 'The Polovtsians devastated the whole of Starodub. I marched with men of Chernigov against the Polovtsians. At the Desna, we seized the princes Asaduk and Sauk, and killed their followers.'[23] As seen, in the end the Kievan Rus and the Polovtsians allied in a futile effort to repel the Mongols and both were destroyed.

Zmievi Vali

It would be very easy if all the linear barriers called the Zmievi Vali* could all be ascribed to the Kievan Rus – not least because they have a common name which is translated variously as snake ramparts or snake walls. This, however, is clearly a later renaming so that any linear barrier in the Ukraine has been attributed to a giant serpent – just as in a similar way linear barriers in the corridor between the Prut and Seret and then the Danube and the Black Sea seem now to be called Valul lui Traian, or Trajan's Wall.

There is a central group – the Zmievi Vali of Kievshchtsni, Pereyslava, and Posulya, around the Dnieper which are generally now seen as having been built by the Kievan

---

* As previously mentioned, if Змієві вали (Zmievi Vali) is put into Google, a Ukrainian Wikipedia site (see Bibliography) comes up. Using the translate function brings up a summary list of the Zmievi Vali or Serpent's Walls. In the case of some of the Zmievi Vali this and an accompanying map (see Bibliography), found only the internet, and unattributed, is the only source of information.

6.2: Kievan Rus

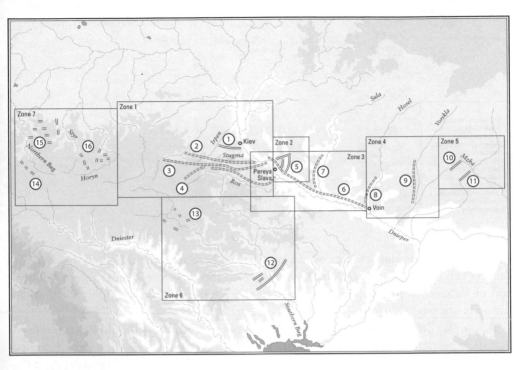

Zmievi Vali of Kievshchtsni (Zone 1) (lines much simplified)

1   Line 1 - Dnieper to Irpen Rivers
2   Line 2 - Trepol along Stugna River at then to Teterev River
3   Line 3 - Trepol over land to further south on Teterev River
4   Line 4 - Roden along Ros River towards Teterev

Zmievi Vali of Pereyslava (Zone 2)

5   Line 1 - double barrier south of Pereyaslavl

Zmievi Vali of Posulya (Zone 3)

6   Line 1 - along Dnieper between Trepol and Voin
7   Line 2 - Sula River (to Voin on Dniester)

Zmievi Vali of Poltava (Zone 4)

8   Line 1 - Horol River (to Dniester)
9   Line 2 - Vorskla River (to Poltava at Kolomak River confluence)

Zmievi Vali of Kharkov (Zone 5)

10   Line 1 - Kolomak to Mzha Rivers (near Kharkov)
11   Line 2 - Oril to Seversky Donetz Rivers (near Zmiev)

Zmievi Vali of Podolya (Zone 6)

12   Line 1 - across Southern Bug River
13   Line 2 – discontinuous lines along near both banks of Southern Bug from Vinnytsa towards Line 1

Zmievi Vali of Volinee (Zone 7)

14   Line 1 – between (northern) Bug River and Dniester north of Lvov.
15   Cluster 1 – between Styr and Northern Bug Rivers
16   Cluster 2 – Between Horyn River and Styr Rivers

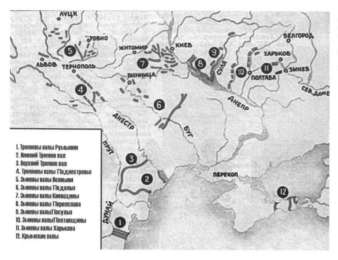

Map of Ukrainian, Moldavian and Romanian linear barriers. *(Widely available on internet – source unknown)*

Rus – either by the state of Kiev or of Pereyslava. There are two outliers to the east, the Zmievi Vali of Poltava and of Kharkiv, and two to the west, the Zmievi Vali of Podolya and of Volinee, which may in part relate to the Kievan Rus period. Overall, though, dating is uncertain.

Below, the Zmievi Vali are summarised in terms of location. It should be emphasised that such barriers were only part of the overall defensive system, as they were designed to operate in conjunction with forts. Also, forts located along rivers often composed the static defence system on their own. To give some idea of the scale of the Zmievi Vali, there were estimated to be about 1,200 kilometres of these earthworks, of which those in the Kiev region totalled about 800 kilometres.

Central Dnieper area of Ukraine

Zmievi Vali of Kievshchtsni (Zone 1) – South of Kiev, leading west from the Dnieper right bank, there were basically four lines of linear barriers. However, this is a considerable simplification as the lines are discontinuous in some places and duplicated or triplicated in others.

- **Dnieper to Irpen Rivers (Line 1)** – The first and shortest line, about thirty kilometres long, ran from the Dnieper west to the Irpen River just below the key garrison town of Belgorod.
- **Trepol along Stugna River and then to Teterev River (Line 2)** – The second Stugna River line extended from near the ford at Trepol along the Dnieper and, after crossing the Irpen River, it split roughly into three, even four, parallel branches. One of these extends to the Teterev River. From end to end it was about a hundred kilometres long, excluding duplicated sections.
- **Trepol over land to further south on Teterev River (Line 3)** – The third line started below the Trepol Ford close to Vitachev and ran across country to the Teterev for about 120 kilometres.

- **Roden along Ros River towards Teterev (Line 4)** – There was a fourth line which followed the Ros River from Roden on the Dnieper to Yuriev where it splits and two branches continued to a Teterev River tributary. This line lay to the south of Pereyaslavl. It might be later and have had as its purpose the defence of the territory to the south of Pereyaslavl across the Dnieper.

Zmievi Vali of Pereyslava (Zone 2) – The city of Pereyslavl lies on the River Trubezh which runs into the Dnieper. A very substantial linear barrier ran from the Dnieper to the Trubezh River, thus creating a protective loop before the city and the confluence of the Dnieper and the Trubezh Rivers. A second large barrier continued along the Dnieper River and joined the first before it reached the Trubezh. The total length was over seventy kilometres. Before Vladimir II Monomakh was invited to become ruler of Kiev in 1113 his main patrimony was Pereyslava whose protection he may have strengthened. He might also have added the fourth line, described just above, from Roden along the Ros to Teterev which protected both Kiev and Pereyslava.

Zmievi Vali of Posulya (Zone 3) – There are two riverine lines.

- **Dnieper between Trepol and Voin (Line 1)** – There was a line which ran from the ford at Trepol near the Dnieper Sula confluence and the fortified harbour at Voin near the Dnieper Sula confluence – a distance of 150 kilometres. This might have served the double function of stopping threats crossing the Dnieper; but it would also have protected shipping on the Dnieper which was a major trade route and where Constantine VII Porphyrogenitus vividly described the Pecheneg threat.
- **Sula River to Voin on Dniester (Line 2)** – Another line ran down the right or west bank of the Sula River from Lubno, a distance of nearly a hundred kilometres, past Voin, to the Dnieper.

Eastern Ukraine

In the eastern Ukraine there were two Zones of Zmievi Vali related to rivers which flow directly or indirectly into the Dnieper. They were not necessarily part of the defence of Kiev and the timing of their construction may be quite different to that of the Zmievi Vali to the south of Kiev.

Zmievi Vali of Poltava (Zone 4) – There appear to be two lines of linear barriers along rivers which flow towards the Dnieper. The builders and the purpose of these barriers remain unclear. They may have formed the forward defences against the Polovtsians of a successor state, Chernigov, after the Kievan Rus broke up in the twelfth century.

- **Horol River (to Dnieper) (Line 1)** – There is a discontinuous linear barrier running along the Horol River to its confluence with the Dnieper.
- **Vorskla River (to Poltava at Kolomak River confluence) (Line 2)** – There is a second discontinuous barrier along the Vorskla River to the confluence of the Kolomak River near Poltava.[24]

Zmievi Vali of Kharkiv (Zone 5) – There were two linear barriers between twenty and twenty-five kilometres long which roughly bridged the gaps between rivers in the Dnieper and the Seversky Donetz Basins. Therefore, they crossed the watershed line. Such lines were often the location of all-weather land routes, and this particular watershed was the location of the Muravsky Shlyah or Trail (discussed in the section below on Russia) which was a major raiding route between the Crimea and Muscovy in the seventeenth century. There appears to be archaeological evidence of much earlier occupation by peoples in the region who may have built linear barriers. It is not really possible, though, to make any very informed comment on the quality of this evidence.

- **Kolomak to Mzha Rivers (near Kharkiv) (Line 1)** – There was a linear earthwork below Kiev which linked the Kolomak River which flows into the Vorskla and then the Dnieper, and the Mzha River which flows into the Seversky Donetz. Local history relates that these were reconstructed in the seventeenth century – as part of the construction of the Izium Line – but were originally Scythian. It is again not really possible to comment on this. Roman coins from the first to third century are reported to have been found in the earthwork. The Chernyakhov culture flourished in the Kharkiv area between the second and sixth centuries. This culture is generally associated with the Goths.
- **Oril to Seversky Donetz Rivers (near Zmiev) (Line 2)** – To the south there is another earthwork between the Oril River which flows into the Dnieper and the Seversky Donetz in the region of Zmiev. A Ukrainian travel magazine says that: 'Among all the Snake Earthworks to be found in the Ukraine, in the best state of preservation are probably those that are situated along the River Oril.'[25] Zmiev may have been a fortified centre built of stone in the seventh century.

Western Ukraine

There are two enigmatic zones of linear barriers to the west of Kiev.

Zmievi Vali of Podolya (Zone 6) – There are clusters of earthworks in a zone around Southern Bug River.

- **Across Southern Bug River** – There is a long linear barrier running across the Bug which was continuous for about 130 kilometres in a north-easterly direction, mostly on the left bank. On the right bank there appear to be two short lengths of earthwork which lay mostly to the north of the main work. The word Bug translates as the Bow and is a Gothic name. This is also an area of Scythian sites. At Zhurzhintsi there is an enormous earthwork circuit attributed to the Scythians.
- **Discontinuous lines along and near both banks of Southern Bug from Vinnytsa** – There were a number of smaller earthworks on both sides of the Bug extending up to the city of Vinnytsia.

Zmievi Vali of Volinee (Zone 7) – There appear to have been a large number of short earthworks between between Lutsk, Rovno, Lvov, and Ternopil in western Ukraine. This is a highly sensitive region in terms of land corridors. Most of the linear barriers lie between the Western Bug and the Horyn River. The Western Bug flows north towards the Baltic – whereas the Horyn runs north briefly but then joins the Pripyat River, which in turn flows into the Dnieper before it empties into the Black Sea. This, therefore, is the junction of the continental divide watershed line and of the route from the south, between the Dniester and the Southern Bug, to the Western Bug towards the Baltic. Watershed lines are often all-weather land transport routes, and linear barriers are often found across or parallel to them. In this case it is not clear quite what function these linear barriers played. They may have blocked access to a bounded area between the Pripyat and its tributaries, the Styr and Horyn Rivers.

There was an amber trade route from the Baltic to the Black Sea. It lay between the territories of Piast Poland and Kievan Rus and was contested between them, with the Rus eventually winning. The Pechenegs raided in the area and later so did the Mongols.

- **East of (northern) Bug River (Cluster 1)** – This cluster lies south of Lutsk in an area where the watershed lines, running roughly east–west and north–south, converge along the Western Bug near the point that the Pripyat and the Horyn Rivers approach it. As such, this would have been a particularly active area in terms of the presence of routeways along watershed lines.
- **West of Horyn River (Cluster 2)** – Another cluster lies south of Rovno and might have controlled access to the bounded area between the Styr and Horyn Rivers which flow into the Pripyat.
- **Between (northern) Bug River and Dniester north of Lvov (Line 1)** – Lvov lies in the land corridor between the north-flowing Western Bug and the south-flowing Dniester. There appears to be a single linear barrier to its north.

Post Kievan Rus break-up

The Kievan Rus broke up in the twelfth century into four federate states and a number of other states. Thus there was the potential for the warring states situation which can result in linear barriers. 'The emergence of many independent principalities in Rus led to the need for fortified lines not only on the external frontiers of Rus but also between the individual principalities.'[26] The problem is that in forest areas, abatis were probably the rule and these tend not to leave physical evidence. Therefore, abatis may have been built between warring Kievan Rus states which have been completely lost if there is no textual evidence to confirm their existence. But it is known, for example, that Prince Igor of Chernigov (1198–1202) built an abatis over 600 metres wide on the Desna and Bolva Rivers against attack from the state of Suzdal. 'Under the instructions of Prince Igor for protection from the north against an attack by Suzdal, Chernigov made a multi-kilometre abatis.'[27]

Analysis – Kievan Rus

The Zmievi Vali lay close to the border between the grassland and the forest steppe. On the former, earthworks might be expected to be found and on the latter abatis. In this border area, where both earth and wood abounded, the materials could be merged to make much higher and steeper linear barriers. In 981 Vladimir I of Kiev campaigned against Poland and might have adopted the idea of building a wooden core from Polish fortresses in order to make Kievan linear barriers. The ramparts were built from the earth excavated from the ditch. They were often covered by a wooden framework of earth and rubble-filled cages. A wooden palisade capped the structure. The earthworks hugged the contours of the land rather than being in a straight line. Indeed, their meandering appearance probably encouraged the name, snake ramparts. The Zmievi Vali did not operate in isolation. There were forts along their length but not necessarily placed directly adjacent to the rampart. These sent out reinforcements against raiders and thus blocked them from either crossing or re-crossing the ramparts.

Between the ninth and thirteenth centuries the Kievan Rus and its successor states fought and made alliances and peace with the Pechenegs and the Polovtsians. They were familiar and ever present, and although probably Turkic in origin and with a range that took them far down the western Black Sea coast, they were local nomads. Given their ever continuing presence over a long period, combined with the difficulty forming reliable treaties – see the Testament of Vladimir Monomakh – it would have made sense to invest in fortifications systems to meet their potential threat. Later on, further barriers were built between successor warring states.

Linear barriers might also be found along the Dnieper whose purpose would have, at least in part, been to stop Pecheneg nomads from attacking the annual trading convoy down the river. As seen above, there appear to have been linear earthworks between the Trepol and Voin along the Dnieper. It is difficult to know much about the situation further downstream, around the cataracts, as the area has been drowned by Soviet era dams. Modern commentators think it probable that linear barriers were built along the Dnieper's left bank. Thus, 'Vladimir made protection of the southern riverway a priority. Fortified harbours capable of accommodating many boats were built … in the vicinity of the Dnieper and one of the functions of the Snake Rampart flanking the Dnieper was to hinder the Pechenegs from positioning themselves on the left bank and ambushing vessels.'[28]

While the Pontic Steppe can be seen in its entirety as a land corridor, attempting to block it would have been futile if not suicidal. What is clear, however, is that linear barriers can be found across the routes off the Eurasian Steppe. Corridors with linear barriers include: the route to Poland between the Carpathian Mountains and the Pripyat Marshes – which is the location of the Zmievi Vali of Volinee; and the route between the watersheds of the Dnieper and Don River basins – where the Zmievi Vali of Kharkiv are found. Although slightly different – in that the corridor is the River Dniester itself which carried the Varangian trade – access to Kiev is blocked by the Zmievi Vali of Kievshchtsni.

The Zmievi Vali may have been important in stabilising the Pecheneg situation as, after their construction, the Kievan Rus was able to go onto the offensive to the west and north. The Polovtsians appear to have been a dangerous threat and forced northwards the southern frontiers of the Kievan Rus and its successor states. That said, no state fell to the Polovtsians and the disunity of the warring Kievan states might have explained their comparative weakness in the face of Polovtsians.

It was not, however, the local and familiar Pecheneg and Polovtsian nomads who ended the Kievan Rus. Rather it was the non-local and utterly ruthless Mongols who destroyed the southern states in the thirteenth century. Already equipped with a formidable siege train – which broke through into the major cities of the Rus including Kiev, Moscow, Vladimir, Pereyaslavl and Chernigov – it was unlikely that the Zmievi Vali could have held up the Mongols for long.

The construction of linear barriers against the Pechenegs might have been aggressive by proxy as it made possible expansion elsewhere to the north and the west. Constantine VII Porphyrogenitus said the Kievans could not go to war without elsewhere being at peace with the Pechenegs. By securing its southern borders against the Pechenegs with what Bruno of Querfort calls the 'longest and most solid of fences because of the roving enemy'[29], the Rus was able to expand to the west and the north. And it was the expansion in the north that ensured the survival of the idea of a Slavic speaking, Cyrillic writing, and Orthodox worshipping Rus, after Kiev was destroyed by the Mongols. This, of course, was not foreseen in the original decision to build the Zmievi Vali.

The Zmievi Vali were part of the solution to obtaining peaceful relations with the Pechenegs and Polovtsians. Without the Zmievi Vali however, the Rus might not have been able to expand north. And without northward expansion there might have been no Russian state which survived the nomad onslaught. (Also, it might be argued that because the idea of an independent Kievan state had taken root a millennium earlier, it was easier for an independent Ukraine to re-emerge in 1991, after the break-up of the Soviet Union.)

Conclusion – State Formation

It is possible to distinguish between the stronger and weaker idea that linear barriers contributed to the formation of longstanding states. The stronger idea says that the actual act of coming together of people physically to construct a linear barrier created such bonds between them that a more durable state developed, united by a group consciousness. Essentially, this was an internal process where barrier building was crucial to consolidating the relationship between the people inside the linear barrier. The weaker idea is that linear barrier building in itself did not contribute to state formation, but that such constructions kept out external threats for long enough for a state to develop in a location guarded by linear barriers.

Given the limited information available about how state formation actually worked, particularly in pre-literate polities, it is very difficult to know quite what role the linear barrier actually played in the process. That said, cases could be made that linear barrier building contributed to the ability of the Bulgars, the Poles and the Kievan Rus to build states in areas where frontiers could easily be contested, and where there were many other peoples roaming the regions who might usurp them.

Chapter Seven

China I – Northern Expansion, Consolidated by Walls, Sets Off Nomad Irruptions

E arlier chapters touched upon the construction of long anti-nomad walls by the three northern Chinese warring states of Qin, Zhao and Yan. In this chapter this great wall building drive is looked at in more detail as it has implications not only for the nomads in the region and for China, but also for the rest of the Eurasian Steppe. The migrations from the Mongolian and Manchurian steppes first provoked by these three walls were of sufficient intensity to force nomads from east to west in explosive movements from one section of the steppe range, to the next – resulting in events at one end of Eurasia having implications for the other.

The earlier analysis of the Warring States period focused on China's internal geography. Now the external impact is considered. China has exceptionally long land borders except to the east where there is salt water in the form of the Pacific Ocean and the Yellow Sea. To the west and, to a lesser extent, the south, there are mountains and forests. The northern border is both long and lacking in a major single natural obstacle capable of blocking all movement in the form of rivers or mountains. The Yellow River, which might have formed a defensible northern border, on the model of the Rhine and the Danube for the Roman Empire, is obstinately situated mostly in the wrong place; it is too far south in the west, while in the east it encloses the semi-arid Ordos, and it leaves out the rich, fertile loess areas outside the loop.

1. Warring States anti-nomad walls

In a comparatively short period, during the last third of the fourth century, all three north-facing states of Qin, Zhao and Yan built very long walls that directly confronted nomad groupings. This action implies both a common challenge and a similar response. All these walls lay well to the north of the main areas of settlement – in other words, deep within nomad territory.

Qin Northern Wall – To protect against the Yiqu semi-nomads, King Qin Huiwen (338–311 BC) built a 300 kilometre-long fortification along the northern border of Qin territory in 330 BC. King Zhaoxiang (307–251 BC), the grandfather of First Emperor Qin Shi Huang, conquered the Yiqu semi-nomads and in 287 BC built a great 600 kilometre wall. As a broad simplification, the Qin wall diagonally bisects the rectangular Yellow River loop, from near the south-west to the north-east corners. The diagonal line of the wall follows the north-east-facing border of the loess plateau. (As seen earlier in the Chapter on Chinese warring states, loess soil is very

7.1: China Warring States Wall and unification: Great Wall

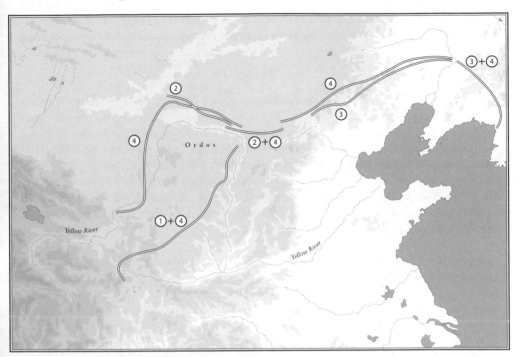

Warring States' North Walls
1.   Qin North Wall
2.   Zhao North Wall
3.   Yan North Wall

Unified China Great Walls of China
4.   Qin Dynasty (221-207 BCE) First Great Wall of China (had possible line north west of the Ordos)

vulnerable, particularly when irrigated in order to exploit its fertility which frequently resulted in the construction of protecting walls.) The walls of tamped earth are only found along relatively flat lands, but for a fifth of its length the barrier followed natural features without a distinct linear barrier but with elevated platforms and forts. There was a complex arrangement of beacons, watchtowers and forts.

Zhao Northern Wall – Zhao was the central of the three northern States. In the early fourth century BC King Wuling (325–299 BC) initiated military reforms. He forced his army to adopt nomad dress, fight as cavalry and practise horse archery. In 306 BC the Zhao military launched expeditions into barbarian territory in the north. In 304 BC the upper reaches of the Yellow River were invaded and taken from the barbarian tribes. Wuling possibly built two roughly parallel walls, a shorter wall north-west of Beijing, and a slightly longer wall in Inner Mongolia north of the Ordos. Basically they ran parallel to the east-west line of the Yellow River loop. They started roughly north of the loop's north-west corner and extended further east than the north-east corner of the loop. Some sections were made of stone.

Yan Northern Wall – King Zhao (311–279 BC) of Yan, the most easterly of the northern States, pushed north-east against the Eastern Hu into the region that is now Manchuria. There he built walls over 500 kilometres long in 290 BC which started some distance to the east of the Zhao walls, roughly due north of Beijing, along the Yanshan mountain range. The intention was to counter the intrusion of Donghu, Lin hu and Loufan nomads. The wall extended east to the Liao River which discharges south into the most northerly part of the Bohai Sea. The wall may then have looped south to the sea. In 254 BC there was another phase of wall building, perhaps the last during the Warring States period. The wall is made of tamped earth or stone depending on locality. One section of this wall was 200 kilometres long.

Analysis – Qin, Zhao and Yan walls

The walls were built after the northward push by Chinese northern states to consolidate the grip over land taken from nomads. 'The states of Ch'in (Qin), Chao (Zhao) and Yen (Yan) needed to protect themselves from the nomads only after they had taken large portions of territory from other peoples and had chased the nomads away from their homelands.'[1] Chinese archaeologists do not believe that the walls mark an ecological boundary between the steppe and the sown. The radical goal was 'to establish a strong military presence that allowed the state to control the movement of people, be they nomads, moving across plains, hills, or mountain passes; peddling merchants; transhumant populations; or hostile armies.'[2] The walls are remote from agricultural land and close to the steppe proper. Their function was to drive out nomads and control lands necessary for horse breeding.

The sheer scale of this construction should challenge the idea that linear barrier generally was defensive, even passive, in motivation. According to the 'traditional interpretation … the fortified lines of defence, the precursors of the Great Wall were built to defend the Chinese civilisation from the incursions of the nomads. Rather, walls were meant as a form of military penetration and occupation of an alien territory that the Chinese states could use in a variety of ways, including horse breeding and trade, and as a reservoir of troops and laborers.'[3] These three walls are extremely important in global terms, for the nomad reaction reverberated eventually all the way to Europe and arguably played a key if indirect role in bringing down the Western Roman Empire.

2. China united by the First Emperor Qin Shi Huang

The mighty Qin First Emperor Shi Huang, having completed unification by conquering all the other warring states, ordered the destruction of all internal walls and the construction of a single wall. Given the amount of Warring State wall that has been discovered however, it is clear that even the First Emperor's order concerning earlier walls was not thoroughly carried out.

Qin Wall of China – In 215 BC Qin Shi Huang drove the Xiongnu from the Yellow River bend. The *Shi Ji*, or *Records of the Grand Historian*, said: 'The Xiongnu were expelled from the north-west. The land occupied from Yuzhong along the eastern side of the Yellow River all the way to Yinshan was then divided into thirty-four counties. In the neighbourhood of the Yellow River, walls were erected and these served as a strategic barricade.'[4]

The *Shi Ji* also reported, 'After Qin had annexed the whole country, Meng Tian was despatched at the head of an army of 300,000 men to drive out the Rong and the Di to the north. He annexed Henan and constructed long walls. In this, he relied on the topography of the land, and built barricades connecting strategic locations. From Lintao in the west to Liaodong in the east, the Great Wall extended for more than 10,000 li.'[5] (a li is about 500 metres.) Archaeologists debate the extent to which Shi Huang Di largely in practice strung together the walls of the existing warring states, Qin, Zhao and Yan.

The Wall may have extended outside of the Yellow River loop as the Helanshan Mountains lie to the west of the Yellow River where it swings north around the Ordos. The Helanshan is an area of loess which extends along the Hexi corridor where the Han later built long walls towards the west. The Qin Great Wall might also have run north to include the Yinshan area which is now extremely dry, but historical and archaeological evidence indicate that in the past it was much more fertile. Also, the plains of Ningxia between the Yellow River and the Yinshan Mountains constituted a cultivable and desirable area of land.

Conclusion – early northern anti-nomad walls

The drive north produced a double reaction: the nomads united in the Xiongnu Confederation and counter-attacked the Chinese; also, more intense rivalry between nomads resulted in nomadic peoples fleeing from the steppe north of China and into the central Asian steppe. This mass flight set off chain reactions which eventually saw Asian nomads moving across the Eurasian Steppe until they reached Europe.

The motivation of the three northern states of Qin, Zhao and Yan in building long walls appears essentially to have been aggressive in purpose: to consolidate the hold on land from which nomads had been suppressed or ejected. The motivation of the First Emperor Qin Shi Huang might have been more complicated as his status as first Emperor was different to the Kings of Warring States. His challenge was now to combine recently fighting polities. Also, he was not conquering new northern territory, but trying to hold it against the resurgent Xiongnu. Construction of the first great wall was arguably a combination of any or all of the following: an exercise in self-projection; empire-consciousness building; or a way of keeping soldiers occupied who until recently had been fighting for the Warring States.

The rapid fall of the Qin under the second emperor, Qin Hu Hai (210–207 BC), cannot be attributed to the failure of the wall in the face of nomad attack since the dynasty was brought down by the Han Chinese. Indirectly, however, the misery imposed on the Chinese by the megalomaniac schemes of the first Emperor, including forcing a reluctant peasantry to build his long wall, may have produced pressures that any less maniacal and weaker personality than the First Emperor could not have managed. Therefore it is arguable that the building of the Great Wall contributed to the failure of the Qin regime, through internal and not external factors.

Nomad irruptions across the Eurasian Steppe

The northern push by the three northern states at the end of the fourth century BC culminated in anti-nomad wall building and eliminated the many semi-nomad peoples as a buffer force. It also, though, brought the Chinese up against the genuine, mounted, composite-bow-armed nomad in the form of the Xiongnu confederation. This resulted in the first of the three trans-steppe irruptions.

1: Xiongnu and the first trans-Eurasian steppe nomad irruption
The earliest known Xiongnu ruler was Touman, who held power between 220 and 209 BC, and who united the nomadic tribes living in Mongolia and invaded Northern China. In 209 BC his son Maodun emerged as leader of the Xiongnu after killing his father. The Xiongnu brought their eastern neighbours, the Donghu, under their rule and defeated the Turkic peoples living in Northern Mongolia. The Donghu later split into the Xianbei and the Wuhuan. (From the Xianbei were descended the Mongols via the Shiwei. The Wuhuan branch disappeared.) In 177 BC the Xianbei defeated the Indo-European Yuezhi and many of the Yuezhi then fled along the Gansu Corridor to Central Asia. There they defeated the Sakas, a Scythian people, displaced the Hellenistic Graeco-Bactrians and became known as the Kushans, founding the great Kushan empire which extended from Bactria to North-east India.

The Xiongnu split into Eastern and Western Xiongnu when Han agents provoked the rebellion of subject peoples in 55 BC. In 54 BC the Eastern Xiongnu withdrew to the Ordos. The Western Xiongnu migrated to Sogdia in Transoxiana and a new Western Xiongnu Empire was established there in 36 BC which the Han later pursued and destroyed. The Eastern Xiongnu, however, revived and briefly overthrew the Han in China in 18 BC.

Famines, plagues and revolts soon resulted in the break-up of the surviving Eastern Xiongnu into the Northern and Southern Xiongnu in AD 48. While the Southern Xiongnu accepted the Han protectorate, after a short time the Northern Xiongnu had to deal with attacks by the Xianbei, who defeated them. The Chinese also attacked them in AD 85 and 89, and they were dispersed. The Southern Xiongnu defeated the Han in 216. While many of the Xiongnu went to western Turkestan some stayed in northern China and established small kingdoms after the Han fell.

The key point is that the Xiongnu, other nomads and the Han linked the north of China to Central Asia, through the Gansu Corridor. Also, nomads from the north of China established states in Central Asia.

Many Xianbei moved south and sedentarised. They founded six of the Sixteen Kingdoms which were unified by the Tuoba tribe of the Xianbei as the Northern Wei. Other Xianbei further split into three groups, the Rouran, the Kitan, and the Shiwei. The Rouran were a confederation; they lasted roughly from the late fourth century until the late sixth century and were led by Xianbei people who remained in the Mongolian steppes.

The confederating of the Xiongnu has been ascribed to the construction of the Qin, Zhao and Yan state northern walls and the Qin Empire Great Wall. The conflicts of the Xiongnu and the Xianbei with the Han dynasty (206 BC–AD 220), and the subsequent period of Disunion Dynasties (AD 220–581) resulted in the great Han wall systems and heroic levels of wall construction by various Northern Dynasties.

The Huns have been identified as descendents of the Xiongnu. Whether this debated link has any direct validity is almost irrelevant in terms of wall-building. What matters is that the connecting up of the Eurasian Steppe resulted in a flow of peoples who split and merged over centuries. To the west the Huns and other nomadic peoples provoked linear barrier building by the Byzantines and the Sasanians, mostly in the sixth century.

2: Turks and the second nomad irruption

With the Göktürks, the Turks burst into history. Within the heterogeneous Rouran confederacy, the Göktürks were probably not an ethnically or linguistically distinct people. Indeed their only specific trait appears to have been functional as they were the metal-working servants of the Rouran elite. The Göktürks rise to power began in AD 546 when Bumin Khan made a pre-emptive strike against the Uyghur and Tiele tribes who were planning a revolt against their overlords, the Rouran. For this service Bumin expected to be rewarded with a Rouran princess. Disappointed, he allied with the Wei state against the Rouran, their common enemy, whose power was destroyed. The Avars have been identified (uncertainly) with escaping Rouran who fled west. From 552 to 745 the Göktürk leadership bound together the nomadic Turkic tribes into an empire which eventually split into Western and Eastern Turks due to a series of dynastic conflicts. The move west of the Turkic peoples had a dramatic impact on Eurasia, as far as Europe, and the Turks provoked a burst of wall building in China and Central Asia, as well as by the Kievan Rus.

Kitan Liao and Jin nomad states

The Kitan Liao split from the Xianbei and occupied a region of Southern Manchuria, north of Korea. From this area of northern China they expanded into Central Asia. The Kitan Liao Empire, founded in the same year (907) that the Tang Dynasty collapsed, ruled over the regions of Manchuria, Mongolia, and parts of northern China proper. The

Kitan had northern and southern chancelleries; they conducted business respectively along nomadic and sedentary lines, thereby resolving the problem of how to govern a people split by very different life styles. In the eleventh century, the Jurchens (a Siberian people) of northern Manchuria had become vassals of the Kitan. The Jurchen overthrew the Kitan in 1125 and established the Jin dynasty which controlled northern China, including Manchuria and part of the Mongol region, until 1234. Both the Kitan and the Jurchen built linear barriers, the former against the latter, and the latter against the Mongols.

3: Mongols and the third nomad irruption
The Mongols, who descended from the Shiwei, were united by Ghengis Khan and went on to establish the greatest land empire in history. Mongols, going south-east towards China, conquered the semi-nomadic Jurchen to the north and the Song in the south and reunited China under the Yuan dynasty. Going west, they crushed and conquered all the way to Hither Asia and Europe. In the fourteenth century the Mongol Golden Horde broke up, but successor Tatar khanates milked the emerging Russian state of goods and people. After the Ming ejected the Mongol Yuan Dynasty and the Russians fought back against the Tatars, there was a last great phase of anti-nomad linear barrier building which stabilised and, in the case of Russia, served to advance the line against the steppe nomads. The Ming fell to the Manchus who were possibly descended from the Jurchen and established the Qing dynasty. Aided by linear barriers, the Russians and the Chinese closed down the Eurasian Steppe.

1. Wall of Qi – Warring States era wall (Jinyangguan). *(Photo by Kim F. Siefert, Great Wall Forum)*

3. Wall of Ston – reconstructed medieval isthmian wall, a type pioneered by the Greeks (Pelješac peninsula, Croatia). *(C. C. license - László Szalai)*

2. Aigaleo–Parnes Wall or Dema Wall of Athens. *(Photo by M.M. Miles)*

4. Hadrian's Wall – looking east from Housesteads Fort. *(Author)*

5. Antonine Wall – looking west from Rough Castle. *(Author)*

6. Raetian Limes (south Germany) – near the watch tower 14/78. *(C. C. license - Heinrich Stuerzl)*

7. *Claustra Alpium Iuliarum* (Slovenia). *(Photo by Mirko Slak, through the Institut Ivan Michler)*

8. Bokerley Dyke – looking south, earthwork faces east. *(Author)*

9. Wansdyke – ditch of eastern section, image right faces north. *(Author)*

10. Dane's Cast (Northern Ireland). *(Photo by Brian Thomas Mcelherron)*

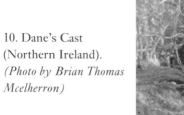

11. Danevirke, Hovedvolden image right facing north. *(Author)*

12. Danevirke, Valdemarsmuren, fired brick wall. *(Author)*

14. Landwehr (Radevormwald in North Rhine-Westphalia). *(C. C. license - Frank Vincentz)*

13. Götavirke (Sweden). *(C. C. license - OlofE)*

15. Letzimauer (Oberarth in canton of Schwyz). *(C. C. license – Pakeha)*

16. Les Fossés-le-Roy (near village of Chennebrun on border of départements of Eure and Orne). *(Photo by Pascal et Nathalie Mercier)*

17. Irish Pale (north of Rathcoffey in county Kildare). *(Photo by Seamus Cullen)*

18. Valul Mare de Pământ
(west of Constanța).
*(Photo by Adrian
Mihălțianu, on Xplorio.ro)*

19. Valul Mare de
Pământ – road along its
top near agricultural
station just north
of town of Valul lui
Traian. *(Author)*

20. Valul Mare de Pământ
– satellite image showing
location, centre upper
left, of previous image –
observe fort bottom right.
(Google Maps)

21. Valul lui Traian de Jos – Valul lui Isac – Lacul Laplug, looking east, image left facing north. *(Photo by Leonid Rosca)*

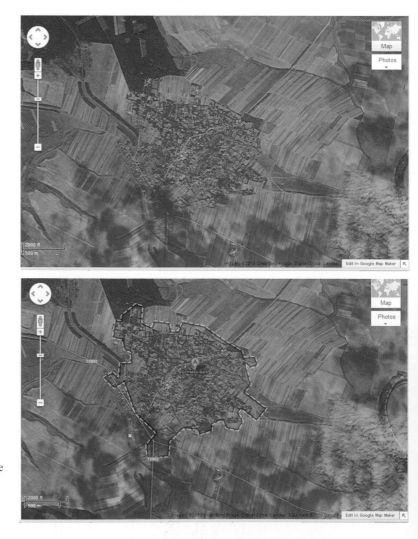

22. Trayanov Vali – Podnestrovya - linear earthwork running from the Zbruch river in the east to the town of Hermakivka. *(Google Maps)*

23. Perekop Val – Crimean isthmus. *(C. C. license - Btxo)*

24. Erkesia, image right looking north (Bulgaria). *(Photo by Geopan)*

25. Zmievi Vali (south of Kiev). *(C. C. license - Vity OKM)*

26. Zmievi Vali
(northeast of
Pereyaslavl).
*(C. C. license -
Maxim Bielushkin)*

27. Qin Wall –
image right facing
north, wall in
characteristic Qin
position forward
of and below peak
(Inner Mongolia).
*(Photo by Andreas
C. Lehmann, Great
Wall Forum)*

28. Zhao Wall
(Inner Mongolia).
*(Photo by Andreas
C. Lehmann, Great
Wall Forum)*

29. Hexamilion Wall – Corinthian Isthmus. *(Photo by David Pettegrew, corinthianmatters. com)*

30. Anastasian Wall – showing ashlar construction. *(C. C. license – Wolfgang Kuhoff)*

31. Sadd-i-Iskandar or Wall of Gorgan, burnt brick, now largely robbed (east of Caspian Sea). *(Photo by Eberhard Sauer)*

32. Wall of Tammisha (south of Caspian Sea). *(Photo by Eberhard Sauer)*

33. Ghilghilchay Wall (west of Caspian Sea). *(Photo by Eberhard Sauer)*

34. Gates of Alexander (Dagestan) – in Sasanian walls of Derbent on western Caspian. *(C. C. license - www. derbent.ru)*

35. Bukhara oasis wall (west of Varakhsha which lay within oasis wall circuit). *(Google Maps)*

36. Han Great Wall (Dunhuang). *(Photo by Bryan Feldman, Great Wall Forum)*

37. Sui Great Wall of China, shows double wall. *(Photo by Kin Jim, Great Wall Forum)*

38. Jin Wall
(Inner Mongolia).
*(Photo by Andreas
C. Lehmann,
Great Wall
Forum)*

39. The Ming Great
Wall of China –
unrestored section
(Shuitoucun). *(Photo
by Bryan Feldman,
Great Wall Forum)*

40. Zasechnaya
Cherta (near
Penza). *(Photo by
Andrey Kolchugin)*

41. *Gului gorod* reconstruction – in contemporary use the sections were linked to form a continuous barrier. *(C. C. license – Лапоть)*

42. Battle of Molodi site - Tatars' view of the Russian position where the gului-gorod was assembled. *(Photo by Sergey Bieloshapko)*

43. Reconstructed Limes watchtower (between Bad Nauheim and Pfaffenwiesbach). *(C. C. license, 1.2 Tadam)*

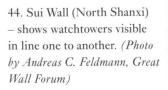

44. Sui Wall (North Shanxi) – shows watchtowers visible in line one to another. *(Photo by Andreas C. Feldmann, Great Wall Forum)*

45. Wall of Qi reconstruction. *(Photo by Bryan Feldman, Great Wall Forum)*

46. Csörszárok - reconstruction near Debrecen. *(Photo by Nagy)*

47. Zmievi Vali – pre-World War Two reinforcement to west of Kiev. *(Photo by Elena Filatova, theserpentswall.com)*

Chapter Eight

Byzantine and Sasanian Empires – Collaboration of Foes

T he Byzantine and Sasanian Empires are seen as mortal enemies. Indeed their destructive wars so weakened them that the Sasanians succumbed to Arabs who they had previously dominated; and the Byzantines lost to them vast tracts of their richest lands. Also, Constantinople nearly fell to the Arabs but for the intervention of the still pagan Bulgars. Yet, faced by the common threat from Eurasian nomads, there was a remarkable cooperation over linear barrier building against common challenges on the Sasanian northern and the Byzantine eastern borders.

1. Byzantine Empire

Justinian's wall building in the sixth century is set out admiringly in Procopius' book about the Emperor's constructions *de Aedificiis*. On reflection these walls appear quite distinctive, even odd, when looked at in the context of imperial defence. Firstly, they are largely sited on the location of earlier walls first built by the Greeks up to a millennium earlier. Secondly, unlike Roman linear barriers they are generally not located near frontiers. This section looks at Byzantine linear barrier building and asks, what was the strategic intention behind it?

Byzantine history begins in the fourth century AD, either with the foundation of Constantinople in 330, or the formal split of Eastern and Western Empires in 395. A defining moment, however, might have been the invasion of the Goths, driven by the Huns, in 375, and the defeat of the Emperor Valens by the Goths at Adrianople in 378. After that, the barbarians were no longer at the gate – they were through it. The Empires of east and west would, from now on, be subject to the great peregrinations of Goths, eastern and western, and Huns. Byzantine history was marked by a desperate attempt to control and direct – or simply avoid being overrun by the flow of peoples.

Great nomad and barbarian *chevauchées*, low level raiding and uncontrolled settlement wreaked havoc. In 395 the Huns attacked the Byzantine Empire's Middle Eastern provinces. In 396 Alaric's Vandals attacked Greece. In 441 the Huns razed Belgrade. Six years later a Hun attack was bought off before Constantinople. By then the Hun Empire had expanded to cover much of eastern Europe and western Asia, and the Byzantine Emperor Theodosius II (408–450) agreed to pay them an annual subsidy which he soon had to double. In 539 there was a major Hun attack on Greece and Thrace which even crossed the Dardanelles into Asia. In 558 the Kotrigur branch of the Huns invaded the Balkans and were finally defeated before Constantinople by Belisarius. Emperor Justin II (565–578) used subsidies to try to control the Avars but he provoked further raids by then withdrawing them.

In the first part of the seventh century the Byzantines and Sasanians fought a war that resulted in the final defeat of the latter in 627. In truth it exhausted the power of both. The Arab semi-nomads, enthused by Islam, now destroyed the Sasanian Empire and the Byzantines lost Syria and Egypt to the new warriors. The Byzantines held out for another eight centuries. It was an originally nomadic people, the Ottoman Turks, who finally extinguished the Byzantine Empire, completed with the siege of Constantinople in 1453.

The areas covered by the Byzantine Empire have largely been outlined in previous sections – particularly the chapter about the Greeks. Outside of Europe there were fertile areas in what is now Syria and Turkey. The problem was that the Sasanians controlled access to them, through and beside the Caucasus. The Sasanians originally took control of the central Darial Pass in the mid-third century. It was probably through this line that the Huns launched their great raid in 395 that took them to Antioch.

The Byzantine Empire effectively became a maritime empire. Most areas were linked by the Mediterranean and Black Seas, with Constantinople, the Byzantine capital, being situated between the two seas linked by the Bosphorus. Land access to Constantinople lay through the land corridor between the Black Sea and the Sea of Marmara. A powerful navy guaranteed free movement by sea, but this was of little value if the intention was to support distant land-based operations if it was difficult to secure safe landing points. In this situation peninsulas might be valuable, both because a living could be made off the land, and because, if walled-off, they could provide secure land points.

Byzantine linear barriers

Europe had already seen steppe nomads like the Scythians and Sarmatians but the Huns posed a completely new problem in terms of scale and ferocity. Throughout the Age of Great Migrations they were followed by a succession of raiding migrant nomads. Also, barbarian Germanic peoples like the Goths and the Gepids appeared on the eastern front while others passed through or went direct to the Western Roman Empire, or what remained of it. Slavs descended into the Balkans and what is now Russia and the Ukraine.

Economically, the Byzantines could not command the resources of the Roman Empire. Furthermore, in the Age of Migrations, the sheer scale of movement of armies and peoples meant that most static defences would simply be swept away; as it was, they were often circumvented. Building and manning linear barriers across whole frontiers might be too expensive; and the exercise probably seemed futile anyway if the barbarians were already through the gates.

How then should the settled powers respond to the grand nomad *chevauchées*? Often, invaded states gathered as much in the way of people, livestock and chattels as possible into a fortified point and looked for an opportune time to counter-attack. This meant fortifying the towns. In certain areas, however, it might be more cost effective and quicker to build or rebuild a linear barrier across a short distance which blocked access to a much larger area. Obvious areas are those that were already fortified by the Greeks – that is, locations like Thermopylae, the Corinthian Isthmus and the Thracian

8.1: Byzantine and Sasanian Walls

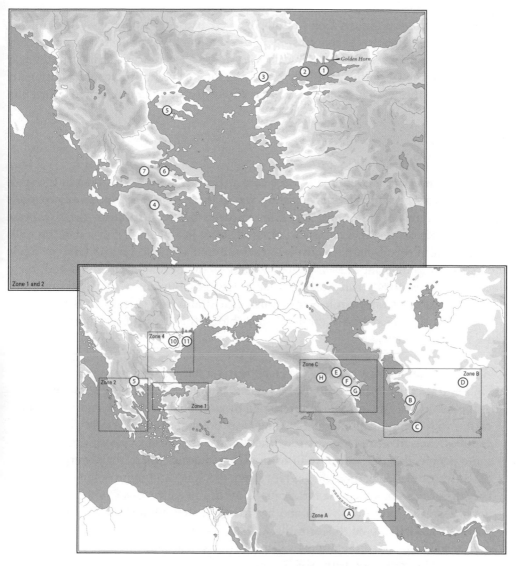

Byzantine Walls
Thrace (Zone 1)
1. Theodosian Wall
2. Anastasian Wall
3. Thracian Chersonesos Wall

Greece (Zone 2)
4. Hexamilion Wall
5. Pallene Pensinsula Wall
6. Thermopylae Pass Wall
7. Heraclean Pass Wall

Crimea (Zone 3) (see Map 5.3)
8. Kerch Peninsula Walls protecting Bosphoran state
9. Dory Wall protecting Crimea Goths stronghold

Dobrogea (uncertain) (Zone 4)
10. Valul Mare de Pământ
11. Valul de Piatra

Sasanian Walls
South Western Border region (Zone A)
A. Khandaq-i-Shapur

East and South Caspian Wall (Zone B)
B. Sadd-i-Iskandar
C. Tammisha Wall
D. Antiochus Wall, Merv

West Caspian Walls (Zone C)
E. Derbent Wall
F. Ghilghilchay Wall
G. Beshabarmak Wall

Also shows:
H. Darial Pass

Chersonesos. Also, although Constantinople itself had very fine walls, first built by Constantine and then by Theodosius, its hinterland could be protected as well with a linear barrier joining the Black Sea and the Sea of Marmara. Strategically placed linear barriers, as at the Corinthian and Thracian Chersonesos isthmuses, could additionally defend many cities with just one barrier, thereby obviating the need for individual city defences.

Pre-Justinian walls

Byzantine linear barrier building is associated with the Emperor Justinian in the sixth century; but as he largely rebuilt existing walls, there must already have been walls in place to rebuild. In the sixth and fifth centuries before Justininan, the Byzantine Empire was already using walls as part of its strategic defence mix. Several of the walls which Justinian rebuilt have already been encountered in the section on Greece. While the location was unchanged their strategic function did develop. When first built these linear barriers generally had worked as local defences, but under the Byzantines this often changed to a strategic role blocking movement into core parts of the Empire.

Procopius described how a great calamity befell the Byzantine Empire when the Huns attacked in 539:

> A mighty Hunnic army crossing the Danube River fell as a scourge upon all Europe …. For from the Ionian Gulf these barbarians plundered everything in order as far as the suburbs of Byzantium… they carried by storm the city of Cassandria … And taking with them the money and leading away one hundred and twenty thousand captives, they all retired homeward without encountering any opposition….. This same people also assailed the wall of the Chersonesus, where they overpowered those who were defending themselves from the wall, and approaching through the surf of the sea, scaled the fortifications on the so-called Black Gulf; thus they got within the long wall …. In another invasion they plundered Illyricum and Thessaly and attempted to storm the wall at Thermopylae; and since the guards on the walls defended them most valiantly, they sought out the ways around and unexpectedly found the path which leads up the mountain which rises there. In this way they destroyed almost all the Greeks except the Peloponnesians, and then withdrew.[1]

Apart from depicting the horrors inflicted by the Huns this passage described the failure of the walls of Thermopylae, the Pallene Peninsula, and the Thracian Chersonesus. But this means there had to be walls there in the first place for them to fail. There is an indication, however, that the walls at the Isthmus of Corinth worked, as almost all Greece was destroyed except for the Peloponnese. The wall built by Anastasius from the Black Sea to the Sea of Marmara was hard to defend – although that does not necessarily mean it failed: 'whenever the enemy descended on any portion of these long walls, they overpowered all the guards with no difficulty.'[2]

The key point here is not so much that the walls failed but that they were already there. Thus, it seems that from the fifth century the Byzantine Empire was already using walls across strategic passes and isthmuses, in order to defend itself, before the reign of Justinian.

Justinian's Walls

This section focuses on Justinian's response to the 539 Hun raid. The possible success of the Corinth Isthmus wall might have encouraged Justinian not to abandon walls as a strategy but instead to build them better. To the extent that Procopius' *de Aedificiis* can be relied on, the greatest period of Byzantine wall building took place under Justinian. The exercises in Byzantine long wall building under Justinian were in Thrace, Greece, and the Crimea. In the first, walls were built across the three chersoneses or isthmuses: those of Constantinople, Thrace, and Gallipoli. In Greece walls were rebuilt across the isthmuses at Corinth and on the Pallene Peninsula. Also, walls were built or rebuilt at the passes of Thermopylae and Heraclea. In the Crimea the Bosphoran State walls were rebuilt and the Mangup heights were given a linear barrier defending the most open of the approach routes.

Thrace (Zone 1)
Before looking at the two walls across Thrace – that is the Anastasian Wall and the Thracian Chersonesos Wall – the walls of Constantinople itself need to be touched upon.

Theodosian Walls – The Emperor Constantine (306–337) built the first imperial walls of Constantinople after he moved the Roman Empire's capital from Rome. By the beginning of the fifth century the city had extended beyond the Constantinian Walls and Theodosius II (408–450) built new walls which were completed in 413. The Theodosian Walls of Constantinople were not full circuit walls. Other walls surrounded the city waterfronts and the Theodosian Walls cut off a small peninsula between the Sea of Marmara and the waters of the Golden Horn. Also, while the Theodosian Walls may have delineated the built-up area of Constantinople at the time of their construction, the city contracted in size, thus leaving the walls enclosing a substantial area that was not built over. Therefore, for much of their history, the Theodosian Walls had some of the characteristics of a small isthmian wall. The walls appear to have been extremely successful for they were repeatedly assailed but were not stormed until 1453 in the gunpowder age.

Anastasian Walls – Walls across the land corridor between the Black Sea and the Sea of Marmara could have had a dual purpose of keeping threats at a safe distance from Constantinople and rich land around it, while also blocking a route into Anatolia across the Bosphoros. (The Gauls in 279 BC travelled to Asia from Europe by this route – thereby becoming the Galatians and meriting the epistle from St Paul.)
  Anastasius (491–518) was credited with the construction of a wall here about which Evagrius Scholasticus made some interesting comments. 'By the same emperor was raised a vast and memorable work called the Long Wall, in a favourable situation in Thrace, distant from Constantinople two hundred and eighty stadia (or over fifty kilometres). It reaches from one sea to the other, like a strait,

to the extent of four hundred and twenty stadia; making the city an island, in a manner, instead of a peninsula, and affording a very safe transit... from the Pontus to the Euxine Sea. It is a check upon the inroads of the Barbarians from the Euxine, ... and from beyond the Caucasus, as well as of those who have made irruptions from Europe.'[3] Thus, firstly, the wall made Constantinople 'almost an island instead of a peninsula'. Secondly, Evagrius makes clear it is intended to block barbarians from regions 'beyond the Caucasus'. Thirdly, it protected a transit route.

Procopius described how rich Romans built outside the walls of Constantinople, thereby creating a form of man-made valued land. 'The people there build and adorn their suburbs, not only to meet the actual needs of life, but they display an insolent and boundless luxury..... Thus, when it comes about that any of the enemy overrun the land of the Romans suddenly, the damage caused there is much greater than in other places .... The Emperor Anastasius had determined to put a stop to this and so built long walls at a distance of not less than forty miles from Byzantium, uniting the two shores of the sea on a line where they are separated by about a two-days' journey.'[4]

Procopius' treatise *de Aedificiis* outlined the building work of Justinian which, when it came to walls, were usually, a great improvement on the ineffectual work which went before – this time by Anastasius – which was itself the cause of great calamities. 'For neither was it possible to make safe a structure of such great length nor could it be guarded rigorously. And whenever the enemy descended on any portion of these long walls, they both overpowered all the guards with no difficulty.' According to Procopius, however, Justinian was determined to make it work by ensuring that each tower was secure.[5]

Further reconstruction work probably took place after an earthquake and a Bulgar raid in the late 550s. The Long Walls continued to be maintained until Heraclius' reign and are mentioned in descriptions of the Avar siege of 626. The Anastasian wall is generally seen as not very successful, yet it appears to have been in use for a couple of centuries. By the seventh century nothing further is heard that unambiguously relates to the subject of Byzantine linear defences generally, that is except for the Theodosian Walls which proved themselves repeatedly as an efficient final line of defence.

Thracian Chersonesos Wall – In 539 the Huns broke through the earlier walls across the Thracian Chersonesos and some even raided across the Dardanelles. Procopius was typically critical about the walls on the Thracian Chersonesos: 'At this isthmus the men of former times built a cross-wall of a very casual and indifferent sort which could be captured with the help of a ladder .... And facing the sea at either side of the isthmus they constructed wretched little bastions.'[6] Justinian, of course, built something much better for he, 'erected another wall, upon the same ground, very broad and rising to a great height. Above the battlements a set-back vaulted structure in the manner of a colonnaded stoa makes a roof to shelter those who defend the circuit-wall. And other breastworks resting upon the vaulted structure double the fighting for those who lay siege to the wall. Furthermore, at either end of the wall, at the very edge of the sea, he made bastions (*proboloi*) extending far out into the water.'[7] These walls worked in 559 against raids by the Kotrigur Huns.

In 1996 the foundations of the Thracian Chersonesos *proboloi* were found in the Sea of Marmara.[8] Their location in the Sea indicates that the wall stood to the east of the Dardanelles, thereby making crossing the waterway to Anatolia more difficult as it necessitated traversing the Sea and not the narrower Dardanelles. The Thracian Chersonesos and the Anastasian Walls together had the strategic function of blocking the land corridor between the Black Sea and the Mediterranean from Europe to Asia.

Greece (Zone 2)

Justinian reconstructed the defences of Greece. He rebuilt the walls of the Pallene Peninsula – making a defensible bulwark to the region approaching Greece. He strengthened the passes at Thermopylae and inland at nearby Heraclea. He also restored the walls across the Peloponnese. All these sites were previously the location of earlier Greek walls. The difference was that Justinian reconstructed them as part of an overall plan of defence after the Hun raids.

Pallene Peninsula Wall – Justinian restored the walls of the small Pallene Peninsula after the Huns' attack. 'The city of Pallene, which stands as a bulwark of the whole region, and the cross-wall at the entrance of the peninsula, became manifestly impregnable and able to defy any who should wish to attack them'.[9] The reason for the importance of Pallene – what Procopius called a bulwark to the whole region – was that there was more fertile land behind the peninsula neck than the other two fingers of the Chalcidike; and the Pallene also had the easiest landing points. Therefore, given early resupply by sea and defence across its neck, the Pallene Peninsula could serve as a base for military operations in Thrace (for the same reasons the Athenians had demanded the destruction of the south walls of Potidaea, an act which led to the Peloponnesian War).

Thermopylae Walls – Procopius describes extensive works by Justinian at Thermopylae which was the gateway to Greece. 'For he made provision for all of them (the sea coast and many inland passages) and especially for the by-paths up the mountains at Thermopylae. First of all he raised the walls there to a very great height.'[10] Procopius makes clear that Justinian understood well that the Achilles' Heel of Thermopylae was the mountain paths. 'Furthermore, he carefully walled off many paths up the mountains which previously had been both unguarded and unwalled.'[11] Justinian built walls with proper foundations and blocked the mountain passes. He also provided reservoirs and granaries to sustain a permanent garrison. In 559 the walls at Thermopylae stopped the Kotrigur Huns.

Heraclean Wall – Justinian also fortified the inland pass about seven kilometres west of Thermopylae at Heraclea (Trachis). 'As one descends from Illyricum into Greece, one is confronted by two mountains which rise very close together for a long distance, forming between them a narrow pass …. A small stream comes down between them… At that point it was possible for the barbarians with no difficulty to effect an entrance both against Thermopylae and into that part of Greece…. Justinian … closed the pass with a very strong cross-wall which he made fast to each of the two mountains, thus blocking the entrance for the barbarians, and the stream when it is in flood is now forced to form a pond inside the wall and then to flow over it and go on wherever it chances.'[12] This sounds a rather peculiar wall with the characteristics of a dam.

Hexamilion Walls – Corinth Isthmus – The Hexamilion Walls across the Corinth Isthmus were first built by Theodosius (408–450) to deal with Germanic invasions, possibly as a response to Alaric's raid on Greece in 396 or the Visigoth sack of Rome in 410. The argument that Procopius provided was hardly original but it was clearly expressed; that building a wall across the short Corinthian Isthmus obviated the need individually to secure the defences of all the cities of the Peloponnesus. 'When the Emperor Justinian … learned that all the cities of the

Peloponnesus were unwalled, he reasoned that obviously a long time would be consumed if he attended to them one by one, and so he walled the whole Isthmus securely, because much of the old wall had already fallen down.... In this manner he made all the towns in the Peloponnesus inaccessible to the enemy, even if somehow they should force the defences at Thermopylae.'[13]

There are extensive remains of the Byzantine barrier which was an ashlar wall with a rubble core which had over 150 towers with spacings of about forty metres. There was a great fortress on its east end. Much of ancient Corinth and surrounding sanctuaries were robbed for its construction. After the seventh century the wall was effectively dormant, but in the early fifteenth century it was repaired by Manuel II in 1415 and by Constantine Palaiologos in 1444 to face the Ottomans. Using cannon the Ottomans took the wall in 1423, 1431, 1446 and 1452. They finally occupied the Peloponnese in 1460.

Crimea (Zone 3)

Justinian re-established Imperial control over the Crimea and constructed or reconstructed walls there.

Bosphoran State Walls – Procopius says that Justinian 'strengthened the defences of the Bosphorus particularly, which in ancient times had been a barbarous city lying under the power of the Huns, but which he himself had brought under Roman sway.'[14] The linear barriers defending the Bosphoran Kingdom go back at least to the time of Asander (44–7 BC) who constructed the Uzunlar wall, according to Strabo.

Dory Wall – Justinian provided the loyal Goths of Dory with long walls that shut off the approaches to the region. 'The land of Dory itself lies on high ground, yet it is neither rough nor hard, but good soil and productive of the best crops. However, the Emperor built no city or fortress in any part of this land, since the men of the country would not suffer themselves to be confined in any fortified places but always lived most happily in an open plain. But wherever the region seemed easily accessible to assailants, he shut off these approaches with long walls and thereby freed the Goths from fear of invasion.'[15] Thus, the walls blocked passages used to access the Goth's valued land.

Later Byzantine wall construction – Budjak and Dobrogea (Zone 4)

After Justinian it is not clear that walls, other than those of Constantinople itself, played a major part in the strategic defence of the Empire. This is maybe because the full force of the Hunnic assault had been broken – in part possibly because of the successful use of linear barriers against the Huns rendering walls subsequently superfluous. After the plagues and wars of the sixth and seventh centuries and the losses of major provinces to the Arabs there may not have been the resources for major wall building; yet the Theodosian Walls of Constantinople proved themselves repeatedly as the last line of defence.

There were, however, two regions where there might have been continuous or later use of wall building. The first is the Valul lui Traian de Jos in the Budjak and the second is the Valurile lui Traian in the Dobrogea. The Byzantines may have continued to occupy the trans-Danubian Budjak region until the seventh century; if so, they would have required some form of system for its defence. Then, after abandoning the Budjak and the northern Dobrogea in the seventh and eighth centuries, the Byzantines would have needed to re-establish a more southerly frontier line. It might be conjectured that the Valul lui Traian de Jos, north of the Danube and the Valurile lui Traian, south of the same river, in the Carasu Valley that crosses the Dobrogea, might have formed respectively the earlier and later lines of defence.

Valul lui Traian de Jos – The Danube, where it flows east to its Delta, was generally not the border of the states to its south. Rather the frontier lay along the northern border of the modern Budjak region. The Romans and then the Byzantines remained in the Budjak after the abandonment of Dacia. Constantine VII Porphyrogenitos in the tenth century described deserted Roman cities. 'On this side of the Dniester River, towards the part that faces Bulgaria, at the crossings of this same river, are deserted cities....Among these buildings of the ancient cities are found some distinctive traces of churches, and crosses hewn out of porous stone, whence some preserve a tradition that once upon a time Romans had settlements there.'[16] This has been seen as evidence of a late Roman presence, which was presumably intended to control the flow of nomads towards the eastern Empire.

Also: 'Late antique sources confirm the existence of Roman domination in the region between Dniester and the Lower Seret, having a specific military function, that is to block the passage of the Turanic (nomadic) peoples towards the Wallachian Plain and Scythia Minor (the Dobrogea) that assured the New Rome's security. This domination was illustrated by the walls, by the cities on both banks of the Lower Danube and in the Northern Pontic Steppe... . The main chronological dates of this Roman 'island' are: Trajan's rule which established its commencement and, six centuries later, the arrival of the Asparuch's Protobulgarians to 680, which ended Imperial Roman domination in the region and the abandonment of the Roman cities.'[17]

The Valul lui Traian de Jos might have marked the northern border of the Byzantine Empire until the late seventh century. (It may then have assumed a new role as a northern frontier of Greater Bulgaria.)

In the second half of the seventh century, the Bulgars fled the Khazars and appeared in the Budjak region. In 681 Khan Asparuch defeated the Byzantines and established the Bulgars in the regions around the lower Danube. A treaty with the Byzantines allowed for the establishment of the first Greater Bulgaria. After the Byzantines withdrew from the Budjak the question became, where should the new more southerly border line lie in the Dobrogea region?

At the beginning of the eighth century the Byzantines lost control of much of Thrace and of the Dobrogea to the Bulgars. Although Thrace was permanently lost – until the reconquests of Basil II in the eleventh century – the Byzantines, the Bulgars, and the Kievan Rus vied for control of the Dobrogea with invasions also by the Magyars and the Pechenegs. It is in this complex period that the date and purpose of the Dobrogea Valurile lui Traian might be sought.

It is possible that in the eighth and ninth century that the Dobrogea was split between the Byzantines and the Bulgars although where the frontier lay is not clear. In the late ninth century Magyars occupied the northern area. In the tenth century the Byzantines began again to exert authority, directly or indirectly over the Dobrogea.

Valurile lui Traian (Dobrogea) – Although there are other candidates the Byzantines do seem the most probable builders of the two north-facing Valurile lui Traian walls, because the scale of these barriers suggests that no other power would have had the expertise to contruct them. The Valurile might have been the new frontier of the Byzantine Empire after withdrawal from the Budjak.

But here there are problems. There is no mention of linear barriers in the *de Administrando Imperio* of Constantine VII Porphyrogenitus (913–959) although there is much detailed discussion of Byzantium's relationship with surrounding peoples. (Admittedly, Constantine could have discussed the Bulgar Erkesia but this might have been a source of embarrassment as it was a Bulgar work and provided, along its length, the location at Derbelt where Byzantium paid the Bulgar's tribute). But if the Dobrogea walls had been Byzantine it is hard to believe the fastidious Constantine would not have mentioned them. That he did not – and that he instead described other strategies for dealing with the Pechenegs and other nomads – seems circumstantial evidence that the Dobrogea Valurile lui Traian had not been built by the Byzantines before 959. Or it may possibly mean that during his reign they had fallen into disuse. (Coins of Constantine VII Porphyrogenitus (913–959) and Romanus II (959–963) have been found in the forts of the Valul de Piatra but their deposition could postdate his death.)

Possible dates for construction might be during the reigns of Nicephoras II Phokas (963–969) and John I Tzimiskes (969–976). In 967 Nicephoras had sought Bulgar cooperation to stop the Magyars from raiding across the Danube. When Nicephoras was rebuffed, he invited Sviatoslav I of Kiev to attack the Bulgars. Nicephoras may have built one of the north-facing linear barriers to stabilise the frontier against whichever peoples the Kievans drove south. Another motivation may have been to stop the Kievans themselves becoming too ambitious and invading Byzantine occupied territory. The Kievans did not go home but resolved to establish a new capital in the Dobrogea. Thereupon, the Byzantines under John I Tzimiskes (969–976) made common cause with the Bulgars. In 971 John recovered the Dobrogea. It is possible that one of the north-facing walls served as a start line for the advance. (Recall that in modern Scotland, 'The Antonine Wall was an offensive, aggressive declaration of intent; it was not simply a means of securing a frontier, but a springboard for advance'.[18]) John Skylitzes wrote that: 'Once the Russians had sailed away, the emperor (John I Tzimiskes) turned his attention to the fortresses and cities along the banks of the river (Danube) and then he returned to Roman territory.'[19] But if the whole of Dobrogea was recovered then it would seem somewhat pointless to have built a linear barrier across the Carasu Valley.

Between 986 and 1000 the Dobrogea, or possibly only the southern part, was part of Khan Samuil's Bulgar Empire. If the Byzantines had held onto the northern part they might possibly have built or rebuilt the south-facing Valul Mic de Pământ. In 1000, during the reign of Basil II, the entire Dobrogea was recovered. Later the nomadic Pechenegs entered the region and there were great raids in 1036 and 1048. The Valul de Piatra could also be dated to this period. After 1064 Turkic Uzes pushed into the Dobrogea.

Another possibility is that the various linear barriers might have been designed for local defence of a transport route, rather than for frontier defence. Examination of the valley's location on the map reveals that it must always have had an important transport function as a way of getting from the Black Sea to the Danube while avoiding the Danube Delta. This would be especially true of the Roman and Byzantine Empires – for control of the valley would have provided a shortcut to the Danube. After the Budjak was lost to the Bulgarians and later to the Pechenegs and other nomads, the Danube Delta area would have been dangerous territory. Linear barriers have been used to protect routes of communications; examples include the portage roads along the Nile by the cataracts and the Greek long walls. The Anastasian Wall protected the land passage from the Black Sea to the Sea of Marmara. It might be speculated that the Byzantines operated a protected route to the Danube in some parts of this period. The forts on the two north-facing barriers might have provided not just a location for garrison troops and patrols but also refuges for travellers and goods during nomad attacks, as well as bases for counter attacks.

Analysis – Byzantine walls

Linear barriers may have formed a key part of the Byzantine strategy for dealing with the nomad threat in periods of intense pressure, particularly during the mid-sixth and later tenth centuries. Unlike the Roman Empire, most early Byzantine linear barriers lay well inside the frontier. There were three key land corridors into the Byzantine Empire: that of Thermopylae which controlled access to Greece; south-western Thrace which controlled access to Constantinople and on to Anatolia; and the Darial Pass in the Caucasus which controlled access to Hither Asia (see next section on the Sasanians). The Byzantines built walls to control the first two and, as will be seen, paid the Sasanians to control the third. Some barriers also had dual roles: the Thracian Chersonesos Wall and the Anastasian Wall, for instance, not only protected their own peninsula hinterland, they also controlled access to and across the Hellespont and the Bosphorus and on to Anatolia.

Byzantine linear barriers also defended interior regions, well populated with cities, where one linear barrier could do the work of many city walls. Examples include the Peloponnese, the Thracian Chersonesos, and the Pallene Peninsula, which were all the sites of pre-Roman Empire Greek walls. Later in the tenth and eleventh centuries, again facing a nomad threat, the Byzantines probably built linear barriers along the Carasu Valley, possibly as part of the military action to recover control of the Dobrogea, or to recover control of and defend a transport routeway along the valley itself.

The Byzantines systematically built walls across the same isthmuses as the earlier Greeks. The Greek and the Byzantine walls differed in that the former generally had a local tactical purpose, whereas the latter generally had a wider strategic role. The phases of linear construction and repair account, however, only for quite limited parts of Byzantine history. For the most part the Byzantines appear to have relied upon the Theodosian Walls of Constantinople to keep alive its beating heart, while the arteries and veins of the Empire came from control of maritime routes which it kept open by its fleets – where its monopoly over the projectile incendiary Greek fire gave it a unique competitive advantage.

The Byzantines usually relied on a range of strategies other than linear barrier building to keep away the nomads. They simply paid subsidies to the Huns, Avars,

Bulgars or Pechenegs to go away. Or they employed the dark arts of setting nomad against nomad. For example, in the 550s Justinian bribed the Utigur Huns from the Caspian steppe to attack the Kotrigur Huns' homeland north of the Danube, while the Kotrigur fighting men were in Thrace and Greece.

Eventually, the Byzantine Empire fell to a nomadic people, the Ottoman Turks, who had mastered the distinctly non-nomadic skills of fortress building (consider the Rumeli castle by the Bosphorus), infantry fighting (the Janissaries), and managing vast artillery trains (which breached the Theodosian walls).

Even if the main periods of construction are quite short, the wall building legacy of the Byzantines is nevertheless substantial. The Hexamilion Wall is the largest archaeological structure in Greece and the Valul de Piatra, if indeed it is Byzantine, is the largest such structure in the Balkans. Linear barriers appear to have played a key part in defending the Empire against the Huns in the mid-sixth century, and in the Dobrogea they possibly did so again against the Bulgars and possibly other invaders in the mid-tenth century.

2. The Sasanian Empire

The Sasanian Empire centred on the area of, but was much larger than, modern Iran. It lasted from AD 224 to 651 yet it is familiar largely as a foil for the Romans and Byzantines. While the Sasanians are generally identified with great battles in the clash of the empires and with a magnificent heavy cavalry there is less consideration of their use of more mundane linear barriers. Yet as the subject was researched an intriguing picture emerged. The Sasanians can perhaps lay claim to being one of the greatest of all builders of walls after the Chinese. Also, if the evidence is put together, it appears that the Sasanians built linear barriers on three open frontiers. Indeed, their combined use of artificial and natural barriers produced a system of near all-round linear defence.

The Sasasian Empire was founded by Ardashir I in 224 who replaced the last Parthian king, Artabanus IV. The Sasasians called themselves, in Middle Persian, the Iranshahr, or the Aryan Empire, and the ruler was the Shahranshahr. At its greatest extent, under Shapur II, the Sasanian Empire covered an area greater than modern Iran, one that included Iraq, Syria, the Caucasus, parts of Central Asia, Turkey, the Arabian Peninsula and Pakistan.

The core of the Empire was the high Persian Plateau. To the north, the Elburz Mountains run close to the Caspian Sea, leaving a narrow land passage along the shore line. The Elburz Mountains continue into the Taurus Mountains of Anatolia. To the north-east there is the Gorgan Plain, named after the river flowing across it which provides open ground until the Kopet Dag Mountains. In the north-west the Caucasus Mountains block the ground between the Caspian and the Black Seas with land passages on both shore lines, and a key gap, the Darial Pass, roughly in the centre. To the south-east the Zagros Mountains separate the Persian plateau from Mesopotamia and the site of its capital Ctesiphon on the east bank of the Tigris. This is the familiar irrigated land of the Tigris and Euphrates.

The northern region of the Sasanian Empire had three land corridors of huge importance, not just to it but also for the Roman and Byzantine Empires. First, there is a broad gap in the Gorgan Plain, crossed by the river of that name, between the south-eastern shore of the Caspian and the Kopet Dag Mountains. Second, the route down the west of the Caspian narrows sharply, in the region of the Caucasus Mountains, reaching its most constricted point at the city of Derbent. Here the mountains come to within nearly a kilometre of the Sea. Third, the Darial Pass through the centre of the Caucasus was the main route from the Eurasian Steppe to Hither Asia. Up until 251 this pass was under Roman control but it was then taken over by the Sasanians.

The Sasanians placed a premium on good agricultural practice and expanded the area cultivated by any Persia-centred Empire to its greatest ever extent. They built many dams and canals and such land, dependent on irrigation, was both valuable and vulnerable. Irrigation was not just practised in Mesopotamia but also on the loess Plain of Gorgan. (As seen with China, where there is loess, old walls might now be sought.) The Sasanian Empire extended into the south-western quarter of Central Asia. It included the great oasis city of Merv where the Hellenistic ruler Antiochus had already built an oasis wall.

Unlike other Empires around the Eurasian Steppe, the Sasanian Empire faced a threat from both the north and the south due to its position between the Eurasian Steppe and the Arabian and North African semi-arid belt. Also, its most valuable and vulnerable irrigated land was not in the core central Iranian plateau area but in the south-west and north-east, thus outside the protection of the plateau's ring of mountains.

In the north, to the east of the Caspian Sea, the Sasanians faced the Hephthalites, a people of uncertain origin but who were almost certainly not Huns, notwithstanding Procopius' identification of them as the White Huns. In 420 they invaded Persia and were driven out in 427; they temporarily defeated Persia again in 454 and 475. In 485 the Hephthalites killed the Sasanian Shah Peroz I and Sasanian Persia became a tributary state until between 503 and 513, when the White Huns were driven out of Persia by Peroz's son Kavad. In 565 the Sasanians and the Göktürks destroyed the Hephthalite Empire.

To the west of the Caspian, the main enemy was initially the Savirs, who managed to push through the West Caspian corridor in 516 until the Avars defeated them at the end of the sixth century. The Turkic Khazars then became the dominant power in the region.

In the south, marauding Arabs were defeated by Shapur II (337–358) who strung the defeated enemy soldiers together with rope through their pierced shoulders – hence his title, the Lord of the Shoulders. He recognised the Lakhmid kings of Hīra and, between the fourth and seventh centuries, Hīra was a Sasanian vassal kingdom. Meanwhile forces under the command of the settled Lakhmid Arabs helped the Sasanians to control the nomadic Arabs from the Arabian Desert. The Sasanians defeated the Byzantines at the Battle of Callinicum in 531 with Hīra's assistance. In 602, Khosrow II deposed Nu'man III of Hīra and annexed his kingdom, thereby eliminating a buffer zone. Later in the century Arabs, enthused by Islam, conquered the Sasanian Empire from the south.

Linear barriers found

Sasanian linear barriers fall into quite a neat chronological and regional pattern. The first barriers were built in the third century in Mesopotamia, those along the east and south coast of the Caspian in the fifth century, and those by the Caspian's west coast in the fifth and sixth centuries. The Central Asian barriers will be investigated last. The concept of Zones can be used to analyse these areas.

South-west – Mesopotamia (Zone A)

There is extensive literary evidence for a system of linear barriers using water to the south of the Euphrates to stop Arab nomad incursions in post-Islamic conquest texts.

> **Khandaq-i-Shapur** – As seen in the chapter on Mesopotamia, Shapur II (309–379) built a moat and fortification system to the west of the Euphrates to stop Bedouin Arabs from raiding. Lakhmid Arabs were settled on the border and they guarded it in return for tax exemptions. For example, Yāqūt said: 'The moat of Shapur is in the plain of Kufa. Shapur dug it between himself and the Arabs for fear of their depredations.'[20] Yāqūt said Anushirvan (531–79) ordered the repair and expansion of the system following Arab attacks. 'He ordered a moat dug from Hit and passing through the edge of the desert to Kāzime and beyond Basra reaching to the sea. He built on it towers and pavilions and he joined it together with fortified points. The reason for that was to hinder the people of the desert from the Sawād.'[21] This is a clear description of an aquatic linear barrier fortified by strong points.

North-east – Gorgan Plain (Zone B)

The Gorgan Plain lies on the south-east corner of the Caspian Sea. There are two land corridors giving access to the Plain which are the sites of walls.

> **Sadd-i-Iskandar** – There is a wall that runs about 200 kilometres from north of the south-east corner of the Caspian Sea to the Kopet Dag Mountains across the Gorgan Plain. It has several names: the prosaic Wall of Gorgan, after the Gorgan Plain; the Sadd-i-Iskandar, or Wall of Alexander; and the Wall of the Red Snake (Qezel Allan in Turkman), where the red reflects the colour of the fired brick from which it is made. If a geological map is searched for loess deposits in Asia there is a clue why such a complicated system might be built in such a 'hot' location. To make the region even more potentially attractive the Gorgan River provided a source of water for irrigation. All this was placed across a land corridor where nomadic peoples might be expected to harass and invade the territory of the Sasanians. The objective of any linear barrier might principally be to defend the region rather than any strategic defence of the Empire in its entirety. 'The line of the Sadd-i-Iskandar follows the approximate divide of between the densely settled landscape to the south from the agriculturally marginal and sparsely settled lands to the north.'[22] It is only comparatively recently that the Wall has been thoroughly examined. Most of its brickwork has been robbed.
>
> This was, however, a proper wall, broad enough for a walkway. There were at least thirty-six forts, implying the need for a very substantial garrison. The structure of the wall was made more complex and effective by a ditch that ran to the north of the wall. It was fed by three canals

running from the river to the wall and then through it to the ditch. The ditch is up to thirty metres wide. A canal that was up to five metres deep conducted water along most of the wall.

Put into perspective, this is the longest complex wall outside China. Altogether it was truly massive as a piece of military and agricultural engineering, greater than anything beyond the borders of China, and in fact not really matched even there until the Ming Great Wall was built. It is far longer than Hadrian's Wall. Only the final stone-walled version of the Raetian Limes is comparable in length; but that structure was much simpler and was comparatively short lived.

Wall of Tammisha – There is a shorter wall running south at the narrowest point between the Caspian Sea and the foothills of the Elburz Mountains to the west of the south-west corner of the Caspian Sea. It is approximately eleven kilometres long with a height of 1 to 3 metres and a width of 2 to 2.50 metres. The barrier begins near the ruined city of Tammisha at the foot of the mountains. The wall faces west and it is difficult to see what strategic function it could have had in the greater scheme of Sasanian defence. It is, however, well placed to defend the western approaches to the loess Gorgan Plain. Yāqūt commented: 'At this place there is a great portal, and it is not possible for any of the people of Tabaristan to depart from there to Jurjan except through that portal, because it extends from the mountains to the sea. (It is made) of baked brick and gypsum. It was Kisra Anusirvan (Xusro 531–579) who made it as an obstacle against the Turks and their raids into Tabaristan.'[23] Thus, the main purpose of the wall might have been local defence, not that of the greater Empire. (Tabaristan was the region that ran along the south coast of the Caspian Sea.) And the Arab historian Tabari said: 'And Sarkhastan (re-)built a wall from Tamis to the sea, a distance of three miles. And (this was the wall that) the Kisras had built between (Tabaristan) and the Turks, because the Turks were plundering the people of Tabaristan in their time. And Sarkastan settled with his forces in Tamis and around it (he had) a vast trench built together with towers for the garrison, and he had a strong gate built for it, and he put it in care of dependable men.'[24]

It seems likely that the Wall of Tammisha and the Sadd-i-Iskandar were intended as much as part of a regional defence system – for particularly valued land which happened to lay in a very border-sensitive area – rather than being designed as a strategic defence system for the Sasanian heartlands on the high Persian plateau.

North-west – Caspian Caucasus Gap (Zone C)
The gap between the Caspian Sea and the Caucacus Mountains is perhaps the most dramatic land corridor linking the Eurasian Steppe to the Hither East. During the fourth century the Sasanians extended their control over the area. There are two very obvious locations for linear barriers where the Caucacus Mountains come within a few kilometres of the Caspian Sea.

The southern narrow passage is about seventy-five kilometres long and just over ten kilometres wide, starting just north of the Aspheron Peninsula. At its northern end is the Ghilghilchay Wall which runs close to the river of that name; it then extends into the mountains. About twenty-five kilometres south is the Beshbarmak Wall which extends only across the coastal plain. To the north of the Ghilghilchay Wall, the Caucasus recedes so there is a coastal plain about forty kilometres broad.

The Caucasus Mountains briefly come down close to the Caspian again about a hundred kilometres to the north of the Ghilghilchay River at the city of Derbent (literally meaning 'narrow way') and this is the site of the Derbent Wall. The location of the Derbent Wall had the advantage of making secure the valuable plain between it and the Ghilghilchay Wall.

Beshbarmak Wall – This wall is the furthest to the south. It blocks the coastal route to the Aspheron Peninsula to the east of the Beshbarmak Mountain. It is nearly twelve kilometres long and consists of two parallel mud brick walls situated about 200 metres apart. The Beshbarmak Wall may date from the reign of Yazdegard (437–457).

Ghilghilchay Wall – This wall ascends from the sea at the mouth of the river Ghilghil. About thirty kilometres along its path it reaches to to a high point in the foothills of the Caucasus, at Chirag Gala, or the 'lamp castle' sited below Mount Babadag Mountain (3,629 metres in height). The first twenty kilometres of the wall is made of mud brick and the last ten kilometres' distance is made of stone. The length is about sixty kilometres with four sections. There are 140 towers spread across its length, and some of these comprise substantial fortresses. The name means Ghilghil River Wall. It was known to the Arabs as Sur-at-Tin or Clay Wall. It is also know as the Shirvan or Shabran Wall (modern Siyäzän) after the city where many caravan routes joined. It may have been built in response to perceived threats from a nomadic confederation led by the nomadic Savirs who were a Turkic or Hunnic people. In 516 they broke through the Derbent passage into Hither Asia. Their power was broken by the Avars at the end of the sixth century. The Ghilghilchay wall has been dated to 508 – in which case it was not successful against later attack by the Savirs.

Derbent Wall – At Derbent the Caucacus Mountains come to within eleven kilometres of the Caspian Sea, which makes this a highly strategic location and the position of the greatest of the West Caspian Walls. The wall itself is properly called the Dagbary – and Derbent is the coastal city and fortress. Descriptions of the Derbent Walls usually focus on the well-preserved and extensive wall of the fortress city and not the less well-preserved long walls that extend east to the Caucasus. The Derbent barrier has three parts: the city of Derbent is built between two parallel walls; these are connected to a great fortress, Karyn Gala, at the foot of the Caucasus Mountains; and then a single stone wall armed with forty fortlets extends thirty-four kilometres into the Caucasus. The Derbent fortifications include a great Sasanian portal called the Gates of Alexander. The historian Yāqūt attributed these walls to the Persian shah, Anushirvan, who reigned 531–79. They were built in the fifth and sixth centuries with financial contributions from the Romans.

Central Asia (Zone D)

The Sasanian Empire extended to the oasis city of Merv which has already been mentioned as Antiochus' *Margiana*.

Merv Oasis Wall – The wall built by Antiochus surrounded Merv and is now called the Giliakin-Chilburj Wall. Confusingly, the Sasanians probably built what is called the Antiochus Wall which was not a full circuit but an inverted 'V' shape; it covered the approaches from the north. (Presumably as Sasanian authority ran to Merv itself a wall facing to the south was not considered necessary.)

Other possibly Sasanian walls

The subject of Sasanian walls has not been systematically studied and there are indications that it may be a much larger subject than generally perceived.

Bazi-Deraz to Qaraviz Wall – Iranian archeologists have recently discovered a wall built by the Sasanian King of Kings, Khosrow II, Parviz (590–628) linking his palace in Qasr-e Shirin (in Kermanshah province) to the west.[25] The wall begins at Bazi-Deraz Mountain in Iran and continues to Qaraviz Mountain in Iraq. Its exact length has not yet been determined. About 40 kilometres of the wall are located within modern Iranian territory. Currently its height is between one metre and 80 cm high, while its width varies between 1.6 and 4.1 metres. Part of the wall in modern Iranian territory has been built of stone slates.

Umm Raus to Samarra Walls – In the earlier section on Mesopotamia, three walls were discussed which lay north of the Tigris and Euphrates convergence point where the alluvial plain peters out and the land becomes hillier. These were the Wall at Umm Raus which extends east from the Euphrates, the El-Mutabbaq which runs west of the Tigris from Samarra, and the Sadd Nimrud in between the other two. The dating of these walls is very uncertain and there has been speculation that they might be Sasanian.[26] Equally, however, they appear never to be discussed in the context of Sasanian walls themselves.

Analysis – Sasanian walls

There is no great originality here in claiming that nomads were the main reason for the construction of Sasanian linear barriers. For example, quoting three different authorities: 'These walls were probably erected in four frontier areas to stop nomadic advances into their territory'[27]; 'The Sasanians built their long walls to keep out the nomads who threatened the irrigated agricultural plots of land'[28]; and 'Sasanian Iran built up three great frontier systems ... whose purpose was to avert the invasions of the nomadic peoples'.[29]

There are also obvious locations to look for linear barriers. 'The narrow strip of land between the Caucasus Mountains and the Caspian Sea at Derbent almost assured the building of a wall there from ancient times.... Nomadic tribes from the north many times moved through this area to the south, so one might expect a defensive bastion here from early times.'[30] On the Gorgan Plain there is the same combination of river, loess soil, irrigation and nomads that produced walls in the region of the Yellow River.

Generally, the linear barriers, when maintained, appear to have been successful. 'The Limes Sasanicus successfully defended the most developed agriculture of the ancient world in the Caucasus, the Gorgan valley, the Merv oasis, and Mesopotamia for several centuries. Both the Wall and the Gate of Alexander the Great (i.e. the Sadd-i-Iskandar and the Dar-I Alān) fulfilled their historical functions.'[31]

Books on the Sasanian military focus lovingly on the heavy, fully armoured, cavalry cataphracts and the great wars with Rome. But linear barriers were clearly essential parts of the defence system on all frontiers; except, perhaps, the one that has been most written about, namely the frontier facing the Roman Empire. These walls are generally considered in the context of the nomad threat but did these nomads threaten the Empire as a whole – that is, did they pose a systemic rather than merely a local threat? It seems perhaps more likely they were usually a local threat to irrigation systems, at least in the case of the north–east and south–west. But defeats here did not threaten the Empire. To do that it was necessary to break into the high Iranian plateau as the last redoubt. This, ultimately, protected the Sasanian Empire against the consequences of defeats by the Romans and Byzantines. So it was only when the Arabs where able to breach the inner sanctum of Sasanian defences, on the plateau, that the Empire collapsed.

The final stand of the Sasanians was at Merv where the great Sasanian oasis wall faced north – in other words, it faced in the wrong direction to be of much use against the Arab threat, which came from the south. Ironically, the Sasanians had discontinued the upkeep of the Khandaq-i-Shapur when they employed the Arab Lakhmids for frontier defence. The main threat to the Sasanians was perceived to come from the north down either side of the Caspian. With hindsight this was mistaken and the Sasanians paid the ultimate price for not maintaining their south-western linear barriers. 'Whereas the Sasanian Empire's eastern and northern walls were well maintained, those facing Arabia were allowed to decay – and it was from Arabia that the Empire's final doom came.'[32]

3. The Byzantine and Sasanian Empires considered together

The relationship between the Romans and the Sasanians might seem one of unremitting conflict. When, however, linear barriers are considered it can be seen that the reality was more complex and interesting and there was much cooperation in the face of the

Table 8.1: Land corridors giving access to the Sasanian and Byzantine Empires.

Caspian		
South-east Caspian	Sadd-i-Iskandar	Sasanian
	Wall of Tammisha	
Caspian west coast	Derbent Wall	Sasanian and Byzantine
	Ghilghilchay Wall	Sasanian and Byzantine
	Beshbarmak Wall	
Caucasus	Darial Pass	
Crimea		
Kerch Peninsula	Four Kerch Walls	Byzantine
Thrace		
Black Sea to Sea of Marmara	Anastasian Wall	Byzantine
Aegean Sea to Sea of Marmara	Thracian Chersonesos Wall	Byzantine
Greece		
Pallene Peninsula	Pallene Wall	Byzantine
Greece coast and mountain pass	Thermopylae Wall	Byzantine
Greece mountain pass	Heraclea Wall	Byzantine
Corinthian Isthmus	Hexamilion Wall	Byzantine

common nomad threat. The result was a collection of linear barriers that extended from the eastern Caspian to the Peloponnese.

Some land corridors in or near the territory of one Empire allowed access into the other. This was particularly the case with the Darial Pass through the Caucasus, which allowed access to the Asia Minor regions of the Roman and Byzantine Empires or to the Persian Empires. It is useful in Table 8.1 to recapitulate the land corridors and the linear barriers built across them in the European and Hither Asian region.

A joint history of wall building and subsidy

The Huns were the first nomads, from beyond the Pontic Steppe, to appear in Europe and Hither Asia. They posed a systemic threat far greater than that of more familiar nomads of the Pontic Steppe, like the Scythians and the Sarmatians. Their first great raid came in AD 395 when they burst through the Caucasus, passing by the Sasanian Empire and attacking the rich cities around Antioch, before being driven off by the Byzantine eunuch leader Eutropius in 398. The Huns also raided Thrace that same year, which prompted the Emperors Theodosius and Yazdegard to enter a treaty sharing responsibility for the operation of the Caucasus passes. The Byzantines agreed to pay the Sasanians 160 kilograms of gold annually. In 425 Theodosius and Varahran confirmed the treaty. The Huns crossed the Danube and sacked Belgrade in 441. The following year saw a further treaty agreed between the Romans and the Sasanians. A chronology of wall building and subsidy runs as follows:

Sometime in the 440s a first mud brick wall may have been constructed at Derbent on the Caucasus. Also, the Beshbarmak Wall may have been built. Attila was bought off before Constantinople in 447. The first Byzantine Hexamilion Wall may date from about 450. In 457 the Byzantines stopped paying for the Caucasus defence when the Sasanians were stretched by the Hephthalites to the east of the Caspian Sea.

In 460 the Huns split into the Onogurs, Utigurs and Kotrigurs. The Sasanian Shah Peroz received payments from the Byzantine Emperor Zenon between 474 and 480. In 484 the Hephthalites killed Peroz. The Hephthalites then plundered Persia but were soon ejected. Sometime during the late fifth or early sixth centuries the Sasanians built the Gorgan and Tammisha walls to block the Hepthalites and protect the rich Gorgan Plain.

The first 'Anastasian' Walls may have been built by Leo or Zeno in the 470s to 490s. This was possibly in response to a Bulgar threat. Between 503 and 508 the, possibly Hunnic, Savirs were at war with the Sasanians. In 505 Byzantium paid the Sasanians 360 kilograms of gold after concluding a peace treaty. The Ghilghilchay Wall may have been built after this treaty and payment. The Savirs and the Sasanians were in alliance during 517–518. The Savirs invaded Roman Hither Asia through the Caucasus.

Anastasius built or rebuilt the Anastasian Wall in 518. The Byzantines and Sasanians were at war between 524 and 531. Justinian succeeded in 527 and secured peace with the Sasanians. In 531 a major treaty was negotiated under which Byzantium was to pay 5,100 kilograms of gold to secure the Caucasus border in the years 531, 545, 550 and 552. During this period a Treaty of Perpetual Peace was agreed in 532. The next year the Byzantines agreed to pay 5,000 kilograms of gold for the Derbent and Caucasus fortifications which the Romans reduced to 225 kilograms in 540.

In 539 a great raid by the Huns destroyed Cassandreia on the Pallene Peninsula and was stopped by the Hexamilion Wall from entering the Pelopponese. Justinian went on a virtual orgy of refortification which included building linear barriers in Thrace, the Anastasian Wall, Thracian Chersonesos Walls, the Pallene Peninsula, at the Passes of Thermopylae, and Heraclea, and the Corinthian Isthmus. In 551 the Kotrigur Huns raided Thrace and Greece but were stopped at the Thracian Chersonesos Wall and the Thermopylae Walls. The Byzantines also paid the Utigur Huns to attack the Kotrigurs in the rear. At last in 557 there was a truce between the Byzantines and Sasanians.

A major treaty was then negotiated in 562 under which Byzantium was to pay 136 kilograms of gold for 50 years to secure the Caucasus frontier. In 562 the Sasanians launched a war with the Hephthalites which led to the latter's total defeat. The Khazars succeeded as the dominant power in their place. In 569 the stone Derbent Wall was built.

Conclusion – Byzantine and Sasanian Walls

The construction of the Derbent Wall marked the completion of a huge system of linear barriers across the land corridors from Greece, south-eastern Thrace, the Caucasus region, and to the west and east of the Caspian Sea. This was the result of the independent and joint endeavours of the Byzantines and the Sasanians. The prime motivator for this work was the appearance of nomads from beyond the Pontic Steppe who came across the Caspian and Pontic Steppes into Europe and Hither Asia. On several occasions these walls held back Hun attacks and the Theodosian Walls of Constantinople consistently held – even against the Arabs who had defeated the Sasanian Empire. In the late sixth and seventh centuries Byzantium and the Sasanians resumed war, disastrously weakening both sides. The latter were defeated by Muslim Arabs from the south of Mesopotamia where linear barriers had been allowed to fall into disuse.*

---

* There is a very substantial but enigmatic stone wall in the Caucasus called the Kelasura Wall. Some estimates make it 160 kilometres long with up to 2,000 towers. It runs from near the coastal city of Sukhumi in roughly a south-easterly direction along the foothills of the south-western Caucasus, to the Inguri River. It defended what is now Abkhazia, which is the part of Georgia that recently seceded. Some historians place this wall in the sixth century which might relate it to Justinian's efforts to block off the Caucasus, but there is no obvious historical record to affirm this. Other historians attribute it to Megrelian princes in the seventeenth century. Such is the uncertainty about some walls.

Chapter Nine

Central Asia – Great Oasis Walls

Central Asia is both part of and adjacent to the Eurasian Steppe, and a region in its own right. It encompasses an exceptionally wide range of terrains from desert to well-watered valleys. Through it passed conquerors, raiders, nomads traders, migrants and the Silk Routes. Although much of it is naturally arid or semi-arid, great rivers and oases allowed ample opportunity for irrigation. As seen already, irrigated areas, constituting both valued and vulnerable land, were often protected by linear barriers. Walls around oases have already been found at *Margiana* and then Merv. Given the presence of both local and migrating nomads and many great oasis cities, Central Asia might seem promising ground for the search for great walls.

There are two great rivers amenable to irrigation, the *Oxus*/Amu-Darya and the *Jaxartes*/Syr-Darya. The more southerly *Oxus*/Amu-Darya gathers in the Basin of that name. It takes waters from the surrounding Hindu Kush Mountains to the south, Pamirs to the east, and the western Tian Shan Mountains to the north. It then flows north-west to the Aral Sea. The more northerly *Jaxartes*/Syr-Darya collects in the Ferghana Valley between the Western Tian Shan Mountains and flows again north-east to the Aral Sea.* Another important river, between the *Oxus*/Amu-Darya and the *Jaxartes*/Syr-Darya, is the Zeravshan which flows east through the valley of the same name and then south to the *Oxus*/Amu-Darya. (Again irrigation projects mean that it no longer joins the *Oxus*/Amu-Darya.) To the west, the *Margos*/Murghab River flows north from the Kopet Dag Mountains to the desert delta which was the site of Merv.

The oases of Central Asia are largely the product of its great rivers. There are man-made riverine irrigation systems as in the regions along the Nile, Tigris and Euphrates and the Yellow River in Egypt, Mesopotamia, or China. The difference is that, rather than covering long continuous areas, the ground worked by irrigation systems in Central Asia tended to be localised around a great city like Merv, Samakand, Bukhara or Tashkent. There a distinct oasis culture became stabilised with a symbiotic relationship between the cultures of the steppe regions and those of the settled oases. This balance might be disrupted by the irruption of nomad hordes from the east.

Geographically there are two types of oasis to be considered in Central Asia. The first is the alluvial fan where a river flattens out and disperses – eventually evaporating if there is not careful irrigation. For example, Merv was sited on the terminal point of the *Margos*/Murghab River which flowed down from the Kopet Dag Mountains. The other

---

* That is to say both rivers did flow into the Aral Sea but over-intensive irrigation projects have cut the flow so much that the Aral Sea is drying out.

is the localised use of water from rivers which continue to flow, if otherwise somewhat diminished – for example, the historic oasis town of Samarkand on the Zeravshan River.

Before the Russians and the British became players in the Central Asian Great Game, the regional contest was between the Persians (Achaemenid, Parthian and Sasanian), Greeks, Chinese and Arabs and the steppe nomads, including the local Saka, a Scythian people, and later Xiongu, Xianbei, Yuezhi, Turkic, Mongol and Tatar peoples from the east. The area's history is known from the sixth century BC when the Persian Achaemenid Empire included three provinces beyond the *Oxus*/Amu-Darya River: Sogdia or Transoxiana, which lay between the *Oxus*/Amu-Darya and the *Jaxartes*/Syr-Darya; Khorezm, to the west of Sogdia and to the east of the Aral Sea; and Saka, north of the *Jaxartes*/Syr-Darya and occupied by nomads of the same name.

The Persian Achaemenids were displaced by Alexander the Great who, after defeating Darius III, crossed the *Oxus*/Amu-Darya. As Alexander's Empire broke up after his death, his general Antiochus founded a Graeco-Bactrian state which extended from the *Oxus*/Amu-Darya valley in the mountains to *Margiana* (later called Merv) built on the oasis in the *Margos*/Murghab River desert delta to the west. In the third century BC the Sakas pushed out the Bactrian Greeks from the area above Samarkand from land north-west of the Hissar Range which delineated the north-west of the *Oxus*/Amu-Darya (Bactrian) Basin. In the following century the Greeks returned to the Zerafshan Valley and recovered Samarkand.

After the mid-second century BC the Yuezhi, fleeing the Xianbei, arrived in the Greek Bactrian state, south of the Hissar Range, and began to displace the Greeks. They established what became the Kushan Empire which extended through Afghanistan to Northern India. The nomad Kangju Confederation of Scythian peoples meanwhile increased their control over Sogdia, the region to the north of the Hissar Range.

The Ferghana Valley was discovered by a Han dynasty era Chinese envoy in the second century BC. He was seeking allies against the Xiongnu, and his silk clothes were much admired, leading to appeals for trade westward of silk. Meanwhile his reports of the 'heavenly horses' in the Valley excited interest in the east and the Han Emperor decreed he must possess them. In the late second century BC a caravan route was opened between China and Persia. China began to export silk to the Parthian Empire, which had replaced the Greek Seleucids in Persia, and to the Roman Empire. The Silk Road, or rather Silk Roads, developed through Central Asia. Some Xiongnu moved west, becoming the Western Xiongnu and established control around Samarkand.

In the third century AD the Sasanians occupied Sogdia and made their military headquarters in Central Asia at Merv. A Turkic Khanate was established in the sixth century. Sasanian nobles, fleeing the Muslim Arabs, settled in Central Asia in the seventh century. In the eighth century Arabs converted most of the region to Islam. Central Asia was focused around the Samanid Dynasty of Muslim Persians in the ninth century AD. In the early tenth century the Samanids were replaced by the Turkic peoples: south of the *Oxus*/Amu-Darya, in Khorasan, the Ghaznavids; and between the *Oxus*/Amu-Darya and the *Jaxartes*/Syr-Darya (and beyond) in Transoxiana, the Qarakhanids.

In 1219 Ghenghiz Khan's Mongols conquered Central Asia. In 1227 his Empire was divided into three parts and Central Asia was given to Chagatai, Ghenghiz Khan's second son. After the break-up of the Mongol Empire, a Turkic people from near Samarkand, led by Tamerlane, took control of Transoxiana and then ravaged lands from India to Turkey. Tamerlane's dynasty, the Timurids, controlled Central Asia until the sixteenth century.

In order to clarify the situation in Central Asia it helps to understand the main regional units, as these might indicate where border linear barriers would be constructed. Bactria was the Greek name for the area around the *Oxus*/Amu-Darya, between the Hindu Kush and the Hissar Range. The Graeco-Bactrians founded several great cities, later notable for oasis walls, including Termez and the capital Balkh. Subsequently the Kushan Empire was centred around Bactria. The Kushans were conquered by the Sasanians. Sogdia was a province of the Persian Achaemenid Empire and its people were eastern Iranian. Sogdian states were based along the Zeravshan River valley and included many of the great oasis cities like Samarkand, Bukhara, and Khujand.

Ustrushana lay to the west of Sogdia on the left bank of the *Jaxartes*/Syr-Darya, and the upper course of the Zeravshan River. In the fifth century it was Hephthalite, and in the sixth to seventh centuries western Turkic. The Ferghana Valley is like a long thin finger extending into the Western Tian Shan Mountains. It was famous for the 'Heavenly Horses' so prized by the Han. *Margiana* was the oasis state built over the *Margos*/Murghab River's desert delta with the capital of Antiochia and later Merv. Merv was the military capital of the eastern Sasanian provinces. In the sixth to seventh centuries it was a western Turkic polity. The Kart dynasty (1245–1381) ruled a compact area from their capital at Herat, in present-day western Afghanistan.

A brief summary of history and geography expressed here indicates the presence of many ingredients for the construction of walls in Central Asia. There are land corridors, both natural, through valleys, and man-made in the form of roads, particularly the Silk Route. There is valued and highly vulnerable irrigated land. There is constant confrontation between states and nomads both local and migrating and between states. A problem in fully understanding the situation, however, concerns the level of destruction of linear barriers. The great oasis states were shattered by the Mongols and Timurids and some never recovered. In other cases the cities survived but the walls did not. More recently, in the twentieth century, there have been huge losses as a result of massive ecologically and archaeologically destructive irrigation schemes. The result is that literary evidence and even oral history is all the more important in establishing the location of walls.

Issues and problems

Earlier Walls revisited

In earlier sections on the Greeks, two linear barriers were considered: the first was the pass wall near Derbent and the second was the oasis wall at *Margiana*. The Greeks may also have built other walls to protect the Graeco-Bactrian kingdom. Indeed it is possible that the Greeks injected the concept of building linear barriers into Central Asia with

9.1: Central Asia

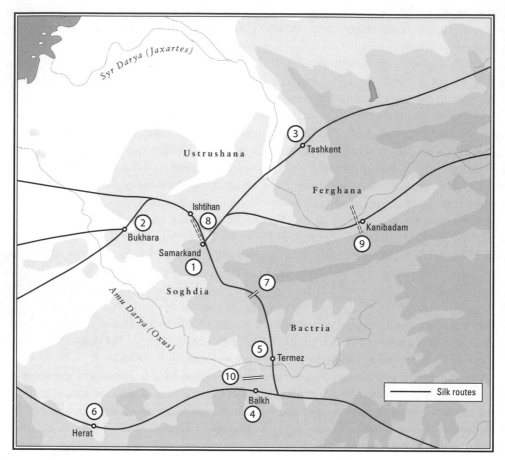

Oasis walls

1. Samarkand (Soghdia)
2. Bukhara (Soghdia)
3. Tashkent (Soghdia)
4. Balkh (Bactria)
5. Termez (Bactria)
6. Herat (Kart)

Walls

7. Derbent Wall (Bactria/Soghdia)
8. Ishtihan (near) Wall (Ustrushana/ Soghdia)
9. Kanibadam (near) Wall (Ferghana/ Ustrushana)
10. Kumsar (near) Kam Pirak Wall

the Derbent and *Margiana* walls. Also, the speed with which generally they could build circuit walls may have encouraged linear barrier building. Famously, the six kilometre circuit wall of *Alexander Eschete* at the mouth of the Ferghana Valley was built in twenty days.

Bactria/Sogdia – Iron Gates near Derbent – There are at least two periods of use of the walls in the Hissar Range. The first has been looked at, discussing Greek walls, when the Bactrian state, to the south, built a wall across a narrow gorge about thirteen kilometres west of Derbent. This wall controlled access to Bactria and Sogdia, and was constructed after the Graeco-Bactrian state lost control of the region to the north of the Hissar Range in the third century BC. The victors in that instance were the nomadic Sakas. In the second century the Greeks recovered the northern region, rendering the wall superfluous. The Kushan empire later sedentarised and integrated into Graeco-Bactrian culture, and then faced the Kangju nomadic confederation. The Kushans rebuilt the Derbent Wall which marked the frontier between Kangju and Kushan territory, or between the settled states and nomads.

As the Kushans settled there emerged 'a new balance of power, once again centred on the frontier-wall of Derbent. As in the Hellenistic period, both sides are characterised by two radically different ways of life: on the one hand the Kushan Empire, recently sedentarised and integrated into Graeco-Bactrian culture; on the other hand, the Kangju who conserved their nomadic structures. The wall rebuilt by the Kushans materialises a conflictual situation.'[1] The wall was about two kilometres long and 6.5 metres thick. Later towers were added to the wall and in the southern part it had a powerful fortress. The structure was known in Antiquity and to the Chinese as the Iron Gates.

Margiana/Merv – The Hellenistic Giliakin-Chilburg Wall and the Antiochus Wall, built respectively by Antiochus and the Sasanians, have already been discussed. *Margiana*, later Merv, became an established post on the Silk Road between Sogdia and the Parthian Empire. Merv was famously terribly sacked by the Mongols.

Central Asian oasis walls

It is the many oasis walls that distinguish Central Asia particularly in what was Sogdia and Bactria. In earlier survey sections it was clear that walls were often built around irrigated land to control access by both men and thirsty animals. These were usually linear, extending between natural obstacles like rivers, mountains and seas. But what form would a linear barrier take around a given object if there were no suitable natural features available to join? As has been seen with the examples of Taif in Arabia and *Margiana* elsewhere in Central Asia, a wall protecting an oasis will curl around into a full circle if the oasis is in open ground without other natural obstacles and the threat can come from all directions.

This, however, is not the same as a circuit wall built around a town or city. With an oasis wall the intention is to protect especially valued land: with a town or city wall it is to protect a built-up area. Great oasis walls, enclosing fertile land surrounding cities, are the special feature of Central Asian linear barriers. The oasis towns had the function of providing sustenance for their inhabitants. But they were also staging posts for caravanserai following the Silk Road. The requirement for the oasis wall comes from managing the relationship of the oasis state and the surrounding nomads. Although associated with polities like Bactria or Sogdia in practice, the oasis states were largely autonomous and responsible for managing ongoing relationships with local nomads.

The Central Asia oasis settlement had up to three lines of defences. At the centre was a citadel occupied by the ruler, his family and key retainers. This was surrounded by a fortified town or shahristan which might have immensely high walls. Some large cities might then be surrounded by a further wall enclosing irrigated land and supporting villages. The oasis state would generally maintain a reasonably peaceful relationship – involving trade and intermarriage – with the mainly Turkic nomads in the region.

Sogdia

Sogdia was the site of several great oasis cities.

Bukhara – Kampirak Wall – Bukhara is located on the terminal oasis of the Zerafshan River. To defend the oasis from nomads' raids it was surrounded by a wattle and daub wall with the length of 250 kilometres. It enclosed an area of approximately 1,300 square kilometres and the Samanids restored the wall in 873. 'The entire area was protected by a wall which measured 12 farsakhs by 12 farsakhs (ca. 72 x 72 kilometres). This wall is mentioned by (tenth century historian) Narshakhi, who said that its name was 'Kampirak',[2] and it 'was of pre-Islamic origin and restored in the early Islamic period. Inside the walls there was scarcely a spot that was not built upon or under cultivation.'[3]

The Samanids came to power in the early ninth century. By 902 their leader, Ismail, had expanded Samanid lands to West Afghanistan, and East and Central Iran. He stopped nomad raiders who previously had frequently invaded the Central Asian oases. The people of Bukhara, however, found the financial burden of maintaining the outer wall too heavy and petitioned Ismail to be released from it. He said, 'While I am alive, I am the wall of Bukhara.' This may have proved sufficient during Ismail's life time but after his death Bukhara fell to the Arabs.

The wall was defined by the irrigation system: 'The entire oasis itself at one point was surrounded by an immense and complicated fortification system, the walls of which extended for a length of 250 or more kilometres. The extent of these walls correlates with the extent of the irrigation system of Bukhara.'[4] The wall also controlled the relation of nomads and settlers. 'It defines the oasis settlement as a distinctive, highly-efficient technological adaptation, a working unit for both the exploitation of the environment, development of a trading economy and successful, albeit defensive, interactions with outside cultural groups, both nomadic and settled.'[5]

Samarkand – Kampyr Diwal Wall – Samarkand lay further east on the Zeravshan River towards Bukhara. It was surrounded by ramparts a hundred kilometres in circumference that covered the whole oasis region.

Tashkent (ancient name Chach) Wall – Chach was on the Silk Road about 200 kilometres north-east of Samarkand on the confluence of the Chirchik River and several tributaries. By the seventh century Chach was a trade centre between Sogdian and Turkic nomads. It had oasis walls that have since been completely lost due to twentieth century irrigation projects.

Bactria

Termez Wall – Termez was founded by the Greeks and lies on the River Amu-Darya. It was an important Kushan and then Arab Islamic centre. A section of oasis wall has been identified.

Balkh Wall – Balkh sits on an alluvial fan built up by the Balkh River. 'In earlier times, there had been a wall twelve farsakhs long, with twelve gates, enclosing both the city and adjacent villages, as a protection from nomads and other marauders.'[6] But by the ninth century this no longer existed.

Kart Kingdom

Herat Wall – The Hari River valley flows from the mountains of central Afghanistan to the Karakum Desert in Turkmenistan and sustains a narrow but fertile oasis. The oasis region was given a protective wall outside the main city walls under the Kart dynasty, though this was quite late, compared to other Central Asian long circuit walls. 'Under Mo'ezz-al-Din Pir-Hosayn (1332–70) an external protective wall was erected in the countryside, where the Enjil canal marked the north-eastern limits of the extended Herat.'[7] In 1381 Tamerlane destroyed the city walls and the Kart outer oasis wall, which was never rebuilt.

Border Walls

Apart from oasis walls there were a number of linear barriers in the region. These might have functioned as frontiers between warring states, to control the passage of nomads, or to exploit trade flows.

Sogdia/Ustrushana – Ishtihan Wall – There was a complex series of linear barriers to the north of Sogdia on the borders with Ustrushana. If Ustrushana were a Hepthalite and then Turkic area then it might be identified as being nomadic compared with the sedentarised Sogdia with its many oasis cities.

Ferghana/Ustrushana – Kanibadam Wall – A linear barrier ran north and west of the *Jaxartes*/Syr-Darya near Kanibadam in Tajikistan. This wall was destroyed by irrigation works in the 1960s. When it still stood it possibly controlled access to the Ferghana Valley and might have been able to exert control over the branch of the Silk Road through the Valley.

Kumsar (Kam Pirak) Wall – There is a defensive wall built of *pakhsa* (mud brick mixed with straw) that runs about sixty kilometres across northern Afghanistan, from Dilbarjīn towards Balkh. Although it has been called Achaemenid[8], the Achaemenids are not associated with linear barrier construction; so this attribution might be unlikely.

Walls requiring further research

Like Sasanian walls, the linear barriers of Central Asia are not a closed subject. There is probably much in Iranian and Russian and even specialist western academic literature that has not been absorbed. For example: 'In the historical stories and fabulous tales narrated from the Kianian period, it is said that during the reign of Goshtasb, his son known as Isandiar, built a battlement 20 kilometres away from Samarghand to stop the invading Turks.'[9] Also, 'The Arabs ... after the conquest of Tranxiana, erected battlements in the Qalas Desert which stood as a barrier between Asfijat and Shash.'[10] And there was a so-called 'Merz rampart' on the northern periphery of the Kopet-dagh'.[11] Again, the subject of linear barriers in Central Asia is still only being unteased and is very much work in progress.

Conclusion – Central Asia

It is the oasis walls which make Central Asia remarkable. These walls were extremely large, as seen particularly in the case of Bukhara, where sides of a rectangle were over seventy kilometres long. Most oasis walls were located along or near the Silk Roads. This was an area of intense activity with a constant flow of travellers, many local nomads and intermittently foreign nomads migrating west. Essentially the circuit defences of the oases are point defences writ very large.

It might be asked why the *Oxus*/Amu-Darya and *Jaxartes*/Syr-Darya region did not evolve into a single great irrigated area, like that surrounding the Tigris and the Euphrates. The explanation might be geography but it could also be political. There were just too many groups passing through the region to make it practicable to control all the flows of peoples, which might have been necessary if there were continuous irrigation along the whole length of the river, as was the case with the Nile or the Tigris and Euphrates. Therefore there were specific focal points based on areas which were particularly suited to intense irrigation. Often walls were built around irrigation projects, because these had created land vulnerable to raiding, trampling by herds and to sand incursion. The purpose of these walls was not to keep out large forces. Instead that duty was performed by the inner city and citadel walls.

The great outer walls only existed in certain periods – mostly perhaps in the period between the *Pax Sasanica* and *Pax Arabica*. This was also the time of migrations – particularly by Turkic peoples – which may have necessitated particular protection to vulnerable irrigation works, necessitating the investment in huge oasis walls. 'The growth of a new urban population presupposed the development of irrigation, which involved a complex technique of underground channels. The need to defend towns against the attacks of Turkish nomads made it imperative to build military outposts (*ribats*) and great circular walls round the larger cities with their suburbs under cultivation and their smallholders' villages. Thus at Samarkand and Bulkhara there were ramparts 100 kilometres in circumference.'[12]

Chapter Ten

China II – Nomad Irruptions and Multiple Great Walls

Exploring the subject of linear barriers was in part provoked by the paradox that the Chinese are regarded as an exceptionally intelligent people but, despite this, they repeatedly indulged in long wall construction – even though this has been considered a futile activity. This raised the question: did the Chinese build walls of such length, over a long period of time, because a peculiarly intense, indeed perverse, sense of Chinese superiority made it impossible to treat with inferior nomads? According to this line of argument, it was preferable – even if quite futile – to wall them out. Or were the Chinese simply responding to the nomad threat – like all other states and empires around the Eurasian Steppe – by building long walls, a practice generally of proven utility? And possibly, the Chinese built walls of such prodigious length, over such a great period of time, because: the Chinese commanded particularly vast resources; the nomad threat was especially great; the border was extremely long; as was the period when the Chinese and nomads confronted each other. So would the Chinese really have had to prove their exceptionalism by not building walls at all?

The first two phases of Chinese wall building, which have been looked at earlier, might invite caution in making sweeping assumptions about the Chinese. Firstly, the earliest Chinese walls – in the Spring and Autumn and the Warring States periods – mostly had nothing to do with nomads and were built by and against similar Chinese states. Secondly, the northern walls of the Qin, Zhao and Yan states, built at roughly the same dates, appeared to have been built well into nomad territories. And – if not seen as straightforwardly aggressive in themselves – they were intended to consolidate the hold of land taken as the result of aggression. Thus, in neither phase were walls being built as a simple, supposedly ineffective, frontier defence against nomads.

Chinese history appears to demonstrate a remarkable continuity. Dynasties came and went but the culture and politics appeared recognisable over millennia. Some dynasties, however, built walls while others did not. Given, that the geography, the general political system and nomad threats were, to varying degrees, similar – were there any particular reasons why some dynasties built walls and others did not? And might the answer to this question reveal something else about the general factors which resulted in linear barrier building?

The combined length of walls built by the Chinese exceeded that of all the other linear barriers in this book put together. In part, however, the aim here is to adjust the balance away from Chinese walls and Hadrian's Wall, because other linear barriers have perhaps received insufficient attention. Additionally if Chinese walls were given attention proportionate to their physical distance and time in use, then this would turn into a book largely on Chinese Walls. Therefore, in this chapter, certain key questions which affect Chinese linear barriers will be addressed generally, but individual walls will not be discussed in detail.*

In the earlier sections on Chinese walls, issues could be treated in isolation from the rest of the world. During the long Han dynasty, however, China, Central Asia and eventually Europe all linked up – through exploration, migration, conquest and trade. After the First Emperor Qin Shi Huang united China, the nation remained for much of the time under one dynasty, but there were long periods when China was divided into multiple dynasties. These dynasties have particular characteristics in terms of linear barrier building; so rather than look at them sequentially, it helps to categorise them.

Major dynasties
The following major dynasties ruled over a united or largely united China.

Table 10.1: Dynasties ruling a united China

Dynasty	Date beginning	Date end	Length in years
Qin Dynasty	221 (BC)	207 (BC)	14
Han Dynasty	206 (BC)	(AD) 220	426
Sui Dynasty	581	618	37
Tang Dynasty	618	907	289
Song Dynasty	960	1279	319
Yuan Dynasty	1279	1368	89
Ming Dynasty	1368	1644	276
Qing Dynasty	1644	1911	267

These major dynasties can be divided into three groups. The Qin and the Sui were two short-lived ethnically Chinese dynasties who followed periods of division and reunited China. There were four long-surviving ethnically Chinese dynasties, the Han, Tang, Song and Ming. And then there were two non-Chinese dynasties, the Mongol Yuan and the Manchu Qing.

Minor dynasties during periods of disunion
There are several phases to the period of disunion between AD 220 and 581. The Three Kingdoms Period (220–280) dynasties were the Wei dynasty in the north, the inland Shu Han dynasty in the south-west and the Wu dynasty in the south-east. The Wei period ended in 265 when the general Sima Yuan usurped the throne, founding the Western Jin. In 280 the Western Jin briefly reunited China until 304. Emperor Sima

---

* There are anyway excellent books on Chinese Walls. To name three, Di Cosmo is very good on earlier wall building and Waldron both generally and particularly on Ming construction. Lovell provides an extremely enjoyable survey on the whole subject. (See Bibliography for full titles).

Yuan then split China by giving a principality to each of twenty-five sons. This act led to the chaotic Sixteen Kingdoms of which the nomadic Xianbei founded six.

The north was united in 386 under the Northern Wei who lasted until 534 when the Dynasty split again. In the east was the Eastern Wei (534–550) followed by the Northern Qi (550–577). In the west the Western Wei (535–557) were followed by the Northern Zhou (557–581). The Northern Zhou conquered the Northern Qi and then, under a Chinese Northern Zhou general (Wen), they overcame the south and reunited China under the Sui dynasty. The Five Dynasties ruled in the north for short periods between 907 and 960 and over varying areas. None survived long enough to become wall builders and they drop out of the analysis.

Basically, during this period of disunion, the interest is focused on dynasties with northern borders which therefore had to deal with nomads. There are periods of overlap when dynasties run co-terminously for periods of time. The important question is what were the various northern dynasties doing on their upper borders in order to deal with any nomadic threat?

Table 10.2: Period of disunion – 220 to 581 – dynasties in the north

Dynasty	Date beginning	Date end	Length in years
Wei	220	265	45
Western Jin	265	316	51
Eastern Jin	317	419	102
Northern Wei	386	534	148
Dynasties ruling co-terminously (1)			
Eastern Wei	534	550	16
Western Wei	535	557	22
Dynasties ruling co-terminously (2)			
Northern Qi	550	577	27
Northern Zhou	557	581	24

Northern nomad dynasties

During the Song dynasty the northern part of China split off and was ruled by two nomadic dynasties, the Kitan Liao (907–1125) and the Jin (1115–1234). These had to defend themselves against more northerly nomads – indeed the first against the second which prevailed over it.

Wall building and non-wall building dynasties

The following table divides the dynasties that either ruled all of or part of northern China according to whether they built walls or not (that is, as far as initial research reveals). Wall builders are further divided into those who built walls immediately on taking power and those where there is a significant gap before initiating wall building. The latter would indicate a major change in internal policy or the nature of the external threat, which might throw light on the reasons why linear barriers were built. Those dynasties which did not build walls are also shown as this may be equally informative as to the motivations why or why not walls were built.

Table 10.3: Dynasties ruling all of China or northern China during periods of disunion

Dynasty	Date beginning	Date end	Length in years
Major dynasties constructing walls early in regime			
Qin	221 BC	207 BC	14
Sui	AD 581	618	37
Major dynasties constructing walls mid-regime			
Han	206 BC	AD 220	426
Ming	1368	1644	276
Other wall building dynasties			
Western Jin	265	316	51
Northern Wei	386	534	148
Eastern Wei	534	550	16
Northern Qi	550	577	27
Northern Zhou	557	581	24
Northern nomad dynasties			
Kitan Liao	907	1125	218
Jin	1115	1234	119

Also of interest are dynasties which did not build walls, as their decisions not to construct them might cast light on the reasons why the others did. These are the Tang (618–907), Song (960–1279), Yuan (1279–1368) and Qing (1644–1911). It might be expected that it was ethnically Chinese dynasties who built walls as this is seen as a Chinese not a nomadic trait; but the table above shows that dynasties of both nomadic and of non-nomadic origin built linear barriers.

Questions arising from Chinese frontier walls

The tables above raise a number of questions:

Looking first at wall-building dynasties – why did the major Chinese Qin, Sui, Han and Ming dynasties build long walls? This question sub-divides into two further questions. Why did the short-lived Qin and Sui dynasties build walls immediately on assuming power? Why did the longer lasting Han and Ming only start major wall-building well after the dynasty assumed power?

Then considering why did the non-Chinese dynasties build long walls, this question sub-divides into three. Why did the non-Chinese Northern Wei and Northern Qi build long walls? Why did the northern nomadic Kitan Liao and Jin states build long walls? And why did the short-lived Chinese Western Jin (265–316) build long walls?

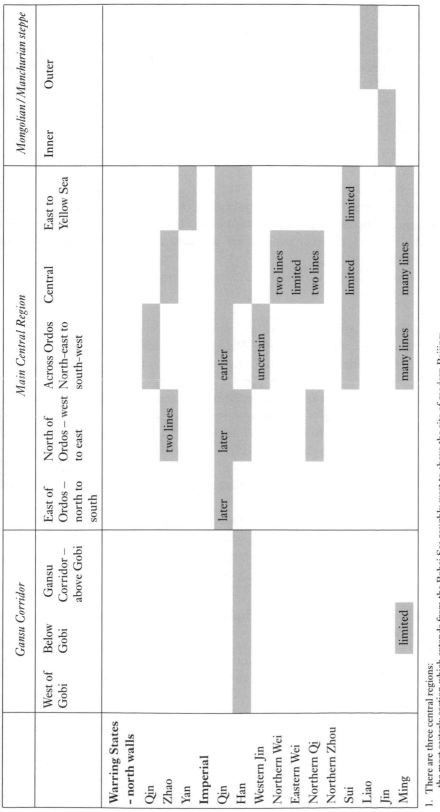

	Gansu Corridor			Main Central Region					Mongolian / Manchurian steppe	
	West of Gobi	Below Gobi	Gansu Corridor – above Gobi	East of Ordos – north to south	North of Ordos – west to east	Across Ordos North-east to south-west	Central	East to Yellow Sea	Inner	Outer
Warring States – north walls										
Qin						▓	▓			
Zhao					two lines					
Yan							▓	▓		
Imperial										
Qin				later	later	earlier				
Han			▓	▓	▓	uncertain	▓	▓		▓
Western Jin										
Northern Wei							two lines			
Eastern Wei							limited			
Northern Qi					▓		two lines			
Northern Zhou										
Sui						▓	limited			
Liao							limited	limited		
Jin									▓	
Ming		limited			many lines	many lines	many lines			

1. There are three central regions:
   - the most easterly section which extends from the Bohai Sea roughly west to above the site of modern Beijing;
   - the central section which continues to the north-east corner of the Yellow River bend around the Ordos; and
   - the easterly section including the Yellow River bend around the Ordos. Here, the routes of walls can take two directions. Either it goes roughly north-west to south-east across the Yellow River bend to the south of the Ordos; or it goes to the north of the Ordos and the Yellow River. The line can then follow the eastern side of the Yellow River bend running roughly north to south.
2. Some walls extend west of the Ordos along the Gansu Corridor. This extension can run initially above or below the Gobi Desert. The latter is identified with the Gansu Corridor, which itself extends to the Jade Gate and Karim Basin.
3. In eastern Mongolia there are two sets of linear barriers. There is a simple line to the far north and a far more extensive set of linear barriers starting to the north of the Ordos and the Yellow River and extending north-east.

Lastly, major non-wall building dynasties are considered. Why did the long-lived Chinese Tang and Song dynasties not build long walls? Why did the nomadic origin dynasties of Yuan and Qing not build long walls?

The Great Walls of China

The maps showing the locations of Chinese walls are frequently baffling. Some maps are totally schematic while other maps, trying to be comprehensive, do a fair imitation of a spaghetti junction. They are damned if they try to show all the walls because they become almost incomprehensibly fussy. However, if they show only one or a limited number of dynasties, then it is hard to determine the relationship of walls constructed by different dynasties. Table 10.4 tries to set out schematically the regions where dynasties built walls.

Review of Table 10.4 shows the walls fit into several groups in terms of the regions covered.

1. **Walls covering a limited number of central regions**. These are the various Warring States period walls of the Qin, Zhao and Yan; and the Period of Disunion walls of Western Jin, the Northern Wei, the Eastern Wei, the Northern Qi and the Northern Zhou.
2. **The Walls covering all three central regions**. These are the walls of the dynasties who reunited China, that is, of the Qin and Sui.
3. **The Walls covering all three central regions and part or all of the Gansu Corridor to the West**. These are the Han and the Ming walls. The former Han walls ran both north and south of the Gobi Desert and along the full length of the Gansu Corridor. The Ming walls covered some of the eastern areas of the corridor.
4. **Walls to the north-east**. There were two sets of linear barriers to the north-east of the lines of the walls outlined so far. These are barriers built by the nomadic Kitan Liao and the Jin barriers. The combined length of the latter is extremely long, many thousands of kilometres.

1. Why did the short-lived Qin and Sui dynasties build walls immediately on assuming power?

Both the Qin and the Sui reunited China under particularly brutal leaders. Emperors Qin Shi Huang (221–210 BC) and Sui Wen (581–604) built great walls along much of the length of the northern border. Also, both the Qin and the Sui dynasties were short-lived. They barely survived the lives of their respective first emperors, and the dynasties lasted fourteen years and thirty-seven years respectively. So what motivated these wall-building efforts – particularly given that they started so early in the reign of the first emperors of the dynasties? Could the reason be that the dynasties faced a very real external nomad threat – which could only properly and urgently be addressed after the Qin and the Sui reunified China respectively in 221 BC and AD 581? Or could it

10.1: China – Imperial

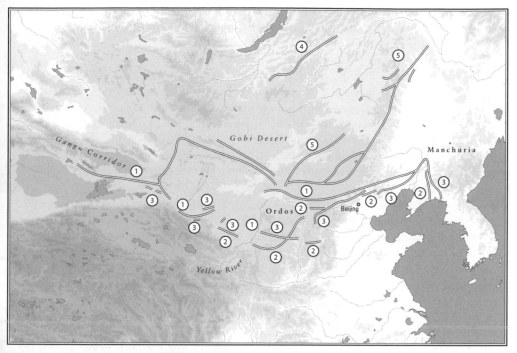

Unified China Great Walls of China
1. Han Dynasty (206 BCE–220) Great Wall of China
2. Sui Dynasty (581–618) Great Wall of China
3. Ming Dynasty (1368–1644) Great Wall of China

Periods of Disunion Walls (not shown)
Western Jin Dynasty (265–316) Wall
Northern Wei Dynasty (386–534) Wall
Eastern Wei Dynasty (534–550) Wall
Northern Qi Dynasty (550–577) Wall
Northern Zhou Dynasty (557–581) Wall

Semi-Nomadic Dynasties' Ramparts
4. Kitan Liao Dynasty (907–1125) Ramparts
5. Jin Dynasty (1115–1234) Ramparts

Please note the walls on this map are much simplified in order to try to clarify the situation. The key points are that the Han Walls extended furthest east to include the Gansu Corridor and extended north of the Yellow River bend over the Ordos. The Sui and Ming walls ran south of the bend across the Ordos. The Sui walls were more continuous than shown as the result of including earlier disunion period walls (not shown). The semi-nomad Kitan Liao and Jin walls ran to the north east of non-nomad dynasties' walls. (The periods of disunion walls largely lay between Beijing and the Yellow River bend.)

have been internal: an act of personal assertion, the construction of a physical symbol of a new unity, or a suitable way of filling the time of otherwise under-employed and possibly dangerous soldiers who had recently fought in wars of unification?

Qin Dynasty Walls – The Qin constructed China's first Great Wall, as already described in an earlier chapter. The key point is that this was the first great wall which extended across the full length of the northern frontier of the newly unified nation. The timing of its construction, following the process of reunification by the megalomaniacal First Emperor Qin Shi Huang, raises the question as to whether construction was driven predominantly internally by the desire to create a symbol of new found unity, which might also enhance the sense of national identity; or whether the impetus came externally from fear of the newly resurgent Xiongnu?

Sui Dynasty Walls – The Sui, who defeated the Northern Qi, rebuilt the Northern Zhou walls. They then went on to unite China at a time of serious Turkic threat and form the Sui Dynasty, which continued the process of Northern Qi and Northern Zhou wall building. The first Sui Emperor and founder of the Dynasty, Wen (581–604), was a Chinese Northern Zhou general who usurped the throne. Emperor Wen refused to pay subsidies to the Göktürk nomads who responded with a great raid in 584 – after which he built walls to keep them out. The Göktürks attacked the Sui capital of Changan, around 600, and demanded that the Sui end interference in the civil war between the Turks. The Chinese responded with more interference and wall-building. There were six major wall building campaigns of which Wen was responsible for four. Wen's son Yang added two projects, which are said to have been intended as expressions of power without strategic purpose: 'These two sections of the Great Wall had no strategic purposes beyond displaying the military power that prevailed during the rule of Emperor Yangdi.'[1]

Qin and Sui compared

Both the Qin and the Sui dynasties were involved in wall-building from very early stages. This seems explicable in terms of the pressure on both dynasties from the Xiongnu (see above) and the Turks respectively. The first Emperors of both dynasties were certainly great builders and their main motivation was to make statements about the strength and permanence of their rule. But, while the walls were great, other efforts, closer to where most people lived, would have been more effective and perhaps less unpopular as dynastic statements. Essentially, long wall building may have been an absolute necessity because of the acute contemporary nomad threat, but an unwanted distraction from other ventures like the construction of tombs, roads, cities and the Grand Canal.

There is a further question of whether the sheer cost and misery involved in wall-building incited revolts and, therefore, was counter-productive; after all, both dynasties proved to be short-lived, and internal disruption might have caused their demise. (It is certainly true that the wall building of the Qin dynasty resulted in a considerable literature describing the miseries caused.) But both Emperor Qin Shi Huang and Emperor Sui Wen were powerful characters and any subsequent ruler would have expected reaction. Indeed, in both cases the successors were seen as vain and weak and this might also have explained the rapid failure of the dynasties. Wall building anyway accounted for only part of the great building exercises of these Emperors. The

First Emperor built roads and canals and, of course, his famous tomb, guarded by the terracotta army. Emperor Wen constructed the Grand Canal.

2. Why did the Han and the Ming only start major wall-building well after their dynasties assumed power?

The Han (AD 206–220) and the Ming (AD 1368–1644) were the greatest of all long wall builders. Yet, in both cases, the dynasties started building walls quite late, and when they first took power, there was no indication that they would later become great builders. Therefore, they may provide useful case studies as to whether it was a change in external factors which resulted in wall building – or in the psychology of the dynastic constructors?

Han Dynasty Walls – The Han were an ethnically Chinese dynasty founded by a soldier who had nothing to lose as he faced execution for late arrival on parade. It was safer to rebel and bring down what was left of the Qin. The Han first emperor Gaodi (206–195 BC) inherited an exhausted state, barely able to defend itself, let alone launch into giant public works. Gaodi was reported to have ordered the restoration of the great wall but it is difficult to believe that his plan was very effective, if anything happened at all.

The early Han tried several strategies to deal with the resurgent Xiongnu who had returned to the Ordos Desert, from which Qin Shi Huang's general Meng Tian had expelled them. The Xiongnu then occupied the Gansu Corridor. In 200 BC Gaodi led an attack on them but was ambushed by the Xiongnu leader Maodun, and suffered a complete defeat at Pincheng. There was little then that Gaodi and the early Han emperors could do except pay tribute – sometimes in the form of sending over reluctant princesses – a policy called *heqin*. *Heqin* offended Confucian moralists who were disturbed by the improper organisation of the universe, where China should be 'first under heaven'. But responsibility for the failure of *heqin* did not lie only with Chinese moralists; it also eventually proved ineffective because the Xiongnu leadership were unable to control all the members of their fissiparous confederation, and this state of affairs resulted in freelance raiding.

Anyway, the early Han had both the qualities of parsimoniousness and durability sufficient to survive sixty years, long enough to replenish the treasuries and turn the tables on the Xiongnu. The later Han sought the wondrous horses of the Ferghana Valley and extended Imperial China along the Gansu Corridor. Emperor Wu (141–87 BC) started to expand the Empire and sent envoys to Central Asia to find allies against the Xiongnu. He recovered the Ordos and conquered the Gansu Corridor.

There was then a renewed campaign of wall-building to secure land retaken from the Xiongnu and to protect the Gansu Corridor to the west. It was during the Han period that China's walls reached their greatest extent. These walls had a number of functions which were not purely defensive. They protected land that had been retaken from the Xiongnu, so they were partly aggressive in that they supported expansion. They protected the transport route that linked China to Central Asia so the Han could strike at the Western Xiongnu's power base far from China. They defended the major trade route to Central Asia. Also, much of the eastern part of the Gansu Corridor is loess and there are oases along the route. Thus, one clear function of the walls was also to protect valued irrigated land.

The Western Han collapsed in AD 24 in a civil war which saw the destruction of the capital Xuan. The Han survived from 25 to 220 at the new capital Luoyang and the dynasty become known as the Eastern Han. Defence of Luoyang against the Xiongnu required the further construction of walls in the east.

The key issue is what had fundamentally changed, so that the Han, who had lived without walls for over a century, suddenly went in for a near orgy of wall-building? Under their reign China saw the greatest length of walls constructed – over 10,000 kilometres – at any time in its history. The reason was not initially based on a defensive mentality: rather it was to consolidate expansion at the expense of the Xiongnu, and to guarantee trade routes that extended to Central Asia. Of course, it was important to have the money to fund aggression and growth – and one reason why there was little wall building in the first half of the dynasty's life was that the Han were refilling their coffers. Furthermore, the *heqin* policy worked – even if it was deemed rather shameful to Chinese sensibilities.

The Xiongnu also played their part in creating the conditions for renewed wall building. As time passed their increasing claims for brides, bribes and hospitality became less acceptable to an Empire that was recovering the power to reject such claims. Also, the inevitably loose nature of the Confederation meant that, even if agreements held at the centre, it was impossible to control outer tribes who might indulge in some independent raiding. While the Han may have been much more outward looking than many other dynasties, accommodation with barbarian nomads was still seen as demeaning – especially in the face of increasingly arrogant demands and the growing capability to wall them out.

But the process of defeating one set of nomads created its own dialectic through the emergence of another. The effective elimination of the Rong and Di by the three northern states of Yan, Zhao and Qin had provoked the emergence of the Xiongnu. The Han defeat of the Xiongnu by AD 89 meant that the way was clear for another nomad Confederation, the Xianbei, to slip into the breach. Anyway, the Han, like most dynasties, ultimately lost vitality, and the Empire broke up into ethnically Chinese not nomad-ruled states. By the early third century the Ordos was abandoned and the Han collapsed.

Ming Dynasty Walls – The Great Wall of China is generally associated with the Ming Dynasty Walls. Yet not only did the wall-building enterprise of the Ming Dynasty (1368–1644) come late in China's history, but such building also came quite far on in the period of Ming Dynasty rule. The major phases of Ming building arrived after a nine century gap following the last episode of Chinese wall construction, under the Sui Dynasty in the sixth century. Without this burst of late Ming building, Chinese wall construction, if it had attracted much attention, would have been seen in the context of the major period of trans-Eurasian linear barrier construction that took place in the second half of the first millennium BC and the first millennium AD. What, therefore, provoked the Ming into building walls in two major phases, roughly one and two centuries after the dynasty came to power, and after such a long gap since previous wall building?

The early Ming were a warlike Chinese dynasty who had driven out the Yuan or Mongols by 1368. They strengthened the Juyong Pass with walls to block any return by the Mongols. They also built short sections of wall and beacon systems to secure strategic routes, but they did not rely on linear barriers for general frontier defence. Basically, they could fight off all comers, as initially a militaristic dynasty under the first and second Ming Emperors Hongwu and Yongle who campaigned aggressively in nomad territory.

By the 1440s the situation had changed. The Emperors became effete and a charismatic Oirat Mongol leader emerged in the person of Esen, a powerful Khagan, or ruler, of the Northern Yuan Dynasty in Mongolia in the fifteenth century, who briefly reunited the Mongols. The Ming reverted to a *heqin* policy of gifts but the demands of Esen and his followers became greater, and missions to collect tribute soared in size. The response was to decrease the number and size of gifts and eventually to close the border and reject Esen's demand for a Chinese princess.

In 1449 an effort by the Ming to revert to a more military solution ended in total disaster when the Oirats destroyed a huge Chinese army at Tumu and captured the Emperor Zhengtong. The Oirats were stopped before Beijing and the Emperor eventually returned, but offensive military solutions were ruled out from now on. The Mongols, however, took over the Ordos, creating a challenge that could not be ignored: either the Ming had to accept the presence of nomads south of the Yellow River or try and drive them out. In 1471 the governor responsible for Shanbei Province, Yu Zijun, built a wall nearly 900 kilometres long from Shannxi Province to the Ningxia Hui Autonomous Region. This was the first Chinese long wall for nearly a millennium. In 1476 Ming Emperor Xianzong connected with walls the Shanhaiguan Pass to the Yanmemguan Pass, a venture that included other passes like the Juyong Pass. In 1482 the wall here successfully blocked a Mongol raid. This was the first phase of Ming wall building which was still quite localised.

The major phase of Ming wall building occurred in the mid-sixteenth century and was associated with the emergence of another charismatic Mongol leader, Altan, who lived a long life from 1507 to 1582. Altan alternated great raids with demands for trade. The Ming rejected the trade demands yet lacked mobile armies capable of fighting off the Mongols. In 1550 Altan laid siege to Beijing. The response to the threat was a decision to wall the Mongols out – eventually on a scale never seen before. In this instance the wall-building exercise also made use of expensive durable materials of fired brick and stone. This is when the Ming Wall of China, as popularly understood now, was built. Building started in 1560 and with increased urgency in 1568 after further Mongol raids in 1567. Notwithstanding the wall building, the Chinese conceded a peace and trade treaty to Altan in 1571. The economic benefits gleaned from the latter treaty financed his wars in the west. The Ming walls meanwhile held against the Mongols. The Ming dynasty itself fell to the Manchu Qing in 1644 when a traitor opened the gates.

Han and Ming compared

Looking at both the Han and the Ming dynasties, something happened well after the dynasties' foundations which resulted in a change in policy towards wall-building. The reasons, however, were not the same for the Ming as for the Han – as the balance of power had shifted in opposite directions. The Han became more powerful and able to expand. The Han walls pushed out through the Gansu Corridor into new territories, and walls consolidated this newly acquired territory and protected trade routes. The Ming, however, had become militarily weaker and needed walls to defend their existing territories.

There are, however, common factors. In both cases there was reluctance by the Chinese to enter into trade agreements which in part were seen as demeaning to the station of China and its Emperor in the correct ordering of life under heaven. In practice, the Chinese way with words meant that a lot of humiliation could be rationalised; but the increasingly excessive and importunate demands for bribes and brides pushed the situation past a tipping point where, even for the Chinese, rationalisation became all too obviously humiliation. This was particularly the case as the weakness of nomadic central authority meant that raiding at the periphery was chronic anyway, and agreements generally were unreliable.

The Chinese were able to create strategies for dealing with nomad polities. They would give things which they had in relative abundance. The problem was that the unruly nomad confederations would not keep their side of the bargain, resulting in raiding or invading, unsanctioned by the nomad leadership, or they would demand too much. Sometimes agreements would break down as the nomad leader could not keep his peoples under control.

It is arguable that the Han became more powerful and were in a position to tolerate less nomad misbehaviour and greed and built walls simply to exclude the unwanted and feckless nomads. The Ming, however, became relatively less powerful and could not resist offensively – but hit the point where *heqin* could not be rationalised within the Chinese world order, so walls had to be built as an alternative defensive strategy to endless humiliation by nomads.

3. Why did the non-Chinese Northern Wei, Eastern Wei and Northern Qi build long walls?

Northern Wei Walls (386–534) – The Tuoba tribe of the Xianbei united the sixteen kingdoms and founded the Northern Wei state. This entity became the dominant northern dynasty ruling from 386 to 534. They became progressively sinicised and faced their own nomad threat from the Rouran who raided farming communities. In 423 the Northern Wei, stung by nomad raiding, built a northern wall which increased their territories. In 429 they defeated the Rouran and pushed them north of the wall. This early Northern Wei wall-building can be seen as aggressive: 'More offensive than defensive the early Northern Wei Long Wall was clearly succeeding in its purpose: safeguarding and even expanding the northern reaches of an Empire.'[3]

In 434 the wall was broken through and in 446 Emperor Shizu built another barrier around the Northern Wei capital Pincheng. In 484 a Chinese official at the Northern Wei court, Gao Lü, gave the famous speech giving five reasons for long walls. 'We calculate that building long walls has five advantages. First, it eliminates the problems of mobile defence. Second, it permits the northern tribes to nomadise (beyond the walls) and thus eliminate the disasters of raiding. Third, because it enables us to look for the enemy from the top of the wall, it means we no longer wait (to be attacked, not knowing where the enemy is). Fourth, it removes anxiety about border defence, and the need to mount defence when it is not necessary. And fifth, it permits the easy transport of supplies, and therefore prevents insufficiency.'[4]

All these reasons sound eminently practical and say nothing about keeping nomads out solely because they offended Chinese sensibilities about the proper ordering of earth below heaven. The Northern Wei shifted the capital to Luoyang, previously that of the eastern Han and the western Jin in 493. In 523 the Rouran broke through the walls and Erzhu Rong, a leader descended from the Xiongnu, took Luoyang in 528, which was dismantled ten years later.

Even if the Northern Wei were originally non-Chinese, they sinicised and as such the reasons given for wall construction both have Chinese precedents. The first Northern Wei walls followed the example of the Warring States – Qin, Zhao and Yan – of consolidating gains in nomad territory, followed by the Qin and the Han. Subsequently, the walls around Luoyang followed the later eastern Han example when they built walls after similarly moving the capital east from Xian to Luoyang. Gao Lü's reasons for building walls were based on making defence easier and cheaper for the Northern Wei; and they also made life easier for the northern tribes who could nomadise beyond the walls. The walls may have functioned to keep out the Rouran as the Northern Wei broke up internally over the question of sinicisation, and split into the Western Wei and Eastern Wei states. The Northern Qi followed the Eastern Wei in turn, and the Northern Zhou replaced the Western Wei.

Eastern Wei Walls (534–550) – The Northern Wei (386–534) split into the Northern Qi and the Eastern Wei. The latter built fortresses at strategic points and then a seventy-five kilometre wall across a passage in Shanxi Province, which nomads had used as an entry point. This was a short wall by Chinese standards and fitted the land corridor pattern.

Northern Qi Walls (550–577) – The Northern Qi bore the brunt of nomad attacks which fell upon them with renewed ferocity when the Turks appeared. Although a short-lived dynasty, the Northern Qi were, if anything, more substantial wall builders than the Northern Wei. They are regarded as the most sinicising of the northern dynasties following the Northern Wei split. But they also faced a far more serious threat. The Rouran were defeated by the emerging Göktürks in alliance with the Northern Qi and Northern Zhou in 552. In 555, the Göktürks beheaded some 3,000 Rouran. The Rouran Khagan fled to the Western Wei state where he and his followers were executed at the Göktürk demand. Some Rouran fled south and others west (where they have been identified with the Avars). The Northern Qi continued building walls as a defence against the Göktürks, who demanded prodigious quantities of tribute yet still went on vast raids. The Northern Qi built over 3,000 kilometres of wall in a double line of defence between 552 and 564. When the Northern Qi kingdom was annexed by the Northern Zhou the latter continued to maintain their walls.

The Northern Wei and Northern Qi rulers, who were originally of Xianbei descent, were among the most readily sinicising of the Northern dynasties, and this characteristic might have made walls more acceptable as a strategy. That said, the reasons given by Gao Lü for wall building were practical, not philosophical and ideological, as they clearly faced a very serious nomad threat, first in the Rouran and then, particularly so, from the Göktürks.

4. Why did the northern nomadic Kitan Liao and Jin states build long walls?

For nearly a millennium the ethnic Chinese Tang and Song and the Mongol Juan did not build long walls. Indeed had not the Ming resumed wall building then Chinese long wall building would have appeared to be just a historic phase that finished before the end of the first millennium, rather like that in Hither Asia and Europe. There appears to be a degree of continuity however, because the semi-nomad dynasties in the north during the Song dynasty period erected huge lengths of linear barriers. These barriers were built in very different areas to earlier Sui and later Ming barriers, and should be looked at in their own right. The walls of the Kitan Liao and the Jin, discussed next, often go by the names of the Walls of Ghenghiz Khan.

Kitan Liao Walls – The Kitan Liao were a semi-nomadic Mongol people who ruled northern China when the Song dynasty ruled the south. The Kitan Liao oversaw an empire which extended across the north of China to Central Asia. In order to resolve the problem of how to manage quite different regions, mixed between nomadic husbandry and sedentary agriculture, government was divided between a northern and a southern chancellery which dealt respectively with steppe and Chinese people. Having been comprehensively defeated by the Kitan Liao, the Song paid them an annual tribute. The Kitan Liao in their turn faced a threat in the north from the nomadic Jurchen people of Manchuria. In response the Kitan Liao built linear barriers.

Jin Walls – The Jin, who supplanted the Kitan Liao, built linear barriers against the Mongols just as the Kitan Liao had built walls against them. The Song now paid subsidies to the Jin who supplanted the Liao as defenders of the northern borders. The Jin walls were situated further north of the Kitan linear barriers and were much greater in length. The Jin built a massive system of linear barriers which differed from most other Chinese linear barriers in being substantially composed of earthwork ditches and ramparts. There was an inner barrier about 1,500 kilometres long, called the Mincheng New Great Wall, and a shorter outer barrier of about 500 kilometres in length which was named the Mincheng Old Great Wall.

As to why the semi-nomadic Kitan Liao and Jin built walls, the simple answer would be, in order to mark a border with more purely nomadic peoples. Both peoples were partially sedentarised and sinicised; as such they faced the same challenges dealing with nomadic peoples that the Chinese had and they reached the same solutions. The threat was certainly real, as is shown by the fact that the Jin did overthrow the Kitan Liao in the east and the Mongols in turn overthrew the Jin. The Kitan Liao and Jin linear barriers are usually included in outlines of Chinese walls. They might, however, be seen as *sui generis* for they are barriers set deep in the steppe. Had the Ming Dynasty not resumed long wall-building in the traditional Chinese locations, then the custom of the Chinese building long walls might have died out with the Sui.

Non-wall building dynasties

5. Why did the long-lived Chinese Tang and Song dynasties not build long walls?

For six and a half centuries there were only two major dynasties, the Tang and the Song, the former ruling all of China and the latter southern China. Neither built walls – and, had it not been for the resumption of wall building by the later Ming, China might have been seen as having kicked the habit.

The Tang (618–907) are held by non-Chinese as exemplars of what the Chinese should be: that is open to and curious about the world – qualities seen as resulting in a time of prosperity, longevity and creativity. Although Chinese, the Tang had Turkic blood in them and they professed affection for the Turks. Such was the reciprocated nomad respect for the first Tang Emperor Taizong that the Turks supplicated him to take the title Heavenly Khaghan. But the Tang were also seen as assuming an aggressive policy towards the nomad threat, adopting nomad cavalry techniques, employing Turkic fighters, patrolling aggressively, and fostering the dark arts to divide and rule. Basically, they took the conflict to the nomads rather than staying behind walls. It might also be added that the full force of the explosive arrival of the Turks had blown itself out by the time the Tang assumed power. Many Turks and other nomad groups had moved west to Central Asia en route for further west, and the remaining Turks were riven by internal disputes – which were carefully cultivated by the Tang to keep them divided, weakening their potential threat to the Chinese.

By contrast to the Tang, the Song (960–1279) were seen as sophisticated inward-looking southerners, during whose dynasty the iniquitous custom of foot binding was introduced. Rather than fight the northern kingdoms of the Kitan Liao and the Jin they paid them tribute. As seen, however, the Kitan Liao and the Jin did build linear barriers against the less tamed nomads further north, so perhaps the Song were ultimately defending China with walls by proxy. By the time the Kitan Liao and the Jin had established their northern states they were partially sedentarised. The Kitan Liao also had a southern Chancellery which operated along Chinese lines. Therefore, it was possible to negotiate reliable agreements between the Song and their immediate northern neighbours. (Major settled states and empires seldom build walls against each other as the walls will not stand against major armies and are, anyway, unnecessary if treaties can be expected to hold.)

6. Why did the nomadic-Yuan and Qing not build long walls?

This question might seem pointless. They were nomadic peoples and nomads did not build walls. But various dynasties of nomadic descent, like the Northern Wei, and northern nomad states, like the Kitan Liao and the Jin, did build linear barriers, leading to questions why?

The Yuan (1279–1368) had no need for linear barriers as the Mongols, of which they were part, ruled from China to Europe. Without a border with another state there was no need for a linear barrier. The threat to the Yuan Mongols in China came unusually from the south, not the north, as they were ejected from China itself by the Ming. (Then, as northern Mongols, they resumed pressing down on the Chinese, resulting eventually in the Ming Walls.) Even though the Yuan were a Mongol dynasty they did not, however, automatically face an easy time to the north; they had to pursue an active military policy to control Mongols who did not accept the authority of rulers based in China.

The Qing (1644–1911), having ejected the Ming, remained in control of the steppe and actively suppressed the nomads. By the later seventeenth century the expanding

Chinese Qing and the Russians ran into each other in eastern Asia, effectively closing down the steppe in the east. This left the question of where the border should lie? In 1689 the first treaty between the China and Russia was agreed at Nerchinsk where the principle was agreed that nomads should be subject to agrarian empires, here China and Russia.[5] The Chinese gained control of land north of the Amur River, thus taking control of the northern steppe. Subsequently, in the mid-nineteenth century China lost land all the way down to Vladivostok.

Chinese wall building did not entirely end with the Manchu Qing. Ordinarily they might have been seen as having no need of walls dividing China and Manchuria, especially as they had come down from the north and maintained a strong grip on Manchuria. Also, they actively campaigned to suppress the nomads of Mongolia – eventually meeting up with the Russians as they moved east across Siberia. The situation was, however, more complex and, while neither the Mongol Yuan nor the Manchurian Qing built walls against nomads, both did construct some rather unusual linear barriers.

Mongolian Hunt Walls – The reason why the originally Mongol Yuan did not build was not because they could not. Ögedei, the second son of Ghenghiz Khan, admitted to four wrongs – of which the second was: 'Furthermore, being covetous, and fearing that the wild beasts, born with their destiny determined by Heaven and Earth, would advance onto (the lands of my) elder and younger brother, I had fences and walls constructed.'[6] Building a wall showed disrespect to nature, here wild animals, by artificially constraining it.[7]

Qing Willow Palisade – The Qing built what is known as the Willow Palisade: its objective was largely to keep people in, not out. The Willow Palisade is of note because it was a living barrier, composed of one or two earthworks on which were planted willows whose branches were tied to each other. There were basically three sections of the Palisade. The Inner Willow Palisade separated China from Manchuria and was divided into an eastern and a western section above the Liaodong Peninsula. Its function was to prevent unauthorised movement north by Han Chinese. The Palisade ran close to or slightly north of the eastern end of the Ming Great Wall which faced it. It was built between the 1630s and 1670s and may therefore have originally predated the Qing conquest of China. The Outer Willow Palisade divided the Manchu and the Mongols and was built in the 1680s. As the Manchu increasingly tolerated and then encouraged migration northwards and colonisation, the function of the Palisade changed. It now became to control smuggling, particularly of Ginseng, and to impose taxes. (As such it sounds comparable to the mid-nineteenth century Great Hedge of India which was intended to stop evasion of the salt tax). It continued to function until the early twentieth century.

Conclusion – China frontier walls

This chapter asked whether the Chinese built walls of such length over so long a period of time because a peculiarly intense sense of Chinese superiority made it impossible to treat with inferior nomads. Thus, was it preferable – simply because of Chinese psychology, even if quite futile – to wall them out? Or were the Chinese simply responding to the nomad threat, like all other states and empires, by building long walls?

The walls of China were particularly long, in terms of distance and the time used, because of the length of vulnerable border, the long period while steppe nomads had the upper hand militarily (when they were united), and the wealth of the Chinese state. Linear barriers were built, at some point in time, at every exit point or area where the Eurasian Steppe met more settled areas. These were exceptionally lengthy in the case of China as the frontier was extremely long. Therefore, rather than long walls being symbols of Chinese exceptionalism, the Chinese would have had to prove they were uniquely different from other peoples by not building their various Great Walls against the nomad threat. Recent scholarship on the Great Wall has tended to emphasise its discontinuity in terms of its multiple lengths, and its appearance and disappearance over nearly two millennia. This, however, only serves to emphasise the sheer number of very long walls that were built – and demonstrates that it was a consistent if intermittent response to a nomad threat.

Although Chinese walls were breached and dynasties fell, walls probably bought time and created a certain sense of stability in the border area. If a wall worked during the builder's lifetime then basically it had worked. The builder cannot foresee the weaknesses of future periods or guarantee the vigilance of future guardians. Even where walls failed the invaders were ultimately sinicised and became in turn vulnerable to future attack. This was a cycle that was ultimately broken by the Qing when they conquered the steppe and suppressed the nomads. Imperial China ultimately collapsed in the face of the threat from maritime western states and Japan, a state using western technology. The ultimate vulnerability of the nomad in the face of firearms was revealed in 1860 when Anglo-French cannon blasted elite Mongol horsemen defending Peking to kingdom come at the Battle of Palikao.

A simple calculation shows that, excluding the period of the Kitan Liao and the Jin, there were walls in operation along the northern border for roughly 42 per cent of the years between the beginning of the Qin and the end of the Ming. If the Ming are excluded and the calculation is up to the end of the Sui period, then the figure is 69 per cent. For the Qin to Sui period – that is from 221 BC to AD 618 – it is clear that walls played a major part in the defence of China. If the calculation goes to 1644, the end of the Ming, then walls are still important. But for the majority of the time China had open borders. That said, for over three centuries, there were significant buffer states in the form of the Kitan Liao and the Jin who did use walls. If these are taken into consideration then China had some form of northern linear barrier for over half the time between 221 BC and AD 1644. What is unarguable is that walls formed a major element of China's defence system for far longer than any other empire or state.

Chapter Eleven

Russia – Defeating the Steppe Nomads

Linear barriers might have played a key role in the establishment of the First Russian Empire – that of the Kievan Rus. They stabilised the southern frontier against the Pechenegs and Polovtsians thereby enabling the Rus to expand north. This created a new heartland where the Russian language, script, religion and political culture could survive the complete destruction of the southern Rus states by the Mongols. In China, the Mongols only debated in theory whether to return the land to horse pasture. With the Ukrainian region this was effectively what happened in practice. In what is now the eastern Ukraine, lands overrun by the Mongols reverted to the so-called 'Wild Country' or *Slobozhanschina*, soon to be overgrown with forests and steppe grasses.

With the collapse of the Kievan Rus the centre of gravity for the Russian states moved north definitively into the forest steppe where, although certainly not forbidden territory to Mongol hordes, their assaults were less devastating in the longer term. Eventually the Muscovite Rus emerged as the dominant principality and there began the long hard period of expansion – only brought to an end with the break-up of the Soviet Union in 1991.

The Muscovite Rus and the early Russian Empire was a land almost without natural frontiers – except to the north and east, the Arctic Sea and the Pacific Ocean respectively. It existed in a vast open space of relatively flat lands interspersed by great rivers. Due south of Moscow, there is only forest and grassland steppe, and rivers down to the Black Sea. From east to west Russia is largely plain with the exception of the Ural Mountains which are no great obstacle – the Ural's highest peak, Mount Narodnaya, is well under 2,000 metres high. Nonetheless the Urals do provide a convenient division between Europe and Asia. Russia's rivers are great but mostly slow moving and not very difficult to cross. The western border is open to the north European plain with only the Carpathians forming a natural border. The result is that Russia has the world's longest open frontiers almost unrelieved by big natural obstacles.

Such frontiers can largely only be defined by man and with great effort – and have changed constantly over the centuries. On many occasions only Russia's vast size has enabled it to survive, for its central authority has been able to retreat, while scorching the earth, and still commanding sufficient resources ultimately to expel an enemy increasingly depleted by inadequate supply lines. If there were divisions, they were largely those imposed by climate. Thus, there are bands of tundra, forest and grassland. The section on the Kievan Rus looked largely at the interface between the grassland and forest steppe. This section follows the retreat into the forest – which provided some protection in depth from the nomads – and the subsequent advance back to grassland steppe down to the Black Sea.

The position of the Kievan Rus, near to the grassland steppe, made its position precarious. It had already broken up into warring principalities by the time it was overrun by the Mongols. In the second quarter of the thirteenth century the Mongols effectively destroyed the southern states that emerged from the breakup of the Kievan Rus and subdued the northern ones; the successful invaders then forced both groups of states to pay tribute.

To the north the ground was less fertile, the climate harsher and the wealth from trading less available. But the Russian states here were less vulnerable and could coalesce in this more marginal agricultural area, where sufficient wealth might still be derived from agricultural and forest products. During the same period, largely under the leadership of Alexander Nevsky of the Novgorod principality, the Russians were remarkably successful at driving back the Swedes and the Teutonic Knights while paying tribute to the Golden Horde.

In the early fourteenth century the Muscovite Rus began to expand – absorbing Kolomna in 1301 and the principality of Pereyaslavl in 1302. In 1328 Moscow's Prince Ivan Kalita was granted dispensation from the Golden Horde to become the Grand Prince of Vladimir and the right to collect taxes from the Rus lands. Moscow's central position meant it was devastated less frequently. Prince Ivan encouraged people to flee to Moscow from worse affected outer lands. Also, its control of the trade route from Novgorod to the Volga ensured it became the dominant principality. Ivan, who died in 1340, was careful to maintain good relations with the Horde but Ivan's successors increasingly fought with it.

While the Russians defeated the Mongols in 1378 and 1380 on the River Voje and at Kulikovo Field respectively, in 1382 the Golden Horde burnt Moscow and besieged it again in 1408. 1478 saw Moscow annex Novgorod and in 1480 Ivan III refused to pay tribute to the Golden Horde. Russia duly emerged as an independent state. In 1510 it annexed the principality of Pskov. Crimean Khan Mehmed-Girey reached Moscow in 1521 and was paid off by Vasily III. In 1552 and 1556 Ivan IV, the Terrible, conquered the Kazan and Astrakhan Khanates. To the west there was a litany of wars with Sweden, Lithuania and Poland, for more than two centuries. During this period Russia was frequently invaded and worsted but always eventually managed to expand.

Muscovy suffered terrible deprivations from the Tatars in 1521, 1541, 1570–72, 1591 and 1633. In 1571 Khan Devlet Girey burned Moscow and sacked thirty-five other towns, killed 60,000 Muscovites and took a similar number of slaves. Some 20,000 Tatars invaded in 1632 and in the following year 30,000 traversed the Oka River, the location of the Bereg Line, and laid waste to central Muscovy. Russian troops who were besieging Smolensk in the war with the Poles deserted to defend their homes. The failure to recapture Smolensk at least meant that Russia turned its attention to the southern border, first to secure it and then to expand south.

'The human toll from these raids appears to have been enormous: it has been estimated that in the period 1600–1650 some 150,000 to 200,000 Muscovites were captured and taken to Kaffa and other Crimean slave markets (this out of a total Muscovite population of about seven million, of whom no more than 500,000 resided in the southern forest-steppe and steppe).'[1] The disruption to life caused by the Tatars delayed development of the rich black steppe earth as peasants retreated to the more inhospitable but safer Siberia.

In the early seventeenth century the Cossacks emerged as a formidable force between the Russians and Tatars. 'Cossack' is derived from a Turkic name Kazak, and was applied to largely Slav autonomous and militarised border peoples. In the period from 1654 to 1667 war with Poland resulted in Russia gaining Kiev. In 1736 the Russians successfully stormed the linear barrier built by the Crimean Tatars across the isthmus but did not hold onto the Crimea. It was not until 1783 that the Crimea was formally annexed, thereby completing the Russian closure of the Pontic Steppe.

Nomads and shlyahs or trails

Turning to the nomads, the Kievan Rus was beset by Pechenegs and Polovtsians, who were probably Turkic peoples, and were later crushed by Mongols. The major threat to Muscovy and then Russia came from the Tatars. These were a group of Mongols fused with Turkic people, who became known to Europeans as the Golden Horde. The Horde was weakened by the Black Death in the 1340s and broken up by Tamerlane in the 1430s.

Two subsequent groups are of note: the Crimean and the Nogai Tartars. In 1441, the Crimean Tatars founded an independent Crimean Khanate under Hacı I Girey, a descendant of Genghis Khan. The Crimean Khanate became a vassal of the Ottomans in 1475 who by 1502 had taken over the remnants of the Golden Horde. Notwithstanding their subordinate status to the Ottomans, the Crimean Tatars ravaged Russia over the sixteenth and seventeenth centuries. This Khanate was ruled continuously by the Girey dynasty up to 1783 until annexed by Catherine the Great – making it the longest surviving of the states that followed the Golden Horde.

A second group who raided with the Crimean Tatars was the Nogai Horde – a confederation of Turkic and Mongol tribes that occupied the Pontic-Caspian steppe from about 1500. The Nogai were pastoral nomads and slave raiders whose routes were to the east of the Crimea Tatars.

On their raids the Crimean and the Nogai Hordes moved along the shlyahs or trails. These ran along watershed lines between the basins of the Don, the Dnieper, the Southern Bug and the Dniester. The most easterly watershed was a corridor which ran north from the Crimea between the riverheads of the Dnieper and Don basins. Between these two rivers flows the Seversky Donets which is a major tributary of the Don. There runs a watershed line, between the Dnieper and Don River basins, which provides a major land route, as opposed to a riverine route, both north and south. The most important route, the Muraysky Shlyah, ran from the fortress at Perekop on the Crimean isthmus to the Russian fortress at Tula. This trail went between the basins of the Vorskla and Seversky Donets – respectively tributaries of the Dnieper and the Don.

The route goes through an area of high grass, from which the word Muravsky is derived in Slavic. Tatar raiders stealthily approached Russia through this terrain. They used other shlyahs for the same purpose too, for example, the Kalmius and Izium Shlyahs which ran in the same direction. Also important was the Nogai Shlyah which lay to the east of the Crimean Tatar routes. It started east of the River Don's mouth on the Sea of Azov, and passed through the corridor between the rivers Voronezh, a south-flowing tributary of the Don, and the Tsna, a north-flowing tributary of the Oka.

Linear Barriers

Any search for Russian linear barriers might initially focus on the shlyah, and ought to consider how these might have been controlled using cross-route obstructions. The shlyah would be an obvious place for a linear barrier but a short barrier would be easy to circumvent given the lack of serious natural obstacles on the Russian Steppe and the mobility of the Tatars. Also, a different shlyah could be used meaning there would soon have to be several cross-route barriers on more than one shlyah. Indeed the invaders going through anything other than very dense forest could easily shift their line of approach to any approach route. Therefore, linear barriers were likely to be extended until great lengths of frontier were covered.

The Tatars, while not intending the downfall of the Russian states, stole people and goods in such substantial quantities that the state's viability was undermined. Negotiated agreements were impossible for there was no reason but compulsion to agree not to raid, there being little the Tatars wanted of the Russian in terms of trade; and that which they did want, people for slaves, they could take. Naturally the Russians could not afford to lose people, if only for economic reasons. The only option was to keep the Tatars out altogether which would mean the need to build continuous linear obstacles, given a homogenous geography without natural obstacles. And due to the size of Russia, continuous would mean very long indeed. Considering that the area dealt with consisted largely of naturally forest steppe, one might expect to find abatis – or at least records of the abatis, because physically these do not survive re-growth of the forest or its clearance. Where there was no forest – or where the fear of fire was paramount – linear earthworks might be expected.

Basically, the result was that over more than two centuries, Russia pushed the border south with the construction of a series of defence lines that consisted of fortified towns and lines of felled trees to form an abatis barrier. The trees were cut near the forest edge but concealed behind the forest border line. The resultant herbaceous barriers stood about six feet high and were pointed in the direction of the hostile advance. The objective was to impede advance, restrict the manoeuvrability of mounted forces, and earn time to evacuate civilians and call for support from the fortresses.

Bereg Line (1400s-1550s) – The first line was the Bereg, meaning shoreline, which was constructed in the fifteenth and early sixteenth centuries. This was a natural riverine linear barrier that ran along the north bank of the River Oka, south of Moscow where the man-made defences were focused on crossing points. It began at Nizhni Novogorod in the east and followed the Oka to Serpikov; and then went north across open countryside finishing at Zvenigorod on the Moskva River to the west of Moscow. In 1533 about 250 kilometres of fortifications were added from Kolomna to Kaluga along the north bank of the Oka. There was a fortress, south of the line, at Tula on the Muravsky Shlyah.

11.1: *Russia*

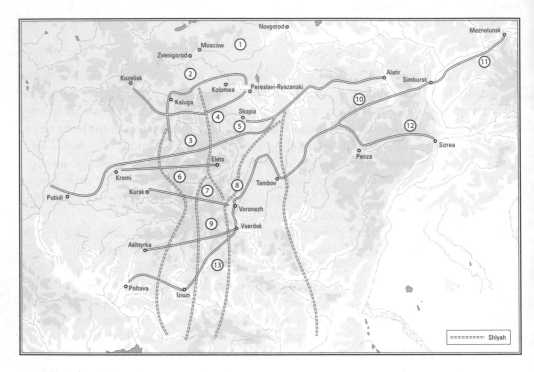

Bereg Line – Pre-Ivan IV
1.   Nizhni Novgorod to Zvenigorod Line (largely riverine line along Moskva river not itself shown)
2   Kolomna to Kaluga Line (along Oka)

Ivan IV (1547–1584)
3.   Novgorod Severski (Desna) Line - Alatir (Sura River) to Putivl'
4.   Zasechnaya Line – Pereslavl-Ryazanski (Oka) to Kozelisk (Zhizdra)
5.   Zasechnaya Line – Alatir to Skopin (Don)

Boris Godunov (1585–1605)
6.   Kromi (Oka) to Elets (near Don)
7.   Kursk (Seum) to Voronezh (Don)

Belgorodskaya Cherta (Seventeenth Century)
8.   Voronezh–Tsna Corridor (1635)
9.   Belgorodskaya Cherta (1635-1646) (Tambov (Tsna) to Akhtyrka (Vorskla))
10. Simbirskaya Cherta (1648-1684) (Tambov to Simbursk (Volga))
11. Zakamskaya Cherta (1652-1656) (Simbursk to Meznelunsk (Kama))
12. Seranskaya Cherta (1683–1684) (Simbirskaya Cherta via Penza to Sizran (Volga))

Izium Cherta
13. (1680s) Userdsk (Belgorod Line) via Izium to Kolomak River)

Although the *Gului-gorod* discussed below was not a static linear barrier, it needs to be considered in the context of the Russian suppression of the threat from nomads. Mobile barriers were specifically designed by sedentary states to take the fight to nomads.

Gului-gorod – Between the fifteenth and seventeenth centuries the Russian army developed linear barriers called *Gului-gorod* or walking towns.[2] These were intended for operation on the steppe where they could provide cover from nomad attacks and arrows, and moveable palisades through which firearms could shoot down mounted nomads. These were unlike earlier war wagons, where men fought from, on and between the vehicles, as they consisted of upright rectangular wooden shields, which moved on bogies or runners and which had gun ports. Before battle was joined, the units of the *Gului-gorod* were coupled together like railway carriages to form a continuous linear barrier. The men stood directly on the ground and there were no gaps between the individual units. Thus something that genuinely looked like a wall was presented to the enemy. Their value eventually diminished when nomads brought with them their own field artillery – as did the Crimean Tatars – but in the sixteenth century they played an important part in the shift of the Russian state from the defensive to the offensive. They were widely used in the sixteenth century wars with the Kazan and later by the Ukrainian Cossacks.

The Battle of Molodi in 1572, during the reign of Ivan the Terrible (1547–1584), perhaps marked a turning point in the fight between settled states and nomads. In 1571 Khan Dovlet Girai of the Crimean Khanate had burned Moscow; he reputedly killed 100,000 people and enslaved another 150,000. The following year Russians used the *Gului-gorod* to shelter their artillery and harquebusiers from Tatar archery. After several days of fighting a detachment of Russians left the protection of the *Gului-gorod* and attacked the Tatars in the rear while those who had remained behind the *Gului-gorod* advanced before it, crushing the Tatars.[3] Dovlet Girai's son, grandson and son-in-law were killed and only 20,000 of an army of 150,000 Tatars returned. The Ottoman Turks had supported their Tatar vassals and the Russian victory at Molodi, although little known in the west, was seen as a key to reversing the northern expansion of the Turks. A crucial role in the victory was accorded to the mobile linear barriers or *Gului-gorod*.

Zasechnaya Cherta – The Zasechnaya System was built during the reigns of Ivan IV, the Terrible, and his able servant, and then successor, Boris Godunov, who served as Regent from 1585 to 1598, and then Tsar, from 1598 to 1605. (Sometimes the system is called the Bolishnya Zasechnaya Cherta or Great Abatis Line.)

- A line ran from Alatir on the Sura River, in the east, via Shatsk to Novgorod Seversky, on the Desna, to the west. Shatsk blocked the Nogai Shlyah.
- The main construction effort was the Zasechnaya Cherta which consisted of two continuous lines joined by the Don River. The more westerly line ran from Pereslavl-Ryazanski via Tula (where the Muravsky Shlyah was blocked) to Kozelisk. To the east, and taking up the earlier line from Alatir to Shatsk, the continuous line finished at Skopin on the Don to the west of Shatsk.

- Under Boris Godunov further shorter lines appear to have been built across the Muravsky Shlyah between Kromi (River Oka) and Elets (near the Don) and to the southern towns of Kursk (River Seym) and Voronezh (Don).

Belgorodskaya Cherta – This line started as a short barrier blocking the corridor that stretched from Voronezh to Tsna. The line extended over the entire southern frontier.

- **Kozlov Steppe Wall – Voronezh-Tsna Corridor** – As Russian estates and peoples expanded south of the Zasechnaya Cherta they remained vulnerable to the Nogai Tatars who were moving up the Nogai Shlyah. So a decision was made in the mid-1630s to build a twenty-five kilometre earthwork to block the open gap in the Voronezh-Tsna corridor across the Nogai Shlyah between the Polnoi Voroneszh, a tributary of the Voronezh, and the Chelnovaia River, a tributary of the Tsna. Initially a palisade was envisaged, but the risk of its being burnt was considered too great and a linear earthwork was constructed. This was designed by a Dutch engineer, Jan Cornelius von Rodenburg to incorporate both cannon and handgun positions. 'The earth steppe wall began at Belyi Kolodez' on the right bank of the Pol'noi Voronezh River, sixteen kilometres west of Kozlov, and ran eastward for twenty-five kilometres until it reached the left bank of the Chelnovaia River.'[4] To the east of the Chelnovaia was an abatis barrier which filled the gap to Tambov on the Tsna River. The barrier was built on time and budget and it worked immediately. In 1636 a force of 10,000 Tatars was driven off. The success of the Kozlov defences convinced the Russians that it was possible to move the main frontier down from the Zasechnaya Cherta (Abatis Line) to a new line running west from a wall on the Kozlov steppe, so as to cross all the shlyahs.
- **Belgorodskaya Cherta** – This ran along the southern edge of forest steppe from, at the west end, Akhtyrka on the Vorskla, and east to Tambov on the Tsna, for 800 kilometres, of which 140 kilometres consisted of earthworks.
- **Simbirskaya Cherta** – The Belgorodskaya Cherta was continued by the Simbirskaya Cherta from Tambov on the Tsna, to Saransk, west of the Sura, on towards Tagay, between the Sura and the Sviyaga Rivers, and then to Simbirsk on the Volga totalling 500 kilometres. It was completed in 1658.
- **Seranskaya Cherta** – Roughly half way between Tambov and Simbursk, the Seranskaya Cherta split off from the Simbirskaya Cherta and ran about 300 kilometres past Penza to Sizran on the Volga.
- **Zakamskaya Cherta** – The move by Russians eastwards disrupted the Turkic Bashkirs and so further linear barriers were constructed that ran east of the Volga. The Zakamskaya Cherta went east of Simbursk on the Volga, to the Meznelunsk on the Kama, for about 400 kilometres.

Izium Line – In 1679–1680 most of the steppe along the Donets and Oskol rivers was enclosed behind yet another new more southerly barrier, the Izium Line. The enclosed area formed a triangle whose base was the Belgorod Line. The Line ran along the lengths of the Oskol and the Donets Rivers, and at their confluence stood Izium as the point of the triangle. Whereas the eastern end diverged from the Belgorod Line near Userdsk, the western end did not quite return to the Belgorod Line but stopped on the Kolomak River. (Kolomak is about sixty kilometres south-west of the west end of the Belgorod Line at Akhtyrka.) The Izium Line brought the Russian lines another 160 kilometres south-east of the Belgorod Line and about 150 kilometres from the Black Sea. The line itself was over 500 kilometres long. The area inside the line corresponds approximately to Kharkiv Oblast and contains the modern city of Kharkiv which began as a small fort in about 1630, and today is the second largest city in the independent Republic of Ukraine.

Pskov-Smolensk-Briansk line – A rare example of a linear barrier which was built by one state against another was seen when Peter the Great ordered the construction of an abatis against Charles XII of Sweden. From 1706 to 1708 a fortified western border was established along the Pskov-Smolensk-Briansk line as a desperate measure. In 1724, Peter I introduced the fortress system of defending borders (primarily in the west), but Russia continued to use frontier lines in the south and east.

Conclusion – Muscovy and Russia

The lines built by Muscovy and then Russia worked on a similar basis to the Kievan Rus' Zmievi Vali: 'The object of all these linear defensive systems was to impede the advance of the Tatars, restrict the mobility of cavalry, and gain time to allow the civilian population to be evacuated and large forces to be summoned from nearby fortresses. The Tatars had no siege machinery or great knowledge of siege warfare, so unsophisticated earth and earth-and-timber fortifications served the purpose well, and were cheap to build.'[5]

By the admission of the Tatars they were successful: 'Even the Tatars themselves acknowledged this (fortification had blocked the Nogai Shlyah), some Tatar princes … admitting to Russian interpreters in 1637 that the new defences at Kozlov and Tambov had 'shut down' the Nogai Road.'[6] Also: 'A 1681 report of the Military Chancellery to the Boyer Duma assessed the impact of the Belgorod Line in the most enthusiastic terms, claiming not only that 'enemy warriors can no longer attack the Borderland towns by surprise because of that defence line,' but that military colonisation along the Line had even transformed the national economy by making the southern frontier safe for private colonisation.'[7] Previously peasants had preferred to risk their chances in Siberia rather than be taken slave by the Tatars. Now they stayed put and opened up the extremely fertile black earth belt. The population of the Moscovite state doubled in the quarter century after the construction of the Belgorod Line.

With the fall of Kiev the heartland of Russia moved to the less hospitable but more defendable north – with Muscovy emerging as the dominant state. It then developed technology involving firearms, linear barriers both moveable (like the *Gului-gorod*) and static, in addition to infantry and cavalry. Using these means Muscovy managed to stabilise the southern frontier and then to move it further south, displacing the nomads in the process. In the eighteenth century, it was the nomads whose own linear defences were stormed by the Russians when the Perekop Wall across the Crimean isthmus was breached. In Russia, as this chapter has hopefully shown, linear barriers played a crucial and aggressive part in the grand exercise of political and military expansion.

Chapter Twelve

Non-Eurasian Linear Barriers

Essentially this book covers the Eurasian Steppe, the borders regions of the Sahara and Arabian deserts, and northern and eastern Europe. So if there is any validity to claims about how barriers have solved and still do solve certain problems, then examples should also be sought and found in the Americas and Africa. It might be said in advance that, certainly outside of north-western Europe, most Eurasian linear barriers have been built in response to the threat posed by horse-borne nomads. Given that these did not exist in the pre-Columbian Americas or in sub-Saharan Africa, then possibly quite different situations are likely to have produced non-Eurasian linear barriers, to the extent that they exist at all.

1. South America – Peru and Bolivia

The Great Wall of Santa – A non-Eurasian long wall was first discovered in 1931 by the Shippee-Johnson Peruvian Expedition in an early use of aerial photography to survey archaeological sites. It was then interpreted as mainly defensive, built by the Chimú people (AD 1000–1460) to prevent the Incas from invading their territory. The wall is described in a compendious volume about the extensive archaeological survey conducted in 1979 and 1980.[1] It was found to have been made in five sections with substantial gaps between the sections and dated to the seventh to eleventh centuries. The 'forts' along its length were dated even earlier. 'The system extends in four major sections along the lower forty kilometres of the north desert margin of Santa, with two additional long sections that extend out across the desert between Santa and Chao valleys, adjacent to steep slopes of the western Andean cordillera.'[2]

The wall was put into global perspective: 'With a total length of slightly over 70 kilometres, the Great Wall system is miniscule compared to its (justly more renowned) counterpart in China. Nonetheless, it is one of the more significant engineering feats in the Central Andes.'[3]

The later report did not consider the wall's function to be defensive. 'The wall system does not presently consist of a single continuous entity, and, judging from the complete lack of any remains (e.g. rock rubble) in the main intervening gaps, never did.... Our research indicates that the wall probably would not have served as an effective defensive barrier, not only because attacking forces could easily have gotten around it in the gaps but also because in no place does it appear to have exceeded an easily surmountable height of 2.5 metres.'[4]

Essentially the wall was seen as having been built at a time of peace: 'Within this context of unprecedented valley-to-valley settlement continuity and interaction, the wall therefore becomes both necessary both as a boundary delineating regional sociocultural groupings and as a means of controlling extensive coastwise commerce.'[5] The overall conclusion is: 'It did not serve as a defensive wall; rather, ... it probably served as a corvée labor project that divided different ethnic groups in the only period when population was not limited to each valley oasis, but ran almost continuously across the intervening desert.'[6] The message is sent very strongly that there could not be a military defensive function.

The Great Wall of the Inca – An expedition in 1984 to South America searched for what has been named 'The Great Wall of the Inca' and associated fortifications. The wall was 240 kilometres long but only a few feet high at altitudes between 3,000 and 4,000 metres, as it ran along mountain ridges between Peru and Bolivia. The proposed background for its construction was the expansion of the Inca in the fifteenth century which took them across the high plains of Bolivia into what is now Chile and Argentina. Around 1490 the Inca apparently experienced an unexpected setback when the rainforest tribe from the eastern Andean slopes, the Chirimayo, counter-attacked: 'Whatever the incentive, the Chirimayo's attack evoked a massive response from the Inca which resulted in construction of a north-south defensive wall linked by large stone forts.'[7]

The 1984 expedition found along the top of a ridge: 'A wall of broken stones – at first intermittent and then continuous – that stood along the edge of the drop. This wall would have acted as a deterrent to attackers, who would have already been fatigued by storming up the steep slope.'[8] At this altitude a wall did not need to be too high and its purpose was to discourage less acclimatised lowland Indians who would have been too exhausted to climb over a low wall after ascending several thousand feet. Unlike the Great Wall of Santa, this wall is seen as having a clear defensive purpose: 'Only a fraction of this defensive system has been discovered and mapped to date, but the wall clearly is comparable in concept, if not in scale, to the Great Wall of China. With a length of at most 150 miles and standing at no more than a few feet high, the wall originally stretched along a high eastern ridge of the Andes.'[9]

2. Central America – Guatemala

The Earthworks of Tikal – Tikal was a Mayan rainforest city in the centre of the Yukatan peninsula in what is now modern Guatemala. Excavations by the University of Pennsylvania started in 1955 and uncovered a great city. It is now a Unesco World Heritage Site in partially cleared forest with archetypal great tiered stone pyramids and wide plazas. It constituted one of the dominant kingdoms of the Maya and reached its peak during the Classic Period between 200 and 900. The king lists are known and many of their tombs identified. The city covered at least sixteen square kilometres and is located in fertile upland soils. Despite its size and political prominence, it had no water supply other than rainwater which was stored in ten reservoirs.

In the late 1960s an earthwork was discovered about 4.5 kilometres to the north of the city. This structure was about twelve kilometres long and bounded by two swamps. It faced the city of Uaxactum.[10] Pottery dated it to between AD 600 and 800. 'The magnitude, construction, and orientation suggest that they (the earthworks) functioned first to repel organised bands of hostile invaders from Uaxactun, rather than to control friendly traders headed for markets in the city or subjects of the realm of Tikal itself.'[11]

Speculating as to motivation: 'Why was so much effort expended to protect this land so far from the concentrations of wealth and authority in the center? ... The inhabitants of Tikal... were interested in protecting the agricultural resources on which they ultimately depended. In answering the next question as to how hostilities between Tikal and Uaxactun could have reached such a level, it seems plausible to surmise that tensions increased as populations expanded. Surely, as the agricultural sustaining areas of the various centres grew and at last began to infringe upon each other, disputes over land could have developed into deep-seated enmity between the cities, and eventually, war.'[12] In other words, the area of valued land which was necessary for food production was being expanded and defended at a time of increasing population. This sounds very like the valued land and warring states patterns encountered in the Old World.

Work in 2003 showed that the scale of the earthworks had been underestimated; a later figure reached 13.6 kilometres. At the same time its military function was questioned. 'Of the many explanations for it, the most durable is that it was intended as part of some sort of territorial boundary.... On the other hand, what was long considered to be one of the principal nails in the coffin of Maya pacifism might not be a fortification at all.'[13] Recently a hypothesis has been advanced that the 'earthworks as a limestone filtration trench that could have been used to collect subsurface water to mitigate the effects of canicular (that is related to the rising of the Dog Star Sirius) drought or to support off-season agriculture.'[14] It is not possible here to determine the function of the linear barriers around Tikal, but it is interesting to note among some archaeologists and academics the apparent increasing rejection of a pure military function involving warring states.

3. Africa – Nigeria

In Nigeria there appeared to be two great earthworks in areas of what are, or were, equatorial rainforest. One barrier is actually a single great circle, to the north of Lagos, and thus not far from the coast in the western part of the country. The other is a set of barriers which form a dense mosaic of earthworks which is located around the inland Benin City (which also has vast city walls). In their extent and mass, they match or exceed anything else on the globe. 'For the last half millennium, the wet forests of southern Nigeria have brooded silently over what is arguably the largest single archaeological feature on this planet.[15] It must have taken centuries of dry season toil to build; and by the time this colossal task was abandoned in the mid-fifteenth century, an intricate network of over 16,000 kilometres of banks and ditches (*iya*) enclosed a 4000 square kilometre cluster of community lands – a vast legacy in earth.'[16] That they are barely mentioned in the literature on linear barriers is testament to the exclusion of Africa from broader historical contextual analysis. But it is also difficult to interpret these barriers, at least on the basis of the usual assumptions, as to purpose made by western analysts.

Sungbo's Eredo – In south-west Nigeria there is a continuous irregular earthwork ring called Sungbo's Eredo. Its total circumference is over 160 kilometres and the diameter varies between thirty-five and forty kilometres. The ring surrounds the Yoruba town of Ijebu-Ode in Ogun state of south-west Nigeria. It encompasses several towns and villages. Carbon dating has given date range of AD 800 to 1000 – covering a period of political confrontation and consolidation in the southern Nigeria rainforest. 'Traditional lore links the construction of this impressive boundary to the legendary Sungbo, a wealthy childless widow, giantess, priestess/goddess, devil woman or even erstwhile Queen of Sheba, to whose grove and magically bare grave flock many long-distance pilgrims'.[17] When built it may have been part of a kingdom-building exercise in the equatorial rain forest.

The moat is between five and seven metres wide and is unusual in that its sides are vertical, not V-shaped. This is possible because it is excavated out of laterite, a mixture of clay and iron-oxides, which can hold an upright shape. It is thought not to have had a defensive function as the constant factor is the level of the groundwater in the moat. As a result the depth varies from shallow to up to twenty metres. The water contained in it may have been what conferred its protective quality, rather than the trench itself. It may be a spiritual rather than a physical barrier occupied by swampland demons. 'It was not a physical but a spiritual line of defence – perceived to be peopled by swamp land demons, which surrounded and protected the kingdom over one thousand years ago.'[18]

Edo State Iya – In western Nigeria, in the area of Benin City, the capital of Edo state, there is a series of earthworks that extend over 16,000 kilometres in length surrounding discrete but broadly contiguous areas. The question of purpose becomes very interesting. The usual assumption is that the physical barriers are built to keep out physical entities – something solid like a warrior. But what if non-physical entities were considered more dangerous than solid bodies? 'One important dimension, absent in Western theoretical models, is the role of earthworks as barriers against the spirit world outside: into the ditches were cast the corpses of those with no sons to propitiate their restless spirits with the proper burial rites and, at City wall entrances, annual ceremonies augmented old charm pots to keep evil forces at bay.'[19] Also, 'Outermost earthworks were known as *iya n'uwa* (boundary ditches), which only women were allowed to cross, calling out as they did so – faint clues that predynastic settlements were lineage-based, and their earthworks demarcated exogamous units (with no intermarriage).'[20] This is to enter a world of ritual and taboo that is very different to the motivation behind most of the linear barriers encountered in the previous survey section.

4. Easter Island

Easter Island developed a hugely vigorous stone-based culture that erected over 300 statues up to 10 metres high between about AD 1000 and 1700. It is also the site of a substantial ditch. Easter Island is shaped like a slightly flattened isosceles triangle with the two acute angles being peninsulas where there are high ground peaks and isthmuses. The Poike Peninsula is the longer of the two and has a narrower point. There are only about nineteen kilometres between the peninsulas and thirteen kilometres between the apex and the base.

Poike Peninsula Ditch – The great ditch across the peninsula was first cut in the fourth century, about four metres deep, thirteen metres wide and three kilometres long. There were about twenty-six trenches over a hundred metres long with gaps about eight metres between them. The location of the ditch might indicate that it had a defensive function. 'The Poike-ditch feature is considered a defensive structure on the basis that it was once filled with grass and branches to burn the defeated 'Long-Ears' after a battle which took place about A.D. 1680. The explorer, anthropologist and archaeologist Thor Heyerdahl thinks of the 'Long-Ears' as descendants of the pre-Polynesian population.'[21]

Revisionist analysis, however, rejected Thor Heyerdahl's analysis. Carbon dating of the ditch shows that its origins are nearly 2,000 years ago, in a time when population pressure and resource depletion were not an issue. No archaeological evidence of fighting has been found in the ditch. The ditch might have been used for agricultural purposes or to demarcate a ritual zone around a magic mountain. The burning could be associated with slash-and-burn agriculture or even cooking: 'The two mile ditch is claimed by tradition to be only an earth 'oven', and in reality seems of little, if any, defensive value. As in the case of similar fosses dug by the Polynesians of the Tuamoru archipelago to the west, it would appear to have served to provide moist soil and protection from the wind and the sun in the growing of bananas, sugar cane, and taro, which the Easter Islanders cultivated. It apparently was dug where it is situated, not because this was a strategic position for defence, but to take advantage of a soil-filled fissure across the island at this point.' [22]

There is also the possibility that the ditch was a barrier controlling access to the end of the Poike Peninsula, a barrier that terminated in what was literally a magic mountain. The linear barrier might first have had an agricultural or ritualistic role when earlier times were good: more than a millennium later it could have had a defensive purpose when changed conditions meant it could no longer function in its original role or roles. The military historian John Keegan identifies the ditch with warfare: 'At one end of the island a ditch had been dug to separate a peninsula from the mainland, surely a strategic defensive undertaking.... The existence of the entrenchment at the Poike Peninsula suggests that some of them (the Easter Islanders) agreed with his (Clausewitz) dictum that the strategic defensive is the strongest form of warfare.'[23]

Conclusion – non-Eurasian walls

Outside Eurasia there is physical evidence of linear barrier building in the Pacific, the Americas, and Africa. But it appears to be the exception rather than the rule. Possibly this is because the major factor leading to Eurasian linear barrier building did not exist – that is conflict between settled (usually literate) states and less developed, often nomadic, polities. Also, movement was by foot – there being no suitable beasts of burden at the time of construction.

Linear barrier building in these regions may have been the result of factors that do not fit into Eurasian patterns apart from warring states. Societal and religious organisation, particularly to do with taboo, may have driven linear barrier construction for reasons which do not fit into any known Eurasian mould.

Eastern Asia

There are some linear barriers built in Vietnam that might be remarked on here although they were built by developed literate states.

Nguyen Walls – In the seventeenth century Vietnam divided into a separate Trinh north and Nguyen south – a division which would continue for 150 years. 'The Nguyen in the South constructed two enormous walls at narrow points near the centre of the country. In seven major campaigns, some lasting several years, the Trinh armies from the North never succeeded in breaking through both of these barriers.'[24] Here, walls are explicitly built at the 'narrow points'.

Viet/ Hrê Wall – In 2011 the discovery of a 127 kilometre length of wall in central Vietnam from Quang Ngai Province to Binh Dinh Province was announced. Construction was started in 1819 – so it is later than the linear barriers covered in this book but is perhaps worth noting because, given the then historic context of the region, it is pre-modern. Sections reach four metres high and it is built of alternating sections of stone and earth. Over fifty forts have been identified. It was constructed along an older road and may delineate the border between the Viet people in the plain and the Hrê tribal highlanders. 'Research suggests it may have been built in cooperation between both the Viet and the Hrê.'[25]

Chapter Thirteen

Summary of Survey Material Through History

In the survey section three great regions of linear barrier building have been identified: first, the Eurasian Steppe; second, northern and eastern Europe; and third, the North African and Middle Eastern semi-arid belt. There are overlaps between the regions, and nomads and migrants also moved from one region to another. It is still, however, useful to look at these three regions and consider how the conditions which gave rise to linear barrier building arose and why they ended. In the first and third areas, the relationships largely involved nomads and settled states because adjacent fertile and semi-arid regions lay in great but discrete belts. The second area was temperate, fertile and increasingly consisted of cleared and farmed land. It featured a wide range of relationships between states and surrounding peoples. The relationships described in this area usually involved peoples at different phases of development – generally, settled states with nomads and barbarians who might also have been migrants.

A further condition found in all three regions, and which sometimes resulted in linear barrier building, was that of warring states of similar ethnicity and culture, located within an area increasingly constrained of resources. Such 'warring states' linear barriers could emerge at any time in any region when the conditions were right. These were first identified with the Chinese Western Zhou period from 770 to 221 BC.

This chapter's summary focuses on the regions where states and nomads, barbarians and migrants, had to manage relationships. In this summary the African and Middle-Eastern semi-arid belt is looked at first. Second, Europe is considered. Third and last, the great irruptions across the Eurasian Steppe are reviewed.

1: African and Middle-Eastern semi-arid belt – local nomads and transhumance

Since the very early recorded history of Egypt and Sumer four millennia ago, foot-slogging nomads and their herds have posed a problem for riverine civilisations – particularly when nomads and their herds, made desperate by drought, threatened to trample delicate irrigation schemes. Climate change resulted in such a rapid alteration in the environment that desperation over sheer survival forced more belligerent intrusions by nomadic pastoralists, and weakened the ability of sedentary states to resist. Egypt had chronic problems with Asiatics, and Sumer III was in part brought down by the semi-nomadic Martu. Both of these settled civilisations built some form of linear barriers, in response to the nomad threat.

By the first millennium BC nomads were mounting small tough horses with great endurance and a fair turn of speed; and they were carrying the short but very powerful recurve composite bow of wood, sinew and horn. Again, climate change around 800 BC reduced the steppe range, yet it conferred a relative advantage to those nomadic groups who could travel long distances. The new, fully mounted, nomads appeared to have a near invincible military technology combining speed of movement with outranging projectile weapons. In response, sedentary states and empires experimented with a great variety of strategies for dealing with the nomad threat. These strategies ranged from diplomacy to aggressive counter-attack, and included the construction of linear barriers.

Nomad attacks are recorded from Hither Asia to China. The Cimmerians destroyed Phrygia. The Scythians assisted the Medes and Babylonians in sacking Nineveh in 612 BC. Nebuchadnezzar, mindful of the threat of the Medes who with Scythian assistance had brought down the Assyrians, built two linear barriers across the Tigris and Euphrates convergence point. Further east the Chinese were afflicted by the 'very swift' Xianyun.

Later the Romans built linear barriers in North Africa to control transhumance in the form of the Fossatum Africae and the many *clausurae* or short walls across passes. The Sasanians constructed a fortified canal along the right bank of the Euphrates against Arab raiders. There are also a number of linear barriers of uncertain date, roughly following the line of the Fertile Crescent in Syria and Cappadocia to the area before the Tigris and the Euphrates converge.

By the seventh century linear barriers, albeit of different dates, could be found all along the semi-arid belt from the Atlantic to Mesopotamia. These fell out of use after the Arabs, ignited by Islam, irrupted across the region and then provided a unifying religion and culture after becoming sedentary themselves. While the Sasanians stoutly defended their northern borders with linear barriers they mis-identified what turned out to be the critical threat, and allowed the southern Mesopotamian aquatic linear barriers to fall into disrepair. Instead, they relied on alliances with Arab Lakhmids, who proved deficient when the recently Islamised Peninsular Arabs attacked from the south. The Sasanians were destroyed while the Arabs quickly spread to Central Asia and across North Africa. Linear barriers then ceased to be built in this African, Middle-East region.

2: Europe – barbarians, empires and colonisers

Although nomads caused problems to settled empires, as long as the steppe zones remained isolated, generally the empires and states could contain the nomad threat. Greek states built walls to resist the other Greek states. Both the Greeks and Romans constructed linear barriers to deal with the non-nomadic barbarian threat.

The Greeks had a landscape full of narrow peninsulas and passes through land corridors. Here their investment in linear barriers of limited length could produce high returns in terms of defending strategic routes or regions of valued land. They developed a unique form of linear barrier specifically to protect transport routes, namely the long wall from acropolis to harbour. Hellenistic expansion into Central Asia and the Crimea resulted in the construction of full circuit barriers around *Margiana*, later Merv, and multiple lines across the Kerch peninsula, protecting the Bosphoran State. Alexander's

Hellenised Macedonians later built pass frontier walls to the north of the Graeco-Bactrian state.

The Romans built linear barriers not only to deal with north-western barbarians in Britain and Germany but also to control transhumance. Linear barriers were built in what are now Algeria, Tunisia and Libya – and possibly in Romania, Moldavia and the Ukraine. There are linear barriers around the trans-Danubian parts of the Great Hungarian and Wallachian Plains which might have been constructed by nomadic and sedentary peoples to assist the Romans in the protection of the Empire.

Overpopulation resulted in Germanic and Slavic barbarian peoples pushing out from around the Baltic region by the beginning of the first millennium. The Roman trans-riverine linear barriers were too demanding to be retained by the mid-third century. The Rhine and the Danube then marked the Roman Empire's frontiers – against which pressure constantly rose, caused by population growth among Germanic tribes.

As the outer frontiers became increasingly vulnerable in the later third century, inner walls were built or rebuilt across the Julian Alps and the Isthmus of Corinth. These protected core areas of Italy and Greece. In the early fifth century the Romans were losing control of north-western Europe. The Rhine froze in 406 and the Germanic peoples, and the nomadic Alans, became permanent migrants into the Empire. In 410 the Emperor Honorius responded to a request for assistance from the Romano-Britons by telling them to look after their own defence. Hadrian's Wall was abandoned at this date, or possibly slightly earlier, and there was no further line, natural or man-made, to hold until the Channel. Britain now faced the full force of invasion by migrants from Ireland, Jutland and Frisia. The Western Roman Empire collapsed under pressure from migrant nomads and barbarians. As Britain broke up into sub-Roman warring states, linear barriers were built across the Roman and pre-Roman route system. Peoples from Jutland, and particularly the Angles, may have also brought their own tradition of linear barrier-building as they sought to consolidate their hold on land taken from the Britons. Separately, a series of linear barriers found in Ireland might mark the retreat of the people of Ulster, who had been forced back by southern expansion into their territory.

Throughout Europe, newly dominant powers were uniting their respective nations: Denmark was unified by the Danes, Central England by the Angles and Mercians, and southern England by the Saxons. In the case of the first two, the construction of the Danevirke and Offa's Dyke probably marked this unification, and the sustainable limits of territory that could be assimilated. Also, frontiers which may have incorporated linear barriers in the form of abatis possibly delineated the limits of Frankish expansion, along the Limes Saxoniae and the Limes Sorabicus. Polish state creation might have involved the construction of linear barriers; these possibly included abatis which have since been lost.

Between the ninth and eleventh centuries linear barriers appear largely to have fallen out of use in Europe. The possible reasons are considered in more depth later but might be related to the development of more effective point defences and mobile mounted defence forces. And in the case of waterborne Viking raiders it may have been impossible to predict from which direction assault would come, thus rendering traditional linear defences nearly worthless.

3: Eurasian steppe – trans-steppe nomad irruptions

In the fourth century BC, the northern Chinese states of Qin, Zhao and Yan eliminated the adjacent semi-nomads, which led to confrontation with the far more dangerous true steppe nomads. There followed three great nomad outbursts across the steppe, each of which resulted in the creation of vast if generally short lived nomad empires.

The Eurasian Steppe was not a smooth unbroken and empty road. Rather it had many obstacles in the form of naturally constricted regions, like the Gansu Corridor or passes such as those through the Carpathians. In addition, several polities already occupied certain particular regions. As a result, movement from one part of the Eurasian Steppe to the next tended to be violent, as pressure built up until there was an irruption of peoples, often creating havoc in the process.

1. Xiongnu to Huns – the first phase of Eurasian linear barrier building
In the later fourth and early third centuries BC the three Chinese states of Qin, Zhao and Yan suppressed the semi-nomads to their north and built walls to consolidate their hold on the territory acquired. In response the newly formed Xiongnu confederation then forced the Chinese back. There was a recovery after the First Emperor reunited China and built the First Great Wall. But then nomads burst west through the Gansu Corridor and into Central Asia and beyond. This time the nomadic genie was truly out of the bottle and the direction of people flows switched. In the fourth century BC Europeans under Alexander the Great had established themselves in Central Asia. The appearance of nomads from the east ended these Hellenistic kingdoms and meant that Central Asia became part of the Asian and not the European world.

The Xiongnu created an eastern empire to the north of China and a western empire in Central Asia. The possibly Indo-European Yuezhi fled the Xianbei confederation, established the Kushan Empire that extended from Bactria to India. By the fourth century new and terrible nomads appeared on the western Pontic Steppe – the Asiatic Huns. The extent of any connection between the Xiongnu and the Huns is disputed but both form part of same overall flow of peoples.

The Xiongnu to the east and later the Huns to the west provoked the first great phase of Eurasian linear barrier building. This was mostly spent by the sixth century when the Chinese Han, Sasanians and Byzantines – in part using linear barriers – largely mastered the steppe nomads. As the Chinese Han dynasty restored China's finances and developed its military skills, it took control of the Gansu Corridor and the route west. As it did so, it built huge lengths of walls west along the Corridor to protect the route, and the loess soil and oases along it. Later, when the Han shifted their capital eastwards to Luoyang as walls to the north of China were built, they had embarked upon the building of the greatest length of walls, 10,000 kilometres in total, that was constructed by any one dynasty, anytime or anywhere.

After the Roman Empire split, the Greek Byzantine east was unable to control its outer borders. So it created a core interior defence system with the Theodosian Walls between the Sea of Marmara and the Golden Horn, the Anastasian Walls between the Black Sea and the Sea of Marmara, and walls across the Corinthian Isthmus. Following the great Hun raid of 539 the Byzantine Emperor Justinian built or rather largely rebuilt earlier Greek barriers at the Thracian Chersonesos, the Corinth Isthmus, the Pallene and Kerch Peninsulas, the Thracian Peninsula, the Anastasian Walls and the Thermopylae and Heraclea Passes.

The Sasanian Empire of Persia first built linear barriers in the form of a fortified canal in the third century AD in Mesopotamia to the west of the Euphrates, in order to protect against raids by semi-nomadic Arabs. By the fifth century the opening up of the Eurasian Steppe resulted in far greater pressure on the northern Sasanian border areas – particularly the very fertile Gorgan Plain and the gap between the west Caspian and the Caucasus. Despite constant war with the Romans, the Sasanians also cooperated with and took subsidies from them in order to defend the Caucasus passes and land corridors. The result was that individually or collectively there was a line of barriers, going from east to west, which were the Sadd-i-Iskandar, the Tammisha Wall, the Derbent, the Ghilghilchay and Beshbarmak Walls, the central Caucasus Darial Pass, the Anastasian Wall, the Thracian Chersonesos Wall, the Pallene Peninsula Wall, the Thermopylae and Heraclea pass walls and the Hexamilion Wall across the Isthmus of Corinth. This campaign of sixth century linear barrier building may have played a critical role in stopping the Huns from breaking up the Byzantine Empire. In that sense, one might say that barriers played a key part in the Byzantines avoiding a repetition of the earlier fall of the Western Roman Empire.

2. Turks and the second phase of linear barrier building

The dramatic emergence of the Turks in the sixth century provoked prodigious wall building by the Northern Qi and the Sui Dynasties. Although the Chinese Sui Dynasty proved short-lived, it fell to a largely Chinese Tang dynasty who developed a range of strategies to deal with steppe nomads, and one which eschewed linear barrier building.

The full force of the Turkic explosion, however, was by this time moving west, and causing both Turkic and other peoples to flee before them. Certainly Turkic nomads challenged the states and polities of Central Asia and around the Pontic Steppe. The Turkic Khazars split apart the Bulgars, who themselves may have been descended in part from the Huns. Further west, the Bulgars combined with the Slavs to create a state surrounded by linear barriers which would rival the Byzantine Empire. In the east the Volga Bulgarian state might have been protected by a linear earthwork between the Volga and the Kama Rivers. The Avars, possibly the same people as the Rouran, may have reused the Csörszárok system around the eastern Great Hungarian Plain.

The construction of the great oasis walls of Central Asia appeared to coincide with the period of Turkic expansion into Central Asia. The Turkic Pechenegs were a constant threat to the emerging Kievan Rus state, which had been formed by Vikings and Slavs who had migrated to the borders of the forest and the grassland steppe. Ultimately this Pecheneg threat was contained by the construction of a massive series of linear earthworks by the Rus, subsequently named the Zmievi Vali. When the Pechenegs were displaced by another Turkic people, the Polovtsians, the linear barriers performed the same function against the latter as they did against the former.

The Byzantine Empire eventually fell to the Ottoman Turks. But by the fifteenth century, when the Turks took Constantinople – whose walls had held out against numerous nomad armies before – they were no longer fighting like nomads but used a powerful Janissary infantry and blasted the ancient walls with mighty artillery. Most significantly, for the purposes of this book, the Ottomans had built great fortresses, like the Rumeli Castle on the Bosphorus, first begun in 1451, with which they isolated and weakened Constantinople, setting up the Byzantine capital for its final fall two years later.

3. Mongols and Tatars and the third phase of linear barrier building
There is a long gap between the later first millennium and the mid-second millennium when there was comparatively little linear barrier building. The Chinese Tang and Song dynasties did not build walls – except in the case of the latter by proxy. The Song left upper China to the semi-nomadic Kitan Liao and then the Jin – who both built linear barriers to the north of the Chinese Great Walls against steppe nomads further to the north. First, the Kitan Liao were ranged against the Jin, and then the Jin against the Mongols. Eventually the Jin and the Song fell to the Mongols who formed the Yuan dynasty.

It was the Mongols and the Tatars who provoked the third and last great phase of linear barrier building on the borders of China and the emerging Russia. The Mongols ruled an Empire from Europe to the Pacific – the greatest the world has ever known. Although the Mongols lost control of China and broke up into various sub-groups, known collectively as the Golden Hordes, they remained a potent force for centuries afterwards. To the north of China the Ming contained the threat with a final grand efflorescence of wall building in the fifteenth and sixteenth centuries, after a gap of nine centuries.

After the destruction of the southern Rus states by the Mongols, the centre of gravity of Rus politics moved north and eventually Muscovy emerged as the most powerful principality. Russia developed the strategies finally to defeat the steppe nomads, using a combination of firearms and fixed and mobile linear barriers. The Muscovite Rus stabilised its borders with the construction of the Bolishnya Zasechnaya Cherta or Great Abatis Barrier. At the Battle of Molodi in 1572 the army of Ivan the Terrible defeated the Crimean Tatars. The Russians protected themselves from nomad arrows with their *Gului-gorod* or walking towns.

The Crimean and Nogai Tatars continued to raid and carried off tens of thousands of Russian annually, until they were blocked by the Belgorodskaya Cherta which the Russians built between 1635 and 1646. The Russians moved south behind new lines of linear barriers until, in the eighteenth century, they stormed the Perekop Wall across the Crimean Isthmus and eventually annexed the Crimea itself.

Closing down the Eurasian Steppe
In the fifth century AD nomadic peoples ruled empires covering the four steppe ranges in Mongolia, Central Asia, the Pontic and Caspian region, and the Great Hungarian Plain. In the thirteenth century the Mongols ruled the world's greatest ever Empire, but by the eighteenth century the nomads had largely been crushed throughout the steppe range and the Eurasian Steppe highway was effectively closed down.

The first Eurasian Steppe zone to be lost by the nomads was the Great Hungarian Plain which the nomadic Huns, then the Avars, and lastly the Magyars had occupied. The Huns were defeated in Europe by the Gepids, an eastern Germanic tribe related to the Goths, in 454 at Nedeo. In turn the Avars with their Lombard allies drove out the Gepids. The Avars were defeated by an alliance of the Carolingians and the Bulgars. After that the Plain was occupied by the migrating Magyars who possessed it once they became sedentary. Soon the area ceased to be a habitat for nomads.

At the other end of the Eurasian land mass, the Ming drove the Mongols out of China and stabilised their northern border with linear barriers. It was the Russians who closed down the nomads of the Pontic and Caspian, and later the Central Asian Steppe. Between the fifteenth and seventeenth centuries, static and mobile linear barriers played a central role in defeating the nomads.

The Ming fell to the semi-nomadic Manchu from the north-east, who formed the Qing dynasty, thereby eliminating the need for walls. The Qing pursued a campaign of aggressive pacification of the Mongolian steppe and, in the later seventeenth century, the steppe north of China was mastered. The Chinese and the Russians moved respectively north and east, and eventually met. In 1689 they signed the Treaty of Nerchinsk, which settled the borders between their empires. There, it was agreed that nomads should be subject to agrarian states. By the nineteenth century the Russians had completed the takeover of most of Central Asia.

The defeat and dejection of the nomad in the face of increasingly powerful agrarian and industrialising states was perhaps symbolised by two events. The year 1771 saw the last great nomad migration, but this time from west to east, when the western Mongol Kalmyk nomads quitted the Volga region and returned to Dzhungaria (in modern far north west China) which they had left in 1607, unable to bear any longer Russian and Volga German migrant intrusion. In 1860, at the Battle of Palikao, south-east of Beijing, Anglo-French artillery blasted away the best Mongol cavalry, in service of the Chinese. Perhaps this debacle for the Mongols symbolised the complete reversal of the previous nomadic/sedentary military imbalance. (Ironically, the destruction of China's dynastic Imperial system came, not from the nomad north but from the maritime east with the arrival of the Europeans and the Japanese.)

It might be asked why it was the Russians and not the Chinese who continually advanced, consolidating ground taken from nomads? It was, after all, the Chinese who first pushed up into nomad territory when the three northern warring states of Qin, Zhao and Yan built walls in what had previously been nomad territory. The question then is why did the Chinese stop at that point – while the Russians kept advancing behind further lines of barriers? The reason is probably simply one of geography. The Chinese were moving north where it got progressively colder and the land less fertile and hospitable. The Russians were moving south into warmer climes with much more fertile soil into territory that had belonged to the Kievan Rus and its successor states before the Mongols' devastation. The Russians had a progressively stronger incentive to keep going while the Chinese had increasingly less. But ultimately both China and Russia had survived the nomad assaults, from the north and south respectively, and linear barriers should be accorded a key role in this process.

Part III

Questions And Issues

Chapter Fourteen

How Valid Are Those Four Linear Barrier Patterns?

T he introduction described four patterns which could be used as hunches to predict where linear barriers might be found. The two geographical patterns were summarised as: the land corridor pattern; and the valued land pattern. The two political patterns were: the states, nomads and barbarians pattern; and the warring states pattern. In this section the validity of the four is reviewed in the light of the material covered in the survey section.

1. Land corridors

Land corridors are deemed to be areas that are particularly likely to have had linear barriers. Why might that be? A land corridor is a more easily traversable area between two more difficult to negotiate areas. Therefore, it is the route that people will tend to take when on the move – whether it is for the purpose of invading, raiding, trading or migrating.

Often the land corridor itself will have a specific narrow point which will tend to be the location of the linear barrier. For example, the Derbent Wall lies where the Caucasus range comes to within a few kilometres of the sea. If Scotland is seen as a peninsula on the island of Britain, then the Antonine Wall lies at the narrow point between the Firths of Clyde and Forth, and Hadrian's Wall between the Firth of Solway and the River Tyne.

A land corridor is usually regarded as created by geography because it lies between two natural obstacles. But it can also be man-made, as the construction of a road creates a corridor, the road itself, which is more easily traversable than the terrain on either side. Of course, the routeway's location will be partly determined by nature; for example, ancient roads often followed watershed lines.

In the course of researching both primary and secondary sources there are a number of explicit references to linear barriers being built across peninsulas, and particularly at the narrowest points along land corridors. For example, Xenophon described how the people of the Chersonesos invited Dercylidas to build a wall to protect the abundance of good land. 'The peninsula needed only to be walled across from sea to sea, and there would be abundance of good land to cultivate.'[1] Crassus' anti-Spartacus wall was constructed: 'from sea to sea, across the neck of the land'[2], although this was not intended as a permanent linear barrier. The Ravenna Cosmography, compiled around 700, listing place names from Ireland to India, outlined the forts along the Antonine Wall: 'Here are listed the stations within the said Island joined together along a straight

Table 14.1: Black Sea, Sea of Marmara, and north-eastern Mediterranean land corridors

Location	Type	Name (if known or other descriptor)
Caspian Sea		
Eastern Caspian	sea to mountain	Wall of Gorgan
Southern Caspian	sea to mountain	Wall of Tammisha
Western Caspian	sea to mountain	Derbent, Ghilghilchay, Beshbarmak Walls
Caucasus Mountains	pass	Darial Pass walls
Crimea		
Main body	sea to sea	Perekop Wall
Kerch Peninsula	sea to mountain	Blinded Slaves' Sons' Trench
Kerch Peninsula	sea to sea	Tyritake, Beskrovnyi, Uzunlar, Akmonai Walls
Cape Kazantip	headland	Linear barrier
Heraclean Peninsula	sea to sea	Unnamed wall
Mayak Peninsula	sea to sea inlet	Unnamed double wall
Other Black Sea sites		
Sinope Peninsula	sea to sea	City walls across narrow point
Cape Kaliakra	headland	Walls across headland
Sea of Marmara		
Sea of Marmara to Black Sea	sea to sea	Anastasian Wall
Kapıdağ Peninsula (originally an island)	sea to sea	Wall built by time of Ottoman expansion
Sea of Marmara to Mediterranean Sea	sea to sea	Thracian Chersonesos Wall
Carpathians to Black Sea		
Dobrogea	river to sea	The three Valurile lui Traian barriers
Aegean Sea		
Reşidaye Peninsula	sea to sea	Cnidian Canal (unfinished)
Gallipoli Peninsula	sea to sea	Thracian Chersonesos Wall
Three fingers of the Chalcidike		
Agion Oros Peninsula	sea to sea	Xerxes' Canal
Pallene Peninsula	sea to sea	Justinian's wall
Greece		
Thermopylae	sea to mountain	Phocian Wall and later walls
Thermopylae	pass above sea	Justinian's wall
Heraclea	pass	Justinian's wall
Corinth Isthmus	sea to sea	Hexamilion Wall and previous walls
Peloponnese	pass above sea	Mount Oneion Walls
Balkans		
Pelješac peninsula	sea to sea	Walls of Ston

track where Britain is at its very thinnest from ocean to ocean.'³ Procopius described how the Emperor Anastasius, 'built long walls at a distance of not less than forty miles from Byzantium, uniting the two shores of the sea on a line where they are separated by about a two-days' journey.'⁴ The Valurile lui Traian are located at the narrowest point across the Dobrogea. In 1854 *The Times* reported, 'The real defence of the Danube is more to the south, at Trajan's Ditch – Vallum Trajani – on that line which traverses the country in its narrowest part of the Danube to the sea from Chernavoda to Kostandjé.'⁵ The Cambridgeshire Devil's Dyke, 'completely blocked a *narrow land corridor* (author's italics) between the southern edge of a region of water-logged marsh in the north-west and dense woodlands in the south, so making circumvention difficult and forming an effective defensive barrier for the lands to the east.'⁶

Overall, the eastern Mediterranean, the Black Sea and the Caspian Sea region are particularly rich in land corridors, and a journey around the seas reveals the near ubiquity of linear barriers across peninsulas, headlands, and passes near to the sea. Table 14.1 shows the land corridors in the region and the walls across them.

Basically, nearly every land corridor in the region has a linear barrier across it. It could be added that in North Africa most of the passes and land corridors that were built through the mountains of eastern Algeria, Tunisia and Libya have walls and *clausurae*. In Mesopotamia the convergence point of the Tigris and the Euphrates is the location of multiple linear barriers.

So were there any land corridors *without* linear barriers? Sithonia, the middle of the three fingers of the Chalcidike Peninsula in northern Greece, does not have a barrier, but this peninsula is rather more mountainous than the Pallene Peninsula and therefore less worth defending. (Agion Oros, another 'finger', was by contrast the site of Xerxes' Canal.) The Kapıdağ Peninsula off the south coast of the Sea of Marmara did not have a linear barrier in ancient times, but that was because it was not then a peninsula; it only became one after Alexander the Great built a causeway linking it the mainland.

In northern Europe the narrow points of north Britain between the Firths of Forth and Clyde, and the Firth of Solway and the River Tyne, are the sites respectively of Hadrian's Wall and the Antonine Wall. On the southern Jutland Peninsula the Danevirke links the Schlei inlet to the Trene River which leads to the North Sea. As has been seen, the Chersonesoses of the Crimea and Thrace and the Peloponnese all had linear barriers. Therefore, the following table shows how all major European isthmuses had linear barriers.

Table 14.2: Major European Isthmuses and Peninsulas

Britain – Firth of Forth to Firth of Clyde	Antonine Wall
Britain – Firth of Solway to Tyne River	Hadrian's Wall
Jutland – Trene River to Shlei Inlet	Danevirke
Corinthian Isthmus	Hexamilion and earlier walls
Thracian Chersonesos	Walls of Miltiades, Pericles, Dercylidas, Justinian
Crimean Isthmus	Perekop Wall

Overall, a high proportion of significant land corridors, both natural and man-made (in the form of routeways) appear to have had linear barriers built across them – at least, when the political situation was appropriate. Basically, the land corridor pattern appears a strong one.

2. Valued land

A pattern can be discerned where the linear barriers were built about land which was differentiated as more valued from that around it. A particular patch may have been intrinsically more fertile or made so as the result of irrigation or intense working. Or it may not obviously have been different in terms of the quality of the land, but a decision has been made to differentiate it as a sanctuary region in which people and animals could be gathered in – or possibly as a sacral zone of special religious or taboo significance.

In Greece and Hellenistic Anatolia quite small parcels of fertile land were protected by field walls. Oases were also protected by linear barriers which might have been incorporated in the defences. Often these formed full circuits if there was no natural barrier. For example, the City of Taif south-east of Mecca was circled by a wall. The great oasis cities of Central Asia appear to have been surrounded by walls at some time in their histories.

Another reason why land was particularly valued and vulnerable was because of loess soil. The Warring States Qin anti-nomad wall ran diagonally north-east to south-west along the loess plateau within the Yellow River bend. The First Great Wall of China, built after Qin had reunified the Empire, may have extended outside of the Yellow River loop to include the Helanshan Mountains. This is an area of loess which lies to the west of the Yellow River where it swings north around the Ordos. In Sasanian Persia the Sadd-i-Iskandar ran along the northern edge of a region of loess, and the Wall of Tammisha was built to the west of the same loess region.

Perhaps the most obvious form of valued land is that which is irrigated. The earliest riverine civilisations of Egypt and Sumer produced textual evidence of linear barriers four millennia ago, particularly the Walls of the Ruler and the *Muriq Tidnim*. In China, following the development of irrigation in the fifth century BC, the pace of wall building sped up during the Warring States epoch. The Seguia Bent el Krass section of the Fossatum Africae protected an irrigated area along the Oued Djebi in modern Algeria. In Mesopotamia, 'El-Mutabbaq was more probably intended to help protect the irrigated land from unwanted settlers and raiding parties coming from the desert.'[7]

Linear barriers of great length were almost the rule, as opposed to being the exception, at certain periods in history around the major oasis cities of Central Asia. At Balkh, Bukhara, Herat, *Margiana*, Samarkand and Tashkent, these were circuits, and at Merv (previously *Margiana*) and Termez they appear to have been linear.

The land inside the territorial oppidum may not have been very different in terms of fertility from the surrounding area, so there must be other reasons why it was held to be of value. Conceivably the enclosure was worth defending because of tribal cults or taboo protection. Areas of refuge for livestock needed space if the animals were to have some opportunity to forage for themselves – if only for a limited period. Territorial oppida in north-western Europe might, however, have been intended for protection in times of stress, or enforced concentrations of people or livestock. At Pliska in Bulgaria a very large area of land is incorporated within a rectangle roughly seven by three kilometres. This could have protected the men, horses and other animals and tents of a sedentarising nomadic people.

Xenophon described how the Thracian Chersonesos could be walled to protect an 'abundance of good land to cultivate.'[8] The same writer said that the Theban stockade 'encircled ... the most valuable parts of the land of the Thebans.'[9] Procopius described how 'rich Romans' built outside the walls of Constantinople and suffered calamities whenever the region was overrun as the 'damage caused there is much greater than in other places.' It was precisely that sense of vulnerability that prompted the construction of the Anastasian walls.[10]

Many secondary sources describe the construction of walls to defend land that was far more valuable agriculturally than that adjacent to it. Thus, regarding the Chinese Warring States: 'Zhao and Wei built walls to protect their valuable irrigated land.'[11] And of the Sadd-i-Iskandar, or Gorgan Wall, near the south-east corner of the Caspian: 'The line of the Gorgan Wall follows the approximate divide between the densely settled landscape to the south from the agriculturally marginal and sparsely settled lands to the north.'[12] In speculation as to motivation behind the construction of the Tikal linear barrier: 'the inhabitants of Tikal... were interested in protecting the agricultural resources on which they ultimately depended.'[13]

The idea of valued land – somehow differentiated from surrounding land either naturally or by the work of man – is a useful means of explaining why linear barriers have been built in certain areas where there are no obvious land corridors or frontiers. In the case of irrigated land or loess soil the pattern seems sufficiently strong to be able to use it to predict with some confidence those areas where linear barriers are likely to be found. Such a forensic understanding is particularly true where there were periodically nomads present. This was land where it was necessary to keep the threat out entirely, and it was often wholly encircled by a combination of natural and man-made linear barriers if the threat could come from any direction.

3. States, nomads and barbarians

The core idea behind the state, nomad and barbarian pattern is that along border areas, where generally literate settled states had to deal with non-literate peoples, it was effectively impossible to negotiate treaties or even reliable holding deals regarding management of the border. Therefore, it was necessary to find a natural obstacle line or, if this was absent, to construct a linear barrier which made it indisputable where the border lay. Once such a clear line was determined, any unauthorised crossing of it would incur severe reprisals. The barrier itself may or may not have been much of an obstacle but it produced absolute clarity in dealings with non-literate polities which had limited centralised authority able to stop raiding at the fringes.

In AD 484 (the Chinese adviser to the Northern Wei) Gao Lü gave the famous speech giving five reasons for long walls. The second reason was: it permits the northern tribes to nomadise (beyond the walls) and thus eliminates the disasters of raiding.'[14] Yāqūt described how the Moat of Shapur 'was dug ... between himself and the Arabs for fear of their depredations.'[15] He says that Anushirvan (531–79) ordered the repair and expansion of Shapur's Moat: 'The reason for that was to hinder the people of the desert from the Sawād.'[16] In 1008 Bruno of Querfurt reported back to Henry II that the lord of the Rus 'enclosed (his kingdom) on all sides with the longest and most solid of fences because of the roving enemy.'[17]

In terms of secondary material, and if one just looks at the Sasanian Empire, three different authorities all make the same point. 'The Sasanians built their long walls to keep out the nomads who threatened the irrigated agricultural plots of land.'[18] 'Sasanian Iran built up three great frontier systems ... whose purpose was to avert the invasions of the nomadic peoples dwelling in Ciscaucasia.'[19] 'What can be said with greater confidence is that the Sasanid Emperors had indeed built walls against the attacks by nomadic tribes that threatened their borders in the north, north-west, and western Iran.'[20] And this is a description of the wall near Derbent that lay between Bactria and Sogdia: 'On the one hand the Kushan Empire, recently sedentarised and integrated into Graeco-Bactrian culture; on the other hand, the Kangju who conserved their nomadic structures.'[21]

The Roman Empire did not have nomads along all its frontiers but it did have some, in the North African region now in eastern Algeria, Tunisia and western Libya, and in eastern Romania, Moldavia, and western Ukraine. There were certainly Roman walls intended to deal with nomads in North Africa, and possibly in the region around the western Pontic Steppe. But in north-western Europe the Romans dealt with Barbarian peoples who mostly lived settled lives in agrarian communities and Hadrian's Wall was built to 'separate the barbarians from the Romans.' Evagrius said the Anastasian Wall 'is a check upon the inroads of the barbarians from the Euxine, ... as well as of those who have made irruptions from Europe.'[22]

Essentially, the question arises: were linear barriers generally built in situations where more developed states were confronted with a threat from less advanced peoples? These may have been nomads or sedentary barbarians, the former moving annually due to transhumance; and both the former and the latter due to occasional migration? The answer is yes – generally, but not always.

The Egyptian, Sumerian, Chinese, Roman, Byzantine, Sasanian, Kievan Rus and Russian Empires and States all at some time built linear barriers to deal with nomads along the steppe and semi-arid belts of Eurasia, Hither Asia and Africa. That said, they did not build linear barriers at all periods because at different times the political equation was different; for example, when Empires like the Tang were strong enough to dominate the steppe nomads. Some linear barriers were built not as simple defences against nomads or barbarians, but in order to consolidate the hold on territory taken from them. One example is found in the practice of the three northern Chinese states of Yan, Zhao and Qin; another and later example is that taken by Russia. Nomadic peoples themselves also built linear barriers as they became more sedentarised. The joint Bulgar-Slav alliance constructed linear barriers around the nascent Bulgarian state and it was the Bulgars who built the Erkesia that faced the Byzantines, and not the other way around.

Generally, however, the state, nomad and barbarian pattern, particularly with respect to nomads, has proved to be a very useful predictor as to where twenty-first century investigators might expect to find linear barriers.

4. Warring states

The germ of the idea of the warring states pattern or hunch came from the observation that the Chinese kingdoms of the Warring States period were prolific builders of linear barriers against each other, and not against northern nomads. This raised the question whether polities of broadly similar peoples, culturally or ethnically, and who occupied an increasingly resource-constrained area, might tend to build linear barriers?

There proved quite a consistent pattern regarding walls that were built between warring states, providing that certain other conditions were met. One condition was the breakdown of conventions governing the ferocity of war in its treatment of agricultural resources and non-combatants. Another was the existence of vulnerable agricultural land that required the total blocking of any incursion.

In the survey section a number of situations were described where linear barriers were constructed by broadly similar states. These included China in the Western Zhou period, the mainland Greek city states, pre-unification Denmark, pre- and post-Roman Britain, Ireland, post-breakup Kievan Rus, Central Asia and the western states in the medieval Holy Roman Empire.* This does not, however, capture, by any means, all the situations where similar states in close proximity have fought with each other and where there is no evidence of linear barrier construction. Take, for example, the Italian states before unification by Rome, or China during various periods of disunion in the first millenium, or the Christian and Moorish states of Spain. Therefore, other factors must be involved in explaining why walls were actually built.

Here are some descriptions of the warring states condition that gave rise to linear barrier building. For example, 'Another factor that may have favoured the building of long walls among Chinese states was the reduced space for territorial expansion. By the fourth century BC the competition had become limited to a few powerful states, thus increasing the pressure to improve both defensive and offensive capabilities.'[23] Looking at Greece, 'Because warfare in the age after the Peloponnesian War tended to be destructive to state economies and civilian populations, Greek poleis expended considerable efforts to exclude enemy forces from economic and population centres.... Athens, Thebes and probably other poleis as well constructed elaborate systems of border fortifications intended to preclude enemy forces from entering and ravaging the interior.'[24] On the situation after the breakup of the Kievan Rus: 'The emergence of many independent principalities in Rus led to the need for fortified lines not only on the external frontiers of Rus but also between the individual principalities.'[25] Describing the *Landwehren* that petty German states constructed in the south-western Holy

---

* In modern times in the interwar period nearly all European countries built lines, of which Maginot's is only the best known.

Roman Empire in the High and Late Middle-Ages: 'Growing friction and blurred judicial boundaries, particularly concerning the petty territories, were other arguments justifying constructions of this type.'[26] It has been speculated as to motivation behind the construction of the Tikal linear barrier: 'It seems plausible to surmise that tensions increased as populations expanded. Surely, as the agricultural sustaining areas of the various centres grew and at last began to infringe upon each other, disputes over land could have developed into deep-seated enmity between the cities, and eventually, war.'[27]

One reason for an increased proclivity to build linear barriers in certain situations might have been the increased ferocity of war. Typically this resulted from the breakdown of earlier conventions that limited the damage caused, as can be seen in both Warring States China and Classical Greece. In both situations the conventions that had governed warfare between elite groups were increasingly disregarded as armies became larger and more professional. The consequences of defeat were not limited to small numbers of combatants: following the break down of conventions agricultural land might be ravaged, and non-combatants slaughtered or taken as slaves. With the stakes raised, it became more important to keep the enemy out of strategic areas altogether.

The idea that warring between similar states might produce linear barriers is far from being a generally consistent pattern and usually requires some additional factors. One example is the breakdown of conventions governing the conduct of war. That said, the construction of linear barriers in such circumstances was sufficiently common for the condition of warring states to be seen as a significant contributory factor leading to the construction of linear barriers.

In some instances, the unification that ended the warring between polities was marked by the construction of a linear barrier. This is seen with the First Emperor Qin Shi Huang's Great Wall, the Danevirke in Jutland, and possibly Offa's Dyke in England. Barriers behind the post-unification linear barrier then became superfluous and fell into disuse – or in the case of China they were (supposedly) destroyed.

Conclusion – validity of patterns or hunches

These various hunches have proved to have varying degrees of strengths and weaknesses. The 'land corridor' and the 'states, nomads and barbarians' models have proved very strong, in certain periods of particular intense movement of peoples and animals. This is evinced by the fact that nearly all land corridors in the Black Sea and north-eastern Mediterranean region had linear barriers, mostly built between the fifth century BC and the sixth century AD. Also, all Empires around the Eurasian Steppe built linear barriers against the nomad threat between the third century BC and the seventeenth century AD.

The 'valued land' and the 'warring states' hunches have proved weaker (although they remain useful) as, generally, other conditions needed to apply for linear barriers to be built. For example, additional factors were the use of chariots, the need for a sanctuary for animals still on the hoof, or the breakdown of conventions of war.

The 'states, nomads and barbarians' and 'land corridor' hunches, however, appear to allow considerably more confidence in their predictive quality. Therefore, when all Empires around the Eurasian Steppe were investigated, relatively unknown or unfamiliar linear barriers like the Kievan Rus' Zmievi Vali (Snake Ramparts) or Russia's Zaseschaya Cherta (Abatis Line) were found. Also, searches along the land corridor of the west Caspian revealed the Derbent, Ghilghilchay and Beshbarmak Walls. Indeed, looking at the peninsulas off the eastern Mediterranean and the Black Sea and the Empires around the Eurasian Steppe those without linear barriers look the exception rather than the rule.

Chapter Fifteen

Motivations Other Than Pure Defence –
Aggression and Assertion?

T he patterns in the last section inform as to the political and geographical
situations in which linear barriers might be found. These patterns, however,
do not necessary help in understanding motivation. Generally, it might be
assumed that the motivation was defensive – and linear barriers were built against a
perceived threat from invaders and raiders who might be nomads or other barbarians or
adjacent states at war. In the course of the survey however other motivations have been
seen. These can be divided into those which are essentially aimed at peoples outside or
peoples inside the linear barrier – or, to use modern communications parlance, external
or internal audiences.

External audience – to consolidate aggressive expansion

Many linear barriers have been built in advance of what were previously frontier lines.
Therefore, their purpose was not the defence of existing lands but to consolidate
aggressive expansion into new territory. The most familiar example of using walls in
this way concerns those built by the northern warring states of Qin, Zhao and Yan
in the late third century BC. 'It is likely then that the walls were erected to defend the
surrounding non-agricultural territory and to establish lines of communication and
facilitate the movements of troops as they patrolled this territory, having occupied it by
forcing the local population to submit and driving away recalcitrant nomadic groups.'[1]
Later the Han Dynasty's linear barriers in the Gansu corridor were offensive in that
they consolidated the hold on recent western expansion. 'The fortifications the Han
built in the Gansu corridor ... were designed to support conquest of the western
regions.'[2] Also, 'The 'long' walls appear also to have been strategic fortifications aimed
at asserting a state's political and military control over a given area.... Military walls
could be an integral part of an expansionist 'offensive.'[3]

On a smaller scale the walls built by the Greek colonists, on the Thracian Chersonesos
and on the Crimea Peninsula, consolidated the hold over land previously inhabited by
Apsinthian and Taurian peoples who would have regarded the walls as aggressive and
not defensive. The Romans built linear barriers across the Rhine in Germany and the
Danube in Dacia, and possibly in what is now Moldavia, in order to consolidate their
hold on trans-riverine territories. Under Antoninus Pius the frontier line was advanced
from Hadrian's Wall to the Antonine Wall and from the Neckar-Odenwald Limes to the
Vorderer Limes.

The move south-west along the Ichnield Way by a series of dykes attributed to the Anglians in Cambridgeshire might have been intended to consolidate their advance forward from an East Anglian kingdom. When the Franks and the Bulgars destroyed Avar power between 791 and 796, in what is now Hungary, they pressed in on the former Avar kingdom. Widekund says the Franks fenced the Avars in with earthworks. The Groß Römerschanze, which faces north-west between the Danube and Tisza Rivers, has been attributed to the Bulgars. Generally, given that the Bulgars built linear barriers around their Thracian conquests, such linear barrier building might be interpreted as aggressive.

The very roughly parallel lines of the Zmievi Vali below Kiev were moved south as they controlled progressively greater areas of land. When Russian expansion resumed, initially under the Muscovy state around Moscow, southward expansion took place along the successive lines of the Zasechnaya Cherta, Belgorodskaya Cherta, and the Izium Line.

When surveyed systematically a substantial proportion of linear barriers are found to have been built not on established frontiers but as new frontiers, *ahead* of recently occupied land. Therefore, in many situations linear barrier building can be seen as an aggressive and not a defensive operation. The nomads, of course, did not see the construction of such lines as defensive. From the Tatar viewpoint: 'Zaseka is a Slavic term for a continuous bulwark Russians were using to cut off the pastoralist herdsmen from their pastures in staged appropriation of their territory by force.'[4]

External audience – to deter attack

A linear barrier might be built with the objective of deterring attack, because it looked as though the sheer effort and skill that could be invested in its construction would inspire such respect in any intending attacker that it would abandon hope before assailing it. Thus, the intention would be to avoid any actual fighting at all on the linear barrier.

There are a few linear barriers which were undoubtedly magnificent. These include Hadrian's Wall, the Sadd-i-Iskandar and the Ming Great Wall of China. But all three were also built at a time of intense military activity when pure grandstanding would have been counterproductive, if not downright dangerous. Hadrian built his wall after correcting 'many abuses' in Britain as part of the consolidation of the Roman Empire's frontiers following what he considered unsustainable expansion by Trajan.[5] In Britain the border had been drawn back in stages from the Inchutil Line, through the Gask Ridge and Newstead Lines indicating an unsettled frontier. The Sadd-i-Iskandar was probably built not long after the Hephthalites had killed a Sasanian Shar, Peroz, in battle. The Ming Great Wall was constructed at the time of resurgent Mongol threat under two charismatic Mongol leaders, Esen and Altan, in the fifteenth and sixteenth centuries.

On a smaller scale – but impressive nevertheless if appraised through contemporary eyes – were the Cambridgeshire Devil's Dyke, the Danevirke in Jutland, the Erkesia in Thrace, the Valul Mare de Pământ and the Valul de Piatra in the Dobrogea, and Anglo-Welsh border Offa's Dyke. But little is known from textual sources about the reasons for constructing any of these linear barriers. The Frankish Royal Annals described the construction of Danevirke as a response to the threat of the expanding Franks; and the Byzantine Bulgar treaty of 816 might refer to the building of the Erkesia. In both cases, however, archaeology shows that the linear barriers or parts of them were started possibly a century before the textual references. The Dobrogea linear barriers are astonishingly mute, given their size, but they seem most likely to have been constructed or reconstructed in the tenth century. At that time the Dobrogea was a very lively and dangerous place with Pechenegs, Magyars, Bulgars, the Kievan Rus and the Byzantines raiding, invading and occupying. It simply does not sound like the right time for grandiloquent but non-functional linear barrier building.

In practice it is difficult to find linear barriers that conform to the idea that constructors would be confident that the act of grand scale construction would, in itself, be sufficient deterrent. Linear barriers were largely functional affairs made of local materials and not in a grand manner. Anyway, those that were indisputably grand – like Hadrian's Wall, the Sadd-i-Iskandar and the Ming Great Wall – were built in times of high tension.

It is possible that some raiders might have been deterred by the sheer vision of a linear barrier and turned back. This would have been on the basis that any state able to construct such a marvel would be too powerful and dangerous to attack. But really there is no point in constructing a linear barrier if it could not be operated effectively. A magnificent but ultimately undefended or indefensible line will eventually be tested and quickly its reputation and effectiveness would be hollow. The consequences of chronic raiding and intermittent invasion, however, were so horrible that most states would probably have constructed a linear barrier they saw as fit for purpose rather than pointlessly grand. Also, it seems likely that many linear barriers were expected to be breached and they functioned by slowing the advance and helping to cut off the retreat of any invader. Therefore, the fact that they did not look impregnable or capable of being constantly fully manned does not mean they had no function.

Internal audience – an expression of state building and power

A number of linear barriers mark the final frontier line of expansion of a state and may also follow a period of warring between states and mark eventual unification. The construction of such barriers might be seen: positively, as a grand communal effort which strengthened the bonds between groups who had previously been at war; or, more negatively, as a way of keeping otherwise now unemployed soldiers occupied and out of trouble.

It is certainly the case that after the Emperors Qin Shi Huang and Sui Wen reunited China, following centuries of disunion, they embarked on great campaigns of wall-building. But these also came at a time of severe nomadic threat, in earlier periods from the Xiongnu and later from the Turks, which alone might have justified wall building. Also, building walls was only part of these Emperors' construction efforts, which also included roads, canals and bridges. Linear barriers like Offa's Dyke, the Danevirke, and the Erkesia marked the limits of Mercian, Danish and Bulgar expansion – and while their construction might have helped make those, within the line, feel more involved and committed, they were also built when all three were constantly at war with their neighbours. The massive construction effort by the Kievan Rus, to deal with the Pecheneg threat, consisted of hundreds of kilometres of wood reinforced earthworks. They surely must have impinged on the consciousness of the people, but then given the fear then inspired by the Pechenegs – who had turned Prince Sviatoslav's skull into a cup in 971 – simple self-interest may have been sufficient incentive. The writings of Constantine VII Porphyrogenitus and Bruno of Quefurt make clear how feared were the Pechenegs. The construction of Sungbo's Eredo could have been an exercise in state building: 'The Eredo may have been built in order to unite diverse communities into a single kingdom.'[6]

Just as linear barriers may have been intended to deter, as expressions of power, an external threat so they might have been intended to forge a sense of internal group consciousness. Yet one can only speculate as to whether the act of wall building was meant to or actually had this effect.

It is known that linear building work was divided between groups from different localities, and that these were often incentivised with rewards for completing their sections first. This exercise would certainly gather together people from different regions of the newly unified state together, but whether it might then encourage coherence or division is debatable.* People probably just wanted to get their sections done as quickly as possible and the main incentive to finish might have been release to go home.

Wall building work under the First Emperor was hugely unpopular and there is an extensive literature devoted to the woes it caused. The construction campaigns of these two Emperors of the Qin and the Sui dynasties placed a huge burden on the state which the less adequate sons of both Emperors could not deal with. The result was that both dynasties collapsed internally. So, ironically, the walls may have contributed to the external security of China, but internally they were counterproductive, to say the least.

On a practical note, linear barriers might have aided state formation by keeping people in rather than out. The purpose of the Qing Willow Palisade was to stop Chinese fleeing north, the Russian Belgorodskaya Cherta prevented serfs from joining the Cossacks, and the Han Great Walls may have had a secondary function of keeping Chinese peasants from escaping along the Gansu Corridor.

---

* Although this is a description of a city circuit, the passage in which Nehemiah 3:1 outlines the reconstruction of the walls of Jerusalem shows how intimately involved a people could be involved in building wall – coming if necessary some distance.

1 Eliashib the high priest and his fellow priests went to work and rebuilt the Sheep Gate. They dedicated it and set its doors in place, building as far as the Tower of the Hundred, which they dedicated, and as far as the Tower of Hananel.

2 The men of Jericho built the adjoining section, and Zakkur son of Imri built next to them.

3 The Fish Gate was rebuilt by the sons of Hassenaah. They laid its beams and put its doors and bolts and bars in place.

4 Meremoth son of Uriah, the son of Hakkoz, repaired the next section. Next to him Meshullam son of Berekiah, the son of Meshezabel, made repairs, and next to him Zadok son of Baana also made repairs.

5 The next section was repaired by the men of Tekoa, but their nobles would not put their shoulders to the work under their supervisors.

And so on for 32 verses.

Internal audiences – an expression of personal assertion

During both the Roman and the Chinese Empires, the Emperors would have naturally associated with Louis XIV's dictum, *l'état c'est moi*. Given that political reality, it is hard to draw the line between the idea that a linear barrier could express the personal authority of the ruler, or the cohesion of the state. Linear barriers were sometimes named after their constructors although this is often a subsequent rationalisation by historians, and the original name is not known or certain. It is, therefore, very difficult to speculate as to motivation.

One who did speculate on this issue, however, was Herodotus, who pondered on the effort of Xerxes in constructing the canal across the neck of the Mount Athos Peninsula. 'It seems to me, when I consider this work, that Xerxes, in making it, was actuated by a feeling of pride, wishing to display the extent of his power, and to leave a memorial behind him to posterity.'[7] If, however, the intention was to cow the Greeks into submission, then Xerxes failed.

Hadrian's Wall might look massively over-engineered but he built it at a time when he was regularising frontiers generally, and after he had had to resolve disturbances on this northern frontier. Of all emperors, given the extent of his travels, he would have had an exceptionally broad perspective of the different needs of different frontiers and could have judged the situation accordingly. Perhaps, given the opportunity, he indulged himself in making real the vision of the ideal Greek wall. Yet as a realist it would seem improbable that he would have overdeveloped such a vision. Anyway, the effort would have been largely wasted as few top Romans or Greeks would have travelled to the wilds of North Britain to see it. He could not even have been certain that he himself would ever return to see it completed.

The reasonably elderly and generally peaceable Antoninus Pius may have expanded the Empire in Germany and North Britain in order to establish his authority with some military *gloire*. 'Although he (Antoninus) had committed the conduct of war to others, while sitting at home himself in the Palace at Rome, yet like the helmsman at the tiller of a ship of war, the glory of the whole navigation and voyage belonged to him.'[8] But it was prosecution of the war, not the building of the wall, which gave Antoninus glory. Reputation was made by glowing reports of conquering new territories for the Empire, and not by building walls around them that most people would never see. Great rulers built magnificent palaces, castles and religious edifices in order to impress visitors and their own peoples. But these were close to centres of power where they would have been visible. It is hard to imagine building anything other than a largely functional structure on a distant and probably dangerous frontier that most people would want to stay well away from.

Quite possibly, without certain individuals there might have been rather less wall building. Hadrian and Justinian respectively built or rebuilt most of the walls around the Roman and Byzantine Empires. In both cases, however, this does not appear to have been simply down to self-aggrandising personalities. Hadrian had to stabilise the frontiers after previous Flavian and Trajanic over-expansion. Justinian was responding to the devastating Hun raids of 539 – by building various walls in strategic locations from the Corinth isthmus to eastern Thrace – as he could see the Peloponnese had escaped attack. This was possibly because the predecessor of his Hexamilion Wall had worked and provided an example of a successful defence strategy. The Emperors Qin Shi Huang and Wen were both great builders generally and built or rebuilt Great Walls of China after they had reunified China. But these were not their only construction works – the infrastructure and tomb building may have been more visible to more people than just the reluctant wall builders who resented their enforced labour on the walls. Anyway, the Xiongnu and Turk threats were in themselves possibly sufficient explanation for the wall construction.

Conclusion – other motivations

The simple fact is that very little can be determined about precisely who, why and when linear barriers were built or indeed rebuilt. It is, however, quite certain that many were aggressive rather than defensive in intent, in that they were intended to consolidate the hold on recently taken land, and possibly to serve as a springboard for further advances. But one can only guess as to whether they were seen as sufficient in themselves – as expressions of power to deter external attacks – or intended to act on the consciousness of the people within the linear barriers.

The view taken here is that linear barriers were largely built in response to what was perceived as a real external threat, and they were intended to function as such. In the absence of detailed contemporary commentary, it is only possible to look at broad patterns. In the case of construction of linear barriers by settled states faced by nomads – the ubiquity of such construction indicates that the primary motivation for building them was to deter nomads. Thus considerations of the image projected, by the individual or the state, were secondary. That said, the building of a wall or linear barrier can be the result of multiple motivations and serve more than one purpose.

Chapter Sixteen

Why Did Some Polities *Not* Build
Linear Barriers?

S ome rulers or dynasties put their faith in linear barriers, and others, who ruled during what appears to have been broadly similar circumstances, did not – despite apparently being similar people in a similar geography. For example, the major, long surviving ethnically Chinese Han and Ming dynasties built linear barriers but the Tang and the Song did not. The Angles appear to have built many linear barriers in England but not, with any certainty, the Saxons.

Or different peoples in broadly similar situations can be considered. The early riverine civilisations of Egypt, Sumer and China all built linear barriers; but not apparently that of the Indus Valley. In the ninth century the Danevirke and the Erkesia blocked land corridors to control respectively access to Denmark and to the First Bulgar Empire with linear barriers; but when Alfred the Great made a treaty with Guthrum in 878 the gap between the river Lea and the Ouse was not covered by building an earthwork. (The treaty defined the border simply as follows: 'First concerning our boundaries: up on the Thames, and then up on the Lea, and along the Lea unto its source, then straight to Bedford, then up on the Ouse to Watling Street' without saying how the non-riverine lengths were defined or protected.[1]) The Russians built a series of linear barriers as they moved south and closed down the steppe; there appears, however, to be no indications of linear barriers being built by Christian states on the Iberian Peninsula during the *Reconquistora* of Muslim Spain. In the Crimea Greek colonists built linear barriers against local Tauric and Scythian peoples; then why did not later colonists in North America build linear barriers against Native American peoples?

Also, why were so many large areas seemingly devoid of linear barriers? In Europe linear barriers mainly seem to be concentrated along a crescent that runs from the British Isles, Denmark and northern Germany, southern Sweden, Poland, then both sides of the Carpathians and down into the Balkans. Apart from the *Claustra Alpium Iuliarum*, what about Italy, France and the Iberian Peninsula?

Generally, it is possible to hazard a guess at explaining why linear barriers might or might not have been built. The situations of the Han and the Ming, and the Tang and the Song, all appear somewhat different on examination – as seen in the section on Chinese Great Walls. The Han and the Ming faced powerful Xiongnu and Mongol confederations. By the time the Tang came to power the full force of the Turkic expansion was shifting westwards. The Song simply let go of northern China to semi-nomadic Kitan and Jin states – and paid them tribute – some of which financed linear barrier building by the Kitan and Jin.

The Angles came to England with a tradition of linear barrier building already established in Jutland. There is little indication that the Saxons had a similar tradition in Germany. It seems that the Saxons pioneered systems of point defence based around burghs. As seen above, when Alfred made a treaty with Guthrum, linear earthworks do not appear to have formed part of the frontier.

As for the early riverine civilisations, why did Egypt, Mesopotamia and China build linear barriers while that of the Indus apparently did not? The common factor in all situations was the use of irrigation which created intensely valuable but vulnerable agricultural systems. It might be speculated that the Indus region was protected by mountain ranges and lacked a continuous nomadic threat, so linear barriers could not be justified. But equally, given the lack of textual records, the answer may simply not be known. One theory is that there was actually no war during the Indus Valley civilisation's mature period (2600–1900 BC): 'Strangest of all for the archaeologists is they found no evidence of war and conflict.'[2] It is hard not to concur that the absence of war is indeed strange.

When asking why the Russian built linear barriers as they expanded south but the Spanish Christian states did not – certain observations can be made. Geographically, the line of the rivers was different. In Russia the north-south line of rivers aided raiders as they could move easily along the watershed lines – whereas in Spain and Portugal the east-west line provided riverine frontiers to Christian states moving south. (It is worth noting that the Oka ran east-west south of Moscow and, given its convenient location, it did form the first defence line ahead of Moscow as the Russians expanded southwards.) The harsh Iberian country did not readily provide material for easy long linear barrier construction – either in the form of malleable earth or quick growing trees. This same impediment did not stop the ancient Greeks building short stone field walls; however, such barriers might have been too short in the Iberian context. Also, both Christian and Muslim states were highly developed and war tended to be intermittent in terms of actual reconquest. Other than that, the relationships in Iberia were very complex as often Christian states fought for one Muslim state against another.

The early American colonists might have been candidates as linear barrier builders against 'barbarian' Native Americans. The fact, however, that no such barriers were built does not mean that they were not considered: 'In the session of 1676 it had been proposed to build a fence of stockades or stone eight feet high from the Charles [River] where it is navigable to the Concord at Billerica and thence to the Merrimac and down the river to the Bay, by which meanes that whole tract of land will (be) environed, for the security & safety (under God) of the people, their houses, goods & cattel: from the rage & fury of the enemy.'[3] The palisade or wall was not constructed as there were insufficient resources, but it was indeed planned as a means to deal with native peoples by colonists.

Sometimes it is simply not possible to recreate the reasons why or why not a linear barrier might be built. If it is known that there was a linear barrier, either because of physical remains or textual sources, then it is a matter of speculation as to the reasons why it was there. But there have been situations where the patterns or hunches might predict the existence of linear barriers but they do not appear to have been built as predicted. This could be for a number of reasons: a linear barrier was built but it has not been found or recorded; a linear barrier was intended but not actually built due to the lack of funds or necessary skills; situations which appear superficially similar were actually not so in practice; a cost benefit analysis would have shown it was not worth the effort to build one; and military practice had already developed, in the light of experience, so other solutions were adopted. It is anyway necessary to adopt a degree of realism – and humility – and recognise that the past can be a mystery where certain issues and questions simply cannot be fully resolved.

India, mentioned above, represents a particular mystery. In the Harappa period (3300–1300 BC) the Indus valley contained an irrigated riverine civilisation but – unlike those of the Nile, Tigris and Euphrates, and the Yellow River – there is no evidence of linear barriers. It has been suggested that this time and region was almost uniquely free of conflict.[4] Given the human record elsewhere it is difficult not to be sceptical. There were certainly many invaders in subsequent periods who established rule over much of the sub-continent. These included the Aryans, Kushans and the Mughals. There were also Hun and Mongol *chevauchées*. These came through the Khyber Pass. It might seem surprising that there were no linear barriers across the pass or in strategic regions in the north-east. Central Asia and Afghanistan had linear barriers and there was constant movement between the two regions.

The fact remains, however, that even though peoples who moved across the Eurasian Steppe frequently ended up in India, linear barriers do not seem to have been used to try to stop them. The explanation might be that India was not composed of steppe with the associated nomads – or even adjacent to steppe given that the mountains of the Hindu Kush separated it from Central Asia. Linear barriers mostly controlled the day to day relations of nomads and settled states – and if there were no nomads, irritating on a chronic basis, then linear barriers were unnecessary. Elsewhere however linear barriers were built to stop great nomad hordes at key strategic passes. For example, the Byzantine walls of Justinian and the contemporary Sasanian walls were both built to stop the Huns. Possibly the passes of the Hindu Kush were situated too far away from the Indian heartlands to be seen as defensible in practicable terms. India, notwithstanding, remains a lacuna as far as linear barriers are concerned.[*]

Why did linear barrier building cease in a particular area?

At some point construction largely ceased, even in those areas where linear barrier building was formerly common. Three overall reasons might be suggested for this phenomenon. The first was that the threat that provoked the construction of linear barriers overwhelmed the polity which constructed them; that is to say, the barriers failed. Secondly, the threat was overcome, in a process where the linear barriers may

---

[*]   Although the nineteenth century Great Hedge of India eventually reached 4,000 kilometres in length and might lay claim to being the longest continuous single linear barrier in history.

have played a part. Thirdly, the polity and the threat to it continued to exist but there was a major change in strategy as to how to deal with it.

In Africa and Hither Asia linear barrier construction appears largely to have ended with the conquest by the semi-nomadic Arabs in the seventh century. Although the Caliphate split, the divisions between nomads and settled states diminished as both sides broadly adopted Islam. Since the Arabs who originally spread Islam were often themselves the nomad threat, this is an instance where linear barriers stopped being built as it was the nomads which overwhelmed settled states and themselves became sedentary civilisations. The Sasanian Empire, which was the greatest power in the region, failed in part because it did not maintain the fortified canal linear barrier system, first developed by Shapur II, and relied instead on local Arabs.

The situation in Europe was more complex. Here, linear barriers appeared to fall out of use without either settled states, nomads and migrants resolving the conflict by one group gaining domination over the other. The early Byzantine Empire seemed to rely on linear barriers to block strategic land corridors, and this tendency culminated in the flurry of wall building and rebuilding under Justinian in the sixth century. Then, with the uncertain later exceptions of linear barriers in the Budjak and the Dobrogea, the Byzantine Empire appeared to rely on its mobile army and navy. The phases of intense linear construction and repair however lasted for only quite limited parts of Byzantine history. For the most part the Byzantines depended upon the Theodosian Walls of Constantinople to keep alive the beating imperial city's heart. The arteries and veins of the Empire were its control of maritime routes which it kept open by its fleets. Furthermore, the Empire's monopoly over Greek fire perhaps gave it a unique competitive advantage.

On the Great Hungarian Plain the Avars and Sarmatian peoples built north-east, east and south-east-facing linear earthworks. By the ninth century, the trans-Danubian Great Hungarian Plain appeared to have ceased to have been defended by linear barriers. The reason may have been that the Magyars had no tradition of or interest in linear barriers; but also by then a combination of improved point defences and mobile cavalry might have been seen to be more efficient.

The Bulgars barged their way into Europe, like many nomad peoples of the time; but unlike most others, they managed to grip onto the territory they occupied. A key factor was probably the part played by the construction of linear barriers as a means of securing contested territory into which the Bulgars had expanded. Bulgarian historians say that Bulgaria was surrounded by earthen and wooden linear barriers and strongholds from the seventh to the tenth centuries. These were, however, subsequently replaced by stone fortresses. Again, the pattern seems to be that by the ninth century linear barriers were seen as less efficient due to advances in point defences and mobile cavalry.

After Offa's Dyke there is little evidence of linear barrier building in Britain. Linear barriers only function effectively if there is certainty as to which direction the threat will come from. In an area with a long coastline, and many rivers, linear barriers would be almost futile in the face of a threat, similar to that of the Vikings, which could come from anywhere, by land, river and sea. In Britain the Burghal Hidage, listing thirty-three fortified towns, shows how Wessex was mobilised to construct a comprehensive system of point defences.

The Christian advance eastward in the thirteenth century at the expense of pagan peoples was conducted without linear barriers. When the Teutonic knights expanded in the Prussian Crusade into largely pagan Lithuania, the progress was consolidated using man–made point not linear defences, and by taking advantages of rivers. A forward line of frontier castles was built, wherever possible along rivers; and to the rear they built forts for refuge for non–combatants when invasion threatened. The forward castles did not intercept raiders, but warned the people of the enemy's advance. When sufficient militia gathered at the castles, knights would lead the pursuit – they expected to overtake the raiders who might be slowed by captured livestock or people.[5]

There were exceptions. The Les Fossés-le-Roy were constructed in the twelfth century in southern Normandy. The Danevirke continued in use until the twelfth century. The Swiss constructed the *Letzimauern* and the minor polities of the western Holy Roman Empire the *Landwehren* between the thirteenth and the sixteenth centuries. But it is difficult to avoid the impression that linear barriers were increasingly falling out of use by the ninth century across Europe, and the reason was not that either the builders or the threats overwhelmed the other.

There was probably a multiplicity of explanations for the increasing reliance on point defences. Greater skill in working in wood and stone meant that stronger multi-storey point defences could be developed. Men at arms became better armed and mounted and more numerous. Whether they actually fought on horseback or on foot, they could intercept intruders more rapidly and effectively. When and where linear barriers *did* continue to be built and maintained, specific reasons particular to each individual barrier meant they could perform their intended purpose effectively. The Danevirke continued to be used until the thirteenth century although in the much shortened and reinforced form of fired-brick Valdimarsmauren. The point is that both the Les Fossés-le-Roy and the Danevirke linear barriers faced threats unambiguously from one direction, here from the south, as opposed to from all directions.

Eventually it was inevitable as artillery improved that linear barriers, constructed above ground level of shatterable materials, would eventually become completely ineffective. The Hexamilion Wall was repaired by Manuel II in 1415 and by Constantine Palaiologos in 1444 to face the Ottomans. Using cannon the Ottomans took the wall in 1423, 1431, 1446 and 1452. They finally conquered the Peloponnese in 1460.

The construction of the Zmievi Vali linear barriers stopped after the eleventh century – probably again as it was more beneficial, from the military and economic standpoint, to construct a fortress–city network. In addition the Kievan Rus could manage the troubled southern border with support–warning outposts and mobile squads of professional soldiers, including paid nomads. The linear barriers were not intended to stop incursions altogether but to gain time for retaliation and to impede booty-laden retreat. As more forts were built, in a system that had always combined linear barriers with forts, it may simply have been found that the linear barriers themselves were increasingly superfluous. In the fifteenth century however, linear barrier construction resumed in use against nomads, now the Tatars, and gathered pace in the sixteenth and seventeenth centuries. As the Muscovite Rus and its successor Russia became more assertive, and nomad raids more devastating, clearly linear barriers were seen as – and indeed proved to be – effective in stopping raids and closing down the steppe. The Russian use of linear barriers was essentially defensive not aggressive.

After the wall-building Sui dynasty, the Tang dynasty ceased such constructions. The Tang relied on mobile cavalry often deliberately copied from the nomad model. The Song preferred to pay off the Kitan Liao and the Jin (both of whom did build linear barriers). The Mongol Yuan actively took the conflict to any other Mongols who were determined to maintain a fully nomadic existence. Had it not been for the return by the Ming (1368–1644) to wall building, half way through the dynasty's history and mainly during the sixteenth century, then wall building by the Chinese might have ceased after the Sui.

The first Ming Emperor Hongwu (1368–1398) built a line of inner fortresses and then eight outer fortresses deep in nomad territory. For reasons which are not entirely clear – but probably having to do with cost – the Hongwu's son Yongle (1402–1492) withdrew from all but one of the eight forward fortresses, and thereby lost control of the steppe. So the Ming started off with point defences and, unusually, reverted to a linear barrier system. Ultimately, the return to a linear system was the result of the failure of other strategies, intense nomadic pressure under the Mongol leaders Esen and Altan, and a particularly strong later Ming aversion to consenting to trade with the Mongols. In terms of general global trends however, this Indian summer of defensive wall building appears anachronistic. The Manchu united the sown and the steppe, thus obviating the need for linear barriers and suppressing such nomads as remained. Eventually this new ruling dynasty met up with the Russians and together they determined the border at the Treaty of Nerchinsk in 1689. The Qing Willow Palisade was largely an internal anti-migration and smuggling barrier.

Linear barrier building ceased in a particular area because one side triumphed. So it remained until such time as the political situation reverted to the divisions that had earlier created such barriers; or something else changed, in the relationship between the wall builder and the perceived threat, for example, military technology had developed, thus rendering linear barriers no longer the most efficient response to the same threat; or the threat had changed perhaps by becoming more multi-directional, and that made a barrier facing in one direction only pointless.

Changes in military technology probably resulted in major changes in the balance of power. As point defences, and the mobile mounted forces contained in them, became more powerful and better armed, the linear barrier that linked or lay forward of the point defences possibly proved no longer cost effective and therefore became obsolete.

Chapter Seventeen

Strategies or Barriers – Which Really Defined Relations Between States and Nomads?

Essentially this book is about how the relationship between static and turbulent states was managed, and particularly the role of linear barriers in that process. But linear barriers were often not used at all; or, when they *were* employed, it was generally in conjunction with other strategies. Usually, when just one strategy was employed, particularly wall building in isolation, the result was failure.

The contrast between the apparent freedom of life on the move and the constraints of living in settled polities might evoke philosophical, moral or even hedonistic judgements. Yet in practice the settled and the nomadic existences were not a matter of choice but rather a function of what particular environments could sustain. Problems arose when the two groups mixed – as was inevitable due to the greater need of nomads for the goods which only settled states could produce or store. Thus strategies had to be devised to manage that relationship. Evolving such strategies was generally the task of the settled states as they had both more to lose and were the more reflective political organisations better able to devise solutions.

Strategies for dealing with nomads, other than linear barrier building, might be divided into three basic categories: diplomatic; aggressive non-military; and aggressive military.

Diplomatic – cooperative and conciliatory strategies

If the relationship was stable the sedentary state and the nomads or other barbarians might trade. The exchanges could be for manufactured goods, particularly luxury items, for livestock, furs and forest products. But it might be for protection – either in the mafia sense of payment for not being attacked, or for the provision of services as border troops. Of course bribery could be wrapped up in all sorts of rituals which affected to conceal the fact that this was effectively protection money. The relationship might become more aggressive if the sedentary state refused to trade, or to provide de facto protection money in the form of goods, feasts and princesses. Ultimately, however, nomads understood who had the higher civilisation and they could not help but be impressed, even intimidated, by the grandeur of, for example, Hagia Sophia in Constantinople. Sometimes nomads would be satisfied with recognition and a grandiose honorary title – perhaps with a wife thrown in.

Another strategy, to pay tribute to stay away, was both obvious and old. The Scythians were paid to depart by the Egyptian Pharaoh Psammeticus in the seventh century BC. The Han Chinese gave the Xiongnu bribes and brides under the peace and friendship policy called *heqin* – until they felt they had recovered sufficient power to retaliate militarily. In AD 681 the Bulgars invaded Thrace and forced the Byzantines to make peace with the new Bulgarian state and pay an annual tribute. The Byzantines also bribed the Huns and the Avars to stay away. In 1521 the Tartar Khan Mehmed-Girey reached Moscow and was paid off by Vasily III. The Danegelt that Ethelred, King of the Saxons, paid to the Vikings might be seen as a tribute payment to Vikings, who in a sense were practising a form of raiding seaborne nomadism.

Brides were another commodity that settled polities could trade in. During the seventh century BC the Assyrian King Esarhaddon made peace with the Scythians by presenting rich gifts and by marrying off his daughter to the Scythian king, Partatua. In China the Han provided brides as well as bribes as part of the *heqin* policy. The Kipchak Turks sought brides from the Kievan Rus. The Mongol leaders Esen and Altan wanted Ming royal brides – requests which were turned down by the Ming, which in turn provoked onslaughts by the rebuffed nomads.

The problems came when demands became excessive – to a degree that the fundamental humiliation of paying them became intolerable. Constantine VII Porphyrogenitus of Byzantium said that even Pecheneg hostages and hired hands were extravagant in their demands: 'Now these Pechenegs, who are ravenous and keenly covetous of articles rare among them, are shameless in their demands for generous gifts, the hostages demanding this for themselves and that for their wives.'[1]

Aggressive non-military strategies

These strategies did not involve overt military action but covert disruption. Settled states frequently tried to neutralise or defeat nomads by provoking divisions or through simple treachery. The Medes devised a successful strategy for handling the Scythians: first they treacherously got them blind drunk, and then they massacred them. The Chinese were adept in these dark arts. After Maodun's death he was succeeded by his son Jizhu (174–160 BC) who married a Han princess and opened the Xiongnu territories to Han spies disguised as officers and diplomats. These spies provoked the subject peoples to revolt, thereby contributing to the collapse of the Xiongnu Empire. The first Göktürk Empire split after the death of the fourth Khagan, Taspar Khan, in around 584. Four rival claimants to the title of Khagan were successfully played off against each other by the Chinese. In 551 the Kotrigur Huns raided Thrace and Greece and the Byzantines paid the Utigur Huns to attack the Kotrigurs in the rear, which effectively brought an end to Hun assaults.

Aggressive military strategies

Some states preferred or were equipped to take on the nomads in open ground by deliberately learning nomad methods of fighting. Others employed nomads to fight with or for them. The Chinese studied nomadic cavalry tactics and created their own light cavalry forces. Or they simply recruited the tribal horsemen into their armies. During the early years of his reign King Wuling of Zhao (326–299 BC) was constantly harassed by the Donghu; and the Zhao copied the nomads and abandoned chariots for light cavalry. The Han Dynasty was at a disadvantage in lacking the number of horses the northern nomadic peoples mustered in their armies. Minister Chao advised Han Emperor Wen (202–157 BC) that Han armies should have far more cavalry to match the Xiongnu. Wen advocated the policy of 'using barbarians to attack barbarians' incorporating Xiongnu horsemen into the military. Han Emperor Wu (141–87 BC) went to war in the Ferghana Valley to capture its heavenly horses.

The twelfth century ruler Daniel I Romanovich of Galicia re-united the south-western Rus. He acknowledged the supremacy of the Mongol Golden Horde, at least nominally, reorganised his army along Mongol lines, and equipped it with Mongolian weapons. In 1256 Daniel succeeded in driving the Mongols out of Volhynia. The approach of a large Mongol army in 1260 forced him to accept their authority over him and to raze the fortifications he had built. But, remarkably, he had resisted the Mongols and survived.[2]

The late Roman Empire agreed to defend nomad and barbarian allies who would promise to refrain from raiding imperial territory and prevent neighbouring tribes from doing the same. Although the allies would officially be denoted *tributarii*, in practice the loyalty of the ally was often secured by gifts or regular subsidies from Rome. The Sarmatians undertook to defend borders and not attack the empire in return for stipends.[3] And: 'On the desert frontier of Syria, the Romans would appoint a Saracen sheikh… according him an official rank in the Roman hierarchy … (who in) return for food subsidies … would defend the desert frontier against raiders.'[4]

The Chinese Song paid tribute to semi-nomadic Kitan Liao and Yuan who defended the northern borders by proxy. The Byzantines employed the Pechenegs against the Rus and the Magyars. The defences of the southern Kievan Rus against the Polovtsians were manned by allied nomads. The Sasanians employed Lakhmid Arab semi-nomads to defend their southern border. The Tang employed Turks as light cavalry to defend their borders as well as adopting such techniques themselves. The Russians used Cossacks from the Turkic Kazak, armed with long spears and sabres, as light cavalry.

Linear barrier building by proxy

Linear barrier building was another strategy adopted by settled states to manage the relationship with nomads. Settled states could build walls by proxy. 'The Romans continued to assist the client tribes to defend themselves in the fourth century e.g. the construction by Constantine's army of two massive lines of defensive earthworks (the Devil's Dykes in Hungary and the Brazda lui Novac de Nord in Romania) well beyond the Danube (100–200 miles forward) to protect the client tribes of the Banat and the Wallachian Plain against Gothic incursions.'[5] The Byzantines financed the Sasanians to build and man walls in the Caucasus. The semi-nomads Kitan Liao and then the Jin were paid tribute by the Song and they built walls on the northern border.

Conclusion – strategies other than linear barrier building

In practice settled states tried a variety of strategies to deal with the nomad threat. Relying simply on a single defensive strategy of staying behind the barriers was almost certainly a recipe for failure. This might help explain why walls have received a bad name – as leading to the so-called Maginot mentality whereby a defensive strategy leads to conceding the initiative to the enemy. While linear barriers could be a valuable part of the mix, aggressive patrolling across the border was also necessary for effective frontier management, combined with the use of spies and fifth columnists to gain intelligence and spread discord.

Chapter Eighteen

Linear Barrier Building –
A Successful or Failed Strategy?

How can linear barriers be judged as successes or failures? One way might be to break the question down into parts. First, did individual linear barriers succeed or fail in terms of their immediate objective? Second, when a particular state used the strategy of constructing linear barriers to further its objectives, was that strategy broadly successful or not? Thirdly, over the longer term, did the construction of linear barriers aid settled states in managing the relationship with nomads and migrants?

1. Did individual linear barriers succeed or fail in terms of their immediate objectives?

The constructor of an individual linear barrier would have had a particular immediate objective in mind when he decided to build it. Given generally scarce resources, it is unlikely that the time and cost involved in building such a barrier would have been expended, except in the face of or in close anticipation of a real threat. The success or failure of that linear barrier might be judged in terms of whether it achieved that particular objective.

As might be expected, some linear barriers succeeded and some failed. The difficulty in judging success is that the textual record is very patchy. If it is known that a linear barrier was built – because of its physical survival or literary references – archaeology alone is unlikely to provide a record of whether it succeeded or failed.

If, however, textual sources are gleaned, examples can be found where linear barriers succeeded. An example of a linear barrier which was an immediate success was that constructed by Dercylidas across the Thracian Chersonesos, because subsequently the region thrived. 'Within these lines he established eleven cities, with numerous harbours, abundance of good arable land, and plenty of land under plantation, besides magnificent grazing grounds for sheep and cattle of every kind.'[1]

It is possible that the pre-Justinian wall built across the Corinth Isthmus by Leo (457–474) or Anastasius (419–518) blocked the Hun *chevauchée* in 539, an assault that devastated the region around the Aegean Sea. 'A mighty Hunnic army... destroyed almost all the Greeks except the Peloponnesians, and then withdrew.'[2] Justinian's wall building efforts also appear to been have rather successful. In 539 the Thracian Chersonesos was ravaged and its walls overrun by the Huns, but in 559 a young officer named Germanus held the walls, rebuilt by Justinian, against the Kotrigur Huns and then forced back the assailants. At the same time Justinian's walls at Thermopylae blocked another group of Kotrigurs. (So many other barriers had previously failed there, that maybe the success in this case is explained by the care that Justinian took, not just to block the land corridor between the mountains and the sea, but also to control the passes in the mountains which were usually the weak point of the defences.) In 1482 the early Ming wall successfully blocked a Mongol raid. In 1635 a twenty-five kilometre-long earthwork was built to block the open gap in the Voronezh-Tsna corridor across the Nogai Shlyah on time and within budget and it worked immediately, stopping completely the next Nogai Tartar raid.

An example of the failure of a linear barrier, known from records or as a reasonable deduction because the state that built them failed soon after, is the Sumerian *Muriq Tidnim* which failed to stop the Martu advance.

A number of linear barriers had a mixed record but were on balance successful – or failed for reasons that were beyond the control of the builder. Hadrian's Wall was finally abandoned not because it failed but because the supporting legions could no longer be justified due to the demands placed on Rome of a greater threat on the Continent. The Antonine Wall was abandoned (twice) because it was 'a wall too far' that could not be justified by anything other than an individual emperor's aggrandisement. (Antoninus Pius, however, might have considered the barrier as a success because it helped him to burnish his military credentials during his own lifetime.) The Zmievi Vali kept the Pechenegs and the Polovtsians at bay but could not withstand the unstoppable deluge that was the Mongols.

It is clear that some linear barriers succeeded and some failed. On balance, it appears that many linear barriers were immediately and consistently successful. Where they failed they did so because of overwhelming force in changed circumstances – after having worked successfully for many generations. 'Attributing causality to an event almost three hundred years after the barrier's construction is an absurd standard by which to judge barrier building effectiveness.'[3]

Many linear barriers were planned not as a response to great armies but to deal with persistent low level raiding and marauding. Unsung success here was, by definition, unlikely to be recorded, but the continued survival of a viable state might be evidence of it. 'History shows that walls, provided people are prepared to do what is necessary to defend them and prevent other people from crossing them, by using lethal force if necessary, work. If not for technical reasons – there never has been, nor can there be, such a thing as an impregnable wall – then for psychological ones; and if not forever, and perfectly, then for long periods and to a very large extent.'[4]

2. Were states' strategies of constructing linear barriers successful or not?

If the question is moved beyond asking whether individual walls achieved their purpose, to whether over time the strategy adopted by particular states of building linear barriers worked generally – then a bigger picture can be derived about the success or failure of such barriers. In the survey section various states and polities which adopted linear barriers were considered.

Very briefly, Egypt's linear defences appear largely to have worked against nomads. Ur III fell to the Martu despite the *Muriq Tidnim* but the situation was probably already hopeless. China's 'Warring States' walls may well have prolonged the survival of individual states – and walls certainly worked for the Qin who were able to roll up all the other states. Also, the experience of building walls developed during the time of Warring States, and this meant that China had the construction skill needed to hold back steppe nomad confederations when these emerged as a major threat. Nebuchadnezzar's semi-aquatic linear barriers worked during his lifetime but the Medes and the Persians broke through during the reign of his less able son, Belshazzar. With the Roman Empire, linear barriers had been largely abandoned for riverine defences by the time nomads and barbarians burst in. Rome's walls in Africa appear to have been very successful in managing that frontier. In terms of state formation, linear barriers may have played a key role in establishing the idea of a Bulgarian and Polish identity. The Danevirke kept Denmark independent within northern Europe and by the eleventh century Denmark was a great Empire. Switching to the Eurasian Steppe, although the Kievan Rus fell to the Mongols, the Zmievi Vali had maintained southern defences against the Pechenegs and Polovtsians. This factor enabled the Rus to expand northwards, thus facilitating the survival of Russian states after Kiev fell. Linear barriers appear to have played a major part in defending the Byzantine and Sasanian Empires against nomads from the east and north in the fifth and sixth centuries. The Byzantine Empire held out in increasingly attenuated form; and when it finally fell it was to nomads who adopted artillery, infantry and castle building. The Chinese repeatedly built Great Walls against ferocious Xiongnu, Turkic and Mongol irruptions. In sum, dynastic Imperial China survived until it fell to maritime powers from the east. Russia aggressively and very successfully used linear barriers to close down the steppe.

If the brief comment on state survival or failure is not totally rejected as being overly simplistic, then the construction of linear barriers must be seen as forming part of a successful survival strategy for at least some states and empires. This should cast doubt on the frequent assumption that linear barrier building was a strategy doomed to failure. Indeed, it could be argued in several cases that it was the decision *not* to maintain linear barriers which contributed to state failure. Examples are seen from the history of the Sasanians and the Samanids, and possibly even the Western Roman Empire. (Of course, when the linear barriers ahead of the Rhine were abandoned earlier, this might have been the only economically sustainable solution. Also, the greater dangers in later generations could not reasonably have been anticipated.)

Overall, linear barrier building can hardly be written off as having been a record of unrelieved failure. Indeed, as part of a balanced strategy, it appears to have been rather successful. Failure generally occurred when the defending polity had anyway lost internal vigour, unity and strength, or when the external force was utterly overwhelming. Recently, analysis of the success of linear barriers has become much more nuanced. 'That even sophisticated linear barriers were only effective, if they were adequately garrisoned and patrolled, and that even then they were not impregnable is self evident. However, instances of enemies managing to break through such barriers do not disprove that they could considerably reduce the number of such incidents and considerably raise the threshold, in terms of military strength and risks, for enemies attempting a raid beyond such a line, especially if they lacked experience in siege warfare or launching an effective sea-borne attack.'[5]

3. Over the longer term did linear barriers aid settled states against nomads and migrants?

Looked at individually, nearly all linear barriers either failed or eventually their upkeep became futile. Some may have failed at once. Others may have worked and then failed while they were still required as defences. Some may have succeeded but when they were no longer needed they just quietly decayed or suffered the indignity of being robbed of their *matériel*. It is more important, however, to look at their record collectively. Settled states and civilisations could not have developed if their domains were constantly overrun, destabilised, robbed, or their populations massacred and generally exhausted by encroaching peoples.

Some time in the mid-first millennium BC the balance of military technology tipped strongly in favour of the steppe nomad with his combination of the hardy sturdy horse, the short composite bow and an organisation where every male was potentially a warrior.

It was not until the invention of mobile and portable firearms, nearly two millennia later, that the balance of military technology moved decisively back in the favour of the settled state. Just as settled states could not function if every male had to become warrior, so the nomad polity could not operate an arsenal and an artillery train comparable to a major settled state. That is, unless it essentially ceased to be nomadic like the Ottoman Turks.

But for two millennia settled states had broadly to contain nomads who, if they did not actually destroy them, could bleed them dry of people, food and goods. During this period linear barriers made a valuable contribution in literally holding the line. Of course, individually linear barriers failed. But enough held for long enough that settled states could survive and eventually gain the upper hand.

Analysis – linear barriers: success or failure?

When viewed collectively, the evidence indicates that linear barriers were a more important solution to strategic threats than perhaps current military history allows. Perhaps the lack of textual material and the preponderance of rather romantic, and clearly non-original, names (looked at later) may mean that historians have not accorded linear barriers the importance given by their contemporary builders. (China is the exception to this general rule because of its relative abundance of texts.) But if the massive amount of surviving physical evidence and remaining literary material is considered systematically, there was a period of more than 1,000 years in Europe, and much longer in Eurasia, when linear defences were a key element of the strategic mix. Moreover, it was a blend used by settled and settling states and polities alike, both for defining, defending and consolidating their hold on large areas of territory.

Chapter Nineteen

Visualisation and Functioning

Pre-modern visualisation of the world

In a world of compasses, portable and accurate timepieces and aerial and, more recently, satellite photography and navigation systems – all of which make possible increasingly accurate maps and positioning – it is difficult to conceptualise how the world must have been viewed through most of history. Certainly this is true of nearly all the period covered by this book. Yet one must still attempt to understand such contemporary world views if one is to glean how the constructor's decision process gave rise to the building of effective linear barriers.

This was a world determined largely by the eye and the ear – where, for most people, it was impossible to know what was over the horizon or even the next hill, without having actually having been there or obtained a reliable verbal report from someone who had. Even if people had a clear idea of their own immediate territory – then after moving to another, as a migrating nomad or barbarian, it was hard to know what movement and to where was permissible.

The Roman Peutinger Map of the fourth century AD survives as a thirteenth century copy. This might seem rather odd to modern eyes, as it is so extremely long and thin. It is more of a diagrammatic route plan than a conventional map, essentially a series of largely horizontal lines between occupied and fortified points in the form of cities and forts. The map would not have been much use to someone actually on a frontier, trying to work out where it went. Yet the Peutinger Map does give an insight into how the world was perceived and navigated. Essentially, this is almost a one dimensional narrow linear world, not a two dimensional spatially broad one. Without compasses and maps people moved from known point to known point, and if the next point were not visible from the last, then one could follow a natural linear feature, like a river or a man-made road or a line of watchtowers.

A line on the ground creates clarity for those on both sides of it. The story of Offa's Dyke is almost certainly apocryphal but, 'it was customary for the English to cut off the ears of every Welshman who was found to the east of the dyke, and for the Welsh to hang every Englishman whom they found to the west of it'.[1] The message was clear: that there was a line on the ground and Welshmen who wanted to keep their ears and Englishmen their lives should stay on the appropriate side of it. In the absence of a clear marker, endless disputes were possible and, as Robert Frost observed in his poem *Mending Wall*, 'Good fences make good neighbors'.

Functioning: approach, encounter, and reaction

The function of a linear barrier might seem to be to stop a threat along its line – after all, that is where what might seem the crucial encounter actually took place. In fact, this might be one of its least important functions – as the barrier might itself have been relatively easy to force by a determined enemy, particularly along an isolated stretch. At the simplest, there are three stages of encounter that both the aggressor and the defender considered: the approach; traversing the line; and the subsequent responses.

There are also a number of key imbalances which need to be borne in mind when considering the functioning of linear barriers. These imbalances are inherent in the nature of continuous defence over time. The defender of a region can only devote a limited number of men and resources to protecting a large area over a protracted period. Also, unless there is clear intelligence as to the time and location of an attack, those men and resources have to be spread along the line, or be tied to particular points along the line or in forts associated with it. Thus, the attacker generally has the advantage in terms of numbers brought to bear on a particular point. He could also more easily move to that or another point, and he enjoyed more control over the timing of the assault.

Two assumptions are made here about the attackers. The first is that they generally intend to return after the attack to their place of origin. Most linear barriers were built to deal with the constant threat of incursions or raids by people who were expected to go back from whence they came having achieved their objective. Generally linear barriers were not effective in stopping great armies planning occupation and were not intended to function in that role. If it was reasonably assumed that the attacker was going to return – probably slowed down with cattle, people, or goods – then that significantly affected the design of the linear barrier as it did not need to be over-engineered so as to be impermeable. (There is the caveat that if this were very vulnerable irrigated land, then it was critical to keep intruders out completely.) Anyway, this would probably have been an impossible drain on resources. Instead the barrier needed to slow attackers down, particularly if they were laden with booty which could be recovered. While the linear barrier itself might seem relatively flimsy, much effort would be put in the location and construction of forts and of signalling systems.

The second assumption is that the attacker's forces consisted entirely of cavalry or had a very significant cavalry element. (That is after the second millennium BC when nomads took to horses.) Horses greatly enhanced the impact of even small groups, as they could now change the location of attack and break off in response to changes in the situation. Most linear barriers, certainly around the Eurasian Steppe, were designed to deal with horse-borne warriors. Infantry might find it relatively easy to cross ditches and dykes; but the former could be made too wide to jump on horseback, and the latter too steep to ascend mounted, a task rendered even harder by a palisade. 'Long walls hardly could stop a determined army with means to scale or breach them, but they were effective against horsemen who travelled without heavy baggage.'[2]

Just as horses added energy to the force of the attack – equally, linear barriers sapped that energy. A linear barrier constituted an investment of energy by the defender at a time when this was in surplus. Then it could be drawn upon at the time of attack.

Equally, the attacker would have had to expend energy and time: move along the linear barrier to find the best place to effect a breach; then actually break through the barrier; and finally retreat back over the barrier with whatever booty had been taken.

Linear barriers eliminated or greatly reduced the element of surprise afforded by horse-borne mobility. Even if the making of the breach were unobserved or unreported, perhaps because the defenders were killed, patrols could quickly determine where it happened simply by locating any gaps or damage. The linear barrier was not just an obstacle to the enemy; it also provided a routeway for the defenders so that they could move warriors to the point of an expected initial breach or return.

In certain situations, however, the barriers needed to be impermeable in the face of unauthorised crossings. This would have been the case with particularly valued and thus sought-after land, like irrigation systems where either raiders or herders' animals could do irreparable damage.

Approach

The presence of the linear barrier would have hampered reconnaissance patrols and perhaps spies who wished to gain intelligence as to what was going on behind the line. It is possible that a linear barrier might have deterred an attacker, particularly one unfamiliar with the obstacle. But presuming this was not the case then, if there were a linear barrier, perhaps with watchtowers, the attacker would have been visible in the distance, looking for a place to make a breach. The defenders would then have had time to evacuate people, animals and key goods into strongholds – while assembling a reaction force from nearby forts and garrison towns. A signalling system involving watchtowers, beacons and riders was often part of the overall design. Indeed, many continuous linear barriers may have started as discontinuous lines of watchtowers and forts. The problem with forts was they could have been bypassed, so even a fairly modest linear barrier between them may have greatly enhanced the efficiency of the defence system and certainly helped determine the precise location of the breach.

Encounter

The encounter occurred when the threatening party attempted actually to traverse the linear barrier. Generally, if a barrier had a ditch below ground level and a rampart above it, then the overall height of the barrier was increased by their combination. This extra height would force a mounted enemy to dismount, thereby losing speed and mobility. Enemies, whether mounted or on foot, tend to lose momentum when striking upwards against defenders who enjoy greater elevation. The defenders can in turn rain down blows with greater force.

Linear barriers had varying degrees of penetrability. They may have been intended to stop a breach altogether or just to slow down progress. Naturally their effectiveness depended on what resources were available, and how important it was to stop any kind of damage to what lay behind the linear barrier. Very high priority was placed, as seen, on stopping access to irrigated land. At the other end of the scale, where breaches were considered inevitable, the important consideration was not stopping the breach itself but having an efficient signalling system to summon response forces to the best point for retaliation. For example, in the Ukraine: 'The Snake Ramparts were not in general designed to be constantly manned. Rather, they served to slow down the nomad horsemen, denying them the advantage of surprise. The ramparts were not particularly high … but they were fronted by ditches as wide as 12 metres; these prevented even the lithest of horses from clearing the ramparts at full trot.'[3]

Reaction

A reaction force might have been summoned by the signallers who were placed along a line of point defences or a continuous linear barrier. Presumably if the attacker was somewhere in the vicinity, he would probably try to return through the breach he made rather than try to effect another. By following the linear barrier, defenders could quickly determine the location of the breach which could be blocked while the return of the raiders was slowed down by animals, people and booty – perhaps requiring a further breach to be made. Consequently, for example, the function of linear barriers in Russia was described as gaining time. For example: 'The object of all these linear defensive systems (Russian abatis) was to impede the advance of the Tatars, restrict the mobility of cavalry, and gain time to allow the civilian population to be evacuated and large forces to be summoned from nearby fortresses.'[4]

Analysis – visualisation and functioning

Without modern maps and navigation aids the world would have been visualised very differently and a linear barrier would have provided much needed clarity – because it was obviously there.

Unless the priority was completely to stop any kind of breach, as with highly valuable and vulnerable irrigated land, then it may have been assumed that the linear barrier would at least slow down any attack. In addition, in a forensic sense, it would have made clear where the break through took place, so as to gain time for a reaction and to slow down the retreat of the attackers.

Often linear barriers where considered to be too expensive to man over their full length and for long periods of time. If, however, the assumption is made that many linear barriers were expected to be lightly manned and often breached, then their main function was to make clear that there was a line which, if crossed, would provoke a reaction. On such grounds, any criticism that they had no serious military function, because they could not be heavily garrisoned, suddenly seems much less valid.

Chapter Twenty

Construction and Maintenance

There is little detailed textual information about how the construction of linear barriers was organised and financed. Probably most available information relates to later Chinese and Russian linear barriers. If, however, the sources are carefully gleaned, the results of excavations considered, and reasonable analogies made from other works involving large numbers of people – like the construction of city and fortified town walls, canals and bridges – then quite a lot can be deduced. Basically, the construction can be broken down into phases: location and quantity surveying, and cost benefit analysis; organising and stimulating construction; and maintenance.

Location and quantity surveying, and cost benefit analysis

Some kind of cost benefit analysis was necessary as part of the decision to construct a linear barrier. This would not have been a highly detailed economic affair similar to that conducted in modern times. Indeed, the choices were often stark: the cost in terms of resources could indeed be cripplingly huge; however, the benefit was (possibly) not being killed, sold into slavery, or starving.

Some kind of pre-calculation exercise must have been carried out. For example, having heard reports of the fertility of the soil, Dercylidas conducted a survey of the Thracian Chersonesos: 'This district, he soon discovered, not only contained something like a dozen cities, but was singularly fertile. The soil was of the best, but ruined by the ravages of the Thracians. Accordingly, having measured and found the breadth of the isthmus barely four miles, he no longer hesitated.'[1]

The Chinese adviser to the Northern Wei dynasty Gao Lü counselled: 'I calculate that the area of the six garrisons is no more than one thousand li from east and west (a li is about half a kilometre), and if one soldier can build three paces of wall in one month, then three hundred men can build three li, three thousand men can build thirty li, and thirty thousand men can build three hundred li, so that a thousand li (about 500 kilometres) would take one hundred thousand men one month to complete.'[2]

Procopius, when commenting on walling the Peloponnese, said Justinian calculated that it would be more cost-effective to build a wall across the Isthmus of Corinth than to wall each city individually. As quoted above in reference to the Hexamilion Walls: 'When the Emperor Justinian ... learned that all the cities of the Peloponnesus were unwalled, he reasoned that obviously a long time would be consumed if he attended to them one by one, and so he walled the whole Isthmus securely, because much of the old wall had already fallen down.'[3]

Planning to block the Voronezh to Tsna corridor in Russia against attack by the Tatars involved the following estimates of timings and work loads. 'Birkin suggested that it might take as little as two weeks to build all this provided at least 2,000 workers were levied, the lumber was prepared beforehand over the course of the winter, and the weather proved favourable.'[4] Also, 'Rodenburg estimated that construction of the steppe fortifications ought to take no more than seven weeks if the redoubts were omitted and the project was assigned 1,200 foot laborers and 100–150 mounted laborers for grading and hauling.'[5]

In an age without carbon-sourced energy, time and cost calculation largely depended on adding up what an individual could dig in a day – and, therefore, how many people could be made available and for how long.

Organising construction

After deciding the location, materials and form of a barrier, it was of course necessary to actually build it. One theme recurs consistently, that is the division of labour between units. Usually teams would work together who were familiar with each other or who had some kind of collective identity. Herodotus described how Xerxes constructed the canal across the Agion Oros Peninsula. 'Along this the various nations parcelled out among themselves the work to be done.'[6] Note that the nations appeared to have done this themselves without instruction – as if this were the natural thing to do.

When Dercylidas set about building the wall across the Thracian Chersonesos, Xenophon described the operation as follows: 'Having offered sacrifice, he commenced his line of wall, distributing the area to the soldiers in detachments.'[7] Both Hadrian's Wall and the Antonine Wall were built in sections by the Legions occupying Britain. For the former, the second, sixth and twentieth legions each built the wall in sections of about five Roman miles. The Antonine Wall was built by the same units and the length of each section built was recorded on distance slabs. The wall was divided into three lengths, each about thirteen Roman miles, with a section of about four and two thirds Roman miles being allocated to each legion.[8]

The Frankish Royal Annals wrote of Godfred's construction of the Danevirke in 808: 'Once he had apportioned the work among the leaders of his troops, he returned home.'[9] Danish historian Arild Hvitfeldt (1546–1609) in his *Chronicle of Denmark*, described how the Danevirke work was shared. 'The men of Skåne received the western section from Karlegat to Trene. Zealanders and Funen dwellers received the section east from Slien (Schlei Bay) to Karlegat. Jutlanders provided provisions to the whole army.'[10] This text has to be regarded with some scepticism as the Danevirke was built well before Queen Tyra's reign. The point, however, is that the chronicler knew how such structures would have been built.

In 1495 the thirty-fourth act of the Drogheda parliament in Ireland, 'enacted that every earthtiller and occupier of said Marches shall build and make a double ditch of six foot of earth above the ground at that end of the said land that he occupies which joins next unto Irishmen before next Lammas (1st August),'[11] and in addition the inhabitants of the whole four counties were to contribute to the building of similar ditches in the wastelands that lay between the marches and the territory of neighbouring Irish Lords. Excavations on the Devil's Dyke in Cambridgeshire show that gangs were responsible for different sections.[12] When the Japanese built a wall around Hakata Bay, in anticipation of Mongol attack in 1274, the Shogun (military dictator) divided the barrier into lengths which were allocated to vassals, according to the precise standard of the holdings of their fiefs.[13]

Incentives

Digging dykes and ditches and erecting walls was not automatically fun – or even an honourable pursuit fit for warriors – although Roman legionaries were probably inured to it. Given that diggers were often divided into units who would be expected to have a group consciousness, it must have been natural to incentivise them with a sense of competition and the promise of rewards. Thus, Xenophon tells us that Dercylidas 'distribute(d) the area to the soldiers in detachments and promise(d) to award them prizes for their industry – a first prize for the section first completed, and the rest as each detachment of workers might deserve. By this means the whole wall begun in spring was finished before autumn.'[14]

Although this was strictly speaking not about the construction of a linear barrier, the story of Dionysius and the defence of Syracuse is informative about incentivisation. 'For Dionysius, in order to excite the enthusiasm of the multitude, offered valuable gifts to such as finished first... so that great rivalry was engendered and some added even a part of the night to the day's labour, such eagerness had infected the multitude for the task. As a result, contrary to expectation, the wall was brought to completion in twenty days.'[15] The Chinese took a harsher view about incentives. This is a world where legalism was a profound tradition, and in the harshest of states, Qin, punishments were common, rewards rare. The Chinese would labour because they were told to do so for the common good: 'The men would understand (the) long-term advantages of the wall, (and) they would work without complaining.'[16]

Maintenance

A linear barrier required maintenance if it was to be effective. What little information is available specifically about linear barriers appears to conform to the pattern for the upkeep of city and burgh defences and engineering projects, like bridges. When the ninth century Leonine Wall was built around the Vatican in Rome, the surrounding communities were responsible for a section. Carolingian Worms imposed *Mauerbaupflicht*, or 'wall building duty', on villages around that German city, with groups of villages required to build and repair specific stretches. The Burghal Hidage shows how many tax hides (five to twelve hectares) were needed to maintain each burgh – the number of hides correlating to the length of the walls.

According to the Rochester Bridgework List of the parishes surrounding Rochester, the manors and estates which belonged to the king, the archbishop, and the bishop of Rochester, were each responsible for keeping a section of the bridge in good repair. In 869 Charles the Bald made his ecclesiastical magnates, bishops and abbots, responsible for raising men to man and repair the fortified bridges across the River Seine to block the Vikings.[17]

By the 1200s Denmark's kings charged communities near to the Danevirke, in North Friesland, the North Sea islands, and the coastlines of Schleswig-Holstein, with its regular upkeep. The *Liber Census Daniae* (The Danish Census Book) from the thirteenth century consists of notes used by the Royal Chancery of Valdemar II on Royal income and Royal land property; it also outlined the contributions made towards particular enterprises including the Danevirke.

> Isted syssel (Schleswig-Holstein Coast) 200 (units of) pure silver besides Sleswig and Menten and Danevirke and Egernborg. Slæsmynnæ 20 (units of) pure silver Arns herred (district to west of Schleswig). Danevirke with Eidersted and Lundebjerg district 120 (units of) pure silver and arrangement of three nights (stay) in summer with the men as the king has assembled to cross over in Jutland. Also arrangement of three nights (stay) in winter or 800 silver pennies Lundæbyargha Thunninghæreth. Giæthninghæreth. Holm. Hæfræ (North Sea Islands). 12 pure silver. Of these the King has 50 pure silver for wingift (presents showing friendship) and 50 pure silver for stud (horse herds), besides the provision of six-night stay accounted for by the Danevirke.[18]

Analysis – Planning, organisation, logistics and maintenance

The point which emerges is that there were clear patterns for linear barrier construction and maintenance and none of this was modern rocket science. The emphasis was on doing what was doable within the administrative capabilities of the time. That was, to assess the benefits in raised security and increased productivity; to calculate the man-days necessary; to divide constructions workers into groups who knew each other and could be expected to work well as teams; to encourage each group with rewards for completing their section first; and to allocate maintenance to particular localities which might be expected to benefit from the protection afforded by linear barriers.

Chapter Twenty-One

Tactical Use of Static and Mobile Linear Barriers

In the earlier survey section there were several mentions of the use of static and mobile linear barriers on the battlefield. Formally these lie outside the definition of linear barriers, as given in the introductory section, which was: barriers built in anticipation of a threat intended for more than one-time use. That said, the distinctions in the case of static barriers can become blurred. For example, in certain locations some linear barriers appear originally to have been temporary in intention, but may have then become long term fixtures. Looking at the Corinthian Isthmus, the stone wall built by Anastasius and rebuilt by Justinian was intended to be permanent and some of it is still there. Other walls which were built to stop Xerxes or Epameinondas were clearly temporary. The site of Artaxerxes' Trench may have been reused for the Wall at Macepracta, described by Ammianus Marcellinus, and is possibly now the location of the Wall at Umm Raus. Also, while the objective may be different, the working principle was similar – namely, the use of a continuous physical object (a wall) or a void (a ditch) to obstruct the progress of the threat in the direction of the builder.

The use of mobile linear barriers has been mentioned in the context of sedentary states fighting battles against nomads. Static linear barriers provided the means to block the progress of mounted nomads and as a defence against their stinging arrows. Therefore, it might be a logical progression, rather than to wait until the threat comes to the fixed barrier, to make the barrier mobile and take it to the threat.

The exercise of looking at the use of temporary and mobile barriers might be valuable in showing how linear barriers fitted into a broad spectrum of such barriers in general.

1: Role of linear barriers on the battlefield and in passes

One-time threats

Many very substantial linear barriers have been constructed across areas where an expected one-time threat would cross. Linear barriers which have already been mentioned include the following: Cnidus' Reşidiye peninsula canal, which was started but remained unfinished during the reign of Cyrus; the Corinth Isthmian walls, built to block Xerxes' Persians; Ataxerxes' Trench, cut before the Battle of Cunaxa (401 BC); and the Wall of the Judean King Alexander Jannaeus (103–76 BC), who tried to stop the Seleucid King Antiochus Dionysus.

Other examples include: Crassus' Servile War Wall, built across the toe of Italy on the Rhegium Peninsula, in order to contain Spartacus and his rebel slave army; Caesar's earthwork to block the Helvetii who were trying to migrate to Gaul in 58 BC; the Teutoburg

Forest Wall, built parallel to the routeway, from behind which the Germans could attack the Romans; and at Hakata Bay where in 1281 the Japanese faced a second attack from the Mongol and Korean forces commanded by Kubilai Khan. (The Japanese had built a stone faced embankment more than twenty-two kilometres along the coast about three metres high and wide, after the first attack in 1274 was broken up by storms and Japanese resistance.)

Passes

A clear category emerges where passes were fortified or refortified with linear barriers in order to strengthen the positions of the defenders. A pass is an obvious place for a defending power to force a battle, as the narrowness of the location helps make the task of the defender easier against a larger attacking force.

Thermopylae, where the Greeks delayed the Persian advance in the fifth century BC, has already been discussed. In the following century the situation was reversed. In 330 BC Alexander the Great advanced on Persepolis, leading 20,000 troops across the Zagros Mountains and onto the ten kilometre-long pass of the Persian Gates. The local satrap Ariobarzanes built a wall across the pass and forced Alexander to retreat. Reversing the story of Thermopylae, the Greeks followed a local guide up treacherous paths onto the plateau above the pass, and then crept up behind the Persians who were annihilated in a joint attack from behind and in front. This manoeuvre left open the road to Persepolis for Alexander.

In 192 BC the Seleucid King Antiochus III invaded Greece and was confronted by the Romans. As mentioned before in Chapter 2, here the invader, rather than the defender, built the wall. 'There Antiochus built a double wall on which he placed engines. He sent Aetolian troops to occupy the summits of the mountains to prevent anybody from coming around secretly by way of the hill called Atropos, as Xerxes had come upon the Spartans under Leonidas, the mountain paths at that time being unguarded.'[1] The Romans, under Marcus Porcius Cato, like many others, got round behind Antiochus using the mountain path – forcing him to withdraw. Later in 146 BC the Romans forced their way through Thermopylae in order to put down a Greek revolt.

The Bulgars and the Byzantines had a joint history of battles in barricaded passes. In 811 the Byzantine Emperor Nicephoras I laid waste to Bulgaria and burnt the capital Pliska. On hearing that the Bulgarians were defending the passes, Nicephoras set out for the Vărbitsa Pass on the route back to Constantinople where the Bulgars had built a wooden wall. The Byzantines tried to burn the barricade and were either themselves burned or drowned in the moat built behind the wall. Victory went the other way in 1014 when Bulgar Khan Samuil built a wooden wall across the pass at the village of Klyuch, or Kleidion meaning key, in the Haemus Mountains which provided the main invasion route into Bulgaria. In the summer of 1014 the army of Basil II was repelled at the wall. Again, a path behind the wall was found and the Bulgarians were overwhelmed.[*]

---

[*] 15,000 Bulgarians were captured and blinded with the exception of one in a hundred who left with one eye. Samuel was reputedly so shocked by the return of the blind that he died of a heart attack and Basil earned the name *Bulgaroctonus* or Bulgar-slayer.

A *Letzimauer*, or Swiss stone wall, played a key part in the Battle of Stoss Pass in 1405 in the Appenzell Wars between 1401 and 1429, when the local populace from the region fought off the Hapsburgs. Appenzell's force of 400 men defended the wall at the Pass against which 1,200 Hapsburg soldiers were suffocated or halberdiered.

Battlefields

Although many battles have been fought at passes most took place on more open ground. Even here there was a consistent record of the use of linear barriers.

When heavily outnumbered, Caesar built a linear barrier in 48 BC, around the forces of Pompey who were camped on the coast of north-western Greece below Dyrrhachium. The barrier was twenty-two kilometres long and included four forts. Pompey's forces also constructed a linear barrier. If anything, this was testimony to the wall-building capacity of the legionary which could be put to use making more permanent linear barriers.

In 484 the Sasanian Shah Peroz led an army against the Hephthalite chief Akhunwar who was crossing the Gorgan Plain to the east of the Caspian Sea. Procopius describes how the Persians (Sasanians) 'gave chase at full speed across a very level plain, possessed as they were by a spirit of fury against the enemy, and fell into the trench, every man of them.'[2] Peroz was killed and his army routed. The Sadd-i-Iskandar may have been built subsequently by the Sasanians in order to counter the Hephthalite threat.

The nomadic Arabs proved adept users of tactical linear barriers. In AD 627 Mohammed led roughly 3,000 defenders of Medina against a confederate Arab and Jewish army more than three times its number. The Muslims dug a trench – hence the name the Battle of the Trench – which negated the enemy's superiority in numbers and cavalry; soon the siege was lifted and the confederacy collapsed. Having proved impossible to dislodge from Medina, Mohammed was able to return in triumph to Mecca.

After the ninth century, linear barriers intended for long term use appear increasingly to have fallen out of use in Europe. This might have been because of the improvements in the military technology of point defences, like burghs and castles, and the mobility of mounted men at arms. The technology employed by infantry improved in turn, to the extent that they could fight off heavily armoured mounted knights by using a combination of weapons of extended reach, like pikes. They also used projectile weapons, for example longbows, and battlefield linear barriers which might be either static or mobile. Thus, linear barriers returned to the military repertory in a somewhat different and now predominantly tactical, battlefield form.

By the fourteenth century, infantry had increasingly got the measure of cavalry. Obstacles were built on the battlefield in the form of ditches – often filled with spikes and other horrors to increase the lethality of plunging into them. These served to channel and break up the momentum of mounted men at arms. In 1385, for example, the Castilians invaded Portugal, met an army reinforced by a contingent of English archers, and were soundly beaten. Excavations of the Aljubarotta have revealed a ditch about 240 metres wide across the Portuguese front and numerous pits. In 1387 the English commander of the mercenary White Company in Italy, Sir John Hawkwood, drew up archers behind drainage dykes at Castagnaro. At Agincourt in 1415 the English archers built a barrier of sharpened stakes which they carried with them. These allowed the construction of a mobile palisade. Indeed, when the French declined to attack, the English literally upped their sticks and reformed closer to the French lines, the better to provoke them into attack with a barrage of arrows.

Linear barriers used on the battlefield demonstrate that ancient and Middle Ages rulers and commanders did not suffer from any prejudice against their deployment. The point is that earlier leaders were flexible in their willingness to consider the value of linear barriers in a whole range of situations, both immediate and long term, and tactical and strategic.

2: Defeating nomads on open ground – mobile linear barriers

The armies of sedentary states found it almost impossible to defeat a nomad horde that was well-led on open ground. The combination of mobility and bow-and-arrow power meant that such armies could destabilise and decimate the more static armies of sedentary states. Even if the body armour of elite troops could stop the nomads' arrows, a terrible toll would still be taken of less well armed soldiery and horses. Nomad armies were, however, occasionally beaten. Crusaders defeated a Turkish force of mounted archers at the Battle of Dorylaeum (1097) where a line of heavily armed dismounted knights defended less well armed compatriots, until reinforcements attacked the Turks in the rear. At Ain Jalut (1260) the Mamluks induced the hitherto invincible Mongols into an ambush by feigning retreat. The Mamluk forces used *midfa*, or portable hand cannons loaded with explosive gunpowder, to incite fear and disorder among the Mongol cavalry.

These battles anticipated the means to defeat nomad forces – the protected line that blocked arrows, and the explosive energy from gunpowder. If the line could be composed of a solid yet moveable inanimate material, one that obstructed nomad arrows, and incorporated crossbows and firearms that could outrange nomad projectiles on a flat trajectory, then the terms of battle could be more than equalised.

Linear barriers did not need to be static. They could be put on wheels or sledges and taken to the enemy. That way protection could be provided against nomad arrow storms and cavalry attacks. Meanwhile, the mobile barrier could provide a fortified screen through which the defenders' bows, crossbows, firearms and cannon raked the enemy.

At the Battle of Mobei in 119 BC the Han general, Wei Qing, used rings of heavily armed chariots, or *wu gang*, first to break Xiongnu charges, and then to launch a successful counter-attack. These vehicles protected infantry and crossbowmen from Xiongnu arrows and gave them the security to be able to shoot back accurately. Han cavalry dealt with any Xiongnu who broke through.

Mobile linear barriers could be improvised of the most obvious available vehicle used by most armies, that is, the wagon or cart, which had always been used to protect camps during halts and to defend camps behind the main battlefield. Mobile defences in Europe were developed first against non-nomad forces. For example, in 1428 at Rouvray, Sir John Fastoff, anticipating attack by larger forces, formed their convoy of carts into an enclosure. By the fifteenth century war wagons were being specially designed so that mobile barriers could be formed. The most famous war wagons were perhaps those of the Hussites, led by Jan Žižka in the early fifteenth century, and known as *vozová hradba* or wagon walls.

The Russian *Gului-gorod*, used in the sixteenth and early seventh centuries, have already been discussed. The Battle of Molodi in 1572 – where the protection afforded by the *Gului-gorod* was critical – perhaps marked a turning point in the fight between settled states and nomads. It has been seen how static linear barriers built by the Russians played a crucial part in closing down the Pontic Steppe. At the same time the Russians also used mobile linear barriers to defeat the nomads in the field.

These developments in military technology ultimately meant that the fight could be taken to the open ground preferred by nomad hordes of mounted archers, and for them to be defeated there. The importance of Molodi is not perhaps sufficiently recognised in the West – for never again did a major nomad army invade a great empire.

Chapter Twenty-Two

Movement of Animals and of People

1: Movement of animals

This chapter explores linear barriers and movement. The first theme is movement of animals across linear barriers, why this might take place, and how it could be managed. The second concerns linear barriers as ways of controlling movement by threats along routeways – and facilitating movement for defenders.

Nomadic pastoralism and transhumance

Usually the immediate association of linear barriers with living beings is with human warriors. In fact, in the survey section, it has emerged that many linear barriers were probably constructed with the intention of controlling the movement of herds of animals.

There were several different types of movement of animals on the move depending, essentially, on two factors. The first was whether or not there was an annual range where animals were moved seasonally between two set areas. The idea behind such movement was to maximise food and water supplies; and sometimes movement was driven by the search for food and water, in any direction, after the occupied area was exhausted. The second factor was whether the movement with the herds involved the whole people or just specialist herders like shepherds and cowherds. If it was the whole people, then the term used is transhumance by nomadic pastoralists; otherwise it is simply transhumance.

When considering the construction and management of linear barriers, another issue was whether the regular transhumance route actually went across the linear barrier. If so, its constructor would have had to decide whether to stop transhumance altogether, or whether to manage and possibly to tax it. Even if the transhumance route did not traverse frontiers, but there were nomadic pastoralists in the region, it might still have been necessary to make plans for managing their movement. This was particularly true of times of famine or drought, which often led to frantic attempts to access vulnerable irrigated land.

The literary texts which mention the Egyptian Walls of the Ruler described it in the context of controlling the movement of Asiatics and their herds. The earliest reference to the Walls was probably in the prophecy of a time when Egypt would be overrun by Asiatics. The Prophecy of Neferti said there would come a ruler, Ameny, and it stated further: 'Men will build the Walls of the Ruler, and there will be no letting the Asiatics go down into Egypt, that they may beg water after their accustomed fashion to let their herds drink.'[1] Before Egypt developed, Asiatics may have seasonally shifted herds between the Sinai and the Nile Delta, almost certainly doing so in times of drought.

As Egyptian irrigation systems expanded there would have been increasing clashes between sedentarists and nomads.

There are two areas where transhumance was practiced until recently on the borders of the Roman Empire: in modern Algeria, Tunisia and Libya; and in Romania, Moldavia and the western Ukraine. These regions are full of linear barriers. In North Africa the various walls that constitute the Fossatum Africae and the *clausurae* – short walls across passes – may have had subtle differences in function, but were still planned with the view to controlling the movement of animals. The Mesarfelta to Thubunae section looks as though it was intended primarily to channel seasonal movement south-west of the Aurès Mountains. The Seguia Bent el Krass section may have stopped nomads and their animals from getting to the irrigated areas along the Oued Djebi. The many *clausurae* 'were internal controls on shepherds and herdsmen who traditionally traversed them.'[2]

Until recently certain Carpathian villages practiced transhumance, involving specialist herders. There was 'antipathy towards transhumance on the part of arable farmers which results from the damage caused to crops along the routes taken by flocks as they travelled.'[3] One function of linear barriers might have been to prevent damage to crops. Many nomadic peoples have practised nomadic pastoralism in the region. During the time of the Roman Empire these included the various Sarmatian peoples. The region around the Carpathians, east, south and west, is replete with linear barriers. In Britain the gateway at Knag Burn below Housesteads Fort on Hadrian's Wall was intended to facilitate the movement of animals.

Analysis – animals

Encounters were inevitable if the nomads crossed or came to the borders of settled states. The issue became how to control the nomads and their herds. The image of the relationship between nomads and settled states has often been cast in the image of a Ghengiz Khan or Attila and vast hordes on great *chevauchées*. The truth was probably far more mundane. The dilemma is caught nicely in the musical *Oklahoma*, set in the later nineteenth century:

> I'd like to say a word for the farmer,
> He come out west and made a lot of changes
> He come out west and built a lot of fences,
> And built 'em right acrost our cattle ranges.

> The farmer should be sociable with the cowboy
> If he rides by and asks for food and water.
> Don't treat him like a louse, make him welcome in your house.
> But be sure that you lock up your wife and daughters!

Linear barriers could block the nomads from their traditional transhumance ranges. It is likely however that in most situations ways of managing the process were worked out and linear barriers could play a positive role. In Egypt a canal could have taken water to the nomads, and thereby remove the threat of their intruding into irrigated areas. Some of the Fossatum Africae and the *clausurae* in North Africa may have been designed specifically so that nomads practicing transhumance could pass through them. If managed properly, a relationship advantageous to both sides could be organised; whereby herds might – after the harvest – clear the stubble and provide manure.

2: Transport routes

Clearly when a linear barrier actually crosses a route, its function was to control what was passing along the route itself. But many linear barriers ran parallel to the route and some of these faced the route while others faced away from it. In addition, there often appeared to be ambiguity about whether a raised construction crossing the ground was actually a road or a linear barrier. The relationship between routes and transport with linear barriers had several facets: protection *against* what was on the route itself; protection *for* what was on the route itself; and provision of the actual route itself.

- **Traversing the routeway – controlling moving along the route** – In Northern Europe from Ireland, Britain, Jutland and southern Sweden there are numerous relatively short linear barriers which crossed or lay near ancient routeways and, in the case of England, Roman roads. Their function seemed quite obvious – to block the path of threats moving along such routes. In practice, however, most of the time such linear barriers simply controlled the flow of people, animals, and goods. Some possibly extracted some form of customs dues rather than merely serving as an obstructing feature. Indeed, given that they were generally fairly short, seldom extending more than a few kilometres on either side of the road, they would have been relatively easy to outflank in most situations, if not simply to overcome by a large force.

- **Facing away from the routeway – protection for what is on the route** – Other linear barriers defended the adjacent area from what was travelling along the routeway. Generally these barriers ran on one side of the route, protecting it from a threat which was reasonably expected to come from one direction only. The two cataract walls in Ancient Egypt defended portage routes. The Chinese Han walls ran along the north side of the Gansu Corridor which had the purpose of protecting the trade routes along the Corridor to Central Asia. In Greece there were parallel long walls that defended both sides of the transport route from the polis to the harbour. The most famous were the Long Walls of Athens. The Anastasian Wall which protected Constantinople to the north, 'afford(ed) a very safe transit … from the Pontus to the Euxine Sea.'

- **Facing towards the routeway – protection against what is on the route** – Some linear barriers, however, face towards the routeway. These may have been intended to protect surrounding land from threats which might have been moving along the route. Examples are the Chilterns and Berkshire Grims Dykes, the Dane's Cast in Ireland and the Trældiget in Denmark.

- **Linear barriers providing the actual routeway** – The linear barrier might itself be the routeway or the road might run just behind the raised line of the linear barrier. Given that linear barriers were long, almost by definition, they could not be defended strongly in most instances along their full length. Therefore, the ability to move defenders to areas of expected attack was critical and the line of the linear barrier itself was likely to the shortest and the quickest route. In Ireland, the Black Ditch between Ballyhoura Hills and the Nagle Mountains through the strategic Blackwater Valley, and dated to around 100 BC, had a cobbled road behind the two parallel ditches on either side of an earthen mound. Both Hadrian's Wall and the Antonine Wall had military roads running behind them. The Warring States wall built by the Qi state against the Chu state is described as follows: 'The Wall is in two lanes, 5 metres in height and 25 metres in thickness, with an inner galloping runway upon the wall.'[4] The walls that the states of Qin, Zhao and Yan built to consolidate their hold over lands taken from nomads had a broader strategic function. 'Like roads, walls provide the logistical infrastructure to facilitate communication and transportation, vital elements for armies employed in the occupation or invasion of a foreign territory.'[5]

Ambiguity of use

So closely do raised roads and defensive linear barriers resemble each other that there is sometimes confusion as to whether a linear barrier was or was not actually a road. For example, three sections of the Roman Fossatum Africae were outlined earlier in this book. There is – or rather there was – considered to be a fourth as identified by Barades. Called the Ad Majores section, it ran about seventy kilometres eastwards from the town of that name (the modern Besseriani). It is now thought to be a Roman road. Between the East and West Wansdyke there is a section about twenty-two kilometres long, but it is not clear whether it was really anything more than the London to Bath Roman Road.

Analysis – transport

Linear barriers tend to be identified with frontiers. Actually barriers which protected a considerable length of frontier appear to have been quite rare. More often than not it seems that linear barriers had a more localised function, like protecting a specific area defined by the work of man, such as particularly valued land (often due to irrigation). Or its role might have been to control movement along routeways either selected or made by man. Linear barriers did not just cross routeways, they also ran parallel to them; and they faced alternatively in or out, depending on purpose. Sometimes the linear barrier provided the strategic routeway itself. And in many situations it probably took on multiple tasks.

Chapter Twenty-Three

Harnessing Nature – Abatis and Hedges, Rivers, Canals and Seas

L inear barriers might generally be associated with structures that were wholly the creation of man and tended to diminish in size, once built, due to various forms of erosion. That is to say, a wall or earthwork can get no higher or thicker, once constructed to a certain height; indeed without maintenance it will diminish in size. But, throughout the survey section, there have been many references to abatis and hedges. Flowing water has often formed linear barriers too. This section draws together those references and considers natural plant growth and flowing water as more general themes in the context of linear barriers.

1: Abatis and hedges

The difference between a hedge and an abatis is that the latter involves chopping through much of the girth of a tree to lay the trunk and main branches forward. Consideration of abatis and hedges is useful because it suggests ways to fill gaps in the linear barrier record. This is particularly the case with central, northern and eastern Europe. The forest steppe extended from what is now modern Russia through Poland to Germany. This is a largely flat plain with, it seems, relatively few earthworks. The apparent absence of surviving linear barriers might, however, be explained by the fact that such barriers *were* there, in the form of abatis, but have disappeared through decay, re-growth or clearance. Since evidence of abatis and hedges rapidly disappears without maintenance, their existence may only be known from textual sources or deduced from place names.

Textual sources and toponyms indicate that abatis and hedges might have been relatively common. Julius Caesar described in 57 BC how the Beglic Nervii, as 'they were weak in cavalry... made these hedges present a fortification like a wall.'[1] Nokter Balbulus repeated the description of what an old soldier who said of the Avar Hrings: 'In between the turfs were planted shrubs which were pruned and lopped, so as to make them shoot forth boughs and leaves.'[2] In Cornwall two linear barriers are explicitly called Giant's Hedges. Bamburgh Castle was surrounded with a hedge: the Anglo-Saxon chronicle said Ida, who became the first identified king of Anglian Bernicia in 547, 'built Bamburgh Castle, which was first surrounded with a hedge, and afterwards with a wall.'[3]

Sections of Charlemagne's eastern border, above the left bank of the Danube, have been named the Limes Saxoniae in the north and the Limes Sorabicus in the south. In the border region, toponyms are seen as indicating the presences of abatis.[4] The Silesian Przesieka, literally Silesian Cuttings, consisted of wide strips of dense, fortified forests within which trees and branches were twisted together, with thick bushes and sometimes ramparts and trenches; and these structures blocked movements from the west.

The Les Fossés-le-Roy, built in the second half of the twelfth century in southern Normandy, consisted of a rampart as well as a ditch and hedges between five and ten metres wide and five metres deep. In the fourteenth and fifteenth centuries the petty states in western Germany constructed hundreds of kilometres of *Landwehr* or *Landhege*.[5] The Calais Pale might have been a palisade of fully cut wood or an abatis, similar to parts of the *Landwehren*. A late nineteenth century description of the Irish Pale said it included a living hedge.

Constantine VII Porphyrogenitus describes how a ditch that cut off the Crimea became filled in and forested over. Through it were two roads used by the Pechenegs to travel into the Crimea. 'In the course of many years this same ditch has silted up and become a great forest, and there are in it but two roads, along which the Pechenegs pass through to Cherson and Bosphorus and the Regions.'[6] It is not clear to what extent the forest was intended to be a barrier or it just grew during a period of neglect.

As the Kievan Rus broke up and northern states emerged, new borders formed within the forest steppe itself. The successor states to the Kievan Rus may have constructed abatis barriers as defences against each other. For example, Prince Igor of Chernigov (1198–1202) built an abatis over 600 metres wide in the areas of the Desna and Bolva Rivers as a defence against attack from the state of Suzdal.[7] Later Muscovy and Russia built a succession of lines or *chertas*, such as the Zasechnaya Cherta and the Belgorodskaya Cherta, which incorporated long abatis sections.

The Inner Willow Palisade separated China from Manchuria and Manchuria from the Mongols. It was first built between the 1630s and 1670s and may, therefore, have originally predated the Qing conquest of China. It was a living barrier composed of one or two earthworks on which were planted willows whose branches were tied to each other.

Analysis – linear barriers of living wood
The use of forest or living wood may well explain the absence of physical remains of linear barriers. In some situations this might be why surviving earthworks were discontinuous – as sections of dense forest might be considered as an adequate defence, possibly reinforced by an abatis line. Generally, literary sources foster most knowledge of the existence of abatis; sometimes place names provide clues. Many surviving linear barriers are unattested in any text. Also, there are linear barriers which are mentioned in texts of which nothing survives. Therefore, it is possible that there were many more abatis in the forest steppe than are known of through texts. Indeed, it might be speculated that in the regions of what are now modern Germany, Poland and Russia lost abatis might have formed a very common border system.

2: Rivers, canals and seas

Water is a recurrent theme. In this section a number of issues will be reviewed: firstly, water itself as an aquatic linear barrier; secondly, how a river could be considered as a transport corridor which might need transverse or parallel linear barriers; and lastly, a few points can be made about the sea.

Natural aquatic barriers reinforced

Where there was a natural aquatic barrier it could be supplemented by a man-made linear barrier. More usually, however, the water provided the barrier and was supplemented by forts along its banks. Examples of continuous linear barriers which ran along river and shore lines are those along the Danube, like the Tutrakan and the Belen Dykes. The Bulgarians also built linear barriers along the Black Sea as defences against the powerful Byzantine Navy. Julius Caesar constructed a line along the left bank of the Rhone to stop the Helvetii. The Russians constructed a palisade along the Oka River between Coloma and Kaluga to block the Crimean Tatars before the Battle of Molodi in 1572.

More usually, however, river and sea shoreline defences are associated with forts – the river itself provided the linear barrier. There were multiple Roman forts along the Rhine and Danube which constituted the main defence of the Roman Empire, north of the Mediterranean, particularly after Roman withdrawal from Germany and Dacia. There were also forts along the eastern and southern coasts of England, the Forts of the Saxon Shore, and along the north coast of Gaul. Further, riverine linear barriers provided clear lines of transportation for patrolling and defending forces. A river does this well, given the relative cheapness of water rather than road transportation through much of history.

Rivers

Roads can provide a man-made land corridor where movement was easier than on the surrounding terrain. Linear barriers have been built across and parallel to roads. They served to control movement along and away from the road. This raises the question: were there ever linear barriers across rivers, similarly designed to control movement?

In fact, there were several examples of linear barriers crossing rivers and estuaries. The Île de la Cité in the Seine provided a location where strategically placed low bridges could stop even shallow Viking ships. In a protracted episode, Charles the Bald forced back a Viking fleet under Sigrid, leader of the Danes, in 864. There can still be seen, in the Military Museum in Istanbul, links of the Byzantine era chain that blocked access to the Golden Horn. The chain defence, buoyed up by barrels, was constructed by Leo III (717–741). Twice it was circumvented by dragging ships overland to the Golden Horn, first by the Kievan Rus in the tenth century and secondly by the Ottomans. In 1204 the Fourth Crusaders managed to ram through the chain. In 1628 a seawall was built blocking access to La Rochelle in France, so that the English could not resupply that Huguenot city. A defensive chain was overcome when the Dutch broke through the Medway in 1667.

Linear barriers could protect ships and transport that have been taken off the river, due to cataracts; or boats that remain on the river itself. In Egypt there were linear barriers which ran parallel to the First and the Second Cataracts along the portage route. In the Kievan Rus: 'The journey to the sea remained arduous but Vladimir made protection of the southern riverway a priority.... One of the functions of the Snake Rampart flanking the Dnieper was to hinder the Pechenegs from positioning themselves on the left bank and ambushing vessels.'[8]

Linear barriers also controlled river crossing points. Two linear barriers rather surprisingly face a river loop rather than away from it. The Doon of Drumsa in Ireland overlooked the River Shannon where there are fords. South Oxfordshire's Grim's Dyke faces the Thames at the Goring Gap where several routes converge. The purpose of these linear barriers was not to defend an area of territory bounded by the river loop and the linear barrier, but rather to contain the advance of a threat between the river and the linear barrier.

Canals

In earlier sections there have been several examples of canals which served as linear barriers. In Egypt the Walls of the Ruler and the later Eastern Frontier Canal were possibly fortified canals. Shapur II (309–379) built a moat and fortification system to the west of the Euphrates to stop Bedouin Arabs raiding.

The situation may be more complex than solely the provision of defence, as a canal might perform multiple functions. For example, the Egyptian Frontier Canal 'had three functions, defence, irrigation and navigation – of which the first was the most important.'[9] The main reason herds come to an irrigated area is to find water and food. A canal could serve the purpose of providing the herds with water and keeping them away from the growing crops. This was hinted at in the texts about the Walls of the Ruler. 'Dig a moat and flood the half of it at the Bitter Lakes, for see, it is the navel-string of the desert dwellers.'[10]

Seas

The sea can be likened to the steppe as a medium to support movement by raiders, traders and migrants, with ships and boats filling the roles of horses and wagons. The result was that certain quite specialised linear barriers were built to defend landing points and access to them. Greek long walls made a protected link from the polis to harbour. Thus they provided access to the sea, which was a maritime route system to any number of destinations which might also require protected landing points. Linear barriers across headlands defended landing points like Hengistbury Head, Flamborough Head, respectively on the coast of southern and north eastern England, or Cap de la Hogue at the end of the Cherbourg Peninsula. One function of Byzantine linear barriers across isthmuses might have been not just to defend the peninsula themselves, but also to provide a protected landing area which could serve as a base for further operations in the region. As Procopius said of Justinian, he 'brought it about that both the city of Pallene, which stands as a bulwark of the whole region, and the cross-wall at the entrance of the peninsula, became manifestly impregnable and able to defy any who should wish to attack them.'[11]

The sea itself might be considered as a linear barrier. A river looks like a linear barrier on a map but what, however, if a river's width were to be expanded for dozens of kilometres? It would then in effect become a sea while remaining a linear barrier at the same time – just a particularly wide one. Seen this way, the Roman forts along the Northern coast of France and the forts of the Saxon shore might be regarded as a continuation of the system of forts along the Rhine.

Problems with water and wood

Constructing a linear barrier out of inert material, like stone, earth or dead wood has disadvantages relative to harnessing nature. For a start it requires great expenditure of manpower. A living hedge expands itself, a canal refills, and a river has already been provided by nature. But given that polities persisted in building linear barriers out of inert material, there must have been flaws with natural barriers. What might these have been?

When searching for a suitable defensible border a convenient river must seem like a better solution than going to the effort of constructing a linear barrier. The problem is that rivers were not always in a convenient position. Rome had the fortune in Europe of having the Rhine and the Danube in roughly the right place in terms of the extent of empire it could reasonably manage. In the case of China, however, the Yellow River was either too far north, in the region of the loop around the Ordos Desert, or too far south along its more easterly section. The result was that frontiers oscillated uncomfortably between north and south, particularly in the area of the Ordos, where sometimes the border was north of the Yellow River and included the Ordos and sometimes it was south and excluded the Ordos. The Oka River made a good southern frontier for the Muscovite Rus, but not if the growing kingdom wanted to expand further south. Simply put, there were no suitable rivers for borders running east to west, a factor that necessitated the building of the abatis line system.

Ultimately the problem with a river is that it is not a true dividing line between different land types, as is the border between irrigated land and semi-desert. In many cases the land on both banks of the river are equally attractive – so the people on one side will be tempted to move across to the other, and vice-versa. The result is that rivers were frequently paralleled by linear barriers which defended the river basin on the other side from that occupied by the dominant polity in the region. This can be seen most clearly with the Rhine and Danube where, for much of their length, there were linear barriers situated respectively to the east and the north of the rivers. Across the Rhine were the Upper German Limes, and across the Upper Danube, the Raetian Limes. On the other side of the Lower Danube was the Csörszárok bordering the Great Hungarian Plain, and the Brazda lui Novac de Nord and de Sud on the Wallachian Plain. The Valul lui Traian de Jos runs parallel to the Danube as it flows west to east on its path towards the Delta. Thus, for at least half of the combined length of the Rhine and the Danube, at one time or another, the riverine borders of the Roman Empire were preceded by linear barriers. To the north of the Yellow River loop, linear barriers were constructed to enclose areas of loess between the River and the Helanshan and the Yinshan Mountains.

A river or canal might define a border and normally be difficult to cross. But it can dry out or freeze. The Prophecy of Neferti described how 'The rivers of Egypt are empty, so that the water is crossed on foot.'[12] The point is that an aquatic linear barrier can fail when nomads and their herds are likely to be most desperate – in times of drought. Rome's Rhine frontier was vulnerable to both drought and freezing. In AD 70 'The Rhine, owing to a drought unexampled in that climate, would hardly admit of navigation, and thus supplies were straitened at the same time that outposts had to be established along the entire bank to keep the Germans from fording the stream.'[13] (It might be noted that here the main concern is the function of the Rhine as a transport route supporting the frontier forces, and not as a border itself.)

Freezing could also enable migrating, raiding or invading. Herodotus described how the Royal Scythians moved over their Crimean border of the Trench of the Blinded Slaves' Sons to traverse the Bosphorus, when it froze between the Kerch and the Taman Peninsulas. In AD 406 the Rhine froze and Barbarians invaded the Western Roman Empire and this time transformed from raiders to migrants. In 559 the Danube froze and Huns threatened the Balkans.

Turning to hedge and abatis, these may seem a very good idea but it is pointless considering them except in geographical locations where hedges grow fast or forests are abundant. Thus hedges and abatis are only feasible in the very verdant areas of north-west Europe and along the forest steppe. Also barriers made out of living wood were always in danger of fire: ferocious legal codes proscribed many activities in the region of abatis. And hedges take a long time to grow: in some situations there was not enough time before a threat became imminent to establish a good hedge. Finally, by their very nature, hedges and abatis required constant management to ensure the most effective density of growth.

Analysis – natural barriers

Harnessing nature may seem like a cost-effective solution to providing a sufficient linear barrier. The problem was that natural obstacles, formed of living forest or flowing water, might not correspond with political divisions. Added to that, they were also vulnerable to other natural events or forces, such as drought, frost and fire. Therefore, in practice the majority of linear barriers surveyed appear to have been made of inert, fixed material; although to some extent this might have been due to accidents of survival. That said, in certain regions like Egypt and Mesopotamia, where flat lands made possible the use of fortified canals, and in Europe, where readily growing forests allowed for abatis, natural linear barriers might have been more common than is generally understood from the surviving evidence; and possibly it is the loss of all evidence of canals, abatis and hedges that is the reason for otherwise unexplained gaps.

Part IV

Aftermath

So great was the terror of the nomad that – in revelation, religion and myth – the hordes from the north had to be contained by a wall of brass and iron built by Alexander, the greatest of heroes. When the day of judgement came the hordes would burst through, presaging the end of the world. And indeed, when the Mongols did come, it was indeed literally the end of their worlds for many states and cities – and for peoples, of their earthly existence. Yet eventually, the Russian principalities and the Chinese state rallied and linear barriers had an important role in stabilising the Chinese front and facilitating the expansion southwards of the Russians, leading to the closing down of the steppe.

Probably, given the inherent weakness of the nomad off the steppe, and the greater long term capacity for technological development by settled states, particularly in the use of firearms, there could ultimately have only been one winner. But many rounds were lost and states destroyed and lives ended in the process. And briefly the Mongols ruled the greatest land Empire the world has ever seen.

The defeat of the nomad and the closure of the steppe rendered linear barriers superfluous. In Russia, the abatis barriers merged back into the forests from which they were formed or were cleared when the forests were felled – although the fortress cities and, particularly, their kremlins remained. In China, the Great Wall survived – although the subject of depredations and then of a peculiar genre of history which increasingly emphasised its modern symbolic as opposed to its contemporary functional qualities. All around the Eurasian Steppe there are monuments on the ground of what was an existential struggle between movement and stasis. Despite destruction much survives as testament to this fight, and this *matériel* and how it has been renamed, reused and reinterpreted, is briefly examined in the next section.

Chapter Twenty-Four

The Naming of Linear Barriers

T he nomenclature of linear barriers may be part of the reason perhaps why they have not been studied systematically and accorded the importance they might merit. Often the names are romantic, redolent of heroes and myth, and there is a fascinating commonality across the length of Eurasia where heroes, devils, grims, pigs, serpents and dragons have been avidly building walls and dykes – voluntarily or forcibly, and heroically or mischievously. Great Britain has many Devil's or Grim's dykes and ditches. In Germany the rampart of the Raetian Limes is called the Teufelsmauer or Devil's Wall. In Hungary one name for the huge system of linear earthworks around the eastern edge of the Great Hungarian Plain is the Ördögárok or Devil's Dyke. Animals, real and mythical, were prolific movers of earth. In Ireland there are many Black Pig's Dykes and in Germany the furrow associated with the Teufelsmauer is called the Schweinsgraben, or Pig's Ditch. If all linear barriers could be known by their original titles, and their builders and purpose clearly identified, their military and strategic role might be taken a great deal more seriously.

Stages in naming and renaming

There are generally at least three stages in the naming of linear barriers. The first is that of the original names which survive almost exclusively in texts, as probably almost no linear barrier before the Middle Ages has retained, continuing throughout history, its first name. (An exception might be Offa's Dyke.) Such names tend to be mundane, functional and undramatic. The second stage involves pre-modern renames and it is here that the nomenclature appears more imaginative and fantastical. These names often seem to have been coined by peoples less advanced than the original builders who needed to invoke some supernatural force or legendary power to explain structures, the construction of which such peoples believed to be beyond ordinary human powers. The third stage is the modern rename which may be driven by political factors or academic imperatives. For example, the Drumul lui Troian became the Drumul lui Traian and then the Limes Transalutanus.* (Replacing Troian with Traian gave a Roman as opposed

---

* Modern historians have perhaps complicated rather than simplified understanding of Roman linear barriers by creating a system of 'limes' which sound Latin and therefore Roman, but would have been unrecognisable to contemporary Romans. When examined however, the limes system terminology seems inconsistent. Roman 'Limes' are largely named after the frontier regions in which they were located and have Latin, albeit coined in the modern era, names. Roman frontiers now include the Limes Britannicus, Belgicus, Germanicus, Rhaetia, Porolissensis, Moesia, Arabicus, Tripolitanus. There is a Rhine-Iller-Danube Limes. Some Roman 'Limes' are, however, named after the threat which they

to Slav identity, and applying the Latin sounding name Limes Transalutanus might confer, possibly dubious, academic credibility.)

Renames – factual

Factual names say something real about a linear barrier, like who it was built by or who it was built against, where it was located, or what it was like. For example, some linear barriers are named after the person who ordered their construction, like Offa's Dyke or Valdemarsmuren. Others are called after the whole people like the Danevirke. Some are named after the threat they were intended to confront like the *Muriq Tidnim*, or Fender off of the Tidnim, and the *Teichos Medias* or Wall of Media that kept out the Medes. Some were named after their location, like the *Claustra Alpinum Iuliarum* or the Wei Hexi, or West Wall. Others had names that reflected their appearance like the Great Dyke described by John Skylitzes. The Anastasian Wall was also called the Long Wall. Such contemporary or early factual names might reflect the fact that linear barriers were not regarded as grandiose gesturing but rather were built to perform straightforward functional tasks.

Some renames also appear factual. Black, as applied to dyke, may mean it was covered in dark heather as opposed to green grass. War, as in the Cambridgeshire Warbanks, may be a corruption of wall, referring to the perceived verticality of the combined ditch and rampart. The Ottoman Turks seem quite prosaic about renaming. Hence the individual Dobrogea Dykes, collectively called the Valurile lui Traian, are individually the Little Earth Wall, the Big Earth Wall and the Stone Wall. The name Erkesia means a cutting in the earth. Clearly these Turks were not overawed by the linear barriers they encountered and did not need to give them supernatural names and explanations.

Renames – fantastical

Fantastical names are almost certainly renames where the original term has been lost. Later peoples needed to explain what they saw as grand structures, the construction of which was beyond their capabilities and, therefore, they had to invoke some greater power. Often the names followed from some story which described how the barrier was built.

---

were supposedly intended to confront, like the Limes Scythicus, or their supposed tributary builders like the Limes Sarmaticus. A few specific linear barriers, as opposed to more general frontier systems, have been called limes. These are the Limes Transalutanus, Laupertal Limes, Neckar-Odenwald Limes, Limes Gemellens. One line of fortresses along a road beside a river – the Olt or Alutanus – has also been named a limes, the Limes Alutanus. Even linear barriers which were clearly not Roman or where the contemporary language would not necessarily have been Latin have now been titled limes. The Limes Lombardicus was the border against the Lombards in north-east Italy. The Limes Saxoniae and Sorabicus were eastern frontiers of the Carolingian Empire. There was even a Limes Sasanicus which extended from the Caspian to Merv.

Devils

Devil's dykes, ditches and walls can be found at the two ends of Europe from Britain, to Hungary and Romania. In Britain the devil has been particularly diligent in building linear barriers and there are Devil's Dykes across the country. Even earthworks not directly named after the devil are his work. Cornwall's Giant Hedge is the work of the devil according to an old Cornish Rhyme: 'One day the Devil having nothing better to do, built a great hedge from Lerryn to Looe.'

In Bavaria the Raetian Limes is known as the Teufelsmauer or Devil's Wall. Denmark has a Fandensdiget or Devil Dyke. On the western Great Hungarian Plain in Hungary and Romania the great skein of linear earthworks is called Ördögárok or Devil's Dyke. Traversing the Wallachian Plain, the Brazda lui Novac de Nord has also been called the Devil's Wallachian Trench.

Gods

Britain has many dykes attributed to Grim, which means literally the masked or hooded one, and is a euphemism for the God Woden who habitually disguised himself. Post conversion to Christianity, the unchristian Woden became devilish and a fit builder of nameless but substantial man-made features. The Antonine Wall was known as Graham's Dyke – possibly a corruption of Grim's Dyke. (Scottish fourteenth century chronicler, Fordun, says the Dyke, 'got its name from Gryme, and is called Grymisdyke by the inhabitants.'[1] Fordun was, however, possibly unaware of the Norse origin of the name Gryme, and explains, rather surprisingly, that Gryme was Roman consul in 419.) Grim built prolifically across many counties while Woden, by name, saved his linear barrier energies for the lengthy Wansdyke or Wodens Dyke which extends across Wiltshire.[*]

The linear earthworks and other features named now after the Emperor Trajan (discussed next) in Romania, Moldavia and the Ukraine were probably earlier named Troian. As Romania and Moldavia sought a Roman not Slav identity, structures renamed once as the works of Troian became those of Traian. Troian was possibly a martial Slav god. The Lay of Igor's Campaign against the Polovtsians by the Prince of Chernigov, Igor, took place firmly in the Christian era but refers to the earlier times of displaced but not forgotten gods:

> The times of Troian have passed; the years of Iaroslav are gone; and the campaigns of Oleg, Oleg Sviatoslavich. With his sword that prince forged discord throughout the land and sowed the earth with arrows.

Heroes – once real

There are heroic characters, both male and female, associated with linear barriers which they were most unlikely to have actually built. Perhaps the most evocative hero of the classical world was Alexander. His folk memory survived, if anything, more strongly in

---

[*] Other features, natural or man-made, that are the work of Woden include Wednesbury, Wodnes-beorh, Wednesfileld.

Asia, than in Europe – but then that is where his greatest conquests lay. Alexander lives on not only in place names and history but also in legend. His orientalising alienated his Greek compatriots but made him an intriguing, if not always attractive, figure in Asia where he became part of legend. Alexander dealt with Gog and Magog, forces of chaos from the north, by walling them out. One of the names of the great wall that extends from the south-east Caspian, is the Sadd-i-Iskandar. There are Gates of Alexander within the Walls at Derbent on the west Caspian shore.

The Roman Emperor Trajan did actually build many structures in south-eastern Europe like the bridge across the Danube at Drobeta and the city of *Tropaeum Traiani*. But many things he did not build are also attributed to him. Like Alexander, Trajan has become the hero of legend. He conquered giants who preceded humans. He also fought the Tatars. Trajan has become associated with many of the linear barriers of Romania, Moldavia and the Ukraine – which he cannot have built. In fact his identification with linear barrier building may be quite recent – having supplanted Troian in order to stress Romania's and Moldavia's Roman as opposed to Slavic identity.

There is a folk tale which connects King Csörsz of the Avars to the multiple linear barriers across the Hungarian Plain called the Csörszárok. It is not clear whether Csörsz was a historical king of the Avars but the Avars and the Longobards did combine to defeat the Gepids.

> King Frederick (of the Gepids), however, attacked (King Rád's) people with a great army, and so King Rád (of the Langobards) sent word to his ally Csörsz, king of the Avars. King Csörsz came with a large army, and together they defeated King Frederick.... Csörsz said: 'King Rád, I have rescued your people, your nation, from sure destruction. Give me your daughter's hand in return!' 'She is yours, but only if you take her home over water,' King Rád replied. Csörsz demanded his people to dig a riverbed. As they were hard at work .... bolts of lightning split the ground around them. Suddenly, a fiery bolt of lightning hit King Csörsz, and he died on the spot. The trench itself still bears the name of the Avar king: it is called Csörsz's Trench.[2]

Linear barriers to the north of China have been attributed to Genghis Khan which are probably the remains of the linear earthworks of the Kitan Liao and the Jin. Denmark has a linear barrier called the Dandiget. King Dan was a legendary king summoned by the Jutes to help them fight the Emperor Augustus who stayed and united Denmark under his leadership.

Women were also prolific linear barrier builders. Strabo identified the linear barriers, which had a dual function protecting against the Medes and controlling water to the north of Babylon, with Semiramis who was possibly an Assyrian queen. Herodotus described a Babylonian queen called Nitocris – possibly the daughter of Nebuchadnezzar and the mother of the king Belshazzar brought down by Cyrus – whose constructions in Babylon were mainly connected with diverting the Euphrates. In Jutland there are linear barriers named after Queen Margrethe like the Margrethediget and the Margrethevolden. In Nigeria Sungbo's Eredo is named after a great African queen.

Heroes – fantastical

Some heroes are clearly mythological like Novac after whom the Brazda lui Novacs are named. A traditional story about the Brazda lui Novac runs: 'A gigantic serpent had frightened all the inhabitants of these lands, and his destructions were such, that they even moved a great brave man of that time, Stroe Novac. This brave man decided, either to die, or to kill the dragon. Novac, seeing the serpent coiled above the forest, shoots an arrow on it and chases it all the time, severing pieces of its body, one by one, until only its head is left, which enters the Black Sea, from where later some poisonous flies emerged, which bite the cattle around the nostrils and udders, wounding them.'[3]

Mythological characters may actually have played a role in constructing linear barriers – without themselves providing the barrier's actual name. Another hero who played a central role in creating Ukrainian linear barriers was Kuzma-Demyan. The Zmievi Vali or Snake Earthworks arose when the mighty blacksmith named Kuzma-Demyan harnessed a dragon to the plough and drove the dragon across the country, tilling the earth. 'Once upon a time, there lived a blacksmith of enormous strength, Kuzma-Demyan. One day, there appeared a dragon in the land where he lived, (who) bellows so loudly that the earth shakes, "Hey, Kuzma-Demyan, open those doors of yours, and chase all those people out into the open, or else I'll set your smithy on fire and eat you!" Kuzma-Demyan began to forge a huge plough with his twelve helpers holding it with tongs. Kuzma-Demyan grabs the Dragon's tongue with the hot tongs and starts pounding its head with a sledge hammer. The Dragon gets knocked out and slumps down, and while he lies there senseless, he is harnessed to the great plough. The moment the Dragon comes to, Kuzma-Demyan begins pulling him forward, holding on to the Dragon's long tongue, and Kuzma-Demyan's helpers are taking care of the plough. The plough was making a deep furrow in the ground with earth rising on one side as tall as a high wall. Kuzma-Demyan and his helpers would surely have furrowed the earth from end to end, had not the Dragon burst open. But the wall of earth they left behind is still there.'[4] The Dragon it was that died – but it, and not Kuzma-Demyan, lives on the name of the great earthworks.

In Iraq there is a dyke between the Tigris and the Euphrates called Sadd Nimrud or Wall of Nimrud. The biblical Nimrod was a legendary hunting hero. In early Arab literature he was the constructor of several Mesopotamian cities.

Pigs

Pig's or rather probably boar's tusks look highly appropriate for gouging furrows through the earth. The Raetian Limes' fosse is called the Schweinsgraben ('Pig's Ditch') as the Devil arranged to buy a piece of land from God, and it was to be as large an area as he could enclose with a ditch or a wall in the course of one night. When God agreed, the Devil turned into a pig and began to rout furiously with his snout, plowing a ditch and throwing the soil up on the sides resulting in the Schweinsgraben alongside the Teufelsmauer. Before the Devil had finished, a cock crowed, announcing the arrival of morning. The Devil had tried to enclose too much land and failed to complete his task.[5] In Ireland there are many 'Black Pig's Dykes'. There are several variants to the story but usually a wicked teacher/druid was cruel to students and used sorcery to turn them into different animals. They revenged themselves by tricking him into turning into a Black Pig which they then chased and as he ran he gouged out earthworks.

Dragons, worms and serpents

Dragons, worms and serpents, alone or harnessed by heroes, were prolific workers of earth. If thought of as slimy, eyeless, legless, sub-soil creatures or as scaled, sighted, legged, even flying beasts, then worms and dragons could hardly seem more different. But the two can be reconciled. The Beowulf saga uses synonymously the words draca and wyrm and the creature described has a venomous bite and bending movement – which sounds serpent-like. In Ireland's County Cavan the Black Pig's Dyke is locally known as the Worm's Ditch because it was made by a huge creature wriggling across the countryside. The Ukraine's linear barriers are collectively called the Zmievi Vali, or snake or serpent walls. Iran's Sadd-i-Iskandar is the Qezel Allan in Turkman, or the Wall of the Red Snake. In China, the grassy mounds of early collapsed walls from the Warring States period now bear the folk name 'earth dragons'. Subsequent generations attributed them to a great resting dragon that morphed into the collapsing walls. Even now the east end of the Ming Great Wall, which extends into the Bohai Sea, like a dragon quenching its thirst, is called the Old Dragon's Head. The east end in the Gobi Desert is the Tail of the Dragon.

Analysis – names

What should be done by a people, new to a region, when confronted with great monuments left by the previous inhabitants, who have no idea who built them or why? Such monuments would have been much more imposing than in modern times, in a less cluttered landscape, with fewer other man-made features – such as railway lines, pylons, canals, metalled roads – which now distract attention from comparatively low and much eroded linear barriers. The original names of most European walls north of the Danube, and Eurasian walls, except for China, were lost due to obliteration by the nomadic or barbarian invasions. But as the edifices themselves remain, as very substantial marks on the landscape, they demanded titles.

Such titles can give some clues as to dating, on the assumption that if the name is clearly fantastical then some possibly quite sudden change in the peoples and the conditions in which they lived has occurred which has obliterated historical memory. If linear barriers were seen as the work of gods, devils, heroes and mythological beasts then the world of the people ascribing their construction to such greater beings must have felt diminished and possibly insecure. Since it could not create itself such huge structures it needed to call on supernatural or heroic forces to explain them. This is very much what would be expected of regions devastated by barbarian nomads and migrants.

The renaming of walls can be useful for it tells us that construction was likely to predate some particular event: in Britain, the conversion of the Anglo-Saxons; and in the Ukraine, the Mongol destruction of the Kievan Rus. This is because (perhaps sadly) one may be sure that the devils and dragons were not the actual builders – so construction must have come before some catastrophic event that obliterated all folk memory. The language of the rename, if it is clearly fantastical, can be informative for it indicates which people provided the rename and possibly helps with dating, on the basis that the linear barrier must have been constructed before they moved into the region.

Renaming a linear barrier may have been part of establishing or re-establishing a national identity as when the Romanians replaced Troian with Traian they were establishing a Roman not a Slav inheritance. Similarly, the Hungarians renamed ditches 'arod' in place of the Turkish 'arka' they were exchanging a Turkish identity with a Hungarian one.

If the survey section in this book has done anything it might have indicated the ubiquity of Long Wall construction from the Atlantic to the Pacific. Also, intriguing is the type of commonality of names. Throughout Europe the devil and pigs have been busily up to no good. From Ireland to China worms, serpents and dragons have been astonishingly industrious. Although the names may seem fanciful the implications are serious and useful for the study of linear barriers.

Chapter Twenty-Five

Destruction, Discovery and Protection

1: Destruction of walls

L inear barriers may have been massive, even majestic, but they have proved vulnerable. Over centuries, even millennia, the ravages of nature have taken their course: weather, water, decay, the growth of vegetable matter and the digging of animals have softened the sharp lines. Wind and rain have blasted and washed away tamped earth and mud brick. Ditches have filled, palisades rotted. Roots have broken up walls built of discrete stone blocks or burnt brick, and modified the profile of earthworks. Some barriers have been submerged by changing water levels: for example the Caspian Sea may have covered sections of the Sadd-i-Iskandar.

But if matters were left to nature, there would still be a massive legacy in earth, stone and brick, and understanding the importance of the role of linear barriers would be much easier. It is, of course, man who has done the most harm – and a great deal of it in the last century. There has always been planned destruction and routine robbing, but industrialised agriculture has perhaps done the most damage. Much of the thousand plus kilometres of the Csörszárok on the Great Hungarian Plain has been lost. There might be a very different picture of the linear barriers of Central Asia but for post Second World War irrigation projects.

The treatment of linear barriers informs about the relative value placed on the presence of historic artefacts and the commercial value of the materials that linear barriers are composed of and the land they occupy for other uses. Well meant development, greed and indifference all play their parts. For many, a large object, capable of being dismantled was often just a nuisance. Objections to the levelling of Offa's Dyke in the 1850s that had stood for so many centuries were countered, 'Oh! To make ground of it, Sir; 'tis no use as it is.'[1] Recently in 2006 in Inner Mongolia, workers who dug up the Great Wall for landfill told officials of the Municipal Office on Cultural Relics Protection, 'It's just a pile of earth.'[2]

Often local people, sometimes living in poverty, have little awareness of the great age of linear barriers and anyway feel that they cannot afford to ignore sources of raw materials or isolate obstructions to development. For example, in China: 'Wang Gui, secretary of village Party branch in Xiaolianggou, explained why the cultural relics were ruined. Previously, local residents had only known it (the earthwork) as "an earth dragon." The investigation team from the county authorities recognised it as one section of the ancient Great Wall, but no landmark or sign was erected to claim the relics were cultural and historical sites under protection of counties. As a result, damage caused by the construction to the relics was not promptly stopped.'[3]

In former communist countries linear earthworks have subsequently been threatened by uncontrolled private interests, possibly working with corrupt officials. In 2001 local archaeologists in the Romanian Dobrogea were shocked to find that almost overnight 300 metres of the supposedly protected Valui lui Traian had been bulldozed flat by the local branch of a French company. 'Wall of Trajan destroyed by contemporary barbarians' exclaimed local media.[4] In the Ukraine seventy-seven hectares of land in the vicinity of Kiev, containing a section of Zmievi Vali were bought by business interests for over $70 million in 2008 in questionable circumstances that provoked much media coverage. (It is possible that the Zmievi Vali may be able to protect itself with the curse of Sviatoslav. Supposedly disrespectful hang-gliders launch themselves from the top of the rampart and every year at least one is killed, according to superstitious locals.)

Stone and fired brick are nearly always worth robbing. Both are durable and require skilled and costly working. In 1867 Captain Barnett said of Habl-es-Sakhar. 'The two caravanserais at Khan-ez-zad are … in great measure built of bricks from it and it has doubtless supplied materials for many other buildings.'[5] In agricultural areas walls provide bricks and stone for building. In the 1990s farmers with hoes were still dismantling towers of the Great Wall of China and putting the bricks into baskets to build pigsties and henhouses.[6] The fired bricks of the Sadd-i-Iskandar have similarly disappeared. There is probably not a stone farmhouse or church in the region of Hadrian's Wall that does not incorporate part of it. Tamped or shaped earth barriers may be seen as valuable stores of soil to be exploited to replace eroded areas or expand farmable land.

Sometimes the value lies in what is apparently denied by the presence of linear barriers. They obstruct farming and irrigation projects so, in order that fields, paddies and canals can be larger, linear barriers must be flattened or filled. Deep ploughing has meant that most of the 1,200 kilometres of the Csörszárok in Hungary has been lost. The Black Pig's Dyke has been threatened by quarrying in county Cavan.

Forests can be a mixed blessing. Many sections of linear barrier have survived only because the area has been forested. But this has its own cost. The vision of the exposed linear barrier is limited or lost. Also, root growth and eventual tree death take their toll. Nevertheless such sections of the Csörszárok as survive are largely in areas of forest – as is true of the *Landwehren* of Germany. In 2008 sections of the Chu Wall from the Spring and Autumn period, more than two and a half millennia ago, were destroyed in an insensitive afforestation project. 'The relics are also known as the Earth Dragon, … (have) been damaged. The villagers said that this part of the barren hills had been contracted to a contractor for afforestation. To plant trees, heavy-duty equipment and machinery such as large-scale excavators, were used. The Great Wall relics, which previously had harmoniously integrated into surrounding hills and slopes, were fragmented. Villagers said that the ancient relics site had been a comparatively well-preserved section of the Chu Great Wall.'[7]

In the 1970s lengths of the Eastern Frontier Canal which lay to the east of the Nile Delta were identifiable from satellite photographs and on the ground. These have now largely disappeared as the result of irrigation projects. In Central Asia many linear barriers have been destroyed in the last forty years as vast agricultural projects have

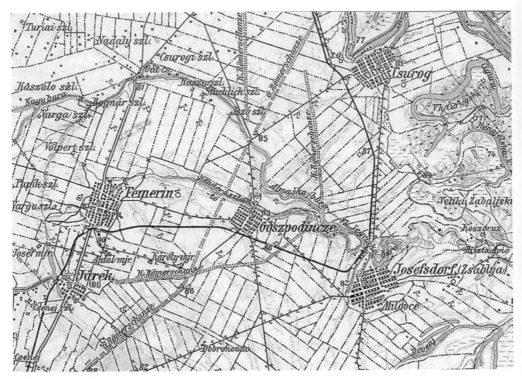

Römaschanzen in the Bačka – shows Groß Römerschanze, Kleine Römerschanze, Römerschanze - Kulpin to Csurog. *(3rd Military Mapping Survey of Austria-Hungary (1910))*

Google Maps view of the Bačka – Römaschanzen no longer visible. *(Google Maps)*

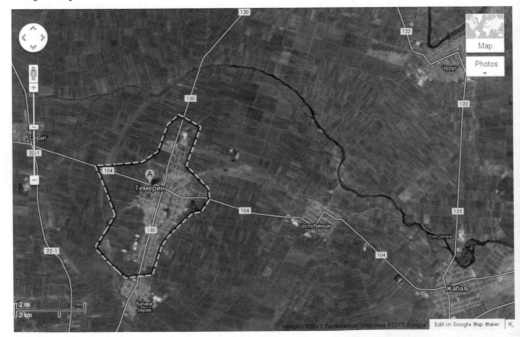

been implemented – often with disastrous environmental consequences. The Soviet era damming of the Dnieper has resulted not only in the loss of the cataracts, where Prince Sviatoslav was killed by the Pechenegs in 972, but also evidence of the Zmievi Vali along the east bank.

Sometimes linear barriers are destroyed through simple carelessness. 'A section of the Great Wall of China has collapsed after workmen dug up a section of a city square in front of it. The work followed weeks of heavy rain. Tons of rubble fell from the 100ft section of the wall running through Zhangjiakou, Hebei Province.'[8]

As interest in the past grows, and more regions are opened up, tourism has added to the damage and erosion to linear barriers. For example, in 2012, 'During the National holiday in China some 60,000 people clamber over the Badalingh section near Beijing. Nearly every brick is carved with, "I visited the Great Wall".'[9] Recently a metal plaque was removed from Hadrian's Wall which read, 'In memory of Nick White, from your Aussie mates'.[410] On balance, however, interest is probably positive in terms of ensuring linear barriers are protected.

The sad fact is that most destruction of linear barriers has taken place within the last century. People have always robbed walls of useful brick and stone, for example, the Sadd-i-Iskandar, Ming Great Wall of China, Habl-es-Sakr, and El-Muttabaq. In some senses, if not commendable, it is understandable and it might be argued that respectable use was made of the material in constructing houses, farms, churches, and caravanserai. There are limits on the speed of destruction imposed by what man or beast can carry or pull. In the twentieth century mechanisation has meant that destruction could be vastly accelerated and there is often absolutely no mitigating gain. The damage caused by the irrigation projects of Central Asia have meant that it is now difficult to grasp quite how important linear barriers were as means to defend and control regions.

2: Recent discoveries

Even if the destruction of linear barriers means sad losses, there have been some compensating discoveries. In recent decades a surprising number of new linear barriers have been found or, at least, become known in the west.

In Germany in 1978 'Lauter Limes' was discovered. This twenty kilometre attachment to the Neckar-Odenwald Limes is dated probably to AD 98 or soon after, when Emperor Trajan built the Neckar-Odenwald Limes. In the early twenty first century about five kilometres of linear earthwork was discovered at the exit of the Crasna river valley, a tributary of the Tisza River. This was thought to be a forward defence of Roman Dacia, possibly built by tributary people.

Archaeological work on the Syrian Steppe, as part of the process of promoting it on the World Heritage list of agro-pastoral cultural landscapes, revealed a Bronze Age 220 kilometre-long stone wall.[11]

In Cappadocia about twenty kilometres of wall has been identified to the south-east of *Sarissa*/Kuşakh but it might have extended a further hundred kilometres. It is dated possibly to the eighth century BC and marked the northern border of Assyria.[12]

In 2006 Iranian archaeologists said they were planning the examination of a recently discovered wall that started seventeen kilometres from the palace of Khosrow II (590–628) at Qasr-e-Shirin in the Bazi-Deraz mountains and ran to Iraq's Qaraviz mountains.[13]

New stretches of the Chinese walls are frequently being discovered. In 2002 it was announced that a lost section of the Ming Great Wall had been found which was hidden for centuries beneath shifting sands in the north-western region of Ningxia some eighty kilometres along the southern slope of Helan Mountain. The section was built in 1531 in a meandering line with three watchtowers added in 1540.[14] In 2009 the Cultural Relics Bureau of Shandong said that the western starting point of the double line of the Qi wall had been reconfirmed and extended at the junction of Ji'nan and Feicheng cities.[15] In 2012 the National Geographical described new Han Wall discoveries, as well as a tamped earth linear barrier probably built by the Mongols to channel hunted game.[16]

The Great Wall of Santa in Peru was discovered in the 1920s but not thoroughly investigated until the 1980s[17]. In the late 1960s an earthwork was found about 4.5 kilometres to the north of the city of Tikal that was about twelve kilometres long and bounded by two swamps. Further lengths have subsequently been discovered.[18] An expedition in 1984 to South America described the 'The Great Wall of the Inca'.[19]

2011 saw the discovery of a 127 kilometre length of wall in central Vietnam from Quang Ngai Province to Binh Dinh Province.[20]

The discovery of linear barriers in Germany, Romania, Turkey, Syria, Iran, China, Vietnam, and Central and South America perhaps shows that the subject has not really been systematically studied. The book is not closed and further discoveries remain to be made.

3: Protection, Restoration and Education

While the scale of losses over the last two centuries has been tragic there have been signs that the situation is improving. A first step took place when the decision to demolish the Theodosian Walls at the end of the nineteenth century and sell the stone for the public purse was defeated by popular opposition. At least in Romania and the Ukraine the destruction and the threat of destruction to the Valul lui Traian and Zmievi Vali provoked a media outcry. Modern construction works need not be totally negative in impact if done sensitively. Much dating of linear barriers in Great Britain appears to result from sectioning to build motorways or lay high pressure gas transmission pipes.

Attitudes have changed. In 2006 China introduced new laws obliging; 'all citizens, legal entities and organisations' to protect the wall and report illegal activity to local government offices. Taking away earth, bricks and stones is forbidden, as are planting crops on it, daubing and inscription, installing facilities unrelated to Great Wall protection, driving across the Wall, exhibiting articles that may damage the Wall, organising activities in sections of the Wall declared off-limits.'[21] Also: 'At the end of the year the Hongji Landbridge Investment company was the first to be fined under the new regulations for removing sections of the Great Wall for an illegal motorway in Inner Mongolia.'[22]

Many linear barriers have obtained, or are lobbying for, inclusion on Unesco's list of World Cultural Heritage sites. The Great Wall of China has been on the list since 1987. The Qi wall in the Dafeng Mountain Tourist Area is being restored as a tourist attraction to rival the Ming Great Wall. 'Currently, the Changqing government has decided to renovate the Great Wall of Qi Kingdom and turn it into the second tourism area centering on Great Wall in China.'[23] Much restoration work generally is underway on the Great Wall of China – although some is asserted to be over vigorous.

Elsewhere, the Croatia Travel Blog now contains the rather breathless announcement: 'Great Wall of Ston opens after Renovation. It's been a long process but finally the magnificent Ston walls are fully renovated and open to the public. The walls of Ston, on the Peljesac Peninsula, comprise the longest fortress system in Europe and second only to the Great Wall of China internationally…. Not only is it hoped that these amazing new walls will bring in tourists, but they just might make in onto the list of UNESCO World Heritage Sites.'[24]

Arguably, after so much destruction in the twentieth century, the situation is improving. Linear barriers can be useful sources of income, attracting tourists. Also, they provide a visually impressive link to the history of a region, bringing the past to the present.

Chapter Twenty-Six

Reuse, Marking Borders, Renewed Building

1: Reuse of walls – military

L inear barriers were located for strategic reasons that made sense at the time to their builders. While political situations developed and changed, geography remained constant. Therefore it might be expected that linear barriers would be reused when the political or military situation demanded it, by very different polities at much later dates because their location continued to be strategic.

Pre-20th century

In the early fifteenth century the Byzantine Emperor Manuel II Palaiologos rebuilt the Hexamilion Wall across the Isthmus of Corinth in order to defend the Despotate of Morea on the Peloponnese against the Ottoman Turks. It was attacked by the Ottomans in 1423, 1431, 1446 and 1452.

In the 1590s the English reused the Dane's Cast and the Black Pig's Dyke as a defensible base line from which to attack Gaelic Ulster and Hugh O'Neill. This was an example of the location remaining the same but the direction of use changing. These dykes had been built originally to face south but in the sixteenth century were being used as a starting point for an attack north.

In the Ukraine local histories claim that a Scythian earthwork was remade in the seventeenth century to block the routes taken by the Tatars on their slaving campaigns. 'The Perekipsky Val, which had been built way back in the Scythian times, was restored. This rampart crossed the Muravsky Shlyakh between the upper courses of the Mzha and Kolomak rivers.'[1]

When the Chalcidike rose in revolt against the Ottomans in 1821 the old fortifications on the Pallene Peninsula were repaired and reused.

In 1848 the Danevirke was hastily strengthened by the Danes, who were, however, unable to hold it in face of the superiority of the Prussian artillery, and it was stormed. From 1850 onwards it was again repaired and strengthened at great cost, and considered impregnable; but in the war of 1864 the Prussians turned it by crossing the Schlei inlet to the east, and it was abandoned by the Danes on 6 February. The Prussians then comprehensively slighted it. Notwithstanding, it retains a massive presence – if now in Germany.

The Dobrogea Valurile lui Trajan were reused in the fighting between the Russians and the Ottoman Empire during the Crimean War. There is an interesting passage in *The Times* of 1854: 'Russians halted by Ottomans at walls of Trajan. The real defence of the Danube is more to the south, at Trajan's ditch – Vallum Trajani – on that line which traverses the country in its narrowest part of the Danube to the sea from Chernavoda to Kostandjé, where was formerly the mouth of the river.... That line has recently been refortified, and the Turks have near it a corps of from 25,000 to 30,000 men, forming their extreme right of the great line of the Danube from Widdin to the sea.'[2]

20th century

In 1912 and 1913 the Bulgarians advanced against the Ottoman Empire. The Turks made their line of defence the Chatalja Line close to Anastasian Walls. In 1920 this line was made the border of Turkey within Europe under the Treaty of Sèvres. (The Turks subsequently forced its shift to the west so that the border, including much of south-eastern Thrace both west and east of the Sea of Marmara, became Turkish under the Treaty of Lausanne in 1923.)

The Valurile lui Traian again played a part in the Great War battle between the Germans under August von Mackensen, and the Romanians in 1917. The latter, with the support of the Russians, tried to form a south-facing line along the Walls of Trajan against the northward advancing Germans and Bulgarians.

In 1920 the White Russian Army retreated to the Crimea. The Bolshevik southern front commander, Mikhail Frunze, studied the records of the 1737 to 1738 Russian attack on the Perekop Wall and rehearsed on similar ground. The Perekop was stormed leading to the withdrawal of the White Army to Istanbul.

The Zmievi Vali, to the west of Kiev, were reused in the construction of the interwar Kiev Fortified Area. In 1929, by Stalin's order, defence lines were built around the west side of Kiev with some bunkers constructed in the earthworks themselves. There was heavy fighting in 1941 along the line before the fall of Kiev.

In 1933, supported by overwhelming firepower, the Japanese attacked the Great Wall of China and overwhelmed the forces of Chiang Kai-shek. The Chinese did win minor victories in passes by using the wall itself as a routeway to shift troops rapidly to sectors under pressure – as had been intended by the Great Wall's Ming constructors.[3]

In 1941 the Germans and Romanians, fighting together again against the Russians, under Erich Von Manstein, faced a strongly defended position blocking access to the Crimea. 'Tank obstacles were especially formidable since they incorporated the "Tatars' Ditch", an extensive earthwork that was at least 5 metres deep and up to 15.2 wide in most of its length. Called the "Tatarengraben" by the Germans, this ditch, almost a ravine, had been dug straight across the isthmus in the fifteenth century as a defence against invasion by the "Rus" (Russians).'[4] After breaking through the Perekop line the Russians attempted a counter-attack across the frozen Kerch Strait from the Taman Peninsula. The objective was to advance to the Akmonai line. At the Uzunlar line the Russians made their last attempt to stem the German advance across the Crimea in the Spring of 1942. Both the Akmonai and Uzunlar lines were part of the defences of the Bosphoran Kingdom.

The site of the *Letzimauer* in the Swiss Linth valley was reused to build an anti-tank ditch in 1941.

In 1944 the occupying Germans, anticipating invasion from Jutland, decided to transform the Danevirke into a north-facing anti-tank ditch. Archaeologist Søren

Telling personally telephoned SS Reichsführer Heinrich Himmler and persuaded him that the Danevirke was important Aryan monument and Himmler ordered its survival.

The 1960s McNamara Line crossed central Vietnam near the seventeenth century Nguyen Walls.

Analysis – reuse of linear barriers
It is perhaps unsurprising that linear barriers were reused. This is largely a function of their location. Basically most of these reused sites are on land corridors which retain their strategic significance regardless of the change in combatants.

2: Walls as marking future borders

Have early linear barriers had any permanent effect in terms of defining the political landscape? The most consistent patterns established, as the result of surveying linear barriers, was perhaps that linear barriers tended to be found where settled states and nomadic peoples rubbed together. Given, however, that the lines between states and nomads were likely to shift, and that eventually settled states took over the steppe, it is unlikely that current borders would lie along the lines of linear barriers between the steppe and the sown. In the case of the largest states bordering on the Eurasian Steppe, that is China and Russia, the current frontiers lie respectively well to the north and the south of their earlier linear barriers.

In northern and eastern Europe the situation is more complex. While the following linear barriers do not actually define the precise borders they do not lie far away from them. In Britain the borders of England and Scotland lie between Hadrian's and the Antonine Walls and England and Wales near Offa's Dyke. The northern and southern halves of Ireland are split near the Worm's Ditch and the Dane's Cast. The Danevirke is now to the north of the Danish-German border but up to the 1860s was close to it.

Scotland and Wales still have national identities separate to that of England. If asked to say where does the border lie between England and Wales or Scotland many people might use Offa's Dyke and Hadrian's Wall as the most convenient general markers. Also, the Worm's Ditch and the Dane's Cast provide a suitable marker for splitting Ireland.

In Britain there is a very rough correspondence between Roman and Anglo–Saxon expansion which stops at lines where it was simply not worth continuing further given that the costs of further conquest exceeded any benefits. These lines are marked by Hadrian's Wall and Offa's Dyke. Possibly, the construction of Hadrian's Wall and Offa's Dyke had helped define a national consciousness that survived later political unification with England.

In Ireland the case that the Worm's Ditch and the Dane's Cast helped define the division of Ireland seems weaker. The expansion of protestant settlers, mostly from Scotland (many of whom were originally from Ireland) largely defined the Six Counties. Yet, once a separate Ulster was created in the twentieth century, an atavistic justification for its separateness could be made by the existence of the ancient Kingdom of Ulster, defined by linear earthworks, which was destroyed by the southern kingdoms with the sacking of Emain Macha in 331.

In Denmark the Danevirke marks the line where the Danes unified the Jutland Peninsula probably in the late seventh or early eighth centuries. The Danevirke did become a marshalling line against the pressure of German and Slavic states and peoples and may have helped lock in a separate Danish identity that meant Denmark could remain separate from the much larger Empire. (The Danevirke and the English Channel are often considered the dividing lines between North and South Europe, since everything above them was once ruled by the Kingdom of England under Canute the Great.)

In eastern Europe the borders of Poland and Bulgaria were not defined *in toto* by linear barriers of the second half of the first millennium as these were generally relatively short. But the linear barriers themselves, which marked out the Polish Piast state and Greater Bulgaria south of the Danube, are not that far from the current borders. Linear barriers may have played a part in ensuring the early survival of these states, enabling them to dig themselves into regional consciousness.

Some linear barriers appear to correspond to cultural divisions within countries – although this point might not be pressed too far. The *Fossa Regia* in modern Tunisia marks a divide. 'Even today that line has meaning. The Tunisian towns and villages beyond the Fossa Regia have far fewer ancient remains and—more significant—are poorer. There men and women wear traditional head wraps; unemployment seems higher, judging by the number of men hanging out in cafés; bus stations often have no posted timetables. The feeling is more like North Africa and less like Southern Europe.'[5]

The McNamara Line, built by the US between 1966 and 1968 during the Vietnam War, was near the seventeenth century walls built by the southern Nguyen against the northern Trinh ruling families. There are marked cultural and linguistic divisions in Vietnam which approximate to these linear barriers.

Analysis – walls marking future borders
It would be a pleasant conceit to be able to say that ancient linear barriers had frequently survived in the form of modern national borders. Only, however, in north-western Europe does there seem to be much evidence for this and even here each border should be considered separately.

3: Renewed barrier building

After a gap of several centuries, the twentieth and twenty first centuries have seen a resurgence of barrier building – largely to counter renewed migration caused by overpopulation and the depletion of natural resources, but also to divide hostile potentially warring peoples. The Introduction described how interest in walls was provoked by the observation that the collapse of the Berlin Wall in 1989, rather than heralding the end of walls, appeared to usher in a period when, all around the world, new barriers seemed to be being erected to stop the flows of peoples, protect natural resources, and defend hostile borders. In this book a number of patterns were discerned which provided hunches for seeking further linear barriers. These might be applied to the modern world to see if they have relevance both past and present.

Anti-migrant barriers

A consistent pattern was that linear barriers were frequently found where settled states were confronted by nomads and migrants. Nomads barely survive in the modern era and are certainly not the existential threat they once where. (In Mali, however, the conflict between northern Tuareg nomads and southern agriculturists is reemerging.) But the world is certainly entering into another Age of Great Migrations, driven by overpopulation, depletion of resources, political instability and the search for greater opportunity facilitated by greater ease of travel. The result has been the construction of many linear barriers.

The type of migration has changed. In the past it was of whole peoples, but now it is of individuals and small groups, yet collectively the numbers are again significant. The best known anti-migrant barrier is perhaps the fence built by the US to stop illegal immigration from Mexico and other Central American countries. Greece has been considering a fence along its non-riverine border with Turkey. Poland may build fences on its borders with the Belarusia and the Ukraine. Spain has built barrier systems around its enclaves in North Africa at Ceuta and Melilla. Israel has constructed a fence along its Egyptian border, to stop illegal immigration rather than for military defence. In southern Africa, Botswana has built barriers on the borders with Zimbabwe, and South Africa with Mozambique.

Smuggling might be regarded as the migration of commodities – whether people or goods. Increasingly complex fence systems are being built around transport systems to contain illegal immigration – any traveller from Paris to London on Eurostar can see this. There is the wall between Gaza and Egypt, below which runs a warren of tunnels; and an anti-smuggling fence has been considered between Russia and Ukraine.

Warring states

Another pattern, discussed in the survey section, was that states which shared similar characteristics, in an increasingly resource-constricted region with expanding populations, often built linear barriers. There are certainly a number of contemporary regions in which there have been wars and peace is uneasy, where many linear barriers have recently been constructed or are actively under consideration. Around the Arabian Peninsula there are linear barriers, built or planned, between Saudi Arabia and Yemen, Saudi Arabia and Iraq, the United Arab Emirates and Oman, and Kuwait and Iraq. Israel has fences on its borders with Gaza, the West Bank, Syria and Lebanon. In and around the Indian sub-continent there are linear barriers between India and Pakistan, India and Bangladesh, Pakistan and Afghanistan, Iran and Afghanistan. The Caucasus region is becoming increasingly unstable with fences under consideration between Russia and Chechnya, and Azerbaijan and Armenia. China has or may build fences between it and North Korea and Myanmar – and, presumably to keep people in, Hong Kong and Macau. The Turks have built a fence around the Province of Alexandretta which Syria claims. India has fenced off part of Kashmir whose possession is disputed by Pakistan.

There are many individual hotspots, with linear barriers, including Uzbekistan and Kyrgyzstan, Thailand and Malaysia, Spain and Gibraltar. Also, despite the reuniting of Germany a number of countries remain split by linear barriers including South and North Korea, Greek and Turkish Cyprus, and the Western Saharan region of Morocco. The division of Georgia and breakaway Abkhazia may be formalised with a linear barrier. Cities around the world have become warring states in miniature, divided by religion, ethnicity, and wealth and poverty. There are linear barriers dividing Belfast, Mitrovica, Rio de Janeiro and Baghdad.

Valued Land

There are now linear barriers intended to protect ecological systems from climate change and overpopulation. The Greenwall of China is an attempt to stabilise and reverse desertification by mass tree planting. In Kenya the nature parks are being fenced off to protect animals. In many countries, such as the US, Russia and South Africa, residential areas are increasingly being surrounded by walls to create gated areas.

Transport routes

Greek long walls and cataract walls in Egypt are examples, seen earlier, of linear barriers which protected transport routes in the form of roads and portage ways. A wall is under construction in Afghanistan to defend the road to Kandahar. Again, anyone who travels by ferry or Eurostar to and from the continent will be aware of anti-migrant barriers all around along the railway lines.

Analysis – renewed linear barrier building

Increasingly in modern times countries are contesting scarce resources, particularly water and agricultural land. Also, migrants are trying to leave areas of extreme overpopulation – and linear barriers are being used, by adjacent states and those en route to their intended destinations, to block their movements. The extensive modern construction of linear barriers says much about the pressures facing the modern world – which, in turn, can learn from the past. The lesson of history is that linear barriers, intelligently designed and operated, work.[6] It might be expected – as the globe gets smaller and pressure on resources increases – to see a lot more linear barriers.

Chapter Twenty-Seven

Linear Barriers – Historiography and Interpretation

Linear barriers – a forgotten, even taboo, subject

Linear barriers have proved one of the most enduring and consistent strategies used by settled states to deal with the nomad or barbarian at the gate. Yet for a strategy that contemporaries must have trusted and considered effective, it has perhaps received little attention compared to say point fortifications like castles or fortresses. Also, when linear barriers have been the subject of historical attention it has often been hostile, critical or cursory. Thus, the questions can be asked what caused the possibly flawed analyses of linear barriers and what have been the consequences?

Some of these issues were touched upon in the Introduction when challenges to analysing linear barriers were set out. These are now discussed in more detail.

Causes of flawed analysis

Various reasons might be suggested as to why linear barriers have become a forgotten, almost taboo, subject. The first relates to the patchy, possibly distorted nature of the actual evidence itself. The second is the general impact of recent history, particularly that of nationalism and war, which has rendered almost unacceptable anything savouring of militarism. The third is the particular experiences during two World Wars of, in the first, the conflict in the trenches, which became semi-permanent linear barriers; and in the second, of the perceived failure of the Maginot Line. The fourth is the military mentality, almost prejudice, that favours the offensive over the defensive. And the fifth is the moral view that walls are barriers and, therefore, impede freedom which is good: so, ergo, such barriers are bad.

The survival of linear barriers is very incomplete and the archaeological evidence in them can be confusing. Those built using coursed stone or burnt brick are likely to have been robbed; and those fashioned out of earth and mud brick will have been reshaped by the elements if not also by man. Abatis, unless associated with an earthwork, do not survive at all, except possibly in place names. Dating an earthwork is difficult unless it contains wood that is amenable to dendrochronology or carbon dating.

In earlier sections the idea was mooted that the study of linear walls was distorted by perceptions of Hadrian's Wall and the later Ming Great Wall of China. These walls were built in locations that have resulted in great – perhaps disproportionate – study. (Maybe Hadrian was actually prescient – if he was concerned about posterity – in the location of his wall for he placed it in a barbarous island that, centuries later, would become perhaps the keenest student of the classical world and the most avid emulator of its imperial ambitions, virtues and vices.) The consequence however is the impression that, if a linear barrier does not look like the possibly unrepresentative Hadrian or Ming Walls, then it cannot really be a proper exemplar of the type. Therefore, the hundreds of utilitarian but functional earthworks, moats, palisades, and mud brick walls get overlooked.

The Eurocentricism and classical fixation of historians is also to blame. Whole texts are devoted to scraps of Greek wall but as yet there is no book on the massive Sadd-i-Iskandar which was two to three times as long as Hadrian's Wall, built of fired brick and manned by 30,000 guards.

Contemporary texts might be expected to raise confidence but frequently such writings as there are, and the archaeological evidence, introduce their own issues and problems. There are names without walls and walls without names – or clearly not contemporary ones. There are references to walls which must have existed but which themselves are lost, for example, the Muriq-Tidnim built by Shu Sin of Ur in the third millennium BC. Great effort has been expended trying to establish the location of the Wall of Media described by Xenophon in the *Anabasis*. (For once this search appears recently to have been successful.) Disproportionate effort can be expended on matching textual references with surviving linear barriers: witness the (probably misguided) efforts to identify the walls or ramparts of the Greuthungi and Thervingi Goths fleeing the Huns in the fourth century with surviving linear earthworks in Moldavia and Romania.

Such references as do exist in ancient texts tend to be short and laconic. Unlike accounts of battles and sieges there are few tales of derring-do involving long walls that might make them memorable. Only in China does there exist substantial documentation on the construction of walls over a long period, and of the debate over their strategic merit. Also, only in China is there a walls literary genre – but its beauties may be lost in translation; and its substance tends to be grim – emphasising the miseries of forced labour, family separation, harsh weather and diplomatic forced marriage to barbarous nomad chiefs. Such a genre complicates understanding of the utility, as opposed to futility, of walls.

The naming of walls and the associated myths and legends is a fascinating subject addressed in an earlier section. The point made was that few linear barriers survive with their original names. In most cases the original name is not even known. Again, the renames might tend to rob authority. Worms, pigs, snakes, serpents, dragons do not sound the stuff of heavyweight history and nor do devils and gods. When authentic names are met like Alexander and Trajan one of the few things that it is possible to be sure of is that they had nothing to do with the linear barriers attributed to them.

The vision of linear barriers is often contemplated through the prism of recent, particularly twentieth century history, and the conflicts and horrors engendered by nationalism and consequent war. The result of this jumbling of locations is that linear barriers have ended up in perhaps the wrong country and become sometimes a reluctant or even taboo subject for study. The Danevirke is now in Germany following the Second War of Schleswig in 1864. Much of Csörszárok, which protected the Great Hungarian Plain, is in Romania and Serbia after the 1919 Treaty of Versailles. The earthworks which are conjectured to have defended Greater Bulgaria are in Romania, Moldavia and Serbia. The dating of Ukrainian earthworks should be more straightforward than in most places due to extensive internal woodwork structures. In fact this seems to have complicated and confused the issue. Carbon dating carried out in the 1960s appeared to place the linear barriers to the south of Kiev to between the second century BC and sixth century AD. This made the Goths, identified with the pre-history Chernyakhov culture, strong candidates as significant linear barrier builders in the Ukraine and encouraged theories that the Goths had been written out of history due, perhaps understandably, to the poisonous legacy of Nazi irredentism. (Hitler's propaganda minister Joseph Goebbels claimed areas where the Chernyakhov culture was found as German.)

The trenches of the First World War became semi-permanent linear barriers and their problem was not that they did not work but they worked too well – perhaps, it might be speculated, provoking an unconscious horror of linear obstacles. The Maginot Line seems not only to have paralysed the resistance of the French: it appears to have switched off the detachment of historians. For a long period, after the Second World War, it seemed difficult to avoid reference to this Line, when discussing ancient linear barriers, which was inevitably associated with a defensive mentality and failure. For example: 'It is the thesis of this paper that the Sasanians had developed a kind of 'Maginot line' psychology which was rudely shaken by the daring exploits of the Byzantine emperor Heraclius, shortly to be followed by the Arab conquest.'[1]

The Maginot mentality has come to mean a strategy that is purely defensive and, therefore, flawed. It might be said, however, that the analogy itself seems irrelevant or wrong. Maginot's defence system was a non–continuous barrier. It was, anyway, never breached. (The Germans chose to outflank it – as was intended – and the military response failed in the more northerly open battlegrounds.) Therefore, not only is the interpretation of the Maginot Line itself questionable, but also it has made the subject of linear barriers generally harder to analyse.

Criticism of linear barriers is not simply a matter of the effectiveness of their physical substance. The construction of a wall makes the builder cower behind it. Walls, therefore, encourage a defensive mindset. This view is not only recent, it is recurrent through history. For example, Plato's Athenian, debating in the Laws, proposed that the state's land-stewards and *phrourarchs* (country police) duties should be, 'first, in order to ensure that the country shall be fenced as well as possible against enemies, they shall make channels wherever needed, and dig moats and build crosswalls, so as to keep out … those who attempt in any way to damage the country and its wealth.'[2] This proposal was criticised: 'Walls should be made of bronze and iron rather than of earth.'[3] The plan, 'of sending young men into the country every year to dig and trench and build, so as to keep the enemy out and prevent their ever setting foot on the borders of the land' would deserve 'roars of laughter'.[4] Generally Plato says a wall, 'causes a soft habit of soul in the inhabitants, by inviting them to seek refuge within it instead of repelling the enemy.'[5] Yet throughout this book linear barriers have been described which, if not immediately aggressive in function, were built to consolidate the hold on territory recently taken as the result of aggressive advance.

The debate and commentary about walls extends beyond their pure military effectiveness or ineffectiveness. Walls themselves have become immoral. For example: 'Walls have come to mean the opposition of freedom, openness, and diversity: and the manifestation of closure, isolation, narrowness. As such they can only be bad in certain people's eyes. Symbolically, the wall is limitation, discrimination, rejection of the other seen a priori as dangerous. It is the affirmation of fixity, refusal of the living and of exchange.'[6] This anti-wall mindset hardly seems to consider that, in the case of some threats, the danger was not just a few liberal ideas but huge armies with established track records of genocide.

It is perhaps not difficult, however, to see why walls might have got a bad name. For example, the Berlin Wall was emblematic of an ultimately failed effort to restrict human freedom by the construction of a human barrier. Of course, militarily it would have been virtually useless but its purpose was to keep people in, rather than armies out – at which, until the overall political situation proved untenable, it actually proved, distressingly, very successful.

Consequent fallacies resulting from flawed analysis

As the result of the possible reasons for flawed analysis just outlined, the consequence has been a number of fallacies in interpretation and assessment. These are, firstly, an almost perverse determination to apply non-military motives for linear barrier construction. Secondly, a view that, even when a military motive is admitted, linear barriers were an inferior solution that almost invariably failed. Thirdly, a suspension of historical perspective with the result that time is telescoped, and therefore later possible failure cancels out years, even centuries, of success. And lastly, that linear barriers are such an unusual solution that, rather than being an independently derived but common solution to the same problems in different locations, they must have been copied from distant exemplars.

Possibly, the bloody wars of the first half of the twentieth century have provoked a backlash against anything which might be perceived as gratuitously militaristic. There appears, sometimes, to be desperation by many archaeologists and historians to interpret or reinterpret walls and linear barriers as having anything but a military function – that is the building of an obstacle, backed up by human force, designed to impede the movement of armed forces.

There are two principle schools of the non-military interpretation of linear barriers. The first school ascribes functions that are non-military to linear barriers. In recent decades, linear barriers have often been interpreted or reinterpreted as having a non-military, function – for example as: peaceable boundary markers whose gaps would have rendered them militarily useless; exercises in personal status and state morale building; or even grand-scale landscaping, portage lines, water filters, giant vegetable plots, taboo line markers and obstacles to evil spirits.* The second school largely rejects an active

---

* There is, although not wall related, the cautionary tale of Ötzi, the five-thousand-year-old iceman. When his body was first discovered in the Alps he was depicted as a fetchingly grass-dressed, ice-world hippy who got lost in the snow when too deeply communing with nature. Perhaps modern prejudices contributed to the overlooking, for a decade, of an arrow head deep in his shoulder which set off internal

defensive function but interprets them as passive, if grand, physical manifestations of power, built into the earth, sufficient in themselves to deter enemies and meant to build national identity.* The view is taken here that while it is often impossible to determine what the intentions were of linear barrier builders – it seems most logical to conclude that the effort was expended to deal with genuine dangers; and also that there should be caution about imposing modern hopes and fears onto earlier peoples.

Another issue is the tendency to consider that, because one wall predated another, the later wall was a copy of the earlier wall – even if the walls were virtually at opposite ends of the earth. Ultimately, wall building has been presented almost as a perverse notion that had to be copied from some distant exemplar – rather than being simply the common, spontaneous and obvious local solution to a similar problem. For example, the construction of the Roman Limes was quite possibly influenced by the concept of the Great Wall of China. 'Although there is no evidence that the two constructions had any direct connections, indirect influence from the Great Wall on the Roman Limes is certain.'[7] Also: 'The similarity of Alexander's Wall (in Iran) to Hadrian's Wall has already led to speculation on the possibility of Parthian prisoners of War bringing the tradition westwards with them.'[8] (One issue is that the Sadd-i-Iskandar almost certainly post-dates Hadrian's Wall by several centuries and, therefore, cannot be Parthian.)

It is not impossible for this kind of imitation to have happened. The answer simply cannot really be known. But, on one level, this gets 'influence' the wrong way around: it is the copier who has the active role in the transaction – selecting ideas that are useful to him. More seriously, it detracts from the argument that similar situations call forth common responses: and that, therefore, linear barrier building might be a quite normal human reaction to certain situations.

Repeatedly, linear barrier building has been associated with military failure from the *Muriq Tidnim* of Sumer, the Ming Great Wall of China, to more recently the Maginot Line of France. This book has tried to put linear barriers in a more positive light by showing that many linear barriers lengthened the survival of individual states and collectively played an important part in the strategic mix that contained and then closed down the nomad threat.

The historian writing about past events is afforded a perspective denied to the actual contemporary maker of history. He or she knows what happened next. There is

---

bleeding that probably caused his death. Ötzi's world was one of murder, judging by his wounds and the blood of others found on his weapons.

* The recent discovery of the skeletons of women and children in a mass burial at a Peak District hill fort at Fin Cop might encourage caution about assumptions about peacefulness in any era. 'In recent years there has become an almost accepted assumption that warfare in the British Iron Age is largely invisible. *Hill forts have been seen as displays of power, prestige and status rather than places with a serious military purpose.* The gruesome discoveries at Fin Cop have reopened the debate on the purpose of hill forts. For the people living here, *the hurriedly constructed fort was evidently intended as a defensive work in response to a very real threat.*' (Wainright, *The Guardian* – see Bibliography Aftermath section) The words '*defensive work in response to a very real threat*' (all author's italics) should be recalled whenever there is a temptation to impose a non-military motivation on any linear barrier.

a risk that the historian's advantage of hindsight affects judgment of the decisions of contemporaries. Linear barriers may have lasted successfully in use for many generations if not centuries. An individual's life is, however, restricted to decades and there is no way of knowing what happened subsequently. If that individual saw that the building of a linear barrier effectively deterred or actually blocked an expected threat in his lifetime – then he would deem that barrier a success. His immediate descendents would also consider it a success if it functioned as intended during their lifetime. If it subsequently failed, after a century or two, then that does not mean that it was a failure, measured in terms of the builder's objectives. The problem is that, with hindsight, often only the drama of failure is remembered, particularly if such failure were followed by a horrible massacre or what has subsequently been perceived as a change in the course of history.

The Ming Great Wall of China was started in the fifteenth century and is frequently castigated as a vast exercise in futility. But the Ming did not fall until the seventeenth century – and then through treachery to the Manchu, not the Mongols against whom the Ming built the wall in the first place. The Mongols were kept out during the builders' lifetimes and for several generations after. Does that mean the Ming walls were a failure?

Conclusion

For a variety of reasons linear barriers appear to have been almost written out of serious history. They are hard to discuss authoritatively due to the lack of texts and possibly because of the fantastical names. They did not work very well, according to many armchair pundits. They do not inspire great stories of marshal gallantry and *gloire*. They offend the military prejudice that favours the offensive over the defensive. They are difficult to feel comfortable about morally. Yet possibly these judgements say more about the intellectual character of the twentieth century, particularly as conditioned by its wars. Now, in the twenty first century, it may be possible to form more balanced judgements, and linear barriers might be seen as an important element in the strategic mix that kept nomad raiders and hordes at bay for more than two millennia when, militarily, they held the upper hand.

Bibliography

Primary material

Full texts of identified authors
Aelius Spartianus, *History of Augustus, Life of Hadrian.* Magie, L., Loeb, 1921.
al-Juvayni, *History Of The World Conqueror.* Boyle, J.A., Harvard University Press, 1958.
Ammianus Marcellinus, *History of the Roman Empire.* Rolfe, J.C., Loeb, 1912.
Appian, *History of the Syrian Wars.* White, H., Loeb, 1913.
Asser, *Life of King Alfred.* Stevenson, W.H., Oxford University Press, 1904.
Caesar, *Gallic Wars.* McDevitte, W.A. & Bohn W.S., Harper & Brothers, New York, 1869.
Constantine VII Porphyrogenitus, *De Administrando Imperio, (On the Governance of the Empire).* Jenkins, R.J.H., Dunbarton Oaks Texts, 1967.
Diodorus Siculus, *Library of History.* Oldfather, C.H., Loeb, 1954.
Eutropius, *Abridgment of Roman History.* Selby, J.S., George Bell and Sons, London, 1886.
Evagrius Scholasticus, *Ecclesiastical History.* Walford, E., Samuel Bagster and Sons, 1846.
Fronto, *The correspondence of Marcus Cornelius Fronto with Marcus Aurelius Antoninus, Lucius Verus, Antoninus Pius, and various friends (Speech on the War in Britain. 140–1 AD).* Haines, C.R., London: W. Heineman, New York. Putnam, 1919.
Herodian, *History of Rome.* Whittaker, C.R., Loeb, London, 1969.
Herodotus, *Histories.* Rawlinson, G., Everyman, 1992 (first published 1858).
John of Fordun, *Chronicle of the Scottish Nation.* Edinburgh, Edmonston and Douglas, 1872.
Jordanes, *Origins and Deeds of the Goths.* Mierow, C. C., Princeton university, 1908.
Josephus, *Antiquities of the Jews.* Whiston, W., Project Gutenberg, 2009.
Josephus, *Jewish War.* Thackeray, H. St. J., Loeb, 1925–8.
Julius Capitolinus, *Life of Antoninus Pius.* Magie, D. Loeb, 1921.
Livius, *History of Rome.* Spillan, D., John Childs and Son, London, 1853.
Plato, *Laws.* Bury, R.G., William Heinemann, London, 1968.
Plutarch, *The Parallel Lives.* Perrin, B., Loeb, 1916.
Procopius, *Buildings of Procopius.* Dewing, H.B., Loeb, 1940.
Procopius, *History of the Wars.* Dewing, H. B., London, W. Heinemann; New York, The Macmillan co., 1914.
Sima Qian, *Records of the Grand Historian of China (Shi Ji).* Watson, B., New York and London, Columbia University Press, 1962.
Skylitzes, J., *Synopsis of Byzantine History, 811–1057.* Wortley, J., Cambridge University Press, 2010.
Strabo, *Geography.* Jones, H. L., Loeb, 1917–32.
Tacitus, *Annals.* Jackson, J., Loeb, 1931.
Tacitus, *Germania.* Gordon, T. (died c. 1750).
Theophanes, *Chronicle of Theophanes.* Turtledove, H., University of Pennsylvania Press, 1982.
Xenophon, *Anabasis.* Dakyns, H. G., Macmillan and Co., 1897.
Xenophon, *Hellenica.* Brownson, C. L., Loeb, 1915.
Zosimus, *History of Zosimus.* Vossius, G.J., London: Green and Chaplin, 1814.

Other full texts
King James Bible. Cambridge Edition.
Koran. Sale, G., 1801.
The Secret History of the Mongols. Onon, U., (Professor), Psychology Press, 2001.
The Anglo-Saxon Chronicle. about.com, medieval history. http://historymedren.about.com/library/text/bltxtaschron501.htm
The Book of Songs. Waley, A., Grove Press, 1987.
The Tale of Sinuhe. *Notes on the Story of Sinuhe*, Gardiner, A. H., Librairie Honoré Champion, Paris, 1916.
Liber census Daniæ, Kong Valdemar den andens jordebog, Nielsen, O., Copenhagen, 1873.

Primary material – sources other than full text

Quotations from named authors
Adam of Bremen, *Gesta Pontificum Hammaburgensis ecclesiae*. In *Limes Saxoniae*, http://de.wikipedia.org/wiki/Limes_Saxoniae
Bruno of Querfurt, *The Letter of Bruno of Querfurt to King Henry II: On His Alliance with the Pagans*. In *Panstowowe Wydawnictwo Naukowe*, North, W.L., Warsaw, 1973, pp. 97–106.
Cantemir, D., *Descriptio Moldaviae*, 1714. In *Prehistoric Dacia*, Densusianu, N. http://www.pelasgians.org/website1/08_01.htm
Dong Ruoyu (citing Beibian beidui), *Qi guo kao*, Beijing: Zhonghua Shuju, 1956. In 'Trapped behind Walls: Ming Writing on the Wall'. In *China Heritage Quarterly, China Heritage Project*, The Australian National University, no. 6, 2006. http://www.chinaheritagequarterly.org/articles.php?searchterm=006_ming.inc&issue=006
Grammaticus, S., *Gesta Danorum*. In *Dannewerk*. http://www.theodora.com/encyclopedia/d/dannewerk.html
Hvitfeld, A., *Danmarks Riges Krønike*. In *Danevirke*. http://en.wikipedia.org/wiki/Danevirke
Nokter, *Life of Charlemagne*. In *Charles the Great*, Hodgkin, T., Thomas Macmillan, 1897.
Pseudo-Callisthenes, *The Alexander Romance*, iii, 26. In *Gog and Magog*, Bøe, S., Tübingen: Mohr Siebeck, 2001.
Sima Qian, *Records of the Grand Historian of China (Shi Ji)*. In Zhewen, L., 'The Great Wall of China'. In Roberts, C. (ed.), Barmé, G.R. (ed.), *The Great Wall of China*. Powerhouse publishing, 2006.
Tabarī, *History of Prophets and Kings*. In Mahamedi, H., 'Wall as a System of Frontier Defence during the Sasanid Period'. In *Daryaee T., Omidsalar, M., (eds.), Spirit of Wisdom (Menog-i Xrad), Essays in Memory of Ahmad Tafazzoli*, Mazda Publishers, 2004.
de Torigni, R., *Gesta Normannorum Ducum*. In Contamine, P., *War in the Middle Ages*. English Translation Blackwell Publishers, 1984.
Widukind, *Saxonian History*. In *Forgotten Bronze Age*. Lukács, B. http://www.rmki.kfki.hu/~lukacs/SZARMAT1.htm
Yāqūt, *Al-Mushtarik*. In Frye, R. N., 'The Sasanian System of Walls for Defence'. In *Studies in Memory of Gaston Wiet*, Jerusalem, 1977. pp. 7–15.
Yāqūt, *Al-Mushtarik*. In Mahamedi, H., 'Wall as A System of Frontier Defence during the Sasanid Period'. In *Daryaee T., Omidsalar, M., (eds.), Spirit of Wisdom (Menog-i Xrad), Essays in Memory of Ahmad Tafazzoli*, Mazda Publishers, 2004. pp. 145–159.

Attributed quotations from unnamed authors
Instruction of Merikare. In *The Literature of Ancient Egypt*, Faulkner, R. O., Simpson, W. K. (ed.), New Haven and London, 1973, pp. 180–192. http://www.reshafim.org.il/ad/egypt/merikare_papyrus.htm

Pouchenie of Vladimir Monomakh, Primary Russian Chronicle. In Harrington, A.K. http://www.dur.
ac.uk/a.k.harrington/wwwdoc.html

Prophecy of Neferti. In *Ancient Near Eastern Texts*. Wilson, J. A., Pritchard, J. B. (ed.) Princeton, 1969.
http://www.reshafim.org.il/ad/egypt/texts/neferti.htm

Tiberius Plautius Silvanus Aelianus funerary text. In *Tiberius Plautius Silvanus Aelianus*. http://
en.wikipedia.org/wiki/Tiberius_Plautius_Silvanus_Aelianus

Other quotations

Annals of the Kingdom of the Franks, 808. In *Charlemagne: Translated Sources, Kendal, 1987,* King,
P.D. http://www.deremilitari.org/RESOURCES/SOURCES/charlemagne3.htm

Bulgarian Apocryphal Chronicle. In *Dobruja*. http://en.wikipedia.org/wiki/Dobruja

Hungarian folk legend. In *Nemzetismeret*, (adaptation by) Lengyel, D. http://www.nemzetismeret.
hu/?id=1.16&sh=&lang=en

Marriage of Martu. In *Electronic Text Corpus of Sumerian Literature (ETCSL)*. http://etcsl.orinst.
ox.ac.uk/

Ravenna Cosmography. In *The Antonine Wall*. http://www.roman-britain.org/frontiers/antonine.
htm

The giant plough furrow of Novac (Osiris). In *Prehistoric Dacia*, Densusianu, N. http://www.
pelasgians.org/website1/07_01.htm

Quotations from other books – within authored chapters in books

Earle, J., 'Offa's Dyke in the neighbourhood of Knighton'. In *Archaeologia Cambrensis*, 3rd ser. 3,
1857. pp. 196–209, at pp. 197–8. In 'Offa's Dyke: a monument without a history?' Williams, A. In
Walls, Ramparts, and Lines of Demarcation, Fryde, N., Reitz D. (eds.), Transaction publishers, 2009.
pp. 31–56.

Turner, F. J, *The Significance of the Frontier in American History*, Chicago, 1893. In 'The Limes:
Between open Frontier and Borderline', Moschek, W. In *Walls, Ramparts, and Lines of Demarcation*,
Fryde, N., Reitz D., (eds.), Transaction publishers, 2009. pp. 13–29.

Source compilations

Chavalas, M. W., *Ancient Near East: Historical Sources in Translation*, John Wiley & Sons, 2006

Faulkner, R. O., Simpson, W. K. (ed.), *The Literature of Ancient Egypt*, New Haven and London,
1973.

Whitelock D., *English Historical Documents c. 500–1042*, Eyre, Spottiswoode, 1955.

Wilson, J. A., Pritchard, J. B. (ed.) *Ancient Near Eastern Texts*, Princeton, 1969.

Source compilation – electronic

Cuneiform Digital Library Initiative (CDLI). http://cdli.ucla.edu/

Electronic Text Corpus of Sumerian Literature (ETCSL). http://etcsl.orinst.ox.ac.uk/

Linear barriers

Books and papers on multiple linear barriers

Curta, F., (ed.), *Borders, Barriers, and Ethnogenesis: Frontiers in Late Antiquity and the Middle Ages*,
Turnhout: Brepols Publishers, 2006.

Fryde, N. & D. Reitz (eds.), *Walls, Ramparts, and Lines of Demarcation*. Transaction Publishers,
London, 2009.

Jurga, R.M., *Fortress Europe: European fortifications of World War II*. Greenhill, 1999.

Nunn, A. (ed.), *Mauern als Grenzen*. Philipp von Zabern. Mainz, 2009.

Squatriti, P., 'Digging Ditches in Early Medieval Europe'. *Past and Present*, 176 (1), 2002. pp. 11–65.

Sterling, B.L., *Do Good Fences Make Good Neighbors?: What History Teaches Us about Strategic Barriers and International Security*. Georgetown University Press, 2009.

Good discussion of general issues involving linear barriers found in:

Nokandeh, J., Sauer, E. W., Rekavandi, H. O., Wilkinson, T., Abbasi, G. A., Schwenninger, J., Mahmoudi, M., Parker, D., Fattahi, M., Usher-Wilson, L. S., Ershadi, M., Ratcliffe, J., Rowena, G., 'Linear barriers of northern Iran: the Great Wall of Gorgan and the Wall of Tammishe'. *Journal of the British Institute of Persian Studies*, 2006, pp 166–168.

Sauer, E. W., Booth, P. *Linear earthwork, tribal boundary and ritual beheading: Aves Ditch from the Iron Age to the early Middle Ages*. Archaeopress, 2005, pp. 37–42.

Nomads

Anthony, D.W., *The Horse The Wheel and Language How Bronze-Age Riders from the Eurasian Steppes Shaped the Modern World*. Princeton University Press, Princeton and Oxford, 2007.

Boswell, A. B., 'The Kipchak Turks'. *The Slavonic Review*, vol. 6, no. 16, 1927, pp. 68–85.

Cernenko, Dr E.V., McBride, A. (illustrator), *The Scythians 700–300 BC*, Osprey, 1983.

Di Cosmo, N., *Ancient China and Its Enemies: The Rise of Nomadic Power in East Asian History*. Cambridge University Press, 2002.

Draganescu, C., Jones, G., 'Problems of free-ranging livestock systems in Romania'. *LaCañada, Newspaper on the European on Nature Conservation and Pastoralism*, no, 15, 2001/02, pp 7–9.

Nicolle, D., McBride, A. (Illustrator), *Attila and the Nomad Hordes*, Osprey, 1990.

Nicolle, D., McBride, A. (Illustrator), *Rome's Enemies (5): The Desert Frontier (Men-at-Arms)*. Osprey Publishing, 1991.

Rapin C., 'Nomads and the Shaping of Central Asia: from the Early Iron Age to the Kushan period'. The British Academy, Proceedings of the British Academy, 133, pp 30–72. http://claude.rapin. free.fr/1BiblioTextesGeogrPDF/Rapin_Nomads2.pdf

Rapin C., 'Nomads and the shaping of Central Asia', Information about *Symposium After Alexander: Central Asia Before Islam*. http://www.britac.ac.uk/events/2004/asia-rapin.cfm

Stieglitz, R. R., 'Migrations in the Ancient Middle East (3500–500 B.C.)'. *Anthropological Science*, 101(3), 1993, pp. 263–271.

Zakiev, M., *Origin of Türks and Tatars, Part two, Origin Of Tatars*. http://s155239215.onlinehome.us/ turkic/20Roots/ZakievGenesis/ZakievGenesis212-264En.htm

http://www.kutsalkitaplar.net/index.php/history/origin-of-tuerks/origin-of-tuerks-and-tatars/11459-origin-of-tuerks-and-tatars-first-chapter

Other sources

Hizia: Histoire   de   Transhumance.   http://membres.multimania.fr/cheikh07000/hizia/ UStranshumance.htm

Geographical regions surveyed

Egypt

Hoffmeier, J. K., '"The Walls of the Ruler" in Egyptian Literature and the Archaeological Record: Investigating Egypt's Eastern Frontier in the Bronze Age'. *Bulletin of the American Schools of Oriental Research*, No. 343, 2006, pp. 1–20.

Jaritz, H., The investigation of the ancient wall extending from Aswan to Philae: second preliminary report, *MDAIK*, 49, 93. pp. 108–132.
Sneh, A., Weissbrod, T., Perath, I., 'Evidence for an Ancient Egyptian Frontier Canal'. *American Scientist*, vol. 63, no. 5, 1975, pp. 542–548.

- Linear barriers in broader context
Vogel, C., Delf, B. (Illustrator), *The Fortifications of Ancient Egypt 3000–1780 BC*. Osprey, 2010.

- Background
Gardiner, Sir A.H., *Egypt of the Pharaohs: An Introduction*. Oxford University Press, 1966.

Mesopotamia and Middle East
Barnett, R. D., 'Xenophon and the Wall of Media'. *The Journal of Hellenic Studies*, Vol. 83, 1963, pp. 1–26.
Dumper, M. R. T., Stanley B. E., *Cities of the Middle East and North Africa: A Historical Encyclopedia*, ABC-CLIO, 2007.
Geyer, B., 'Die Syrische Mauer', *Mauern als Grenzen*, Nunn, A. (ed.). Philipp von Zabern, Mainz, 2009. pp. 39–46. (Book also cited.)
Jaubert, R., Mohamed al-Dbiyat, M., Geyer, B., 'La patrimonialisation des steppes du Proche-Orient: un instrument pour quelle stratégie?'. *Pastoralisme méditerranéen: patrimoine culturel et paysager et développement durable*, Lerin, F. (ed.), Montpellier: CIHEAM (Centre International de Hautes Etudes Agronomiques Méditerranéennes), 2010, pp 117–138.
Killick, R. G., 'Northern Akkad Project: Excavations at Ḥabl Aṣ-Ṣaḫr. *Iraq* (British Institute for the Study of Iraq), vol. 46, no. 2, 1984, pp. 125–129.
Müller-Karpe A., 'Die Kappodokische Mauer', *Mauern als Grenzen* in Nunn, A. (ed.), Philipp von Zabern, Mainz, 2009. pp. 47–56. (Book also cited.)
Reade, J.E., 'El-Mutabbaq and Umm Rus'. *Sumer*, 20, 1964, pp. 83–9.

- Background
Frayne, D., *Ur III Period (2112–2004 BC)*. University of Toronto Press, 1997.
Gadd, C. J. 'Babylonia, c. 2120–1800 B.C.'. *Early History of the Middle East*. Edwards, E. S., Gadd C. J. Hammond, N. G. L., Cambridge University Press, 1971. Cambridge Histories Online. Cambridge University Press. 30 October 2012.
McIntosh J., *Ancient Mesopotamia: New Perspectives*. ABC-CLIO, 2005.
Morony, M.G., *Iraq after the Muslim Conquest*. Gorgias Press, 2005.

China
Lindesay, J., Lindesay, W., 'Finding Genghis Khan's Wall'. *China Daily*, 8 March, 2012.
Lovell, J. *The Great Wall: China Against the World, 1000 BC–AD 2000*. Grove/Atlantic, 2006.
Man, J. *The Great Wall*. www.rbooks.co.uk, 2008.
Owen, J., '"Lost" Great Wall of China Segment Found?' *National Geographic News*, March 19, 2012.
Pingfang, X., 'Archaeology of the Walls'. *The Great Wall of China*, Roberts, C., Barmé, G.R., Powerhouse Publishing, 2006, pp 52–56.
Roberts, C. (ed.), Barmé, G.R. (ed.), *The Great Wall of China*. Powerhouse publishing, 2006.
Turnbull, S. Noon, S. (illustrator), *The Great Wall of China 221 BC–AD 1644*. Osprey, 2007.
Waldron, A., *The Great Wall of China From History to Myth*. Canto, 1992.
Zhewen, L., 'The Great Walls of China'. *The Great Wall of China*, Roberts, C., Barmé, G.R., Powerhouse Publishing, 2006, pp 42–51.

Other sources
'Ancient sites from Zhou Dynasty discovered in the Qi Great Wall in Shandong', *Cultural China*, 2 February 2009.
'China uncovers lost part of Wall'. *BBC News*, 9 October 2002. http://news.bbc.co.uk/1/hi/world/asia-pacific/2314915.stm
'Great Wall ruins discovered in Shandong Province', *The People's Daily*, July 9, 2009. http://english.people.com.cn/90001/90782/90874/6697070.html
'Oldest Great Wall Relics Destroyed'. *Epoch Times, China Central News Agency*, 16 June 2008.
'The Great Wall of China', *TravelChinaGuide.com*. http://www.travelchinaguide.com/china_great_wall/history/sui/
'The Great Wall of the Qi Period', *AnESL.com*. http://www.anesl.com/schools/view.asp?id=656

- Linear barriers in broader context
Peers, C.J., McBride, A. (Illustrator), *Ancient Chinese Armies 1500–200 BC*. Osprey, 1990.
Peers, C.J., McBride, A. (Illustrator), *Imperial Chinese Armies (2) 590 – 1260 AD*. Osprey, 1990.

- Background
King Wuling of Zhao. http://en.wikipedia.org/wiki/King_Wuling_of_Zhao

Greek world
Bakhuizen, S. C., *Salganeos and the Fortifications on its Mountains*. Wolters-Noordhoff Publishing, Groningen, 1970.
Munn, M. H., *The Defence of Attica: The Dema Wall and the Boiotian War of 378–375 B.C*. University of California Press, 1993
Broneer, O., 'The Cyclopean Wall on the Isthmus of Corinth, Addendum'. *Hesperia*, 37, 1968, pp. 25–35.
Gregory, T.E., 'The Hexamilion and the Fortress (Isthmia)'. *American School of Classical Studies*, vol. V, 1993.
Munn, M. H., 'Agesilaos' Boeotian Campaigns and the Theban Stockade of 378–377 B.C.', *Classical Antiquity*, University of California Press, vol. 6, no. 1, 1987, pp. 106–138.
Winter, F. E., 'Notes on Military Architecture in the Termessos Region'. *American Journal of Archaeology* (Archaeological Institute of America), vol. 70, no. 2, 1966, pp. 127–137.
Wiseman, J.R., 'The Greeks had a wall for it'. *Alcade* (The University of Texas Alumni Magazine), Feb. 1962, pp. 12–15.

- Linear barriers in broader context
Scranton, R.L. 'Review of Greek Walls'. *The Classical Weekly*, vol. 35, no. 9, 1941, pp. 104–107.
Talbert, J.A. (ed.), *Barrington Atlas of the Greek and Roman World*. Princeton University Press, Princeton and Oxford, 2000.

- Background
Hanson, V. D., *Warfare and Agriculture in Classical Greece*. University of California Press, 1998.
Ober, J., 'Classical Greek Times'. *The Laws of War*, Howard M., Andreopoulos G.J., Shulman M.R. (eds), Yale University Press, New Haven and London, 1994, pp. 13–26.

Roman Empire
Baradez, J, *Fossatum Africae. Recherches Aériennes sur l'organisation des confins Sahariens a l'Epoque Romaine*, Arts et Métiers Graphiques, Paris, 1949.

Breeze, D.J., *The Antonine Wall.* John Donald Publishers Ltd., 2006.

Daniels, C., 'The Frontiers, Africa', in *The Roman World*, J. Wacher (ed.) Routledge, 2002. Vol. 1, p. 244.

Matei, V., Gindele, R., 'Fortificatia romana de pamant de tip burgus, atasata valului şi şantului roman descoperit la supurul de Sus, Jud. Satu mare'. *Acta musei porolissensis*, Zalau, Muzeul Judetean de istorie si arta, Zalau, 2004, vol. 26, pp. 283–307.

Mitford, T. B., 'Cappadocia and Armenia Minor: Historical Setting of the Limes'. *Aufstieg und Niedergang der Romischen Welt: Principat*, Temporini H., Temporini, H., Haasepp, W. (eds), pp. 1169–1228.

Napoli, J., *Recherches sur les Fortifications Linéaires Romaines*, École Française de Rome Palais Farnèse, 1997.

Wells, P. S., 'The Limes and Hadrian's Wall: Rome's Northern European boundaries'. *Expedition*, Vol. 47, No. 1, 2005, University Museum of the University of Pennsylvania, pp. 18–24.

- Linear barriers in broader context

Breeze, D.J., *The Frontiers of Imperial Rome.* Pen & Sword, 2012.

Cherry, D., *Frontiers and Society in Roman North Africa.* Clarendon Press, 1998.

Parker, P., *The Empire stops here.* Jonathan Cape, London, 2009.

Whittaker, C.R., *Frontiers of the Roman Empire. A Social and Economic Study.* The Johns Hopkins University Press, Baltimore, 1997.

- Background

Ball, W., *Rome in the East.* Routledge Taylor & Francis Group, London and New York, 2000.

Bowman, A.K., 'Provincial Adminstration and Taxation'. *The Cambridge Ancient History*, Bowman, A.K., Champlin, E., Lintott, A. (eds.), vol. 10, 1996.

Garnsey, P.D.A., 'Imperialism in the Ancient World'. *The Cambridge University Research Seminar*, Garnsey, P.D.A., Whittaker C. R., Cambridge University Press, 1978.

Kaplan, R. D., 'Roman Africa'. *Atlantic Magazine*, June 2001.

Parkin, T. G., Pomeroy, A.J., *Roman Social History: A Sourcebook.* Taylor & Francis, 2007.

Whittaker, C.R., 'Land and Labour in North Africa'. *Klio*, 60, 1978, pp. 331–62.

Northern Europe

Britain

Allcroft, A., *The Earthworks of England.* Macmillan, London, 1908.

Barber, J., Lawes-Martay, E., Milln, J., 'The Linear Earthworks of Southern Scotland'. Transactions of the Dumfriesshire and Galloway Natural History and Antiquarian Society, Williams, J., Cormack, W.F., Dumfries, 1999, pp 63–164.

Bowen, H.C., Eagles B.N. (ed.), *The Archaeology of Bokerley Dyke.* Stationery Office Books, 1990.

Hill, D., Worthington, M., *Offa's Dyke.* The History Press, 2003.

Reynolds, A. J. and Langlands, A., 'Social Identities on the Macro Scale: A Maximum View of Wansdyke'. *People and Space in the Middle Ages, 300–1300*, Davies, W., Halsall, G., and Reynolds, A, (eds.), Brepols: Turnhout, 2006 pp. 13 – 44.

Sauer, E. W., Booth, P., *Linear earthwork, tribal boundary and ritual beheading: Aves Ditch from the Iron Age to the early Middle Ages*, Archaeopress, 2005.

Squatriti, P., 'Digging Ditches in Early Medieval Europe'. *Past and Present*, 176 (1), 2002. pp. 11–65. (Offa's Dyke)

Other sources
Devil's Dyke Restoration Project. http://www.devilsdykeproject.org.uk/histarch.html
Devil's Dyke, Cambridgeshire. http://en.wikipedia.org/wiki/Devil's_Dyke,_Cambridgeshire

- Linear barriers in broader context
Lavelle, R., Spedaliere D. & Spedaliere S.S., (illustrators), *Fortifications in Wessex c. 800–1066. Osprey*, 2003.
Laycock, S., *Britannia the Failed State*. The History Press, 2008.
Newton, Dr S., The Defences of the Wuffing Kingdom. http://www.wuffings.co.uk/WuffSites/Dykes/EADykes.htm.
Williams, G. *Stronghold Britain Four Thousand Years of British Fortifications*. The History Press, 2003.
Other sources
Wansdyke Project 21. http://www.wansdyke21.org.uk/wansdykehomepage.htm

- Background
Black, E.W., *British chariotry and territorial oppida*. Essex, Archaeology and History (Transactions of the Essex Society for Archaeology and History, vol. 21, 1990, p 140.
Borrow, G., *Wild Wales*. George Bridge Books, 2009.
Campbell, J., *The Anglo-Saxon State*. Hambleton and London, London and New York, 2000.

Ireland
Condit T., Buckley V. M., Cooney G. (ed.), The Doon of Drumsna: An Iron Age frontier fortification in Connacht (Archeology Ireland Heritage Guide), 1998
Cullen, S., 'The Pale', *Oughterany – Journal of the Donadea Local History Group*. Reid, N. (ed.) vol. I no. 1, 1993. http://seamuscullen.net/pale.html
De Vismes Kane, W. F., 'The Black Pig's Dyke: The Ancient Boundary Fortification of Uladh'. *Proceedings of the Royal Irish Academy. Section C: Archaeology, Celtic Studies, History, Linguistics, Literature*, Royal Irish Academy Vol. 27, (1908/1909), pp. 301–328.
Duke, S., Archeologists discover Irish Hadrian's Wall, *The Sunday Times*, March 8 1998
Feeley, J.M., *The Rathduff Trench. The Gripe of the Pig*. http://glasnost.itcarlow.ie/~feeleyjm/archaeology/rathduff%20dyke.pdf
Wise, P., *Northern Linear Earthworks: Reassessing their Function in the Irish Iron Age Landscape Using GIS Techniques*. Thesis submitted to the Department of Geography, National University of Ireland Galway, 2006.

- Linear barriers in broader context
Elrington Ball, F., Hamilton E., *The parish of Taney: a history of Dundrum, near Dublin, and its neighbourhood*. Hodges, Figgis & Co., Dublin, 1895.
O' Brien, C., *A History of Offaly Through its Monuments*. Offaly Historical and Archaeological Society, 2007.

- Background
Bardon, J. *A History of Ulster*. Jonathan Blackstaff Press, 1992.
Connolly, S. J. (ed.), *The Oxford Companion to Irish History*. Oxford University Press, 2007.
Conway, A. E., Curtiss, E., *Henry VII's Relations with Scotland and Ireland: 1485–1498*, CUP Archive, 1932.

Denmark and Sweden

Andersen, H., *Til Hele Rigets Værn*. Moesgard & Wormianum, 2004.

Neumann, H. *Olgerdiget – et bidrag tils Danmarks tidligste historie*. Haderslev, 1982.

Schmidt, A. F., *Folkevolde i Jylland: en Oversigt*, 1925. (Text available at http://tidsskrift.dk/index.php/historiejyskesamling/article/view/13534/25813)

Squatriti, P., 'Digging Ditches in Early Medieval Europe'. *Past and Present*, 176 (1), 2002. pp. 11–65. (Danevirke)

German and Germanic

Hardt, M., 'The Limes Saxoniae as Part of the Eastern Borderlands of the Frankish and Ottonian-Salian Empire'. Curta, F. (ed.), *Borders, Barriers, and Ethnogenesis: Frontiers in Late Antiquity and the Middle Ages*. Turnhout: Brepols Publishers, 2006, pp. 35–50.

Huser, M., Mortsiefer, J., *Landwehren, was ist das?* Private Project. http://www.*Landwehren*.de/

Lutz, D., 'Territoire et protection des frontiers Quelques exemples de XIVe et XV siècles dans le sud-ouest de l'Allemagne'. *Château et territoire Limites et mouvances. Première rencontre internationale d'archéologie et d'histoire. Préface d'Yves Guéna, sénateur-maire de Périgueux. Périgueux, 23–25 September 1994*. Presses universitaires de Franche-Comté, 1995, pp. 73–92.

Eastern Europe

Hungary, Serbia, Romania

Bernard Le Calloc'h, 'Une curiosité archéologique: le Csörszárok ou 'fossé du diable''. *Études finno-ougriennes*, vol. 37, 2005, pp 205–215.

Crawford, O.G.S., 'Some Linear Earthworks in the Danube Basin'. The Geographical Journal, Vol. 116. Nos 4–6, 1950.

Istvanovits, V., Kulcsár, E., 'The history and perspectives of the research of the Csörsz Ditch'. *XVIIIth International Congress of Roman Frontier Studies*. Amman, 2000.

Romania, Moldavia, Western Ukraine

Croitoru, C., 'Sudul Moldovei În cadrul sistemului defensiv roman'. *Acta Terrae Septemcastrensis I*, pp. 107–120.

Krandjalov, D., *Vallums In Dobroudja / Bessarabia And Proto-Bulgarian Theory*. http://berberian11.tripod.com/krandjalov_ramparts.htm

Valpe, R., *Le Vallum de la Moldavie Inferieure et le 'Mur' d'Athanaric*. Mouton & Co., The Hague Netherlands, 1957.

Other sources

Trajan's Wall by Veltman.jpg http://en.wikipedia.org/wiki/File:Trajan%27s_Wall_by_Veltman.jpg

Valul lui Traian. 1200 de ani de istorie, http://www.xplorio.ro/valul-lui-traian-1200-de-ani-de-istorie/ Valul lui Traian. 1200 de ani de istorie, http://www.xplorio.ro/valul-lui-traian-1200-de-ani-de-istorie/

- Linear barriers in broader context

Plamenytska, O., Plamenytska, E., *Kamyanets Podilsky, A Town at the Periphery of the Roman Empire: Urban Order and Fortifications*. http://www.tovtry.kilometres.ua/en/history/article/mist1.htm

Other sources
Borshchiv Raion. http://en.wikipedia.org/wiki/Borshchiv_Raion.

- Background
'The Passage of the Danube by the Russians', *The Times*, April 2, 1854. http://paperspast.natlib.
   govt.nz/cgi-bin/paperspast?a=d&d=NZSCSG18540722.2.11&l=mi&e=-------10--11----
   0pardessus—
Dobruja, First Bulgarian Empire rule. http://en.wikipedia.org/wiki/Dobruja#cite_note-34
Kingdom of Galicia. http://en.wikipedia.org/wiki/Kingdom_of_Galicia%E2%80%93Volhynia
Podolia. http://en.wikipedia.org/wiki/Podolia

Ukraine (Kievan Rus)
Змиевы валы (Zmievi Vali), Wikipedia. http://ru.wikipedia.org
A map showing theZmievi Vali set out in the above website can be found at:
http://andrew-vk.narod.ru/public/Zmievy_valy/index.htm. (It has not proved possible to establish
   the source of this map.)

- Linear barriers in broader context
Franklin, S., Shepard, J., *The Emergence of Rus: 750–1200*. Longman History of Russia, 1996.
Kirievsky, V.D., *Novgorod-Seversky, Road of the Prince*. http://terra-trajana.narod.ru/novgorod.html
Nossov, K., Dennis, P. (illustrator), *Russian Fortresses 862–1480*. Osprey, 2007.
Rappoport, P., 'Russian Medieval Military Architecture'. *Gladius*, VIII, pp. 39–62.

Other sources
'Valky and Environs: Glimpses of History', *Kharkiv Oblast, Ukraine, Valky County, Town of Valky*,
   http://www.valki.Kharkiv.ua/history-e.htm
'Rivers of milk and creeks of honey, witches flying around at night in the Land of Poltavshchyna,
   Zmiyevi valy — Snake Earthworks', *Welcome to Ukraine*. http://www.wumag.kiev.ua/index2.
   php?param=pgs20051/46

- Background
Borshchevskii, Y.E., *Dzhaxān-nāme*. Moscow, 1960.

Crimea
Braund D., 'Cimmerius Bosphorus', 1997. *Barrington Atlas of the Greek and Roman World*, Talbert,
   R. J. A. (ed.), Princeton University Press, Princeton and Oxford, 2000. pp. 1243 – 1254. (Book also
   cited.)

- Background
Clarke, E. D., *Travels in Various Countries of Europe, Asia and Africa: Russia, Tartary*. T. Cadell and
   W. Davies, 1817.
Henderson, E., *Biblical Researches and Travels in Russia: Including a Tour in the Crimea, and the Passage
   of the Caucasus*. J. Nisbet, 1826.
Von Manstein, E., Powell. A. G. (ed. and trans.), *Lost Victories*. Presidio Press, Novato, California,
   1984.

Poland

Przesieka Śląska. http://pl.wikipedia.org/wiki/Przesieka_%C5%9Al%C4%85ska
Silesian Przesieka. http://en.wikipedia.org/wiki/Silesian_Przesieka.

- Linear barriers in broader context

Buko, A., *The Archaeology of Early Medieval Poland: Discoveries, Hypotheses, Interpretations (East Central and Eastern Europe in the Middle Ages, 450–1450)*, Andrzej Brill Academic Publishers, 2008.

Bulgaria and Greater Bulgaria

Bury, J. B., 'The Bulgarian Treaty of A. D. 814, and the Great Fence of Thrace'. *The English Historical Review*, Oxford University Press, vol. 25, no. 98, 1910. pp. 276–287.

Rashev, R., 'Remarks on the Archaeological Evidence of Forts'. *Borders, barriers, and ethnogenesis: frontiers in late Antiquity and the Middle Ages*, Curta, F. (ed.), Turnhout: Brepols Publishers, 2006.

Rashev, R., Les vallums de Dobrudža dans le développement de la fortifications ancienne bulgare. *Dobrudža, Etudes ethno-culturelles*, pp. 48–56.

Squatriti, P., 'Digging Ditches in Early Medieval Europe'. *Past and Present*, 176 (1), 2002. pp. 11–65. (Erkesia)

Squatriti, P., 'Moving Earth and Making Difference: Dikes and Frontiers in Early Medieval Bulgaria'. *Borders, barriers, and ethnogenesis: frontiers in late Antiquity and the Middle Ages*, Curta, F. (ed.), Turnhout: Brepols Publishers, 2006, pp. 59–90.

Welkow, I., 'Pliska', Akrabova, Dr I.). *Antiquity*, vol. 13, no. 51, 1930.

- Linear barriers in broader context

Randsborg, K., 'A Seagoing Ship of c1650 AD in Bessarabia, Ukraine'. *Archaeological Notes*, 1, 1998. http://www.abc.se/~pa/publ/bessarab.htm

Byzantine Empire

Brezeanu, S., 'Toponymy and ethnic Realities at the Lower Danube in the 10th Century. "The deserted Cities" in the Constantine Porphyrogenitus' *De Administrando Imperio*'. *Istituto Romeno di cultura e ricerca umanistica*, Venice, Marin, S., Dinu, R., Bulei, I., (eds), 4, 2002. Translation available at http://tech.groups.yahoo.com/group/cybalist/message/15243

Sasanian Empire

Aliev, A.A., Gadjiev, M.S., Gaither, M.G., Kohl, P.L., Magomedov, R.M., Aliev, I.N., 'The Ghilghilchay Defensive Long Wall: New Investigations'. *Ancient West & East*, vol. 5, nos 1–2, 2006, pp 143–177.

Frye, R. N., 'The Sasanian System of Walls for Defence'. *Studies in Memory of Gaston Wiet*, Jerusalem, 1977. pp. 7–15.

Harmatta, J. 'The Wall of Alexander the Great and the Limes Sasanicus'. Bromberg, C.A., Skjærvø P.O. (eds.), *Studies in Honor of Vladimir A. Livshits*, vol. 10, Bulletin Asia Institute, 1996, pp. 79–84.

Mahamedi, H., 'Wall as A System of Frontier Defence during the Sasanid Period'. *Spirit of Wisdom (Menog-i Xrad), Essays in Memory of Ahmad Tafazzoli*, Daryaee T., Omidsalar, M., (eds.), Mazda Publishers, 2004, pp. 145–159

Nokandeh, J., Sauer, E. W., Rekavandi, H. O., Wilkinson, T., Abbasi, G. A., Schwenninger, J., Mahmoudi, M., Parker, D., Fattahi, M., Usher-Wilson, L. S., Ershadi, M., Ratcliffe, J., Rowena, G., 'Linear barriers of northern Iran: the Great Wall of Gorgan and the Wall of Tammishe'. *Journal of the British Institute of Persian Studies*, 2006, pp 121–173.

Rekavandi, H. O., Sauer, E., Wilkinson, T., Nokandeh, J. 'The Enigma of the Red Snake'. *Current Archaeology*, no. 27, 2008, pp. 12–22.

Other sources
'In Search of Sasanian Wall', *CAIS (The Circle of Ancient Iranian Studies) Archaeological & Cultural News*, 12 February 2006. http://www.cais-soas.com/News/2006/February2006/12-02-archaeologists.htm

- Linear barriers in broader context
Pazouki, N., 'Defence Buildings in Iran'. *Miras-e-Melli*, no. 13, Page pp. 32–38.

- Background
Nicolle, D., McBride, A. (illustrator), *Sassanian Armies, The Iranian Empire early 3rd to mid-7th centuries AD*, Montvert Publications, 1996.

Russia
- Linear barriers in broader context
Davies, B.L., *State, Power and Community in Early Modern Russia, The Case of Kozlov*. Palgrave Macmillan, 2004.
Nossov, K., Dennis, P. (illustrator), *Russian Fortresses 1480–1682*. Osprey, 2006.
Sanders, R. L., The Strelzi (1550–1705). *Xenophon Group*. http://www.xenophon-mil.org/rusarmy/streltzi.htm

- Background
Davies, B.L., *Warfare, State and Society on the Black Sea Steppe, 1500–1700*. Taylor & Francis, 2007.
de Madariaga, I., *Ivan the Terrible*. Yale University Press, 2005.

Central Asia
Bader, A.N., Gaibov, V.A., Košelenko, G.A., 'Walls of *Margiana*', In the land of the gryphons: papers on Central Asian archaeology. *Antiquity*, Antonio Invernizzi, Le Lettere, 1995. pp. 39–50.

- Linear barriers in broader context
Ball, W., *Warwick Archaeological Gazetteer of Afghanistan*, 2 vols. Paris, 1982.
Frye, R. N., *The History of Bukhara*. Cambridge, Mass., 1954.
Gangler, A., Gaube, H., Petruccioli, A., *Bukhara, the Eastern Dome of Islam: Urban Development, Urban Space*. Edition Axel Menges, 2004.
Niekum, M. *The Role of Shrines and Temples in the Urban Sogdian Community: An Ethnoarchaeological Perspective from Contemporary Bukhara*. http://depts.washington.edu/reecas/events/conf2002/papers02/Niekum.doc)

Other sources
'Balk', *Encyclopædia Iranica*. http://www.iranicaonline.org/articles/balk-town-and-province
'Heart', *Encyclopædia Iranica*. http://www.iranicaonline.org/articles/herat

- Background
Rabinou, H.L., *A Travel to Mazandaran and Astarabad*, translated by V. Mazandarani. Book Translation and Publication Institute, 1957.

Non-Eurasian

Peru and Bolivia
Paddock, F. K., 'The Great Wall of the Inca'. *Archaeology*, 37:62, July/August, 1984.

- Linear barriers in broader context
Wilson, D., *Prehispanic Settlement Patterns in the Lower Santa Valley Peru*. Smithsonian Series in Archeological Inquiry, Washington. 1988.

Guatemala
Puleston, D. E., Callender, D. W., 'Defensive Earthworks at Tikal'. *Expedition*, Spring, 1967, pp. 40–48. http://www.penn.museum/documents/publications/expedition/PDFs/9-3/Defensive.pdf
Silverstein, J. E., Webster, D., Martinez, H. and Soto, A, 'Rethinking the great earthwork of Tikal: a hydraulic hypothesis for the classic Maya polity'. *Ancient Mesoamerica*, 20, 2009, pp. 45–58
Webster, D., 'Lowland Maya Fortifications'. *Proceedings of the American Philosophical Society*, vol. 120, no 5, 1976, pp. 361–371.
Webster, D., *Re-Evaluation Of The Earthworks At Tikal, Guatemala: Phase 2* Final report submitted to the National Science Foundation, 2007. http://www.anthro.psu.edu/faculty_staff/docs/Tikal%20final%20NSF.pdf

- Linear barriers in broader context
Martin, S., 'Tikal Crucible of Maya Civilisation'. *The Great Cities in History From Mesopotamia to Megalopolis*, Norwich, J. J., Thames & Hudson, 2009.

- Background

Nigeria
Aremu, D. A., 'Saving Sungbo's Eredo: a challenge to Nigerian archaeologists'. *West African Journal of Archaeology*, vol. 32, issue 2, 2002, pp. 63–73.
Darling, P. J., 'A Legacy in Earth'. *Historical Archaeology in Nigeria*, Trenton, NJ: Africa World, 1998, pp. 145–197.
Darling, P. J., 'Sungbo's Eredo, Southern Nigeria'. *Nyame Akuma*, no. 49, 1998. http://cohesion.rice.edu/centersandinst/safa/emplibrary/49_ch09.pdf

Other sources
'Sungbo's Eredo – Africa's Largest Single Monument', *Recording West Africa's Visible Archaeology African Legacy*, Darling, Dr P., African Legacy – School of Conservation Sciences, Bournemouth University, http://csweb.bournemouth.ac.uk/africanlegacy/sungbo_eredo.htm
Sungbo's Eredo. http://en.wikipedia.org/wiki/Sungbo's_Eredo

Easter Ireland
Emory, K.E., 'Review of Archaeology of Easter Island', Heyerdahl, T., Ferdon, E.N. *American Antiquity*, vol. 28, no. 4, 1963, pp. 565–567.

Other
- Linear barriers
Brush, P., 'The Story Behind The Mcnamara Line'. *Vietnam magazine*, February 1996, pp. 18–24. http://www.shss.montclair.edu/english/furr/pbmcnamara.html

Linear barriers
Stone Wall in Imazu. http://www.bekkoame.ne.jp/~gensei/ten/eimazu.html
'Archaeologists unearth 127-km long 'Great Wall' of Vietnam'. *Asia News International,* 27 January 2011.

Historical and other background
de Souza, P., *The Ancient World at War*, Thames & Hudson, 2008.
Keegan, M., *A History Of Warfare.* John Random House, 1993.
Laflen, J.M., *Soil Erosion and Dryland Farming.* CRC Press, 2000.
Lombard, M., *The Golden Age of Islam.* Markus Wiener Pub, 2003.
Morris, I., *Why the West Rules – for Now: The Patterns of History, and What They Reveal About the Future.* Straus and Giroux, 2010.
Woods, M., *The Story of India.* BBC Books 2007.

Questions and issues section
Abels, R., *The Fortified Bridges of Charles the Bald, king of West Francia (848–877)* 2009. http://usna.edu/Users/history/abels/hh315/vikingsrevised.html
M. van Creveld, *Defending Israel: A Strategic Plan for Peace and Security*, New York: Thomas Dunne Books, 2004, p. 66.
Urban, W., 'The Prussian-Lithuanian frontier of 1242'. *Lituanus, Lithuanian Quarterly Journal of Arts and Sciences*, vol. 21, no.4, 1975. http://www.lituanus.org/1975/75_4_01.htm
Defence-in-depth (Roman military), http://en.wikipedia.org/wiki/Defence-in-depth_(Roman_military)#cite_note-29

Aftermath section
Bray, A., 'Vietnam's own 'great wall' uncovered'. *Special for CNN*, 25 January 2011
Coonan, C., 'The great repair job of China'. *The Independent*, 30 December 2006.
Golubenko, S., 'Як приватизували Змієві Вали'. *Новини УНІАН*, 7 March 2008. http://www.unian.ua/news/259608-yak-privatizuvali-zmievi-vali.htm
Mehl, J-M., La logique des murs, *Réforme*, 31 August 2006.
Wainright, M., 'Who killed the hill fort nine? Mystery find shakes our iron age assumptions'. *The Guardian*, 18 April 2011.

Other sources
'Great fall of China'. *The Daily Telegraph*, 9 August 2012.
'Romans may have learned from Chinese Great Wall: archaeologists'. *People's Daily Online*, 20 December 2005.

Notes

Prologue

1. Dr E.V. Cernenko, and A. McBride, (Illustrator), *The Scythians 700-300 BC*, Osprey, 1983, p. 5.
2. Herodotus, *Histories*, G. Rawlinson, Everyman, 1992 (First published 1858), 1, 104.
3. ibid. 1, 105.
4. King James Bible, Cambridge Edition, *Jeremiah*, 5:16.
5. *The Book of Songs*, A. Waley, Grove Press, 1987, Song 132.
6. ibid. Song 131.
7. A. Waldron, *The Great Wall of China From History to Myth*, Canto, 1992, p. 38.
8. C. Rapin, 'Nomads and the shaping of Central Asia', *Information about Symposium 'After Alexander: Central Asia before Islam'*. http://www.britac.ac.uk/events/2004/asia-rapin.cfm
9. 'Kharkiv Oblast, Ukraine, Valky County, Town of Valky', in Valky and Environs: Glimpses of History, http://www.valki.Kharkiv.ua/history-e.htm
10. Strabo, *Geography*, H.L. Jones, Loeb, 1917-32, 7, 4, 7.
11. D. Braund, 'Cimmerius Bosphorus', 1997, in *Barrington Atlas of the Greek and Roman World*, R. J. A. Talbert (ed.), Princeton University Press, Princeton and Oxford, 2000, p. 1244.
12. op. cit., Strabo, 7, 4, 6
13. Josephus, *Jewish War*, H. St. J. Thackeray, Loeb, 1925-8, 7, 7, 4.
14. Zosimus, *History of Zosimus*, G.J. Vossius, London: Green and Chaplin, 1814, Book 1.

Introduction – why walls?

1. C. J. Gadd, 'Babylonia, c. 2120–1800 b.c.' in *Early History of the Middle East*. I. E. S. Edwards F.B.A., C. J. Gadd F.B.A and N. G. L. Hammond F.B.A., Cambridge University Press, 1971, p. 611.
2. Sir A. H. Gardiner, *Egypt of the Pharaoh: An Introduction*, Oxford University Press, 1961, p. 162.
3. J. Lovell, *The Great Wall, China against the World, 1000 BC–AD 2000*, Grove/Atlantic, 2006, p. 37.
4. F. K. Paddock, 'The Great Wall of the Inca' in *Archaeology*, 37:62, July/August 1984, p. 62.
5. R. N. Frye, 'The Sasanian System of Walls for Defence', in *Studies in Memory of Gaston Wiet*, Jerusalem, 1977, p. 15.
6. M. H. Munn, *The Defense of Attica: The Dema Wall and the Boiotian War of 378-375 B.C.*, University of California Press, 1993.
7. S. C. Bakhuizen, *Salganeos and the Fortifications on its Mountains*, Wolters-Noordhoff Publishing, Groningen, 1970.
8. T.E. Gregory, 'The Hexamilion and the Fortress (Isthmia)', *American School of Classical Studies*, vol. V, 1993.
9. H.C. Bowen, B.N. Eagles (ed.), *The Archaeology of Bokerley Dyke*. Stationery Office Books, 1990.
10. E. W. Sauer, P. Booth, *Linear earthwork, tribal boundary and ritual beheading: Aves Ditch from the Iron Age to the early Middle Ages*, Archaeopress, 2005.
11. D. Hill, M. Worthington., *Offa's Dyke*. The History Press, 2003.

12. A. Nunn (ed.), *Mauern als Grenzen,* Philipp von Zabern, Mainz, 2009.
13. N. Fryde, D. Reitz, *Walls, Ramparts, and Lines of Demarcation,* Transaction publishers, 2009.
14. F. Curta (ed.), *Borders, Barriers, and Ethnogenesis: Frontiers in Late Antiquity and the Middle Ages,* Turnhout: Brepols Publishers, 2006.
15. B.L. Sterling, *Do Good Fences Make Good Neighbors?: What History Teaches Us about Strategic Barriers and International Security,* Georgetown University Press, 2009.
16. *Valul lui Traian. 1200 de ani de istorie,* http://www.xplorio.ro/valul-lui-traian-1200-de-ani-de-istorie/
17. A. F. Schmidt, Folkevolde i Jylland: en Oversigt, 1925. (Text available at http://tidsskrift.dk/index.php/historiejyskesamling/article/view/13534/25813)
18. *Trajan's Wall by Veltman.jpg,* http://en.wikipedia.org/wiki/File:Trajan%27s_Wall_by_Veltman.jpg

Nomads

1. D. W. Anthony, *The Horse The Wheel and Language How Bronze-Age Riders from the Eurasian Steppes Shaped the Modern World,* Princeton University Press, Princeton and Oxford, 2007, p. 416.
2. 'The Instruction of Merikare', R. O. Faulkner, in W. K. Simpson (ed.), *The Literature of Ancient Egypt,* New Haven and London, 1973, http://www.reshafim.org.il/ad/egypt/merikare_papyrus.htm
3. Herodotus, op. cit., 4, 46.
4. Sima Qian, 'The Account of the Xiongnu', in *Records of the Grand Historian of China (Shi Ji),* B. Watson, 1962, New York and London, Columbia University Press, 1962, 110, http://www.upf.edu/materials/huma/central/fonts/materials/shj110.htm
5. Ammianus, op. cit., 31, 3, 5.
6. ibid. 31, 2, 17.
7. ibid. 31, 2, 21.
8. ibid. 31, 2, 1.
9. *'The Marriage of Martu',* Electronic Text Corpus of Sumerian Literature (ETCSL), http://etcsl.orinst.ox.ac.uk/
10. A. B. Boswell, 'The Kipchak Turks', in *The Slavonic Review,* vol. 6, no. 16, 1927, p. 76.
11. Sima Qian, op. cit., 110.
12. Ammianus, op. cit., 31, 2, 6.
13. ibid. 31, 2, 20.
14. ibid. 31, 2, 17.
15. ibid. 31, 1, 17.
16. Sima Qian, op. cit., 110.
17. Ammianus, op. cit., 31, 2, 7.
18. ibid. 31, 2, 10.
19. *The Pouchenie of Vladimir Monomakh. Primary Russian Chronicle,* A.K. Harrington, http://www.dur.ac.uk/a.k.harrington/wwwdoc.html
20. ibid. 4, 123.
21. ibid. 4, 129.
22. Jordanes, *Origins and Deeds of the Goths.* C. C. Mierow, Princeton University, 1908, 4, 25.
23. Tacitus, *Germania,* T. Gordon, (died c. 1750), 29, 4.
24. Sima Qian, op. cit., 110.
25. *Prophecy of Neferti. Ancient Near Eastern Texts,* J. A. Wilson, J. B. Pritchard (ed.) Princeton, 1969, http://www.reshafim.org.il/ad/egypt/texts/neferti.htm

26. ibid.

27. *The Book of Songs*, op. cit., Song 132.

28. Procopius, *History of the Wars*, H.B. Dewing, Loeb, 1914, 2, 4.

29. al-Juvayni, *History Of The World Conqueror*, J.A. Boyle, Harvard University Press, 1958, p. 162.

30. ibid.

31. 'Ezekiel', *King James Bible*, 38:15.

32. 'Revelations', *King James Bible*, 20:17.

33. *Koran*, G. Sale, 1801, 18.

34. Pseudo-Callisthenes, The Alexander Romance, iii, 26, in *Gog and Magog*, S. Bøe, Tübingen: Mohr Siebeck, 2001. p. 224.

Chapter 1: Egypt, Mesopotamia and China – Early Riverine Empires and Irrigation Defence

1. *The Prophecy of Neferti*, op. cit.

2. ibid.Issues searching for linear barriers

3. *The Tale of Sinuhe*, op. cit.

4. *The Prophecy of Neferti*, op. cit.

5. *The Instruction of Merikare*, op. cit.

6. A. Sneh, T. Weissbrod, L. Perath, 'Evidence for an Ancient Egyptian Frontier Canal', *American Scientist*, vol. 63, no. 5, 1975, pp. 542-548

7. ibid. 545.

8. ibid. 545.

9. Constantine VII Porphyrogenitus, *De Administrando Imperio, (On the Governance of the Empire)*, R. J. H. Jenkins, Dunbarton Oaks Texts, 1967, 2.

10. 'King Lists, Shulgi', *Cuneiform Digital Library Initiative (CDLI)*, University of Oxford, http://cdli.ox.ac.uk/wiki/doku.php?id=shulgi

11. ibid. http://cdli.ucla.edu/tools/yearnames/HTML/T6K4.htm

12. M. W. Chavalas (ed.), *Ancient Near East: Historical Sources in Translation*, John Wiley & Sons, 2006.

13. 'Letter from Carrum-bani to Cu-Suen about keeping the Martu at bay'. *Electronic Text Corpus of Sumerian Literature (ETCSL)*, op. cit., http://etcsl.orinst.ox.ac.uk/cgi-bin/etcsl.cgi?text=t.3.1.15&charenc=j#

14. J. McIntosh, *Ancient Mesopotamia: New Perspectives*. ABC-CLIO, 2005, p. 83.

15. I. Morris, *Why the West Rules - for Now: The Patterns of History, and What They Reveal About the Future*, Straus and Giroux, 2010, p. 194.

16. R. D. Barnett, 'Xenophon and the Wall of Media', *The Journal of Hellenic Studies*, Vol. 83, 1963, p. 25.

17. ibid. p. 25

18. Strabo, op. cit., 11, 14, 8.

19. Herodotus, op. cit., 1, 185.

20. Xenophon, *Anabasis*, op. cit., 2, 4.

21. Barnett, op. cit., p. 19.

22. R. G. Killick, 'Northern Akkad Project: Excavations at Ḥabl Aṣ-Ṣaḫr, in *Iraq* (British Institute for the Study of Iraq), vol. 46, no. 2, 1984, 125.

23. Xenophon, *Anabasis*, op. cit., 1, 7.

24. J.E. Reade, 'El-Mutabbaq and Umm Rus'. *Sumer*, 20, 1964, p. 88.

25. Ammianus, op. cit., 24, 6, 2.

26. Reade, op. cit., pp. 83-9.

27. Barnett, op. cit., p. 7.
28. Reade, p. 88.
29. ibid. p. 88.
30. ibid. p. 88.
31. ibid. p. 84.
32. Barnett, op. cit., pp. 6-7.
33. Reade, op. cit., p. 86.
34. ibid. p. 86.
35. ibid. p. 85.
36. Barnett, op. cit., p. 7.
37. Reade, op. cit., p. 89.
38. Yāqūt, *Al-Mushtarik*, in R. N. Frye, 'The Sasanian System of Walls for Defence', in *Studies in Memory of Gaston Wiet*, Jerusalem, 1977, p. 10.
39. R. R. Stieglitz, 'Migrations in the Ancient Middle East (3500-500 B.C.)', in *Anthropological Science*, 101(3), 1993, p. 266.
40. *The Book of Songs*, op. cit., Song 132.
41. Waldron, op. cit., p. 44.
42. 'The Great Wall of the Qi Period', *AnESL.com*. http://www.anesl.com/schools/view.asp?id=656[SOURCE
43. ibid.
44. X. Pingfang, 'Archaeology of the Walls', in C. Roberts, G.R. Barmé, *The Great Wall of China*, Powerhouse Publishing, 2006, p. 52.
45. Waldron, op. cit., p. 13.
46. 'Oldest Great Wall Relics Destroyed, *The Epoch Times*, Chinese Central News Agency, 16 June 2008, http://www.theepochtimes.com/news/8-6-15/71887.html
47. 'Great Wall ruins discovered in Shandong Province', *The People's Daily*, July 9, 2009, http://english.people.com.cn/90001/90782/90874/6697070.html
48. N. Di Cosmo, *Ancient China and Its Enemies: The Rise of Nomadic Power in East Asian History*, Cambridge University Press, 2002, p. 139.
49. Morris, op. cit., p. 265.
50. Cosmo, op. cit., p. 155

Chapter 2: Greek World and Roman Empire – Barbarians and Local Nomads

1. O. Broneer, 'The Cyclopean Wall on the Isthmus of Corinth, Addendum', in *Hesperia*, 37, 1968, pp. 25-35.
2. Herodotus, op. cit., 9, 7.
3. Diodorus Siculus, *Library of History*, Oldfather, C.H., Loeb, 1954, 15, 68.
4. J.R. Wiseman, 'The Greeks had a wall for it', in *Alcade* (The University of Texas Alumni Magazine), Feb. 1962, pp. 12-15.
5. Herodotus, op. cit., 9, 7.
6. Plutarch, 'The Life of Pericles', *The Parallel Lives*, Perrin, B., Loeb, 1916, Vol. III, 19.1
7. Xenophon, *Hellenica*. Brownson, C. L. Loeb, 1915, 3, 28.
8. ibid., 3, 28.
9. Strabo, op. cit., 7, 4, 6.
10. E. D. Clarke, *Travels in Various Countries of Europe, Asia and Africa: Russia, Tartary*, T. Cadell and W. Davies, 1817, p. 285.
11. Braund, op. cit., p. 1244.

12. Strabo, op. cit., 7, 4, 6.
13. Procopius, *Buildings of Procopius*, H.B. Dewing, Loeb, 1940, 3, 7, 10.
14. Herodotus, op. cit., 7, 127
15. Herodotus, op. cit., 7, 127
16. V. D. Hanson, *Warfare and Agriculture in Classical Greece*, University of California Press, 1998.
17. Xenophon, *Hellenica*, op. cit., 5, 4, 38.
18. Munn, op. cit., p. 107.
19. Bakhuizen, op. cit., p. 109.
20. F. E. Winter, 'Notes on Military Architecture in the Termessos Region', in *American Journal of Archaeology* (Archaeological Institute of America), vol. 70, no. 2, 1966, p. 129.
21. Strabo, op. cit., 9, 10, 1.
22. Strabo, op. cit., 9, 10, 2.
23. A.N. Bader, V.A. Gaibov, G.A. Košelenko, 'Walls of *Margiana*', in *In the land of the gryphons: papers on Central Asian archaeology in antiquity*, Antonio Invernizzi, Le Lettere, 1995, p. 49
24. Herodotus, op. cit., 1, 174
25. Josephus, *Jewish War*. H. St.J. Thackeray, Loeb, 1925-8, 1, 4, 7.
26. Aelius Spartianus, *Historia Augusta*, D. Magie, Loeb, 1921, (1, 12, 6).
27. Livius, *History of Rome*, D. Spillan, John Childs and Son, London, 1853, 1, 33.
28. Caesar, *Gallic Wars*, W.A. McDevitte & W.S., Bohn Harper & Brothers, New York, 1869 , 1, 8
29. ibid., 1, 10.
30. Plutarch, op. cit., *Crassus*.
31. *Tiberius Plautius Silvanus Aelianus*, http://en.wikipedia.org/wiki/Tiberius_Plautius_Silvanus_Aelianus
32. V. Istvanovits, E. Kulcsár, 'The history and perspectives of the research of the Csörsz Ditch', in *XVIIIth International Congress of Roman Frontier Studies*, Amman, 2000, p. 625.
33. V. Matei, R. Gindele, 'Fortificatia romana de pamant de tip burgus, atasata valului éi éantului roman descoperit la supurul de Sus, Jud, Satu mare', *Acta musei porolissensis*, Zalau, Muzeul Judetean de istorie si arta, Zalau, 2004, vol. 26, pp. 283-307.
34. *Tiberius Plautius Silvanus Aelianus funerary text*, in *Tiberius Plautius Silvanus Aelianus*, http://en.wikipedia.org/wiki/Tiberius_Plautius_Silvanus_Aelianus
35. *Podolia*, http://en.wikipedia.org/wiki/Podolia
36. J. Baradez, *Fossatum Africae. Recherches Aériennes sur l'organisation des confins Sahariens a l'Epoque Romaine*, Arts et Métiers Graphiques, 1949, Paris.
37. C. Daniels, 'The Frontiers, Africa', in *The Roman World*, J. Wacher (ed.) Routledge, 2002. Vol. 1, p. 244.
38. Hizia: Histoire de Transhumance, http://membres.multimania.fr/cheikh07000/hizia/UStranshumance.htm
39. C.R. Whittaker, *Frontiers of the Roman Empire. A Social and Economic Study*. The Johns Hopkins University Press, Baltimore, 1997.
40. T. B, Mitford, 'Cappadocia and Armenia Minor: Historical Setting of the Limes'. *Aufstieg und Niedergang der Romischen Welt: Principat*, H. Temporini, H. Temporini, W. Haasepp (eds), p. 1193.
41. Ammianus, op. cit., 31, 11, 3,
42. Zosimus, op. cit.
43. C. Draganescu, G. Jones, 'Problems of free-ranging livestock systems in Romania' in *La Cañada, Newspaper on the European on Nature Conservation and Pastoralism*, no, 15, 2001/02, p. 9.
44. G. Williams, *Stronghold Britain Four Thousand Years of British Fortifications*, The History Press, 2003, p. 57.

45. Aelius Spartianus, op. cit., 1. 10, 3.

46. Julius Capitolinus, *The Life of Antoninus Pius*, D. Magie, 5,4.

Chapter 3: North African and Middle-Eastern Semi-arid Belt – Unification by Nomads Transcends Walls

1. R. Jaubert, M. Mohamed al-Dbiyat, B. Geyer, 'La patrimonialisation des steppes du Proche-Orient: un instrument pour quelle stratégie?' in F. Lerin (ed.), *Pastoralisme méditerranéen: patrimoine culturel et paysager et développement durable*. Montpellier: CIHEAM (Centre International de Hautes Etudes Agronomiques Méditerranéennes), 2010, pp 117-138.

2. B. Geyer, 'Die Syrische Mauer', in A. Nunn (ed.), *Mauern als Grenzen*. Philipp von Zabern, Mainz, 2009. pp. 39-46

3. Jaubert, al-Dbiyat, Geyer, op. cit., p.122.

4. A. Müller-Karpe, 'Die Kappodokische Mauer', in A. Nunn (ed.), *Mauern als Grenzen*. Philipp von Zabern, Mainz, 2009. pp. 47-56.

5. M. R. T. Dumper, B. E. Stanley, *Cities of the Middle East and North Africa: A Historical Encyclopedia*, ABC-CLIO, 2007, p. 342.

6. D. Nicolle, A. McBride, (illustrator), *Rome's Enemies (5): The Desert Frontier (Men-at-Arms)*, Osprey Publishing, 1991 p. 16.

7. Morony, M.G., *Iraq after the Muslim Conquest*, Gorgias Press, 2005, p. 153.

Chapter 4: Northern Europe – Barbarians and Ancient Roads

1. A. J. Reynolds and A. Langlands, 'Social Identities on the Macro Scale: A Maximum View of Wansdyke', in *People and Space in the Middle Ages, 300-1300*, W, Davies, G. Halsall, and A. Reynolds (eds.), Brepols: Turnhout., 2006 pp. 13–44.

2. Asser, *Life of King Alfred*, W.H. Stevenson (ed.), Oxford University Press, 1904.

3. Sauer, op. cit., pp. 30-36.

4. Dr S. Newton, *The Defences of the Wuffing Kingdom*, http://www.wuffings.co.uk/WuffSites/Dykes/EADykes.htm

5. A. J. Reynolds and A. Langlands, op. cit.

6. J. Bardon, *A History of Ulster*, Jonathan Blackstaff Press, 1992, p. 11.

7. T. Condit, V. M. Buckley, G. Cooney (ed.), *The Doon of Drumsna: An Iron Age frontier fortification in Connacht*. Archeology Ireland Heritage Guide, 1998, p. 7.

8. Condit, Buckley, ibid. p. 10.

9. C. O' Brien, The Iron Age in Offaly. *A History of Offaly Through its Monuments*, in Offaly Historical and Archaeological Society, 2007, p. 2.

10. S. Duke, 'Archeologists discover Irish Hadrian's Wall', *The Sunday Times*, March 8 1998

11. Duke, ibid.

12. Duke, ibid.

13. J.M. Feeley, *The Rathduff Trench. The Gripe of the Pig*, http://glasnost.itcarlow.ie/~feeleyjm/archaeology/rathduff%20dyke.pdf

14. *Annals of the Kingdom of the Franks*, 808, P. D. King, Kendal, 1987

15. Saxo Grammaticus, *Gesta Danorum*, in Danevirke, http://Encyclopedia-Britannica-Volume-7-Part-1-Damascus-Education-Animals/Dannewerk-or-Danewerk.html

16. Caesar, op. cit., 2, 17.

17. Tacitus, *The Histories*, op. cit., 4.37.

18. Tacitus, Annals, op. cit., 2, 19.

19. ibid. 2 19.

20. Ammianus, op. cit., 31, 3, 5.
21. ibid. 31, 3, 7.
22. Adam of Bremen, *Gesta Pontificum Hammaburgensis ecclesiae*, http://de.wikipedia.org/wiki/Limes_Saxoniae, 2, 15b.
23. M. Hardt, 'The Limes Saxoniae as Part of the Eastern Borderlands of the Frankish and Ottonian-Salian Empire', in F. Curta (ed.), *Borders, Barriers, and Ethnogenesis: Frontiers in Late Antiquity and the Middle Ages*, Turnhout: Brepols Publishers, 2006, p. 44.
24. Widukind, 'The Saxonian History', Chapter XIX, http://www.rmki.kfki.hu/~lukacs/SZARMAT1.htm
25. M. Huser, J. Mortsiefer, *Landwehren, was ist das?* Private Project, http://www.*Landwehren*.de/
26. R. de Torigni, 'Gesta Normannorum Ducum', in P. Contamine, *War in the Middle Ages*, English Translation Blackwell Publishers, 1984. pp. 221-222
27. S. Cullen, 'The Pale', *Oughterany - Journal of the Donadea Local History Group*, N. Reid (ed.), vol. I, no. 1, 1993, http://seamuscullen.net/pale.html
28. 'English Pale' in S. J. Connolly (ed.), *The Oxford Companion to Irish History*. Oxford University Press, 2007.
29. F. Elrington Ball, E. Hamilton, *The parish of Taney : a history of Dundrum, near Dublin, and its neighbourhood*, Hodges, Figgis & Co., Dublin, 1895, p. 8.
30. Cullen, op. cit.

Chapter 5: Eastern Europe – Multiple Barriers where Steppe and Europe Collide

1. Dimitrie Cantemir, *Descriptio Moldaviae*, 1714, in *Prehistoric Dacia*, N. Densusianu, http://www.pelasgians.org/website1/08_01.htm
2. Nokter, *Life of Charlemagne*, in *Charles the Great*, Hodgkin, T., Thomas Macmillan, 1897, p. 206.
3. V. Istvanovits, E. Kulcsár, 'The history and perspectives of the research of the Csörsz Ditch', in *XVIIIth International Congress of Roman Frontier Studies*, Amman, 2000, p. 626.
4. Widukind, op. cit., (19).
5. Constantine, op. cit., 2.
6. K. Randsborg, 'A Seagoing Ship of c1650 AD in Bessarabia, Ukraine', in *Archaeological Notes 1*, 1998, http://www.abc.se/~pa/publ/bessarab.htm
7. Ammianus, op. cit., 31, 3, 5.
8. O. Plamenytska, E. Plamenytska, *Kamyanets Podilsky, A Town at the Periphery of the Roman Empire: Urban Order and Fortifications*, http://www.tovtry.km.ua/en/history/article/mist1.htm
9. *Borshchiv Raion*, http://en.wikipedia.org/wiki/Borshchiv_Raion)
10. Herodotus, op. cit., 4, 3.
11. ibid. 4, 20.
12. ibid. 4, 28.
13. E. Henderson, *Biblical Researches and Travels in Russia: Including a Tour in the Crimea, and the Passage of the Caucasus*. J. Nisbet, 1826. p. 288.
14. Constantine, op. cit., 42.

Chapter 6: Bulgaria, Poland and the Kievan Rus – Early State Formation

1. Theophanes, *Chronicle of Theophanes*, H. Turtledove, University of Pennsylvania Press, 1982, 11, 24, 2.
2. *Bulgarian Apocryphal Chronicle*, in Dobruja, http://en.wikipedia.org/wiki/Dobruja
3. Bury, J. B., 'The Bulgarian Treaty of A. D. 814, and the Great Fence of Thrace' in *The English Historical Review*, Oxford University Press, vol. 25, no. 98, 1910. pp. 276-287.

4. J. Skylitzes, *Synopsis of Byzantine History, 811-1057,* J. Wortley, Cambridge University Press, 2010, Nicephoras II Phocas.

5. Theophanes, op. cit., 11, 24, 2.

6. K. Randsborg, 'A Seagoing Ship of c1650 AD in Bessarabia, Ukraine', Archaeological Notes 1, 1998, http://www.abc.se/~pa/publ/bessarab.htm

7. *Bulgarian Apocryphal Chronicle,* op. cit.

8. ibid.

9. I. Welkow, 'Pliska', in *Antiquity,* Dr I. Akrabova. vol. 13, no. 51, 1930, p. 296.

10. A. Buko, *The Archaeology of Early Medieval Poland: Discoveries, Hypotheses, Interpretations (East Central and Eastern Europe in the Middle Ages, 450-1450),* Andrzej Brill Academic Publishers, 2008, p. 219.

11. ibid. p. 98.

12. Silesian Przesieka, http://en.wikipedia.org/wiki/Silesian_Przesieka. See also, for map, Przesieka Śląska, http://pl.wikipedia.org/wiki/Przesieka_%C5%9Al%C4%85ska

13. Buko, op. cit., p. 200.

14. ibid. p. 98

15. ibid. p. 99.

16. Bruno of Querfurt, 'The Letter of Bruno of Querfurt to King Henry II: On His Alliance with the Pagans', W.L. North, in *Panstowowe Wydawnictwo Naukowe,* Warsaw, 1973, p. 98

17. Constantine, op. cit., 9.

18. ibid. 1.

19. ibid. 3.

20. ibid. 5.

21. ibid. 2

22. *The Pouchenie of Vladimir Monomakh,* op. cit.

23. ibid.

24. Змиевывалы, http://ru.wikipedia.org/wiki/%D0%97%D0%BC%D0%B8%D0%B5%D0%B2%D1%8B_%D0%B2%D0%B0%D0%BB%D1%8B

25. 'Rivers of milk and creeks of honey, witches flying around at night in the Land of Poltavshchyna, Zmiyevi valy — Snake Earthworks', in *Welcome to Ukraine,* http://www.wumag.kiev.ua/index2.php?param=pgs20051/46

26. P. Rappoport, 'Russian Medieval Military Architecture', *Gladius,* VIII, p. 59.

27. V.D. Kirievsky, Novgorod-Seversky, Road of the Prince, http://terra-trajana.narod.ru/novgorod.html.

28. S. Franklin, J. Shepard, *The Emergence of Rus: 750-1200,* Longman History of Russia, 1996.

29. Bruno of Querfurt, op. cit.

Chapter 7: China I – Northern Expansion, Consolidated by Walls, Setting off Nomad Irruptions

1. di Cosmo, op. cit., p. 143.

2. ibid. p. 149.

3. ibid. p. 8.

4. Sima Qian, 'The Account of the Xiongnu', in *Records of the Grand Historian of China (Shi Ji),* 110 in Zhewen, Luo. 'The Great Walls of China'. *The Great Wall of China,* Roberts, C., Barmé, G.R., Powerhouse Publishing, 2006, pp. 42-51.

5. ibid. Sima Qian, 'The Biography of Meng Tian', 88.

Chapter 8: Byzantine and Sasanian Empires – Collaboration of Foes

1. Procopius, *History of the Wars*, op. cit., 1, 4.
2. Evagrius Scholasticus, *Ecclesiastical History*, E. Walford, Samuel Bagster and Sons, 1846, 3, 38.
3. ibid. 3, 38.
4. Procopius, *The Buildings*, op. cit., 4, 9, 4.
5. ibid. 4, 9, 7.
6. ibid. 4, 10, 5.
7. Procopius, ibid. 4, 10, 10
8. D. Krandjalov, *Vallums In Dobroudja/Bessarabia And Proto-Bulgarian Theory*, in http://berberian11.tripod.com/krandjalov_ramparts.htm
9. Procopius, *The Buildings*, op. cit., 4, 2, 22.
10. ibid. 4, 2, 3.
11. ibid. 4, 2, 27.
12. ibid. 4, 2, 17.
13. ibid. 4, 2, 27.
14. ibid. 3, 7, 12.
15. ibid. 3, 10, 13.
16. Constantine, op. cit., 37.
17. S. Brezeanu, 'Toponymy and ethnic Realities at the Lower Danube in the 10th Century. "The deserted Cities", in Constantine Porphyrogenitus' *De Administrando Imperio*', in *Istituto Romeno di cultura e ricerca umanistica*, Venice, Marin, S., Dinu, R., Bulei, I. (eds), 4, 2002.
18. Williams, op. cit., p. 57.
19. Skylitzes, op. cit., John I Tzimiskes.
20. Yāqūt, op. cit., pp. 8-10
21. ibid. p. 10
22. J. Nokandeh, E. W. Sauer, H. O. Rekavandi, T. Wilkinson, G. A. Abbasi, J. Schwenninger, M. Mahmoudi, D. Parker, M. Fattahi, L. S. Usher-Wilson, M. Ershadi, J. Ratcliffe, G. Rowena, 'Linear barriers of northern Iran: the Great Wall of Gorgan and the Wall of Tammishe', in *Journal of the British Institute of Persian Studies*, 2006, p. 138.
23. Yāqūt, in Mahamedi, H., 'Wall as A System of Frontier Defence during the Sasanid Period'. *Daryaee T., Omidsalar, M. (eds.), Spirit of Wisdom (Menog-i Xrad), Essays in Memory of Ahmad Tafazzoli*, Mazda Publishers, 2004, p. 147.
24. ibid. Tabarī, p. 147
25. 'In Search of Sasanian Wall', in *CAIS (The Circle of Ancient Iranian Studies) Archaeological & Cultural News*, 12 February 2006, http://www.cais-soas.com/News/2006/February2006/12-02-archaeologists.htm
26. Reade, op. cit.,p. 85.
27. H. Mahamedi, 'Wall as A System of Frontier Defence during the Sasanid Period', T. Daryaee, M. Omidsala (eds.), *Spirit of Wisdom (Menog-i Xrad), Essays in Memory of Ahmad Tafazzoli*, Mazda Publishers, 2004, p. 146.
28. Frye, op. cit., p. 8.
29. J. Harmatta, 'The Wall of Alexander the Great and the Limes Sasanicus', in Bromberg, C.A., Skjærvø P.O. (eds.), *Studies in Honor of Vladimir A. Livshits*, vol. 10, Bulletin Asia Institute, 1996, p. 80
30. Frye, 1977, op. cit., p. 11.
31. Harmatta, op. cit., p. 84.
32. Nicolle 1996, op. cit., p. 49.

Chapter 9: Central Asia – Great Oasis Walls

1. Rapin, 2004, op. cit.
2. Narshakhi in Frye, R. N., *The History of Bukhara*, Cambridge, Mass., 1954, p. 128
3. A. Gangler, H. Gaube, A. Petruccioli, *Bukhara, the Eastern Dome of Islam: Urban Development, Urban Space*, Edition Axel Menges, 2004, p. 45.
4. Frye, 1954, op. cit., p. 127-28.
5. M. Niekum, *The Role of Shrines and Temples in the Urban Sogdian Community: An Ethnoarchaeological Perspective from Contemporary Bukhara*, p. 3, http://depts.washington.edu/reecas/events/conf2002/papers02/Niekum.doc)
6. Balk, *Encyclopædia Iranica*, http://www.iranicaonline.org/articles/balk-town-and-province
7. Herat, *Encyclopædia Iranica*, http://www.iranicaonline.org/articles/herat
8. W. Ball, *Archaeological Gazetteer of Afghanistan*, 2 vol .1, 1982, p. 145.
9. N. Pazouki, 'Defence Buildings in Iran', in *Miras-e-Melli*, no. 13, p. 33.
10. H.L. Rabinou, *A Travel to Mazandaran and Astarabad*, V. Mazandarani, Book Tranlation and Publication Institute, 1957, p. 34.
11. Bader, Gaibov, Koshelenko, op. cit., p. 50.
12. M. Lombard, *The Golden Age of Islam*, Markus Wiener Pub, 2003, p. 129.

Chapter 10: China II – Nomad Irruptions and Multiple Great Walls

1. 'Sui Dynasty Great Wall', in *chinatravelguide.com* http://www.travelchinaguide.com/china_great_wall/history/sui/
2. Waldron, op. cit., p. 9
3. Lovell, op. cit., p. 105.
4. Waldron, op. cit., p. 45.
5. Morris, op. cit., p. 458.
6. *The Secret History of the Mongols*, U, (Professor), Onon, Pschychology Press, 2001 p. 278
7. 'Finding Genghis Khan's Wall', *China Daily*, March 8, 2012.

Chapter 11: Russia – Defeating the Steppe Nomads

1. B.L. Davies, *State, Power and Community in Early Modern Russia, The Case of Kozlov*, Palgrave Macmillan, 2004, p. 34.
2. R. L. Sanders, 'The Strelzi (1550-1705)'. *Xenophon Group*, http://www.xenophon-mil.org/rusarmy/streltzi.htm
3. Pro. I. de Madariaga, *Ivan the Terrible*, Yale University Press. 2005, p. 277.
4. ibid. p. 64.
5. K. Nossov, P. Dennis, (illustrator), *Russian Fortresses 1480–1682*. Osprey, 2006, p. 44.
6. Davies, op. cit., 2004, p. 71
7. ibid. p. 74.

Chapter 12: Non-Eurasian Linear Barriers

1. D. Wilson, *Prehispanic Settlement Patterns in the Lower Santa Valley Peru*. Smithsonian Series in Archaeological Inquiry, Washington, 1988.
2. ibid. p. 10.
3. ibid. p. 10.
4. ibid. p. 251.
5. ibid. p. 255.
6. ibid. p. 358.

7. Paddock, op.cit., pp. 62–63.

8. ibid. p. 63

9. ibid. p. 62

10. D. E. Puleston, D. W. Callender, 'Defensive Earthworks at Tikal' in *Expedition*, Spring, 1967, p. 40.

11. ibid. 43.

12. ibid. 48.

13. D. Webster, *Re-Evaluation of the Earthworks at Tikal, Guatemala: Phase 2 Final report submitted to the National Science Foundation*, 2007, p. 49.

14. J. E. Silverstein, D. Webster, H. Martinez and A. Soto, 'Rethinking the great earthwork of Tikal: a hydraulic hypothesis for the classic Maya polity' in *Ancient Mesoamerica*, 20, 2009, p. 45.

15. McWhirter 1980 et seq.

16. Darling, 1998. op. cit., p. 143.

17. P. J. Darling, 'Sungbo's Eredo, Southern Nigeria'. *Nyame Akuma*, no. 49, 1998, p. 58, http://cohesion.rice.edu/centersandinst/safa/emplibrary/49_ch09.pdf

18. 'Sungbo's Eredo - Africa's Largest Single Monument'. *Recording West Africa's Visible Archaeology African Legacy* - Dr P. Darling School of Conservation Sciences - Bournemouth University, UK, http://csweb.bournemouth.ac.uk/africanlegacy/sungbo_eredo.htm

19. P. J. Darling, 'A Legacy in Earth'. *Historical Archaeology in Nigeria*, Trenton, NJ: Africa World, 1998, p. 150.

20. ibid. p. 150.

21. K.E. Emory, 'Review of Archaeology of Easter Island', T. Heyerdahl, E.N. Ferdon, *American Antiquity*, vol. 28.

22. ibid. p. 566.

23. M. Keegan, *A History Of Warfare*, John Random House, 1993, p. 26.

24. P. Brush, 'The Story Behind The Mcnamara Line' in *Vietnam magazine*, February 1996, p. 9, http://www.shss.montclair.edu/english/furr/pbmcnamara.html

25. A. Bray, 'Vietnam's own 'great wall' uncovered' in *Special for CNN*, 25 January 2011.

Chapter 14: How Valid are those Four Linear Barrier Patterns?

1. Xenophon, *Hellenica*, op. cit., 3, 28.

2. Plutarch, *The Parallel Lives*, ibid. Crassus.

3. 'The Ravenna Cosmography', *The Antonine Wall*, http://www.roman-britain.org/frontiers/antonine.htm

4. Procopius, *The Buildings*, op. cit., 4, 9, 4.

5. 'The Passage of the Danube by the Russians', *The Times*, April 2, 1854, http://paperspast.natlib.govt.nz/cgi-bin/paperspast?a=d&d=NZSCSG18540722.2.11&l=mi&e=———10–11——-0pardessus—

6. Devil's Dyke, Cambridgeshire, http://en.wikipedia.org/wiki/Devil's_Dyke,_Cambridgeshire

7. Reade, op. cit., p. 86.

8. Xenophon, *Hellenica*, op. cit., 3, 28.

9. Xenophon, *Hellenica*, op. cit., 5, 4, 38.

10. Procopius, *The Buildings*, op. cit., 4, 9, 4.

11. Morris, op. cit., p. 265.

12. Nokandeh et al., op. cit., p. 138.

13. Puleston, Callender 1967, op. cit., p. 48.

14. Waldron, op. cit., p. 45.

15. Yāqūt, in Frye1977, p. 8-10
16. ibid. p. 10
17. Bruno of Querfurt, op. cit.
18. Frye, 1977, op. cit., p. 8.
19. Harmatta, op. cit., p. 80.
20. Mahamedi, op. cit., p. 159
21. Rapin, 2004, op. cit.
22. Evagrius Scholasticus, op. cit., 3, 38.
23. Di Cosmo, op. cit., 139.
24. J. Ober, 'Classical Greek Times', in *The Laws of War*, M. Howard, G. J. Andreopoulos, M. R. Shulman (eds), Yale University Press, New Haven and London, 1994, p. 25.
25. Rappoport, op. cit., p. 59.
26. D. Lutz, 'Territoire et protection des frontiers Quelques exemples de XIVème et XVème siècles dans le sud-ouest de l'Allemagne', author's translation, in *Château et territoire Limites et mouvances. Première rencontre internationale d'archéologie et d'histoire. Préface d'Yves Guéna, sénateur-maire de Périgueux. Périgueux, 23-25 September 1994*, Presses universitaires de Franche-Comté, 1995, p. 74.
27. Puleston, Callender, 1967. op. cit., p. 48.

Chapter 15: Motivations Other Than Pure Defence - Aggression and Assertion?

1. Di Cosmo, op. cit., p. 149.
2. Waldron, op. cit., p. 38.
3. Di Cosmo, op. cit., p. 139.
4. M. Zakiev, Origin of Türks and Tatars, Part two, Origin of Tatars. pp. 223-24, http://www.kutsalkitaplar.net/index.php/history/origin-of-tuerks/origin-of-tuerks-and-tatars/11459-origin-of-tuerks-and-tatars-first-chapter
5. Aelius Spartianus, op. cit., 1. 10, 3.
6. *Sungbo's Eredo*, http://en.wikipedia.org/wiki/Sungbo's_Eredo
7. Herodotus, op. cit., 7, 24.
8. Fronto, *Speech on the War in Britain. 140-1 AD*. Haines, C.R. London: W. Heineman, New York. Putnam, 1919.

Chapter 16: Why Did Some Polities not Build Linear Barriers?

1. D. Whitelock, English Historical Documents c. 500-1042, Eyre, Spottiswoode, 1955.
2. M. Woods, *The Story of India*, BBC Books 2007, p. 37
3. F. J. Turner, *The Significance of the Frontier in American History*, Chicago, 1893, in 'The Limes: Between open Frontier and Borderline', W. Moschek, in *Walls, Ramparts, and Lines of Demarcation*, N. Fryde, D. Reitz D. (eds.), Transaction publishers, 2009, p.16.
4. Woods, *op. cit.*, p. 37.
5. W. Urban, 'The Prussian-Lithuanian frontier of 1242' in *Lituanus, Lithuanian Quarterly Journal of Arts and Sciences*, vol. 21, no.4, 1975, http://www.lituanus.org/1975/75_4_01.htm

Chapter 17: Strategies or Barriers Building – Which Really Defined Relations between States and Nomads?

1. Constantine, op. cit., 7.
2. *Kingdom of Galicia*, http://en.wikipedia.org/wiki/Kingdom_of_Galicia%E2%80%93Volhynia
3. Aelius Spartianus, *History of Augustus, Life of Hadrian*, L. Magie, Loeb, 1921. 6, 6

4. *Defence-in-depth (Roman military)*, http://en.wikipedia.org/wiki/Defence-in-depth_(Roman_military)#cite_note-29
5. ibid.

Chapter 18: Linear Barrier Building - A Successful or Failed Strategy?
1. Xenophon, *Hellenica*, op. cit., 3, 28.
2. Procopius, *History of the Wars*, op. cit., 2, 4.
3. B.L. Sterling, *Do Good Fences Make Good Neighbors?: What History Teaches Us about Strategic Barriers and International Security*, Georgetown University Press, 2009, p. 2.
4. M. van Creveld, *Defending Israel: A Strategic Plan for Peace and Security*, New York: Thomas Dunne Books, 2004, p. 66.
5. Nokandeh et al., op. cit., p. 138.

Chapter 19: Visualisation and Functioning
1. G. Borrow, *Wild Wales*, Bridge Books, 2009, p. 59.
2. Frye, 1977, op. cit., p. 8.
3. Franklin, S., Shepard, J., op. cit.
4. Nossov, 2006, op. cit., p. 44.

Chapter 20: Construction and Maintenance
1. Xenophon, *Hellenica*, op. cit., 3, 28.
2. Waldron, 1990, op. cit., p. 38.
3. Procopius, Buildings, op. cit., 4, 1, 27.
4. Davies, 2004, op. cit., p. 55.
5. Davies, 2004, op. cit., p. 61.
6. Herodotus, op. cit., 7, 23.
7. Xenophon, Hellenica, op. cit., 3, 2 10.
8. D. J. Breeze, *The Antonine Wall*. John Donald Publishers Ltd., 2006, p. 65.
9. *Annals of the Kingdom of the Franks*, op. cit.
10. A. Hvitfeld, A., *Danmarks Riges Krønike*, in http://en.wikipedia.org/wiki/Danevirke
11. A. E. Conway, E. Curtiss, *Henry VII's Relations with Scotland and Ireland: 1485-1498*, CUP Archive, 1932, p. 127.
12. Devil's Dyke Restoration Project, http://www.devilsdykeproject.org.uk/histarch.html
13. Stone Wall in Imazu, http://www.bekkoame.ne.jp/~gensei/ten/eimazu.html
14. Xenophon, *Hellenica*, op. cit., 3, 2 9.
15. Diodorus Siculus, op. cit., 14, 18, 6.
16. Waldron, op. cit., p. 38.
17. Abels, R., *The Fortified Bridges of Charles the Bald, king of West Francia (848-877)* 2009, http://usna.edu/Users/history/abels/hh315/vikingsrevised.html
18. *Liber census Daniæ, Kong Valdemar den andens jordebog*, O. Nielsen, Copenhagen, 1873, pp. 15, 17, 19 (author's translation).

Chapter 21: Tactical Use of Static and Mobile Linear Barriers
1. Appian, *The History of the Syrian Wars*, H. White, 4, 4, 18.
2. Procopius, *History of the Wars*, H. B. Dewing, Loeb, 1914, 1, 4, 10-16

Chapter 22: Movement of Animals and of People

1. *The Prophecy of Neferti*, op. cit.
2. Whittaker, op. cit.
3. Draganescu, op. cit., p. 9
4. The Great Wall of the Qi Period, op. cit., http://www.impressivechina.com/Dest/Shandong/Jinan/43306552394.html
5. Di Cosmo, p. cit., 139

Chapter 23: Using Nature - Abatis and Hedges, Rivers, Canals and Seas

1. Caesar, op. cit., 2, 17.
2. Nokter, op.cit.
3. The Anglo-Saxon Chronicle, year 547, about.com, medieval history, http://historymedren.about.com/library/text/bltxtaschron501.htm
4. Hardt, op. cit., p. 44.
5. Lutz, op. cit.
6. Constantine, op. cit., 42.
7. V.D. Kirievsky, Novgorod-Seversky, Road of the Prince, http://terra-trajana.narod.ru/novgorod.html
8. Franklin, Shepard, op. cit.
9. Sneh, Weissbrod, Perath, op. cit., p. 545.
10. *The Instruction of Merikare*, op. cit.
11. Procopius, *The Buildings*, op. cit., 4, 2, 22.
12. *The Prophecy of Neferti*, op. cit.
13. Tacitus, *Germania*, op. cit., 4, 26.

Chapter 24: The Naming of Linear Barriers

1. John of Fordun, *Chronicle of the Scottish Nation*, Edinburgh, Edmonston and Douglas, 1872, p. 82.
2. *Hungarian folk legend*, adaptation by Dénes Lengyel, http://www.nemzetismeret.hu/?id=1.16&sh=&lang=en)
3. N. Densusianu, 'The giant plough furrow of Novac (Osiris)', *Prehistoric Dacia*. http://www.pelasgians.org/website1/07_01.htm
4. *Welcome to Ukraine 2005*, op. cit., http://www.wumag.kiev.ua/index2.php?param=pgs20051/46
5. P. S. Wells, 'The Limes and Hadrian's Wall: Rome's Northern European boundaries' in *Expedition*, Vol. 47, No. 1, 2005, University Museum of the University of Pennsylvania, pp. 20.

Chapter 25: Destruction, Discovery and Protection

1. Fryde, op. cit., p. 39.
2. C. Coonan, *The Great Repair Job of China*, 30 December 2006, The Independent.
3. Epoch Times, op. cit.
4. S. Golubenko, 'Як приватизували Змієві Вали'. Новини УНІАН, 7 March 2008, http://www.unian.ua/news/259608-yak-privatizuvali-zmievi-vali.html
5. Barnett, op. cit., p. 19
6. The Great Repair Job of China, 30 December 2006, The Independent
7. The Epoch Times, op. cit.
8. 'Great fall of China', *The Daily Telegraph*, August 9 2012.
9. Coonan, op. cit.

10. Illegal Hadrian's Wall plaque removed without damage, *BBC*, 24 January, 2012, http://www.bbc.co.uk/news/uk-england-tyne-16701305
11. B. Geyer, op. cit., pp. 39-46.
12. A. Müller-Karpe, ibid., pp. 47-56.
13. 'In Search of Sasanian Wall', in *CAIS (The Circle of Ancient Iranian Studies) Archaeological & Cultural News*, 12 February 2006, http://www.cais-soas.com/News/2006/February2006/12-02-archaeologists.htm
14. 'China uncovers lost part of Wall', *BBC News*, 9 October 2002, http://news.bbc.co.uk/1/hi/world/asia-pacific/2314915.stm
15. 'Ancient sites from Zhou Dynasty discovered in the Qi Great Wall in Shandong', *Cultural China*, 2 February 2009
16. J. Owen J.' '"Lost" Great Wall of China Segment Found?', *National Geographic News*, March 19, 2012
17. D. Wilson, *Prehispanic Settlement Patterns in the Lower Santa Valley Peru*. Smithsonian Series in Archaeological Inquiry, Washington, 1988.
18. D. E. Puleston, D. W. Callender, 'Defensive Earthworks at Tikal' in *Expedition*, Spring, 1967.
19. F. K. Paddock, 'The Great Wall of the Inca' in *Archaeology*, 37:62, July/ August, 1984, p. 40-48.
20. A. Bray, op. cit.
21. Coonan, *The Great Repair Job of China* op. cit.
22. ibid.
23. *The Great Wall of the Qi Period*, op. cit.
24. 'Great Wall of Ston opens after Renovation' in *Peljesac Peninsula*, December 1, 2009, http://croatiatraveller.com/blog/great-wall-of-ston-opens-after-renovation/2009/12/01/

Chapter 26: Reuse, Marking Borders, Renewed Building
1. Kharkiv Oblast, Ukraine, Valky County, Town of Valky, op. cit.
2. *The Times*, 1854 op. cit., ('Russians halted by Ottomans at Walls of Trajan')
3. Defence of the Great Wall, http://en.wikipedia.org/wiki/Defence_of_the_Great_Wall
4. E. Von Manstein, A. G. Powell (ed. and trans.), *Lost Victories*. Presidio Press, Novato, California, 1984.
5. 'Le Kef, Tunisia', in *Atlantic Magazine*, June 2001.
6. M. van Creveld, op. cit.

Chapter 27: Linear Barriers – Historiography and Interpretation
1. Frye, 1977, op. cit., 7.
2. Plato, *The Laws*, 760e, 761a, R.G. Bury, William Heineman, London, 1968.
3. ibid. 778d, 778e.
4. ibid. 778d, 778e.
5. ibid. 778e, 779a.
6. J-M. Mehl, 'La logique des murs', author's translation, in *Réforme*, August 31 2006,
7. 'Romans may have learned from Chinese Great Wall: archaeologists', in *People's Daily Online*, December 20 2005.
8. W. Ball, *Rome in the East*. Routledge Taylor & Francis Group, London and New York, 2000, p. 317.

Index

Index of names and terms other than great walls and linear barriers specified above